ST HELENS:

THE GREAT & THE GOOD

(and a few of the not so good!)

Brian Leyland

STELLAR BOOKS

ABOUT THE AUTHOR

Brian Leyland grew up in St Helens and attended St Austin's and St Teresa's Primary Schools followed by West Park Grammar School. He graduated from Manchester University with a degree in Modern History with Economics and joined the Inland Revenue as an inspector of taxes, working in Liverpool and then London.

He stuck around for nearly ten years and then jumped ship to Price Waterhouse (now PwC). He became a partner in 1988 and worked in Liverpool, Düsseldorf, Manchester and London before his retirement in 2010. He is now a director of Hometown Plus Limited, a business which helps restore community and commercial prosperity mainly to towns which have been left behind in the post-industrial era.

St. Helens: The Great and the Good is his first publication and he has no idea if there will be any more. In fact he has no idea at all what the future holds for him, other than that it will feature in some measure drinking decent beer, watching rugby league and attempting to play various sports to a mediocre level.

CONTENTS

FOREWORD BY PAUL SCUNTHORPE MBE

I am not from St Helens - I am a proud Oldham boy and wouldn't have it any other way - but St Helens has played a huge part in my life. It wasn't planned that way and it could quite easily have turned out very differently. But when St Helens agreed to pay Warrington what was then a world record fee for a forward to secure my transfer in 1997, it set in train a series of events which were to have a major impact on my life. It began of course with the stream of trophies which the Saints team won in the period up to my retirement in 2008. However whilst I count myself extremely fortunate to have been a part of that team, it really was only the

Paul Sculthorpe holding aloft the World Club Challenge Trophy 2007 ©Copyright Bernard Platt.

beginning. Both during and since that time I have built many lifelong friendships with persons from the town, I have an ongoing position with the club as an ambassador and, not least, it led to my involvement with the Steve Prescott Foundation, to which all the profits from the sales of this book will be donated.

There are in fact many similarities between Oldham and St Helens. Both are working class towns, both played a pivotal part in the Industrial Revolution and, sadly, both are now suffering from the consequences of social and economic change which has left many of the old industrial towns as a shadow of the communities which they once were. But perhaps the most striking similarity is that both towns have produced a huge number of successful persons in all ranges of life – sport, the arts, sciences and industry are just some of the areas in which the population of the two towns has made its mark. Unfortunately this has for the most part gone under the radar, even amongst the townsfolk themselves – I suspect many readers of this book will be astonished at the number and range of the people featured and that there will be much shaking of heads and comment on the lines of, "Well I never knew he came from round here". But that is why, to my mind, the book is important – it highlights the success of the town in a way that hasn't been done before, and celebrates the fact that it is a great exporter of talent and that its contribution to the nation goes well beyond the sport of rugby league and the manufacture of glass!

I also regard myself as being privileged to be able to count amongst my friends a number of those profiled in these pages. Perhaps foremost amongst these is Steve Prescott himself, who we all know was a truly extraordinary person, an inspiration to everyone who knew him and indeed many who didn't. But there are numerous others as well, whose contribution in their chosen profession or sport we can only stand back and admire.

I hope that you read the book and enjoy it. It will provide not only an insight into the lives of the persons included herein, but at the same time illuminates the fascinating history and rich contribution of a town which only came into official existence just over 150 years ago.

All we need now is someone to write about famous people from Oldham..........

Paul Sculthorpe MBE

INTRODUCTION

"St Helens? I really gotta go that place sometime". Somebody actually said that to me. No, honestly, it's true - unlikely as it may seem. Even more remarkable, it was said without a hint of sarcasm. The year was 1971 and during the late summer I was a teenager hitchhiking around what was then West Germany with a friend. We were not hard core hitchhikers in that we had a little money in our pockets, courtesy of a few weeks summer work on building sites around St Helens. We would also occasionally succumb to the attractions of public transport when the going got tough. It was on one such occasion that caused us to arrive at Heidelberg railway station sometime around midnight with no accommodation having been arranged.

We were approached on the station concourse by someone asking if we needed a roof for the night. His offer of bed and breakfast sounded infinitely preferable to finding a camp site and pitching the tent so we readily accepted and were whisked off to wherever it was that we were going to stay. I remember little or nothing about the place itself but I can vividly recall turning up at breakfast the following morning. The place was exclusively populated by Americans (indeed Heidelberg itself seemed to be a temporary home to more Americans - soldiers, tourists and hippies camped on the side of the River Neckar - than it was to Germans at that time) and the first question we were asked was,

"Hey, where are you guys from?"

"St Helens, in England," we replied which elicited the immediate response,

"Gee, I really gotta go that place sometime". My friend and I looked at each other in bemusement. We both knew intuitively that there was no response which would be in any way appropriate. So we said nothing at all.

My initial assumption was that the name St Helens sounded to the questioner something like Los Angeles or San Francisco, a sort of glamour town. Doubt was immediately cast upon this theory by the experience of the only other new face arriving at breakfast that morning, "South Dakota? Really? Hey that's fantastic," said the same guy. This suggested that he might be the sort of American who would feel the need to show enthusiasm regardless of what the answer had been. On the other hand it may well be that the guy's enthusiasm for South Dakota was dictated by something entirely different, namely that the lady in question, probably in her early twenties, was at the stunning end of the attractive scale. I have occasionally pondered what his response might have been had we said, "We're from Grimsby". Either way, I think it's a safe assumption that he never went to St Helens and probably only went to South Dakota if invited by the attractive young lady to accompany her.

Of course such a conversation would have been inconceivable in this country. In the UK people don't feel the need to fake an enthusiasm about these things and, more pertinently, would already have a very clear view about what St Helens was like. This view was famously and succinctly portrayed in a *Punch* cartoon in February 1978.

"He's utterly convinced that he's being exiled to St. Helen's, poor devil!"

Doesn't look too happy does he?

It is hardly surprising that this was the general view as writers have always been pretty damning in their verdict on the town. *The Liverpool Echo,* as long ago as 1876 stated that, "the only thing remarkable about the town…. is its smoky atmosphere," and a little further afield the *Coventry Telegraph* in 1879 described it as that "far from salubrious town where they manufacture chemicals". Admittedly that was more than 100 years ago, but more recently, Pete McCarthy, who was educated in St Helens, wrote in *McCarthy's Bar* that St Helens was a town so devastated by industry that it made Warrington, where he lived, seem by comparison an area of outstanding natural beauty. History books get in on the act as well, with Alan Crosby in his *History of Lancashire* referring to "squalid and unsewered streets" and describing it as "a peculiarly unhealthy place". And when one grafts on to this image the one created by Tony Lane and Kenneth Roberts in their book about the Pilkington strike of 1970, which depicted St Helens as "a rugby league town*, a man's town" where "the women do as they are told…they play bingo while the men go drinking", one very quickly starts to understand why others view our town in the way that they do!

But if the image is indisputable, it is undoubtedly also the case that St Helens has a name which does not fit this image. It would be difficult to imagine, for example, the likes of Scunthorpe or Hartlepool being attractive spa towns to which tourists might travel in droves. But you could imagine the name St Helens belonging to such a town. After all, it doesn't sound all that different from (Lytham) St Annes or St Ives, both of which, for very good reason admittedly, have a far more positive image. Indeed I do recall occasions when, having disclosed that I was from St Helens, the listener clearly made the mistake of confusing it with St Annes. A response

* You may have noticed that I have made reference to rugby league. Or to be more precise I have used a quotation which includes the words "rugby league". My brother accuses me of shoehorning rugby league into every conversation involving someone who is not a native of St Helens at the earliest opportunity. This is totally untrue. I can remember conversations in which rugby league didn't feature at all, although admittedly not too many. And there are lots of other occasions when I have not introduced rugby league into the conversation until a respectable period had passed. But what I didn't want to do here was to be a rugby league bore. I am told that there are some. However as the association between the town and the game is indelible, it would neither be right nor proper to ignore it completely – hence moderation is the order of the day.

of, "Oh, I believe it's really nice there," was a dead giveaway. One always felt honour bound at such times to put the poor misguided person right.

I am not the first to ponder what might these days be termed *the disconnect* between the name and the place. Charles Nevin, author and journalist, mused in his book *Lancashire: Where Women Die of Love,* in the context of St Helens, whether an ugly town could have a beautiful name. He even went as far as suggesting that the old villages making up the town had a certain poetry attached to them – Pocket Nook, Fingerpost, Thatto Heath and the like. But then Charles does get carried away from time to time - more of that later!

Let's go back to the breakfast conversation in Heidelberg, or at least the sentiment expressed in the conversation. What is it about a place that might make a person feel he's "Gotta go there"? Whatever that might be, you might very reasonably conclude that St Helens doesn't have it. Stratford on Avon is a pretty enough place but we all know that the reason it features on so many tourist itineraries is the ubiquitous presence of its most famous son. You can understand as well why a place like Bath, with its natural hot springs and Roman history, is a honey trap for visitors. And of course there are other places which feature on travel itineraries for reasons we would not wish to emulate. Many travel writers, such as Bill Bryson in *Tales from a Small Island,* go to Wigan, but as far as I can establish this is simply to verify, albeit rather belatedly, the findings of George Orwell, who famously wrote about the wretched state of the working classes there in *The Road to Wigan Pier.*

To the best of my knowledge, St Helens features on only one travel itinerary, whether tourist, writer or otherwise. It was the first port of call for Jonathan Hibbs in the aptly named *The First Tourist: Travels in Search of St Helena* – again, more of that later. But whilst it is certainly understandable that the town does not appear too often in travel literature, it is shamefully ignored in some other works. It is accorded only the occasional reference in Paul Morley's *The North (and Nearly Everything in it)* – yet he manages to produce a list of Lancashire comedians which makes no mention of Bernie Clifton or Johnny Vegas, he refers to Frank Cottrell Boyce as coming from Liverpool, describes the trials of Stephenson's Rocket as taking place in "Rainhill, near Liverpool", discusses the 2012 Olympic Opening ceremony without any reference to the source of its inspiration and, in a book which is in many ways a homage to Lancashire and its part in the industrial revolution, the name of John Rylands does not feature at all. What has St Helens done to upset him? Is it really just one more unremarkable town in the North West of England? Does it have no real identity? Well, I certainly believe it does and there are certainly others who share that view. The aforementioned Charles Nevin once wrote in *The Guardian* that coming from St Helens was a bit like being a Catholic – however hard you tried, you couldn't quite get away from it. It may of course be the case that you could say the same thing about a number of places in the UK but more importantly I think there are many more that you could not. And disclosing in a conversation that you are from St Helens is rarely a conversation killer as it invariably gives rise to some sort of quip – OK often derogatory, but that's far better than no reaction at all. But what is it that gives the town – or what gives any town - its identity?

For many places the answer is obvious – once again Stratford upon Avon is the perfect example. The multiple attractions of capital cities which more often than not are also steeped in history, again make it relatively easy to trace the roots of their identity. But St Helens? A town which only came into being in the latter part of the nineteenth century?

Is it simply the existence of the world famous rugby league team? There is no doubt at all that this makes an enormous contribution to the identity of the town. But is this the full explanation? If it is not, then pinning down exactly what is, is not easy.

Staying in the sporting arena, there is of course Haydock Park. I say "of course", and for many people the association with St Helens does exist, but it has to be said that there is also a substantial body of people who do not actually realise that Haydock Park is in St Helens. Worse still, there are those who believe it is located in – God forbid – Wigan (if my recollection is correct, Wigan did make a bid at some point to have Haydock Park incorporated into its own borders which was, thankfully for all concerned, unsuccessful). My own view however is that, notwithstanding the fact that St Helens is rightly proud of its Grade 1 racecourse, it actually contributes very little to the town's identity.

There is little else sports-wise which has any real profile. The football team, St Helens Town, has had its moments; these include a win at Wembley in the 1987 FA Vase final and a 1-0 victory over Everton in 1909 (I'm not sure if this is true but I remember hearing it at school – the joke at the time was that Everton had refused to give them a fixture since then). Until the club was relegated in 2015, St Helens Town also had the distinction of being the only club to play in the top division of the North West Counties League every year since its commencement in 1982. However this is hardly the stuff of legends – after all the premier division of the North West Counties League is in the ninth division of English football. True Premier League status is still some distance away. And Premier League status is overrated anyway. Just look at some of the towns in the North West which have, or have had, teams in the Premiership. Need I say more?

So, rugby league apart, sport contributes little to the town's identity. What about the town's heritage and the key part it played in the industrial revolution? It is after all the birthplace of both the railways and modern canals; its coal fired many of the first industrial processes and its glass was responsible for introducing light throughout the buildings of the era. But the town's heritage has been disgracefully underplayed over the years – it has never been celebrated in the manner it should have been and is therefore little known, not only outside the town but, perhaps unbelievably, within.

One thing that people did associate with the town for many years was the glassmaker Pilkington, founded in the early 19th century, the town's major employer and, prior to its flotation on the London Stock Exchange in 1971, the world's largest private company. This was the company which pioneered the float glass process which was the dramatic breakthrough in glass manufacture in the 1950s. Sadly these days the company is in Japanese ownership and, in terms of employment at least, is a shadow of the industrial giant which once dominated the town (although to be fair, this is attributable more to advances in technology rather than Pilkington falling off the pace). One legacy which does survive is the museum, the World of Glass (successor to the Pilkington Glass Museum) which in its own literature describes itself as one of the country's most remarkable visitor attractions. Its visitor numbers would suggest this claim to be slightly over the top – it could be so much more than it is - but I think we have to accept that it is unique, even if it only plays a bit part in building the town's image.

The other industrial behemoth founded in St Helens was Beechams, the pharmaceutical manufacturers whose powders were famed throughout the world. Sadly, its successor SmithKline Beecham merged with Glaxo in 2000 and the merged company, GlaxoSmithKline, no longer carries the Beecham name. There is no doubt that Beechams played a huge part in putting St Helens on the map and it certainly made its own contribution to the identity of the town.

However I am still left with the feeling that there is an ingredient we are missing – something which complements the legends of the rugby field and the pioneers of the glass and pharmaceutical industries.

So what are we left with? It seems to me that the answer must lie in the people of St Helens and in particular the character traits that might distinguish them from those who populate other northern towns. Research by scientists at the Universities of Cambridge and Helsinki published in 2009 tells us that different places in Britain have distinct personality traits so it may not be as fanciful as it sounds to contemplate whether or not we are different from anyone else. Some commentators have certainly hinted at it; Charles Nevin wrote in the *New Statesman* in 2005 that one should "not make the mistake of thinking that the people of St Helens are dour and grim up-northerners; they live where Lancashire whimsy meets Liverpudlian wit and they like their life and their rugby the same". Sir Thomas Beecham had expressed essentially the same sentiment many years earlier: "Where *I* come from, we're all a bit vulgar, you know, but there is a certain heartiness – a sort of bonhomie about our vulgarity – which tides you over a lot of rough spots in the path". His view of our brethren from the other side of the Pennines was less favourable, ".... in *Yorkshire*, in a spot of bother, they're so damn-set-in-their-ways that there's no doing anything with them".

This view is consistent with the reaction of the town to the publication of the *Punch* cartoon referred to earlier. As far as I am aware, nobody in St Helens objected to the cartoon at all. There was no outcry nor any letters in the national press expressing outrage. There was no movement to boycott the magazine (although I strongly suspect the *Punch* circulation figures in St Helens were not breaking any records at the time). Word did get around quite quickly but my recollection is that everybody either found it quite amusing or simply shrugged shoulders and returned to complaining about the important things in life – like the cost of a pint. Would the reaction have been different in other towns, particularly those populated by professional northerners? Most of these of course hail from the dark side of the Pennines but much closer to home, you could certainly imagine a furious Stuart Maconie (try reading *Pies and Prejudice*), detecting a treacherous plot by effete southerners and calling for the brethren to march on London in protest. The reaction to Pete McCarthy's unflattering remarks about the town tells the same story. The only criticism I heard was in relation to his suggestion that Warrington might be regarded differently (and anyone who has disembarked from the train at Warrington Bank Quay in the shadows of the Unilever plant would certainly concur!)

St Helens however is a town which can and does laugh at itself. Amusement rather than outrage is generally the order of the day. So it would surprise no-one when the opening of the St Helens Hilton (sadly no longer in existence) was observed by many at the time as representing the ultimate devaluation of the Hilton brand. The Chief Executive of the Arts Council may have described "The Dream" as "Jaume Plensa's stunning, enigmatic sculpture which celebrates the town's industrial past". To many St Helens residents it is simply known as "The Nob of the North". The town's inhabitants may have aspirations but for the most part, they don't take themselves too seriously and they are disarmingly realistic when it comes to talking about it.

It follows then that in determining whether or not St Helens has a particular identity, we should be examining those people from St Helens, both past and present, who have achieved a profile outside as well as within the town. That is what this book attempts to explore. Who are they, what is their background, what have they achieved and how did they do it?

The criteria for inclusion are that someone must have been born, raised or educated in the town. This last category will require the inclusion of some who might more readily be associated with other towns but it is, after all, one's education which generally dictates accent and certainly influences character; the Jesuits knew what they were doing when they adopted the mantra, "Give me the child for the first seven years and I will give you the man". For this very reason, I have opted to exclude those who have simply come to live in the town. As welcome as they are, their inclusion in this collection would be misleading.

Having trawled through as many sources as I could find, I have discovered that there is a wide range of what we might loosely call distinguished persons who hail (or hailed) from the town. Of course what *distinguished* means to one person will be very different from what it means to others but I have tried to be as inclusive as possible – which means not only those who have brought success and honour to the town but also those whom certain members of the populace might have preferred to ignore. And I have tried to include only information which I hope the reader will find interesting and that does mean of course that the nature, length and content of some entries differs from others.

When I shared my intentions with my wife (who hails not from St Helens but from Newcastle upon Tyne) she observed that there would not be many entries in the book, but despite that there would more entries than there would be readers. As you will see she was a long way from the truth on the former and I would love to think that she was very very wrong on the latter as well!

So let us have a look at town's production line, the local lads made good, the famous and the infamous, the distinguished and the disgraced, the legendary and the mythical. Let us explore the characters who have shaped and illuminated the town's history, those who have put the town on the map. And let us consider not only those names which are synonymous with the town, but also those who for many have slipped through the net – where the connection with St Helens will prompt surprise and raise a few eyebrows.

Sporting Towns of the North : 1. St. Helens

St Helens as depicted in a popular cartoon

THE GREAT & THE GOOD....

... (and a few of the not so good!)

Jacqui Abbott

The distinction of being the first person in this compilation goes to the singer Jacqueline Abbott, once of The Beautiful South and now part of a very successful duo with The Beautiful South founder Paul Heaton. The story is reasonably well-known – in 1991, at the age of 17 she was at Sixth Form College when she bumped into Paul outside a night club. He invited her and a friend to a party somewhere close to Taylor Park where the friend encouraged her to sing.

We now fast forward to 1993 when Paul is looking for a replacement lead singer for the band and he decided to track down the "lass from the glass", as he called her. It seems when he found her, she was working in a greengrocer's shop, where she was reputedly earning £1.75 an hour. She readily accepted his invitation and went almost from zero to hero overnight.

Jacqui was born in St Helens on 10th November 1973, daughter of Harry and Margaret and younger sister of Christopher and Steven. She was educated at Grange Park before moving on to Sixth Form College to retake her GCSEs. Quite what path her life would have taken absent the meeting with Paul Heaton we will never know. In the event, she was speedily propelled into the limelight as the lead singer of one of Britain's most successful bands.

Her career with The Beautiful South spanned its best and most successful years. Jacqui sang on four albums from which several top 10 singles were released, the best-known of which were "Rotterdam", "Don't Marry Her" and "Perfect 10". However in 2000 Jacqui left the band, for reasons which were not at the time entirely clear – rumours of disagreements, and that Jacqui had had enough of the band's legendary hard drinking, circulated but were unconfirmed. What is certainly the case is that she had recently given birth to her son, Matthew, who had been diagnosed with autism and to whom Jacqui unsurprisingly, wanted to devote her whole time and attention.

At this point Jacqui pretty much disappeared from public life for over a decade, during which time she returned to St Helens to spend time with her partner Sam and her children and, after doing voluntary work with some local charities, had taken a job as a teaching assistant. She did not resurface until 2nd June 2011, when she was interviewed on BBC Radio 4 by Alan Johnson, the ex-Home Secretary and, by his own admission, a failed rock star. At around about the same time, Paul Heaton tracked her down (again!), this time via Facebook, and invited her to sing at the performance of his concept show *The 8th* (about the deadly sins) at the Manchester International Festival the following month. It seems that Jacqui had missed playing in the band hugely and didn't take much persuading once Paul had been in touch. She met up with him for the first time in ten years and singing together again immediately brought back for her the realisation of how much she had enjoyed singing and performing. Critically, the chemistry with Paul was also still there. Jacqui couldn't resist agreeing to his suggestion that they make an album together at which point the show was once again on the road. Paul, for his part, said that working with Jacqui again was like "going into your garage and discovering a beautiful covered up Rolls Royce that hadn't been started in years".

The duo's album *What Have We Become* was released in 2014 and reached number 3 in the album charts. Television appearances followed, including a slot on *The One Show* and they started to tour together, not under The Beautiful South name, but simply as Paul Heaton and Jacqui Abbott. They played a number of festivals including Glastonbury and also made a video for the song "Loving Arms" from the album with the Grimethorpe Colliery band (which had become world famous after featuring in the film *Brassed Off*).

The following year saw the release of a second album *Wisdom, Laughter and Lines* and 2016 brought a major tour including an appearance at Delamere Forest as part of the Forestry Commission's Music Live series. By then there was no holding them back and their third album together *Crooked Calypso* entered the album charts at number 2 in July 2017.

It would be nice to think that now Jacqui is back, she is here to stay!

St Edmund Arrowsmith

Every town should have its own saint – a proper one that is, not a rugby playing one – and there would of course have been a certain neatness had we been able to construct a case that St Helen(a) herself had been born in the town. We can however boast that we do have a bona fide saint within our ranks in the form of St Edmund Arrowsmith who we can say unequivocally did come from St Helens.

St Edmund was moreover not just any old saint, he is a member of the celebrated "Forty Martyrs of England and Wales" all of whom were elevated from the rank of "Blessed" to "Saint" on 25th October 1970 by Pope Paul VI. What got them over the line apparently was the cure of a young woman with a malignant tumour after Catholics prayed to the Forty Martyrs on her behalf.

St Edmund was born in Haydock in 1585, although he was actually christened Brian rather than Edmund. Edmund seems to have been his confirmation name as well as the name of one of his uncles, who helped train priests in France. Whatever the reason however, Edmund was the name by which he was always known. His mother was a member of the Gerard family, a name which one encounters frequently in the history of Catholic Lancashire. His family was in fact steeped in Catholicism although in the area in which he lived that was not too unusual – Catholics had largely been left alone by the local landowners, who included the Earls of Derby. All that said, this was not of course a particularly good time for Catholics (or Popish recusants, as they were known at the time). During Edmund's childhood the Protestant Elizabeth I was Queen of England and indeed his own parents were jailed in

Lancaster as a consequence of their faith, leaving Edmund and his siblings to be cared for by neighbours. Although Elizabeth died when Edmund was 18, she was succeeded by James I, who was the subject of the infamous gunpowder plot carried out by the Catholic fanatic Guy Fawkes. This event was not good news for others of that faith since it considerably hardened the king's resolve to control non-conforming Catholics.

Edmund's father Robert and elder brother Peter had fought on the continent for Sir William Stanley, a prominent Catholic and opponent of the Elizabeth I. Peter died after being wounded in Spain and Robert himself died soon after his return to England. As a consequence, in order to help his widowed mother Edmund was taken under the wing of a secular priest. He turned out to be a very capable student and in 1605 - the same year as the gunpowder plot - he travelled to Douai in France where he trained for the priesthood. He was duly ordained in 1612 and immediately despatched whence he came to administer to the Catholics in Lancashire. It seems this passed largely without incident until 1622 despite the fact that, according to a 2010 article in the *Catholic Herald*, he went about his business in a "fearless and forthright" manner, "denouncing heretics with an unguarded zeal". It was probably no surprise therefore when he was arrested by the Anglican Bishop of Chester. But his luck held as he was shortly freed on the orders of James I (not necessarily the act of tolerance that it might seem – James was at the time trying to arrange a Spanish marriage for his son Charles and no doubt thought that easing off the persecution of Catholics in his own kingdom might help his case). Clearly not a man to back off after such a minor setback, on regaining his freedom Edmund resolved to join the Jesuits and to this end was required to spend a brief time in London. It was not long however before he was back in his native Lancashire, promoting the faith once more "with his accustomed vigour".

Given the religious uncertainties of the time, this state of affairs was never going to last and in 1628 Edmund was denounced by a man named Holden – something to do with Edmund having reproached him for extra marital activities. On this occasion his luck did run out and he was indicted at Lancaster assizes, charged with being a seminary priest and a Jesuit. It is unlikely that he pleaded not guilty (and if he had it probably wouldn't have done him any good). Retribution was swift and decisive – he was hung, drawn and quartered on 28th August of the same year, his head was set on a pinnacle at Lancaster Castle and his quarters distributed elsewhere upon the building.

Somehow the Arrowsmith family managed to recover Edmund's hand and it survives to this day as a relic of a true saint in the church of St Oswald and St Edmund Arrowsmith in Ashton in Makerfield. Edmund had to wait some 300 years until 1929 for his beatification – in the greater scheme of things his elevation to the higher rank in 1970 was positively speedy!

Recognising that for the great majority of the faithful, the requirement to make five visits to Rome to secure a plenary indulgence was impractical,
Pope Pius XI extended the concession to
a number of other locations, the only one in the UK
being the Church of St Helen and the
Holy Cross in St Helens.

Michael E. Arth

Photo of Michael as a child in his home in Litherland Crescent, St Helens

Michael E. Arth's entry on Wikipedia describes him as a "polymath". I didn't know at the time I read this whether I had ever met a polymath, whether from St Helens or anywhere else, as I had no idea what a polymath was. It is, I have since discovered, an extremely learned person whose knowledge ranges across many and diverse areas. Put more simply, it is someone who knows a lot about a lot. Leonardo de Vinci was, I am reliably informed, a polymath but of course I never met him. I have undoubtedly met people who would like to consider themselves as polymaths (and plenty of those were from St Helens) but I still don't know whether I have actually encountered one or not.

Anyway, back to Michael E. Arth. Michael is an American citizen who lives in the Garden District in DeLand, Florida, an area which had previously been a slum district known locally as Crack Town. In the year 2000 he purchased 32 properties there which were mostly dilapidated and in severe disrepair, and then spent some seven years rebuilding and restoring them. His biggest challenge was not the condition of the buildings but dealing with what he describes as "a mostly transient population of crack cocaine dealers, vagrants, addicts, hookers and criminals engaged in all sorts of unpleasant activities". He changed the name to the Historic Garden District and has transformed the area into one of the most desirable in the city.

Michael's objective in carrying out this work was to put into practice the principles of a new urban design movement that he had founded, known as "New Pedestrianism". As the name suggests, its purpose is to reduce dependency on the motor car. The idea is that you create pedestrian villages close to the "downtown" thereby providing access to all its facilities without having to rely on the automobile – quite a radical proposition in modern America!

A feature-length award winning documentary *New Urban Cowboy: Toward a New Pedestrianism* was released in April 2008. It covers the transformation of the slum district in DeLand and the concepts behind the New Pedestrian movement.

Aside from all of this, Michael is an artist, author, photographer, film maker, landscape designer, social activist and, in 2010, was a candidate for the Governor of Florida (his initial intention had been to run as a Democrat but he clearly upset too many people within the Party and ended up running as an independent. He didn't win). However there isn't room in this compilation to record all his activities which are in any case chronicled elsewhere for anyone who is interested. Suffice to say, this is a guy with opinions, who has a social conscience and is willing to put himself about a bit in order to try and solve them. It is certainly worth at the very least readers taking a quick look at his Wikipedia entry to get a flavour of the sheer breadth of his activities.

The connection with St Helens? Well Michael lived in St Helens until he was 16 months old, initially in Chadwick Street in Haresfinch and then in Litherland Crescent. His father worked as a meteorologist at the US airbase in Burtonwood but he and his wife wanted to live amongst the English, as they put it, "to counter the reputation of ugly Americans". They chose St Helens, liked the town and stayed there for the whole of Michael's father's tour of duty in the UK.

Michael's mother recalled that the people in St Helens were by and large very poor (at the time, in the early 1950s, there was still rationing) and that they shared with their neighbours the provisions they obtained from the air base.

Michael has made the return journey to St Helens on several occasions as an adult, visiting local pubs as well as St Peter and Paul Catholic Church where he and his younger sister were baptised. Returning in 1993 Michael tracked down his entry in the church records written in Latin, which recorded not only the dates of his birth and baptism but also went on to record that he was later confirmed in Midland Texas in April 1962 (do they keep track of everyone that is christened in St Peter and Paul?).

Whilst it might be regarded by some that a period of just 16 months in the town doesn't meet the criteria for entry into this collection, it should be noted that based upon his time in the town, Michael has joint US and British citizenship and, more importantly, believes his first clear memory was of looking at the rows of terraced houses from the back of the car on the day he left St Helens. In the light of this, can there really be any argument against his inclusion?

The bell and the portholes for the
Titanic were manufactured in
St Helens.

Eric Ashton MBE

Born in St Helens on 24th January 1935, Eric Ashton MBE went on to become the first St Helens-born player to captain Great Britain, the first to lift the Challenge Cup as a captain and the first to lift the World Cup as captain. In June 1966 he became the first rugby league player to be awarded the MBE.* He played for Great Britain 26 times before retiring from international rugby at the age of 27 and was one of the most gifted centres ever to play the game. By any normal standards he would be an icon in his home town, lauded by all. There was just one problem – Eric spent the whole of his playing career with the arch enemy Wigan. It is no surprise therefore that for many years he was regarded as the villain rather than the hero.

How and why the St Helens club repeatedly passed over opportunities to sign Eric defies rational analysis but it was arguably the biggest mistake they ever made. And it wasn't as if he was one of those misguided persons who were lured away from the town of their birth by the offer of more money – quite the opposite in that he made it very clear that given the opportunity he would have signed in a flash!

As a child Eric lived in Mulberry Avenue, just a stone's throw from Saints' old ground at Knowsley Road. He and his brother would watch all the home games, albeit rarely via the turnstiles and more often via the top of the wall behind the men's toilets, but then that was the preferred form of entry for many a schoolboy in days gone by. Eric's father, Ernie, had played briefly for Warrington some years earlier so a rugby tradition was certainly present in the family and at Rivington Road School, Eric soon excelled on the rugby field, being selected to represent both the town and county at schoolboy level. In his spare time he would play touch rugby on the Congregational Church Fields (where he also encountered a somewhat younger Ray French). It seemed inevitable that he would find his way into the professional ranks and in due course he was invited to take part in a trial with Saints "B" team. And that was the last time he was called upon by Saints, despite turning up week in week out for the training sessions. At the age of 16, fed up and quite disillusioned, Eric Ashton retired from rugby league, took a job with Pilkington and for the next two years started out on what might have been a totally unremarkable life.

During this era however, National Service still existed and when Eric's turn came he was sent to Edinburgh as a Royal Artillery Gunner. Discovering that being a member of the rugby team would exempt him from many of the boring overnight guard duties, he volunteered to play and the army liked what they saw. He was selected to play for the Scottish Command and sent to London for trials with the national Army side. But more significantly, his scrum-half, Bert Marsh, was from Wigan and persuaded him once his army days were over to go there for a trial. Wigan too liked what they saw. Eric made his first team debut in August 1955 and the rest is all too painful history.

For obvious reasons we will gloss over the next few years quite quickly, pausing to note only that after 18 months at Wigan, he was made captain (and was to retain the captaincy for the rest of his career there), that he continued to work at Pilkington until 1963 (he admitted, unsurprisingly, to taking a lot of stick!) when he became full-time player coach, that he captained Wigan in a record six Cup Finals (albeit he was on the losing side twice against St Helens), and that he scored 231 tries and 448 goals in 497 appearances. Oh yes, and that when he went on to the transfer list in 1961 after a dispute with Wigan, Saints offered £11,000 against an asking price of £13,000 (admittedly more than twice the previous record fee). Saints confidently expected the League to order Wigan to reduce the fee in accordance with the rules at the time in the absence of an offer at the asking price. Everything was scuppered however by a bid from Workington for the full amount. Eric turned down the opportunity to go to Cumbria, Wigan were not required to reduce the asking price and another opportunity went begging!

After retiring from playing Eric went on to coach Wigan for four years before spending a season as coach at Leeds and then, at the age of 39, he finally came home and was appointed coach at St Helens. And it couldn't have started better as Saints, inspired by the return from early retirement of John Walsh, stormed to a championship win in his first season and in his second, won the BBC 2 Floodlit Trophy, the Premiership and the Challenge Cup in the famous *Dad's Army* final against Widnes. But that was where the success ended and it is fair to say that Eric Ashton the coach was never held in the same regard as Eric Ashton the player. He stayed on at Saints until 1980 but the all-conquering side of the early and mid-seventies had grown old and their replacements were not delivering on the field. Eric himself was hurt by some of the

Eric during his time as Saints' coach
© Copyright Brian Peers

criticism that came his way, resorting on one occasion to writing a passionate defence of his coaching in the *St Helens Reporter*. He was replaced as coach by Kel Coslett but there was no quick fix and it was to be another 16 years before the glory days were to return to the club.

His resignation as coach did not however mean he was severing contact with the club. Two years later he joined the board of directors and was to stay on the board for the rest of his life. The three Cup Final defeats to Wigan in 1989, 1991 and 2002 did prompt the rather unkind observation that he was the only man to be on the losing side in all five St Helens versus Wigan Cup Finals, although thankfully that record was put straight when Saints defeated Wigan in the final at Cardiff in 2004. His final moment of glory came when, during his period as Chairman of the Club between 1993 and 1997, he led the St Helens side onto the turf at Wembley in 1996 against Bradford Bulls, and thereby became the only man to win the Challenge Cup as captain, player/coach, coach and chairman. In 2003 in recognition of his many years' service with the club he was made Life President.

Eric passed away in 2008 after finally losing a battle with prostate cancer. He was survived by his wife of 50 years, Doreen, his two daughters Beverley and Michelle and four grandchildren. The accolades came from every quarter and without exception, they would describe Eric not only as a giant of the sport and a fierce competitor, but also as the perfect gentleman who had been one of the finest ambassadors the game had ever had seen. There is no doubt that he was one of the true greats – but why, oh why, did it have to be that Wigan and not St Helens was the main beneficiary of that great talent?

* David Hadfield suggests that Eric may also have been the first rugby league player to pen an autobiography when Glory in the Centre Spot was published in 1966 – however I think that accolade may rest with another legend, Vince Karalius, with the publication of Lucky 13 in 1964.

ROCK GROUP

QUEEN

APPEARED AT THE
ST HELENS CONGREGATIONAL HALL
ON 19TH DECEMBER 1970.

Rick Astley

The purists may still feel a little uneasy with the concept of Newton-le-Willows being part of St Helens. After all, it had been in existence for hundreds of years (it was mentioned in the *Domesday Book*) before it was subsumed into the Metropolitan Borough of St Helens on 1st April 1974. My own recollection is that, certainly in my school days, inhabitants of Newton felt more of an affiliation with Warrington than St Helens. But then St Helens only came into existence in 1868 and was itself made up of four previously independent townships so on the basis that Newton has now been part of the town for more than 40 years, it certainly cannot be ignored. It has to be acknowledged as well that it is an area which has produced some extremely worthy entries in this collection, the first of which is Richard Paul Astley, born on 6th February 1966, just eight years before Newton's big event. And as the MTV website now records his birth place as being Newton-le-Willows, St Helens he must take his rightful and proper place on these pages!

Rick was the youngest of four children but his parents separated when he was five years old. Although he was brought up by his father, Ozzie, in Park Road, his introduction to music actually came from his mother, Cynthia, who was herself a singalong pianist. As a consequence, he sang from a very early age as a member of the local church choir. He was educated initially at St Peter's Primary School before moving to Selwyn Jones High School for his secondary education, during which time he was involved with a number of bands, mainly as a drummer. He left school at 16 and went to work in the garden centre in Newton owned by his dad.

Over the next few years Rick played drums in a number of bands, the last of which, FBI, was quite popular locally. In 1985, the lead singer, guitarist David Morris (who is incidentally currently Conservative MP for Morecambe and Lunesdale), decided to quit and Rick volunteered to take over. He attracted the attention of a local talent agent, Dave Warwick, who in turn tipped off Pete Waterman, who came to watch the band at

Monks Social Club in Woolston. Pete liked him but it took some time to get Rick on board, as he wanted to stick with the band rather than go solo. However after a while Rick did agree to accept the offer of a job in Pete's recording studio in London, and it was there that Rick got to know the ins and outs of the music industry (as well as once making tea for Bananarama, which led to the persistent rumour that he had been employed as a teaboy!) However all was to change with the release of his first solo single "Never Gonna Give You Up" in August 1987. The song was a massive worldwide hit, staying at number one in the British charts for five weeks as well as topping the charts in 24 other countries including the United States. Most commentators picked out Rick's voice as the reason for its success – full, deep and rich, it seemed incongruous that it should belong to a fresh faced, red-haired 21-year-old from Newton. The track was voted Best British single in the 1988 Brit Awards and featured on Rick's first album, *Whenever You Need Somebody*, which was released November 1987 and also made number one in the British charts, helping him become that year's bestselling British artist worldwide.

Rick went on to release another nine singles and a second album with SAW (Stock, Aitken, Waterman). He featured constantly in the chart, being an ever-present in the British top 40 for the six months after his first single was released and in one year selling more albums than any other artist. However he could not quite repeat the initial success of "Never Gonna Give You Up" and he was the subject of some harsh press criticism, some of which arose because of his links with SAW (seen by some as nothing more than a music factory) as well as some hurtful tabloid coverage of his decision to abandon FBI and go alone.

Rick decided to leave SAW in 1990 – although still only 24, he wanted to develop a more mature musical image and to move away from the original dance/pop into his preferred genre, soul music. He went on to release two more albums and five more singles, one of which, "Cry for Help", reached number 7 in both the UK and the USA. But in many ways the bubble had burst and he was no longer seen as one of the world's great musical stars.

Still, what came next surprised everyone. At around the time he left SAW, Rick also broke up, amicably, with the childhood sweetheart he had been with since his Newton days. He then got together with a Danish film producer, Lene Bausager, whom he met at RCA records, and they had a daughter, Emilie, who was born in 1992. In 1993, arriving back in the UK from a trip to America, he was distraught that he had missed Emilie's first steps and, one assumes, also somewhat disillusioned with fame and its trappings. He made the snap decision that he was going to retire from the music business and that was pretty much that for the next four to five years.

During this time, Rick kept a low profile, living in London with Lene and Emilie. He did not return to the recording studio until 2002 when he released the album *Keep It Turned On* in Continental Europe and then three years later he released *Portrait* which reached number 26 in the UK album chart. More successful were two compilation albums, *Greatest Hits* in 2002 and *The Ultimate Collection* in 2008. By then however, his name was on everybody's lips for a different reason - the advent of the internet phenomenon "rickrolling"!

Rickrolling was a trick whereby internet users were unwittingly taken to a video of Rick singing "Never Gonna Give You Up". By April 2008, the BBC was reporting that some 13 million internet users had been rickrolled, including, famously, the New York Mets when they asked fans to vote for a new theme tune for the baseball team – some 5 million votes were inadvertently recorded for Rick Astley! Live rickrolling events followed with the song being played at sporting events, protest gatherings and the like. Quite how this all kicked off, nobody really knows but it certainly gave Rick a somewhat unlikely longevity and a legacy that will not soon be forgotten. It even led Rick to be nominated for – and win – the MTV award in 2008 for Best Act Ever, although he declined to turn up to accept the award on the basis that many who had voted for him did it as a sort of spin off from the rickrolling craze.

Since then Rick has continued to be active and has appeared around the globe, often with other 1980s acts. In 2011 he appeared on stage at Haydock Park Racecourse with his mother Cynthia, now in her 70s. He has also been visible away from the stage, with appearances in Comic Relief and in Peter Kay's "The Tour That Doesn't Tour Tour – Now on Tour". He has DJed on Magic FM and co-hosted an episode of Chris Evans Breakfast Show. In 2016 he was back on the music scene big time - his album *50,* released to mark the end of the first half century of his life made it to number one in the album charts, nearly 30 years after his first album had made it there. On the basis of this, it seems quite probable to me that we will also be seeing plenty of Rick during the second half century of his life!!

Professor Theo Barker

There are many in this collection – possibly even the majority – who have moved away from the town in order to follow the path they have chosen in life. For some, this was to all practical intents and purposes the end of their connection with the town, other than perhaps paying lip service to their devotion to the rugby team. However that was categorically not the case with the eminent historian, Professor Theo Barker. Indeed, far from distancing himself from the town of his upbringing, he positively embraced it, with many of his publications having the town, its industries or its transport as their subject.

Theodore Cardwell Barker was born on 19th July 1923 in Barton upon Irwell. However he attended Cowley Prep before moving on to Cowley Boys Grammar School so the family clearly moved to St Helens at some early point in Theo's life. We do not know very much about his childhood other than that his father Norman, was an electrical power engineer*, his mother's maiden name was Louie Cardwell and the family was living in Swinburne Road in 1939. However it does seem that he was fired up at an early age by the subject of local industrial history; whilst still at school, he and his close friend, John Harris, resolved that they would together write a book recording the growth and development of St Helens during the Industrial Revolution.

Theo would have left Cowley during the Second World War and one presumes he would have been called up by the military, although there appears to be nothing recorded about his activities in the war years. The next we know he has enrolled at Jesus College in Oxford where he obtained a first class degree in history in 1948. His thesis there on the Sankey Canal went on to provide the basis of the Sankey's claim to be Britain's first post-industrial canal. He moved to Manchester for his Master's Degree and went on to complete his PhD in 1951. Next stop was a year at Aberdeen University before he took up a post as lecturer at the London School of Economics in 1953.

The following year saw the publication of the book which he and John Harris (with whom he had renewed his acquaintance as a fellow post graduate student in Manchester) had conceived in their school days. Entitled *A Merseyside Town in the Industrial Revolution: St Helens 1750-1900*, it went on to become something of a classic in economic history circles (OK that might be a bit niche but I also studied economic history which I would like to think qualifies me to make such an observation!) It was one of the first books to approach urban history from an economic and industrial perspective, focusing at the same time on the social change that was taking place. As such it proved quite influential and was the subject of several reprints, the last one being in 1994.

In 1960 Theo married the opera singer Judith Pierce in Munich. Known more commonly as Joy, she had first met Theo whilst he was at Cowley Boys and she at Cowley Girls, albeit she was seven years younger than him. It is said that she acted as a restraining influence on some of his more exuberant notions - it is not entirely clear what these were but one assumes it was something to do with his fondness for eating, drinking and socialising! There was however no slackening off in his work ethic. That same year saw the publication of a history of *Pilkington Brothers and the Glass Industry,* before Theo moved his focus to the history of transport, which resulted in the publication in 1963 of *The History of London Transport: 19th Century,* another joint effort, this time with Michael Robbins.

1964 saw Theo move on from LSE, when he became the founding professor of economic and social history at the new University of Kent in 1964. Although he retained his London flat in Red Lion Square, he moved his main residence to Faversham which was where he was to remain for the rest of his life. During this period he started to take a keen interest in nutrition and authored a book entitled *Our Changing Fare: 200 Years of British Food Habits* and followed this with a number of histories of City Livery Companies which he wrote in collaboration with two former students.

Theo returned to LSE in 1976 as professor of economic history and stayed until his retirement. And next on the writing front it was another, expanded, history of Pilkington in 1977 and then back to transport with the publication of *The Transport Contractors of Rye* in 1982.

After retirement in 1983 he was awarded the title of Emeritus Professor of Economic History at the University of London, in recognition of the distinguished service he had given. His retired status did not however stem the flow of publications – he was to write a history of Shepherd Neame brewery (the oldest in Britain), was a joint author of *The Rise and Rise of Road Transport: 1600-1990* and in 1994 produced his third major volume documenting the history of Pilkington. But there were plenty more strings to his bow. He was the founding chairman of the Oral History Society and did many broadcasts on BBC radio which he delivered, according to the *Daily Telegraph*, with a "no nonsense Lancastrian bluntness". At various times, he was President of the Railway and Canal Historical Society, Secretary and later President of the Economic History Society, Secretary and later Chairman of the British National Committee of Historians, Chairman of the Transport History Research Trust and President of the International Committee of Historical Sciences.

One might reasonably assume from the impressive list of responsibilities above that this was someone devoted to his work with no time to play. Yet Theo and Joy were well-known for their entertaining and Theo in particular for his love of red wine. He also maintained a keen interest in big bands, whilst his warmth, enthusiasm and generosity were remarked upon by many. He was a regular visitor to his home town throughout his life, playing a large part in the founding of the Sankey Canal Restoration Society (of which his thesis had been the original inspiration), making many visits to the Pilkington archives, as well as returning for landmark local events such as the centenary of the St Helens Museum in 1992 and the centenary of the opening of the Gamble Institute in 1996.

Theo died at the age of 78 in November 2001 in Faversham and his obituaries all acknowledged both his innovative approach and the major contribution he had made to the study of economic and social history. Some of the tributes to him made specific mention of the entrepreneurial approach he had brought to the academic world – he had written for example a number of commissioned histories of various businesses (for example the livery companies) and he was also instrumental in raising private finance for the Business History Unit at

LSE and the Dictionary of Business Biography. But for the purposes of this publication, perhaps what stands out most is that this was a man for whom his home town mattered and a man who was prepared to put back into the town as much, and indeed more, than he had taken out.

Theo did not have any children but was survived by his wife Joy. She herself passed away two years later in 2003.

*   This was the occupation recorded in the 1939 National Registration although elsewhere he was recorded as having been an industrial chemist and I have heard anecdotally that he was a policeman.

A St Helens man, Major Norman Pilkington of Pilkington Brothers was the first flight fare paying passenger in 1919 when he flew from London and Paris.

Sir Joseph Beecham

With the exception of Pilkington, Beecham is, or more correctly was, the industry most associated with St Helens and indeed was an industrial giant in its own right. It was not however founded by someone from St Helens. The original Thomas Beecham was born in Oxfordshire in 1820 and was something of an itinerant. He came to St Helens via Liverpool and then Wigan where he had made pills and marketed them. He had acquired his knowledge during a childhood as a shepherd in the course of which he had educated himself and acquired herbal lore. The Wigan business, albeit initially a success, had to close down after Thomas's wife omitted to label a medicine bottle "poison" as a result of which a small child died. Unsurprisingly, this had a negative impact on his business and as a consequence Thomas sold up and moved to St Helens with his family in 1859. Wigan of course was a completely different world (it still is really) and his reputation did not transfer with him. He was therefore able to start afresh and begin the successful business which became so familiar to all of us.

The first Beecham to qualify for entry into this collection is Thomas's son, Joseph (later Sir Joseph Beecham, First Baronet, which I understand elevates him above all knighthoods with the exception of the Order of the Garter). Joseph was born in 1848 whilst his parents were still residing in Wigan but after the move to St Helens was schooled at the Moorflat Church of England School on Baldwin Street. Domestically however it was not a happy situation as his mother struggled with a drink problem (when she eventually died in 1872 the inquest recorded the cause of death as "habitual intemperance") and his father indulged in a number of extra-curricular activities, one of which resulted in the birth of an illegitimate child. At some point in mid to late 1863 the inevitable happened and his parents separated, with Joseph going to live with his mother. Shortly before the separation however, Joseph had left school to join his father in the business and this arrangement survived the domestic rift.

According to Joseph's own account, he worked exceptionally hard during this time, from 5.30am until midnight most days. This doesn't leave a lot of time for any leisure activities, whether of the type enjoyed by his father or otherwise, but he was apparently a member of St Helens Cricket Club and he also travelled to Liverpool to watch the opera, a love of music having been instilled in him by his mother. At a later point he was the co-founder of the St Helens Cycling Club.

The business meanwhile was using the slogan "Worth a guinea a box" to sell its pills and was advertising in the local press as well as selling via a network of agents who were located in London as well as Lancashire and Yorkshire. It was run from a small workshop in Westfield Street (which adjoined the house into which Thomas had moved shortly after the separation) and by 1865 had a turnover of £2,533. This rose steadily over the next few years and the business certainly made headway against its main rivals in the industry. By 1877 turnover had reached £23,000 and the first purpose-built factory in Westfield Street was constructed.

In 1873 Joseph married Josephine Burnett, whom he had met as a result of his involvement in music. Josephine's background is not entirely clear – it seems she claimed to have been born in Lille into the French Bohan family but there is no evidence to support this. Her marriage certificate records her father as William Burnett, whom she described as a silk dealer from St Helens, but there is no evidence either that he even existed. In fact her birth certificate records Everton, Liverpool as her place of birth and no father's name appears. Her mother seems to have been a Martha Dickens, born in New Brunswick, Canada and who was living in Croppers Hill with five of her children when Joseph came onto the scene. At a later date, Martha and three of her younger children emigrated to Australia. It is not known whether she ever made it full circle back to Canada.

Events at the end of this decade marked a critical point in the history of the business. In 1879, Thomas, whose private life can at best be described as chaotic, married his third wife Mary Sewell (his second having died after only four years of marriage, leaving him a widower for the second time). Mary had been raised in Canterbury and was herself, at the tender age of 28, already a widow three times over. Despite being housed in Thomas's new residence, Hill House, built in its own grounds on Croppers Hill, it seems she detested St Helens (there's no pleasing some folk!) and after a year and a half persuaded Thomas to go and live in Buckinghamshire. This marriage didn't last long either, ending acrimoniously when she accused him of trying to poison her, and by the end of 1884 he was back in St Helens. During his absence however, Joseph had been in charge and during this period an event took place which was to have a major impact on the business as well as his private life. It seems despite their shared love of music and the air of mystery surrounding her origins, he and Josephine did not turn out to be soulmates. Josephine had borne him five children by this point (and indeed went on to bear him three more) but it was his meeting with 22-year-old, Scottish-born but US-raised, Helen Taylor which caused him to embark upon a relationship which would endure for the rest of his life. However according to TAB Corley, in his book *Beechams: 1848–2000,* it marked another important change. In his view, Helen's influence, and in particular her cosmopolitan and unconventional view of life, brought about certain changes in Joseph's character and it was at this point that a decisive entrepreneur began to emerge.

As a consequence, by the time Thomas returned from Buckinghamshire, Beechams was poised to become market leader, a position it was to achieve emphatically in the second half of the 1880s. Between 1882 and 1890, turnover increased from £34,000 to £178,600. By then, over 250 million pills were being sold every year, one quarter of the total domestic market. To ensure the firm kept pace with production, Joseph commissioned the construction of a brand new factory on the site of the old one in Westfield Street, grandiose in every respect and reflecting his innovatory ideas. This was completed and opened in late 1887 and coincided with the launch of another initiative by Joseph, an export drive which would make Beechams a household name, not just in this country but in pretty much every English speaking country in the world and which would, after the introduction of prohibitive duties on imports to the USA in 1890, lead to the introduction of manufacturing in New York as well as St Helens.

Joseph had been admitted in 1888 as a partner in the firm alongside his father and in 1895 he took complete control after Thomas handed over his own 50 per cent share in the partnership. Thomas was by this time living in Southport with his housekeeper, Jane Roberts (by whom he had a daughter in 1895 when he was 75 and she was 22 – readers may have detected a certain pattern emerging here). He was to stay there until his death in 1907. His remains however were returned to St Helens for burial in St Helens cemetery.

During this period Joseph was developing a tremendous liking for foreign travel (possibly stimulated by the company of the well-travelled Helen Taylor) including more than 60 trips to the United States as well as a large number to Europe, Egypt and South Africa – never once accompanied by his wife. Indeed it is entirely possible that one of the attractions of foreign travel was that he could spend more time away from the marital home, which since 1885 had been a large house set in 13 acres in Huyton, (supposedly the first private house in England to be lit by electricity). His marriage to Josephine was surviving in little more than name. Josephine was suffering from epileptic fits and was increasingly dependent on alcohol, a situation which possibly led to Joseph in 1895 engaging a widowed headmistress to take charge of three of his daughters. Worse was to follow in 1899, when Joseph arranged for Josephine to be committed to a lunatic asylum (as such places were then known) in Northampton, on the basis that she was suffering from hysteria and delusions. Her children, on discovering this, commenced court action to have her released and in due course she moved in with the in-laws of her elder son Thomas in London. A judicial separation followed together with a rather unseemly public battle over the level of alimony which Joseph should pay, all of which made headlines both at home and in America (and which were described by Thomas Senior as "the best bit of free advertising I ever had!").

By the end of the century, Joseph was a very rich man with annual profits of around £80,000 all of which accrued to him as sole owner. He was also involved in other activities outside the firm, including three separate spells as mayor of St Helens and a very active chairmanship of the town's electricity committee. It is said that he even contemplated retirement after his father's death in 1907 but did not pursue this in the absence of an obvious successor. However the type of innovation which had characterised Joseph's early years in charge did not feature once the 20th century was underway and the progress of the business certainly stalled. Even the advertising campaign which had often been controversial but always effective became less punchy. That said, the firm was generating profits of over £100,000 in the years prior to the outbreak of the Great War in 1914 and these rose still further in the early war years to more than £130,000 (something approaching £6m in today's terms, not bad for a sole trader!) so they were clearly continuing to do something right.

Following the separation from Josephine, Joseph purchased a 30 room residence in Hampstead and fitted it out extravagantly with works of art, his new passion which for a time seemed to have replaced his love of music. This seems to have been little more than self-indulgence as his mistress Helen was moved to another home in Shepherd's Bush, whilst his relationship with his elder son was at best strained and at times hostile. He later spent £300,000 to promote the cause of opera in Britain which certainly helped him achieve the knighthood, awarded to him in the 1912 New Year's Honours list for services to music. Further accolades were to tumble his way in the lead up to the outbreak of war – he was appointed by the Czar to the Order of St Stanislaus for having brought Russian ballet to the rest of Europe, he was invited to a state ball at Buckingham Palace and in the June 1914 Birthday Honours, was advanced to the rank of baronet (it is rumoured that he was offered a peerage but turned it down on the basis that it was hereditary and Joseph did not think it appropriate for Thomas, his son, to use the House of Lords as a platform to expound some of his more controversial views). But it was also in this same period that he made the mistake that was to have major financial ramifications both for the firm and for his descendants, as well as most likely contributing to his own demise.

What Joseph agreed to do was to act as a front man for the purchase of the 19 acre Covent Garden estate in Central London from the Duke of Bedford – the largest chunk of central London ever to be sold in one plot. Joseph's intention was simply to pay out £500,000 of the £2m purchase price and then to sell his rights on for £550,000, a profit of £50,000, to Alexander Ormrod, a Manchester stockbroker. Joseph's involvement was merely to lend respectability to the deal and indeed the Duke of Bedford was by all accounts delighted to be dealing with such a wealthy purchaser. Unfortunately the back to back arrangement was not signed off when Joseph entered into the purchase contract on 6th July and war was to break out on 4th August. The government immediately closed down the London

Stock Exchange and banned new company share issues, thus denying Ormrod (and indeed Joseph) the opportunity to raise money to complete the purchase. There was no way that Joseph could pay off his massive debt and although he renegotiated the payment date with the Duke, it was at the cost of five per cent interest and only put off the day of reckoning to June 1917. This turned out to be hopelessly unrealistic and a further renegotiation took place in late 1916. However although agreement was reached, Joseph died in his sleep at his home in Hampstead before signature had taken place. Joseph was 68 and the cause of death diagnosed as heart failure.

One cannot help but be left with the impression that for all his wealth, Joseph was not a happy man and was rarely at ease with himself. His parents had not stayed together and his own marriage did not provide any contentment. His relationship with his children, particularly Thomas, was often strained. The only affection he appears to have received was from his long-suffering mistress, Helen, who stayed loyal to the end. It is said that despite his decisiveness in matters of business, Joseph suffered from an inferiority complex, being self-conscious about his small size, his strong Lancashire accent and his apparent inability to converse freely on any subject other than business. In the words of his own son, ".....outside the conduct of his own business he was a man of pathetic simplicity and uncertain judgement". He heavily relied on a friend, a Congregational minister, for advice despite the fact that the rest of his family heartily disliked him as he was old-fashioned and bigoted - perhaps not the best source of guidance on matters such as Joseph's children's education and his domestic arrangements. Joseph did succeed in some of his social aspirations, most notably by becoming mayor of St Helens, but he never really felt accepted in the social circles in which he would have liked to have moved. In the latter years, it might even be said that the Beechams firm thrived despite him rather than because of him. But in the final analysis there is no escaping the fact that it was he, more than anybody else, who was responsible for transforming Beechams into the enormously successful concern that it was ultimately to become.

The death of Sir Joseph Beecham in 1916 was the start of the end of the connection between the Beecham family and the firm which was to grow into the pharmaceutical giant familiar to all. Joseph's elder son,

Thomas, was to achieve fortune and fame in a world far removed from pharmaceuticals, whilst his second son Henry could at best be described as unremarkable and was effectively squeezed out of the business during the legal wrangles that ensued after Joseph's death. He was convicted of manslaughter in 1921 after a car he was driving too quickly had skidded, killed one child and injured two others. Not long after his release, he was paid off in full when the new Beechams Estates and Pills Limited was floated on the London Stock Exchange in 1924.

St.Helens Council

Sir Thomas Beecham

As noted earlier, Sir Joseph's elder son Thomas was to become famous in a quite different arena and is deserving therefore of his own entry in this collection. Indeed there have probably been more words written about Sir Thomas Beecham than any other person from St Helens including, as well as his own autobiography, a number of biographies which tell the story of an extremely colourful character who was a major influence on 20th century musical life in Britain. There is even a book wholly dedicated to his quotations and anecdotes about him (*Beecham Stories* by Harry Atkins and Archie Newman).

Thomas was born in Westfield Street in 1879 and lived initially at the back of the Beechams factory before moving with the family to "Ewanville", a 13 acre estate in Huyton, when he was six years old. Music was about the only thing that his parents had in common and after they took Thomas to his first concert at the age of five, he reportedly arose in the middle of the night, came downstairs and announced to a bemused assembly of adults that he wanted to learn to play the piano. Arrangements were made for a tutor to come over from St Helens twice a week and it seems Thomas was very soon demonstrating a precocious ability. Even more excitement was injected into his life by the installation in the family home of an orchestrion, a sort of machine that is intended to reproduce the sound of an orchestra, and which provided the young Thomas with an opportunity to listen every day to, and to learn by heart, the works of all the great composers. Every opportunity was also taken to attend orchestral concerts and operas.

In 1892 Thomas was despatched to Rossall School in Fleetwood and for most of the first year was thoroughly miserable. In time however he did settle in, striking up a good relationship with his music master and involving himself in various sports albeit, as he put it, "with a well calculated absence of zeal". He progressed to become Captain of his House and one of the privileges accorded to him was a study with its own piano – an apparently unique event in the school's history both before and after. His reputation as a maverick character was further enhanced when he took time off school to travel to New York with his father in 1893, returning on his own and apparently taking the opportunity on both voyages to accompany singers on the piano during the ship's concerts.

In 1897 Thomas gained admission to Wadham College, Oxford where he read, or more correctly was supposed to read, classics. In fact he showed little or no interest, preferring to play the piano that he had arranged to be installed in his room out of his handsome allowance. He apparently took a couple of trips to Dresden to watch opera when he should have been attending tutorials and, perhaps predictably, he and Wadham College parted company at the end of the first year.

Thomas at this point wanted to travel but did not get a sympathetic hearing from his father who arranged for him to enter the family firm as a trainee. This did not go down too well with young Thomas who loathed the routine and the monotony of the production process. He continued to pursue his musical interests by founding the short-lived St Helens Orchestral Society and his first big break arrived in 1899. The Hallé Orchestra had been invited to play at Joseph's inauguration as town mayor but their conductor, the eminent Hans Richter, pulled out at the last minute. The 20-year-old Thomas stepped up and by all accounts performed admirably. He was however unable to build on this opportunity as he was about to experience a major falling out with his father, as a consequence of which he was to move away from St Helens.

It seems that when, in 1899, Joseph had arranged for Thomas's mother, Josephine, to be committed to the lunatic asylum, he was not altogether open with his children. Thomas however became aware of the true situation and informed his elder sister, Emily. Together they managed to trace their mother's location but when they confronted Joseph about this and also about his relationship with Helen Taylor, he went into a rage and threw them out of the house. Thomas was taken in by Dr Welles, a US-born physician to the American Embassy, with whose daughter Thomas had struck up a friendship. Welles funded Thomas's musical studies and the legal actions which eventually resulted in Josephine's release (she also went to live at the Welles residence), the grant of a formal separation and the payment of alimony of £4,500 per annum. One consequence of all of this was that Beecham family relations fell to an all-time low.

Although Thomas went on to marry Utica Welles in 1903 (his mother attended the wedding but not his father) it did not turn out to be a "happy ever after" story. His only independent means of support was an income of £300 per year (a wedding present from his grandfather Thomas), so he was forced to rely upon the Welles family, a situation not to his liking. He saw himself stagnating and as a consequence made overtures to his father as early as 1905, offering even to move back to St Helens and rejoin the business (for some reason Utica did not approve of this bit but it didn't seem to bother him). His father was having none of it initially – it was not until 1909 that his attitude softened in any way, but even then the reconciliation was not straightforward and involved various intermediaries and numerous meetings. Thomas was however by now making his way in the world of music and after Joseph's attendance at a performance of the opera *The Wreckers*, at which Thomas was conducting, the reconciliation finally took place – perhaps Joseph concluded that Thomas was indeed going places and wanted to be associated with this. Whatever the reason, Thomas now had the benefit of Joseph's not insignificant wealth to provide him with financial support at a time when he was starting to develop from a shy young man into a self-confident operator with a very distinctive personality.

The timing was particularly good because Thomas had got himself into something of a financial pickle as well as a lot of unwelcome publicity after being named as co-respondent in a divorce case involving the American-born Maud Foster. The jury unanimously found Mrs Foster guilty and costs were awarded against Thomas – absent the reconciliation with his father he would have had no way whatsoever of paying these.

It was also timely in that Thomas had just formed the Beecham Symphony Orchestra, despite the fact that he didn't have any money to support it. He was gambling on the fact that he had now attracted considerable attention in London musical circles, partly because he had conducted in a number of highly acclaimed concerts and partly because of the close relationship he had struck with the composer Frederick Delius.

Now armed with Joseph's financial backing, he was in 1910 able to launch three musical seasons, two at Covent Garden and one at His Majesty's Theatre at which his orchestra would play. The seasons received only mixed reviews and expenses exceeded revenues by some £40,000, but undeterred, in 1911 and again in 1912 Joseph authorised Thomas to enter into a contract with the Russian impresario Sergei Diaghilev, to bring over to London the Imperial Russian Ballet for whom the Beecham orchestra played. The 1911

Sir Thomas rehearsing in the US in 1948. Photo by Culver Pictures.

season in particular, which coincided with the coronation of King George V, was undoubtedly a success, but once again both years came at a considerable cost, a major factor being that Diaghilev was living up to his reputation as a notorious spendthrift – up to 100 dancers and 200 other supporting staff often being engaged for each performance.

Over the next two years, Beecham's seasons continued with a mixture of opera and ballet at Covent Garden, His Majesty's Theatre and Drury Lane. Meanwhile, Thomas had also been admitted back into the family firm in August 1913 although this may simply have been a mechanism to get him on the payroll, given that there was never any real prospect of him providing any services to the business.

During this time Thomas's personal life had become increasingly difficult. He had two sons with Utica and although for a period he had taken his paternal duties seriously, as the years passed his sons came to regard him as a sort of visiting uncle figure rather than their father. Joseph purchased for them a home in St John's Wood, as Utica wanted to be nearer to her husband's sphere of activities but it made little difference. After engaging in a series of affairs, Thomas finally left Utica in 1912 although they did not divorce until many years later.

Notwithstanding his father's financial backing, Thomas still managed to run up personal debts from moneylenders which by early 1914 amounted to some £50,000. Joseph bailed him out more than once but the outbreak of World War 1 and his father's disastrous transaction involving the Covent Garden estate were to change the landscape quite dramatically.

It seems that Thomas, still only 35, more or less exempted himself from military service by dedicating his time and efforts to keeping alive the performance of live music. To this end he conducted a series of wartime concerts around the country with various orchestras but not only refused to take a fee from any, he freely subsidised them despite the family's financial difficulties. In 1916 he was knighted for his services to music and following his father's death that same year succeeded to the baronetcy. After the war he continued in the same vein, ignoring the financial consequences of the legal battles now taking place, claiming later that he had been unable to bring himself to let down the "hundreds of worthy people….." who were "dependent on the continuance of my efforts". It was no surprise therefore when a petition for his bankruptcy was lodged with the courts in 1919. His financial affairs were quite shambolic, with gross liabilities of well over £2 million but, with the assistance of the executors of his father's estate (Joseph had sensibly not appointed Thomas to this position) he did avoid bankruptcy and was finally discharged from his debts in March 1923. He took much of the credit for this himself but the claim of one biographer that this showed he was a "first rate businessman" is seriously doubted by others who concluded exactly the opposite.

Thomas now returned to the musical scene with a vengeance, involving himself once again with the Hallé, London Symphony Orchestra and the Philharmonic, as well as the British National Opera Company (effectively the old Beecham Opera Company), bolstered in 1924 by the sum of £950,000 which he received from the sale of his family shareholding. In 1926 he announced, in a very dramatic fashion, that he was to leave England for good (it seems to have been the Labour Party and the BBC which prompted this disillusionment) and after a farewell concert, departed for America. He was to return quietly a few months later and carried on as if he had never been away.

Another Beecham orchestra was to emerge in 1932, this time bearing the name The London Philharmonic Orchestra. Its personnel included a significant number who had played in the original Beecham Symphony Orchestra, most of whom were prepared to forget unpaid debts in exchange for the prospect of guaranteed work. The orchestra was regarded as the best in Britain (and possibly in Europe) and played every summer season in Covent Garden until 1939. During 1936 Thomas took his orchestra to Nazi Germany where, on one occasion when Hitler himself was present, he pointedly entered the concert hall late to avoid having to join in the otherwise mandatory salute to mark Hitler's arrival.

After splitting from Utica in 1912, Thomas had been involved in a number of affairs, the most famous, and indeed the most enduring, of which was with Lady Cunard, an American who was the ex-wife of Sir Bache Cunard, grandson of the founder of the shipping line. Not long after the commencement of the Second World War, Thomas went to America and she followed him, moving into the Ritz in New York. However whilst in America Thomas encountered Betty Humby who, as a child in London, had played piano for Thomas after winning a scholarship to the Royal Academy of Music. He appointed her as his concert pianist for his engagements in America and very soon they were living together. Both needed to divorce their previous spouses, but once that process was complete, they were free to marry. Lady Cunard apparently fainted upon hearing the news and immediately returned to London (quite a dangerous trip during the war years). The wedding took place in New York on 23rd February 1943, Thomas being 63 and Betty just 34. Later that year they returned to England.

Once the war was over, Thomas went about his usual business, raising yet another new orchestra, this time bearing the name of the Royal Philharmonic. But life in austere post-war Britain was not to his liking, especially after it was made clear that he was no longer required at Covent Garden where he had been expecting to pick up where had left off. With his well-earned reputation for profligacy, Thomas didn't really stand a chance.

The Royal Philharmonic did however become the resident orchestra at Glyndebourne and also played some 92 concerts, at the Royal Festival Hall all of which Thomas conducted. In 1950 he took his orchestra on a strenuous tour of the United States, Canada and South Africa. He also continued to act as a guest conductor, including for the Liverpool Philharmonic, made some studio recordings of operas for the BBC and managed to conduct at Covent Garden again as part of the Festival of Britain celebrations in 1951.

Thomas's activity in this country was considerably reduced from 1951, the reason being that he became one of Britain's first tax exiles, locating himself in the South of France and in Italy for much of the year. He did perform abroad and gave concerts in the United States in 1952, 1955, 1956 and 1957. In the summer of 1958 he conducted five operas on a tour to Argentina but the trip was marked for him by tragedy when Betty, to whom he had been devoted and who had accompanied him everywhere since 1943, died in Buenos Aires of a heart attack.

Thomas was devastated by his loss and, although nearly 80, reacted by throwing himself into his work. He conducted a number of concerts as a tribute to Betty and finally published his biography of Delius which had taken some 30 years to complete. He returned to the United States in January 1959 to conduct with the Philadelphia and Chicago Orchestras and then to Lucerne in Switzerland to conduct at its festival. Whilst there (his grieving for Betty presumably complete!) he surprised everybody by disappearing off to Zurich and marrying 27-year-old Shirley Hudson, who had worked for the Royal Philharmonic Orchestra and been part of his household for the last eight years.

On returning to Britain, he conducted a number of concerts with the Royal Philharmonic and then it was off to the United States again, for what was to turn out to be his last tour. He returned to Britain in April 1960 and gave his last two concerts, the first at the Royal Festival Hall and the second at the Portsmouth Guildhall. However his advanced years and ill health had now caught up with him and he spent the rest of his days holed up in a flat in Marylebone Road, the secrecy being dictated by the fact that he had exceeded his allotted days in the UK for tax purposes. On 8th March 1961 he passed away, a month short of his 82nd birthday, the cause of death being diagnosed as thrombosis. He was buried initially in Brookwood cemetery in Surrey but in 1991 his remains were moved to Limpsfield, also in Surrey, where they rest beside those of his great friend, Frederick Delius.

Sir Thomas was undoubtedly one of the great British musicians of the 20th century. To describe him as a character would be something of an understatement although there is no doubt that he deliberately cultivated both the image of eccentricity and his northern roots. He would generally speak in impeccable Edwardian English, albeit with a detectable Lancashire accent, but according to his biographer Alan Jefferson, "When he told a tale, the St Helens lad would pop out". He would at times deliberately play this up – irritated (or perhaps just amused) by a doorman in the United States who had been in the habit of addressing him as "Your Grace" in deference to his baronetcy, he started to respond with, "Hiya old cock". But having said all this, it does seem that Sir Thomas's attachment to his home town was real – he may not have performed there after 1911 but in 1949, when addressing the audience at the Liverpool Philharmonic he observed, "I am not exactly a Liverpudlian, or even a Mancunian, but if there were any spot in the world that I would call my own, it would be somewhere in this neighbourhood".

Sir Thomas may have had his detractors and would not necessarily qualify for many titles as a role model, but notwithstanding all that, he is certainly in the running for the title of "St Helens finest"!

Judge Barry Cotter from St Helens
found Theresa May (as Home Secretary)
guilty of contempt of court in 2012.

Andy Bell

U ntil relatively recently, Andy Bell was not a name that would have inspired instant recognition amongst most St Helens townsfolk, although he has been well-known in the rather more esoteric world of investments and pensions for some time. This has of course changed

somewhat. It began with the renaming of the Sale Sharks and Salford City Reds stadium as the AJ Bell stadium, continued when AJ Bell became the main sponsor of the AJ Bell World Squash Championship, the AJ Bell National Badminton League and the AJ Bell London Triathlon, and there was also the partnership with Lancashire County Cricket Club. A random Google search of the name will generate 111 million hits (only a few of which relate to the gun supplier of the same name in West London and the singer from Erasure). Yet all that said, it is a fair bet that the majority of the followers of these sports would be hard pushed to tell you much about him or what he does.

Andy was born on 6th April 1966, son of Jim, a sales engineer, and Carol, a housewife. He had two younger sisters and, although born in Liverpool, was brought up in Rainford. He was educated at Brook Lodge Primary then at Rainford High School. He continued his education at Nottingham University where he gained a first class honours degree in mathematics. At the time he saw his future as an actuary and in 1987 he joined the Royal Insurance Company as an actuarial student. My own personal experience of both the actuarial profession and the insurance industry has not been a stimulating one and Andy appears to have shared my feelings at least in regard to the insurance industry. His own observation was that he was in danger of becoming part of something in which he did not believe. And demonstrating the sort of maverick tendencies which many would regard as alien to actuaries, in 1990 he jumped ship and went to the United States to coach tennis and football.

Importantly though, this did not involve Andy bailing out of the financial world entirely. He split his time between the UK and the US, in his own words enabling him on the one hand to put back America's chances of ever winning the World Cup whilst on the other to finish off his professional exams in the UK. His professional focus had by then turned to what was in due course to propel him into the big time – the SIPP. For those not familiar with the term, this is a government approved Self-Invested Pension Plan, which allows an individual to make his or her own investment decisions with the funds that have been put away to finance their pension, and most importantly without the need for an insurance company.

Andy completed his professional qualifications to become a fellow of the Institute of Actuaries in 1993. Two years later he decided to set up an actuarial consultancy in Manchester with his colleague Nicholas Littlefair. The initial capital required to begin the venture was £10,000, funded out of personal savings. As the internet revolutionised that market, the business branched out into wider stockbroking services and it is fair to say, it has experienced success upon success.

At the time of writing, AJ Bell Limited is one of the largest providers of online investment platforms and stockbroking services in the UK, with over 140,000 clients and more than £30bn of assets under administration. It has continually been at the forefront when it comes to innovative ways of doing business – from launching the UK's first online SIPP in 2000 to becoming the first investment platform in the world to launch a service enabling customers to make investments via Facebook's Messenger service in 2016. It owns the very popular *Shares Magazine* and various other investor information websites. Andy himself is still at the helm as both a major shareholder and as Chief Executive and indeed remains the driving force behind the business. In 2013 he wrote a book called *The DIY Investor,* aimed at people looking to take control of their own investments. .

There has been no shortage of industry recognition for either Andy himself or the business in recent years. In 2010 he reached number nine in Management Today's list of Britain's Top 100 entrepreneurs and

AJ Bell has also picked up a whole stream of industry awards, with 2016 alone bringing four major accolades encompassing the whole breadth of its service offering. And with neither Andy nor the company showing signs of slowing up, it is a fair bet that there will be many more to come over the next few years.

It is no surprise either that much of AJ Bell's profile has been in the sporting world. Throughout his life, Andy's spare time has been taken up with one form of sport or other. He has been a lifelong supporter of both St Helens RLFC (and was in fact a board member from 2009 – 2012) and of Everton FC (though, unlike his fellow entrants in this collection, Chris Foy and Elton Welsby, he has yet to make the list of Celebrity Blues supporters on Toffeeweb.com!) He is also a keen skier, enjoys flying helicopters and owns a boutique racehorse stable called Blythe Stables.

More recently Andy has engaged in a project in another arena, refurbishing Moor Hall in Aughton, and opening there a fine dining restaurant in partnership with Mark Birchall, previously head chef at the 2 Michelin starred *L'Enclume*. Andy clearly hasn't lost the Midas touch – it had been trading for only six months, when it was awarded a Michelin star in September 2017!

Married to Tracey and with four children, Andy lives in Lathom so has clearly been drawn back to his roots. However notwithstanding his impressive list of achievements above, he has yet to fulfil his dream of scoring at Goodison Park, despite having had the opportunity to play there on three occasions. Whilst he has not yet lost all hope, the likelihood of him being offered a professional contract is fading very rapidly indeed.

David Bernstein CBE

I have always thought that David Bernstein was an unlikely inhabitant of St Helens. I suppose there were a number of reasons for this. The Jewish community in the town has always been very small. He clearly prefers football to rugby. And most of all, he comes over as a very smooth operator indeed (not that there are no smooth operators in St Helens but you know what I mean). The following is a passage from *The Guardian* of 16th May 2012 on the occasion of the appointment of Roy Hodgson as England football manager.

> *"At his unveiling, England's manager had been led out by the elbow under the spell of the marvellously polished David Bernstein, an FA chairman blessed with the wincingly refined condescension of the poshest estate agent in the world, the kind of estate agent who emerges magisterially from his panelled back office once a year wearing a shirt composed almost entirely of cufflinks and wing-collar in order to hobnob with the Earl of Sandwich".*

For what it's worth David was not an estate agent but, originally at least, a chartered accountant. And we all thought accountants were boring!

To be fair, David did not spend a great deal of time in St Helens before moving to pastures new. He was born on 22nd May 1943, was an only child and lived initially on Bold Street, Greenbank. His father, Henry, ran a ladies wear store in the St Helens town centre called Annie Cooper, which was named after David's mother, whose maiden name was Annie Coopersmith. His parents both originated from London and in 1946 the family upped sticks and moved back there.

Notwithstanding his relatively short period of tenure in the town, the *St Helens Star* reported after an interview with him that he still regarded St Helens as his emotional home and that he always followed the fortunes of St Helens RLFC – though I suspect not too avidly as I have come across no evidence that he has attended a game in the recent past. And when advised by a friend of mine that he was to appear in this compilation, he apparently looked uncomfortable and commented that he did not really regard himself as being from St Helens, which is somewhat at variance with the *Star* interview. But he qualifies for inclusion and that is the end of that.

David was educated at Christ's College, Finchley, left after his GCE A levels, and joined accountants Robson Rhodes. He qualified in 1966, spent a further year at a different firm, Hacker Young and then joined Bright Grahame Murray where he became a partner at the tender age of 26. One of his clients was the Pentland Group and in due course he joined them and progressed to managing director. The Group was extremely successful during his time there, which was particularly notable for the development of the Reebok and Speedo brands. David then hit the headlines as Chairman of the retail chain French Connection when he oversaw the introduction of the controversial (but once again extremely successful) "FCUK" advertising campaign. He has retained his link with fashion retail, sitting on the board of Ted Baker and, previously, Black's Leisure. Other non-executive appointments include the restaurant chain Carluccio's. However it is for his activities in the sporting arena that most people will remember him.

His first foray into the football world came with his appointment as chairman of Manchester City in 1998, the team which he had supported since his childhood. It was not the most auspicious of times for the club which was then at its lowest point ever, having been relegated to the third tier of English football, then known as the second division. Bernstein oversaw the first stages of the revival that would ultimately lead to the club becoming Premiership champions some 14 years later. They were promoted back to the first division at the first attempt and went on to recover Premiership status a year later. In 2001 he was instrumental in bringing in Kevin Keegan as manager, a hugely popular move amongst the supporters. But Manchester City and David Bernstein always seemed to me to be an odd combination – on the one hand the measured, sensible chartered accountant and on the other, the club with the rollercoaster reputation and with a majority of supporters who (at the time anyway) firmly believed that, whatever the circumstances, everything would end in tears. In 2003 the inevitable happened and the two parted company. Many Manchester City supporters however recall David's time at the club fondly and believe him to be at least in part, responsible for re-establishing the club amongst football's elite.

Let us now fast forward to 2011. David reemerges in the football world as Chairman of the Football Association, regarded at the time as a safe pair of hands who could be trusted with a job which had not been without its embarrassments in the past (the last one of which had been the debacle of the failed bid to host the 2018 World Cup). And broadly speaking, that is exactly what they got. There were certainly mistakes, one of which was the handling of the Hillsborough tragedy, but when the Minister of Sport describes your performance in a role as "exceptional" and laments the archaic FA rule that required the chairman to stand down at the age of 70, you can be satisfied that you have achieved something of significance in very difficult circumstances.

Bernstein's other legacy to the football world was his involvement in Wembley Stadium. He was a director from 2003 and chairman from 2008 of Wembley Stadium Limited and played a major part in stabilising the finances of a company which had been something of a shambles. This is clearly a man who relishes the challenge of sorting out basket cases.

Although David is 75 years of age at the time of writing, few would bet on us having seen or heard the last of him. He has retained a number of non-executive appointments and took on a new challenge as Chairman of the British Red Cross on 1st January 2014. He also had a brief foray at Aston Villa in 2016, joining the Board in March of that year, only to resign a month later.

Married for 50 years to Gill (a lifelong Tottenham Hotspur supporter!), David has four children and eleven grandchildren. He was awarded the CBE in the 2014 New Year's Honours list. He can certainly count himself in the upper echelons amongst those from St Helens who have succeeded in the world of business – even if he doesn't regard that accolade as one of the greater achievements of his life!

Henry Berry

H enry Berry, Liverpool's second Dock Engineer, was the man primarily responsible for the construction of the world's first modern artificial canal which was the Sankey (also known as the St Helens) Canal. As such he must take his place on the pantheon of the great and the good from the era of the industrial revolution.

Although there is no actual record of his birth, he was almost certainly born and raised in St Helens. His tombstone at the St Helens Congregational Church, which then stood in Ormskirk Street, stated that he died in 1819 in his 93rd year, which would suggest he was born around 1726. Nothing is known of his childhood however, other than that he had an elder brother, John, who was a trustee of the Independent Chapel in the town. Henry's first appearance in any surviving documents is also in a Trust Deed, dated 1742, in which he is described as "of Parr Battchelor". In the next few years he makes several further appearances in the Parr township papers – at one point he is a highways surveyor and then later an Overseer for the Poor. In 1850 however he surfaces in the Liverpool Town Books when following the death of Thomas Steers, Liverpool's first Dock Engineer, it is recorded that his "late clerk" Henry Berry was to take temporary charge of all the ongoing works. Henry obviously made a decent fist of it as the following year he was formally appointed to the top job and became Liverpool's second Dock Engineer. Whether he had any formal training in engineering we do not know, although one assumes he would have learned a huge amount from the tuition of Thomas Steers, the founder of Liverpool's world famous dock system and widely regarded as one of the finest engineers of his time. Critically Thomas had experience not just in the construction of docks but also in inland waterways, and any knowledge that Henry picked up in that arena would certainly prove useful to him in the fullness of time.

After Henry had been in the job for three years, the Salthouse Dock was opened and it is generally accepted, notwithstanding that its construction had begun before the death of Thomas Steers, that most of the credit belonged to

Henry Berry. It may well have been a consequence of his good work there that he was then entrusted by the proprietors of the Sankey River (all of whom were on the Liverpool Council which had appointed him as Dock Engineer) with the responsibility for investigating whether or not it could be made navigable. By 1755 he was giving evidence in Parliament on behalf of those proprietors as they needed Parliamentary approval for their project. It was Henry however who concluded that the proposal was impractical and who instead suggested the construction of an artificial canal along the Sankey Brook valley. It seems this suggestion may have been withheld from some of the proprietors on the grounds that they would not have given their approval, but one way or the other Henry got the go ahead and as a consequence can be acclaimed as the person responsible for the construction of the first post-industrial canal*, which opened for business in 1757.

Henry had been granted two days a week off from his job as Liverpool's Dock Engineer to supervise the Sankey project but nonetheless his work continued there as well – he was responsible for a graving dock which was constructed in 1756 (and also two later ones which he constructed in 1765) all of which formed part of what later became Canning Dock. He then supervised the construction of George's Dock which was completed in 1771 and finally King's Dock which opened in 1788.

Liverpool was not the only port with which Henry was involved. His reputation spread quickly – there is evidence that he was consulted by the Hull Corporation in 1756 although it is probable his other commitments prevented him becoming engaged on the other side of the Pennines at that point. However he was later heavily involved in the construction of Hull Dock which opened in September 1778 and was the largest single dock with which he was associated. He was also consulted by the Port of Lancaster and asked to provide an estimate for the construction of a dock there but again turned down the opportunity as he could not "make it convenient to attend to this business".

Henry was employed for a while to investigate the possibility of extending the navigation of the River Weaver after powerful Liverpool merchants had exerted pressure on the trustees of the river to improve the waterway. This project did not end well for Henry however – it seems that whereas he had had no problem in harnessing the stream from Sankey Brook, when he tried to do the same with the more variable currents in the river, he caused a minor flood and was relieved of his position. Whether his dismissal was fair or not is debatable, as there was certainly at the time considerable friction between the Cheshire gentlemen, who made up the trustees and the somewhat less genteel merchants from Liverpool, and Henry was very much regarded as the agent of the latter!

Despite all the above activity, there was clearly not enough dock and canal construction taking place to keep Henry fully occupied and there are several references to him being used by Liverpool Corporation for other services, particularly as a surveyor on the construction of roads in both Liverpool and surrounding areas.

Henry's retirement as Dock Engineer came in 1789. He had lived on Duke Street in Liverpool since 1865 and it seems retired with an annual income of about £1,000 – not an insignificant amount in the early 19th century. When he died in 1819, in accordance with his will, his remains were interred "at the Dissenters Chapel at St Helens, but not within the chapel where my mother and father were buried, but in the chapel yard as I would not have their grave opened". His remains were later moved from Ormskirk Street to the Borough Cemetery when work was being carried out to widen the road.

We know precious little of Henry's private life. He certainly had no wife or children who survived him and probably never married. He took no part in public life, though his dissenting views would probably have prevented him from doing so. His obituary in the *Liverpool Mercury* observed that despite his age, there were "no marks of imbecility" which is borne out by the clarity of his will which he wrote at the age of 88. His assets included, inter alia, an estate in Parr as well as a number of properties in Liverpool. He left the Silver Cup, which had been awarded to him by the proprietors of the Sankey Canal, to his great nephew.

Henry does however have one surviving legacy – Berry Street, in Liverpool which adjoins Duke Street at the point where Henry's house was situated, was named in his honour, albeit, as with much of his life, details of when and by whom are sadly lacking.

---

*   It should be noted in passing that there are some who contest the assertion that the Sankey or St Helens Canal was the first post-industrial canal on the somewhat specious basis that its final 400 metres were shared with the Sankey Brook. I do not think we need to consider the merits of this argument further.

Frank Cottrell Boyce

Remember the opening ceremony for the London Olympics in 2012? The bit where the Olympic rings rose from the ground to create a cauldron of brightly lit petals? It was in fact inspired by the Latin phrase *"Ex Terra Lucem"* or "Out of the ground comes light", which was from 1974, and then again from 2013 (after a successful campaign to reinstate it), the town motto of St Helens and which features on its coat of arms. Indeed the words *Ex Terra Lucem* were posted on the Olympic site noticeboard throughout the construction period and even found their way into the final programme for the opening event.

The link with St Helens is Frank Cottrell Boyce, who was the scriptwriter for the opening ceremony. The immortal words uttered by the Queen to Daniel Craig, "Good evening, Mr Bond," were also scripted by him - not, in most likelihood, the greatest challenge in his career as a scriptwriter but they may turn out to be the four words for which he is most remembered. Interestingly, during an interview on BBC Radio 4, Frank told listeners there had been no initial expectation that the Queen would take part in the opening ceremony. He had simply written to the Palace to ask permission to include the scene, but the Palace had written back with full details of the Queen's availability for filming. Had she not actually been involved, few would have remembered the scene but then it is upon such happy (and in some cases unhappy) accidents that history is built.

Frank Boyce was born in Rainhill in 1959 into a deeply religious Catholic family and attended St Bartholomew's Primary School and later West Park Grammar School. Already with a keen interest in reading, this was further stimulated by his English teacher, "Ned" Biggs, who was something of an institution at West Park. Ned and Frank in fact struck up a working relationship outside of school and at weekends would run Punch and Judy shows in rural Lancashire. Frank became the first in his family to attend university when he went to study English at Oxford

University, staying on there to complete his doctorate. It was there that he met Denise, a theology undergraduate who was thinking of becoming a nun. Instead, she married Frank and he took on her maiden name Cottrell to complement his own. Whilst still in Oxford they had their first child together. Six more were to follow in the fullness of time.

Frank began his writing career with the *Brookside* team during its very early days before moving on to *Coronation Street* (he was also a critic at the time with the publication *Living Marxism* as a consequence of which this magazine sat rather incongruously on the shelves in Rita Fairclough's newsagent's shop The Kabin). A meeting at Thames TV studios with Michael Winterbottom, who was at the time toiling away in a fairly junior position, was the catalyst to the next stage in Frank's career. He wrote a script for Winterbottom to film, and although it was never released, it did enough to alert the producers to the duo's potential. Their next effort *Forget About Me* did make it, being released in 1990 and kicking off a partnership which was to generate a further six films over the next 15 years – *Butterfly Kiss* (1995), *Welcome to Sarajevo* (1997), *The Claim* (2000), *24 Hour Party People* (2002), *Code 46* (2003), and *A Cock and Bull Story* (2005). During this period Frank also worked on *Hilary and Jackie* with Anand Tucker.

The break with Michael Winterbottom was prompted by Frank's desire to move on and reach new audiences. He took an unfinished film script and, prompted by Danny Boyle, not only completed the film but also turned it into his first novel, *Millions,* both of which were released in 2004. Recognition came very quickly, as Frank was awarded the Carnegie Medal for the best children's book published in the UK as well as three separate awards in Germany. His next two books *Framed* and *Cosmic* were also shortlisted for the Carnegie award and in 2011, after a neighbour recommended him to the Estate of Ian Fleming, he was commissioned to write a sequel to *Chitty Chitty Bang Bang* (two more were to follow, mirroring the original which was also published in three parts). That same year, he co-presented the Papal Visit alongside TV personality Carol Vordermann.

In 2012 Frank was appointed to the newly created post of Professor of Reading at Hope University in Liverpool before his profile unsurprisingly increased as a result of Danny Boyle's invitation to him to script the Olympic ceremony. Frank found inspiration in Shakespeare's

The Tempest as well as the smoking chimneys and burning metal scenes from Humphrey Jennings's *Pandaemonium*. His responsibilities extended to the brochure, the stadium announcements and the television presenters' media guide.

The next award to come Frank's way was the 2012 Guardian Children's Fiction Prize for *The Unforgotten Coat*, inspired by the true story of a Mongolian girl Frank had met on a school visit who had left her coat behind before she was deported – a touching story which is both humorous and melancholic. The book was commissioned by the Liverpool charity, the Reader Organisation, something very close to Frank's heart.

As well as his novels, film and TV work, Frank wrote and staged the theatre production *Proper Clever* at the Liverpool Playhouse and he has also made the occasional appearance as an actor. However notwithstanding all these different strings to his bow, he continues to regard himself primarily as a children's writer. He retains a lifelong passion for literature and reading which explains in part the strength of his relationship with Danny Boyle, who is also a compulsive reader. Frank sees it almost as his mission to promote reading, especially in the eight to twelve year group and with both parent and child involved together. He also spends time as part of his responsibilities at Hope University trying to develop a "reading for fun" culture amongst the trainee teachers with the hope that they will in due course pass this on to their pupils.

A keen Liverpool supporter, Frank now lives in Crosby with his wife and those children who have not yet flown the nest. His children are home schooled and Frank is quite disciplined in ensuring he doesn't work at weekends which for him is sacred family time. And in 2014 he grabbed the opportunity to take his children to see the Tardis and to meet Dr Who (Peter Capaldi), after Frank had been asked to write an episode for the series, fulfilling one of his own lifetime ambitions!

Dr Henry Ambrose Grundy Brooke

If you are unlucky enough to contract Brooke's disease (sometimes known as the Brooke – Spiegler syndrome) it will probably be of scant comfort to know that the disease was named after St Helens most prominent medical practitioner and one of the country's leading dermatologists. The disease is not the only modern day reminder of his work – there is also a Brooke's tumour (and there was at one point a Brooke's ointment) whilst Brooke Building at Salford Royal Hospital also carries his  name as a mark of recognition of his contribution to advances in the field of dermatology in the late 19th and early 20th centuries.

Henry was born in St Helens in 1854 as Henry Ambrose Grundy. His father William practised as an architect* and his mother Maria was a member of the Blinkhorn family who had come to St Helens from Bolton and owned the Sutton Glass Works. Henry had an elder brother, also William, and two younger siblings, Edith and Robert. There may also have been a fourth son, Alexander, who died as an infant.

It is not entirely clear when the family left St Helens, but Robert's birthplace is recorded as Eccles and his birth was registered in 1857 in Stockport. However the family appear to have been living in Southport when the father, William, passed away in 1859. In 1861 Maria remarried and her new husband William Brooke was a merchant from Manchester. They lived initially in Southport but the trail then goes blank for some years. The next we know is that the 1871 Census records the family, minus Maria, living in Hale in Cheshire – William Jnr, Henry (actually Harry in the census), Edith and Robert have all by then adopted the surname of their stepfather but have retained Grundy as a middle name. Sadly, Maria is at this point living in Clifton Hall Asylum in Salford, her entry in the census bearing the annotation "Lunatic". She appears to have remained there until her death in 1887.

Despite all the disruption to his family life, Henry was obviously a diligent scholar. We know nothing of his schooling but, according to his brother Robert, he was a fervent and enthusiastic reader, rising at 5am to work at his books by candlelight. Remarkably, at the age of 16 he entered medical school at Owens College (which was in the fullness of time to become Manchester University). He then trained at Guy's Hospital London, obtaining a BA in 1874 at London University, followed in 1880 by a medical degree and a diploma from the Royal College of Surgeons. At this point he appears to have returned to Manchester to work as a house doctor and surgeon at The Royal Infirmary before tracking back to London again to work at The London Fever Hospital. He married Sarah Lightbown in 1880 in Salford.

Henry's next move was to continue his studies on the continent where he worked under some very prominent dermatologists. During this time it seems he became fluent in both German and French albeit, according to a fellow prominent dermatologist, Arthur Whitefield, "with a perfectly astonishing Manchester accent". On returning to the UK he worked briefly as a physician at The Manchester Royal Infirmary before in 1883 taking up a post as a consultant physician at the newly opened Manchester and Salford Hospital for Skin Disease, which has been described as one of the greatest hospitals in the country at the time**. Henry had soon built up what was to become an enormous private practice whilst at the same time becoming heavily involved in teaching, being appointed as the first clinical lecturer in dermatology at the University of Manchester.

Henry was instrumental around this time in setting up the North of England Dermatological Society but maintained links also with the dermatological societies in both Paris and London. Along with Malcolm Morris he founded the *British Journal of Dermatology* in 1888 and stayed as joint editor until 1891. The journal was to flourish and indeed remains an established internationally respected and highly cited publication to this day.

Although Henry did publish a number of papers (which often included his own sketches as he was by all accounts also a talented artist) he was not a prolific writer. It had apparently been his intention to write a book about dermatology, but unfortunately his work was curtailed in 1906 by a cerebrovascular accident (which involves the death of some brain cells as a consequence of a lack of oxygen resulting from a blockage to the blood flow to the brain). His wife Sarah, with whom he had one daughter, Audrey, born 1892, also died in 1907 but Henry soldiered on, continuing with his clinical duties and regularly attending meetings over the next few years. Indeed he married once again in 1908 to Dorothy (some 27 years his junior) and together they had a son Henry Leslie who was born in 1911, when Henry Senior was the ripe old age of 55! It seems that Malcolm Morris's observation that during these years Henry fought on "as a wounded warrior" was pretty near the mark. Inevitably however, the end had to come and in 1919 after a further stroke he passed away at the age of 65.

Henry was described in one of his obituaries as a delightful companion, unfailingly genial and having a real kindness of heart. As well as his scientific and artistic talents, we are told that he was also an accomplished musician. In another obituary, we learn that he was an intensely humorous man who was surprisingly easy to approach. A combination of a fine build but a pronounced stoop (caused by a short sightedness that meant he had to bend forward to study his patients) made him a very distinctive figure and in a way creates a fitting image for someone who was described by the aforementioned Arthur Whitfield as one of the "great five" and "the most notable figure in dermatologists in the North of England".

---

*   Henry's father William was in fact the son of William Grundy, who was headmaster at Cowley School, and Margaret Grundy. They later ran a boarding school for girls in Parr Hall which was the subject of a book written by Ruth Brandon entitled *Other People's Daughters: the Life and Times of the Governess.*

** In his obituary in the *British Medical Journal* on 19th April 1919, he is described as having founded this hospital although that does not seem to have been the case.

Rob Broughton

The term "cage rage" conjures up some very vivid images, which I suspect is the reason it was chosen in 2002 as the name for a new mixed martial arts competition. It was televised by Sky Sports but survived only for six years before folding. However during that time it did produce, in Rob Broughton, a St Helens British heavyweight champion who won the title in 2006 after being given only one week's notice that he was to challenge for the crown. Known as "The Bear", Rob went on to resurface in the M-1 Challenge, the Ultimate Fight Championships and later fought briefly in the ICE Fight Championships.

Rob was in some ways an unlikely champion. In fact he was an unlikely sportsman in that he was advised by the medics that it would be stupid and dangerous for him to engage in sport. The problem was that he had been born with a condition known as talipes (sometimes referred to as club foot), caused by the feet twisting round in the womb which means they have trouble facing forward. Rob recalls that he had dozens of operations before the age of 12 and that he seemed permanently to have his leg cased in plaster. However ignoring the advice of the medics, Rob continued to engage in sport as he was convinced it was helping rather than hindering his condition and his determination was ultimately to pay off.

Rob was born on 12th January 1982, son of Tony, a painter and decorator, and Angela. He was the eldest of three children and the family lived just off Duke Street in the town centre. Rob was schooled at Windlehurst and then Hurst School, followed by Sutton High School. After leaving school he attended St Helens Technical College and qualified as a fabricator welder. However he had by then already had his introduction to the fight world, after taking up amateur boxing at Lowe House. He had also played amateur rugby league at Haresfinch and Blackbrook before giving it up at 17 after he had started to get involved in wrestling. With this now his main focus, he trained at Atherton Wrestling Club and started to win competitions. However he was also attracted by the martial arts and went to Thai boxing schools in St Helens and Warrington. He then moved on to learn Brazilian jiu jitsu and judo. At the age of 20 he was 6 foot 2 inches tall and 18 stone and it was therefore in many ways natural that he should be attracted by mixed martial arts (known as "MMA"). His first cage fights were to take place in the now defunct CFC Cage Carnage in 2004.

His career had a relatively subdued start, with a loss and a draw in his first two fights. However by the time he came up against the Cage Rage British Heavyweight Champion, James Thompson, in July 2006 he had won four of his last five fights and, despite the fact that he was a late replacement, he won by a third round knockout to take the heavyweight title. He went on to defend it successfully later that year and won another non-title bout before losing his crown to the Georgian Tengis Tedoradze after the doctor stopped the fight because of cuts Rob had suffered.

A snapped Achilles tendon (ouch!) then side-lined him for the best part of a year but in March 2008 he returned to the cage, won his first fight and then came very close to taking the Cage Rage World Heavyweight championship against the American Ricco Rodriguez (another challenge he accepted at a week's notice!) The writing was however already on the wall for Cage Rage – Sky Sports had withdrawn their coverage earlier that year – and this turned out to be Rob's last fight in this competition.

He spent most of 2009 fighting in M-1 Challenge, a Russian based mixed martial arts

© Copyright Rob Broughton 2018

51

promotion. He fought in Japan, Kansas City and in Russia and acquitted himself pretty well, winning all three fights in the M-1 Challenge and losing just the one in M-1 Global Breakthrough. With his reputation now further enhanced as one of Europe's leading heavyweights he went on to win the ZT Fight Night Heavyweight Tournament in January 2010, winning three bouts in just one evening! This performance earned him his chance to compete in the top competition worldwide, the US based Ultimate Fighting Championships, known generally as the UFC. Rob described it at the time as equivalent to a footballer playing in the Champions League!

His career there got off to a flying start with a win in his first contest at the London O2 arena in front of 22,500 screaming fans. The future at this point looked bright – Rob was enjoying the competition, training hard and also turning out when he could for Blackbrook second team. However he then had shoulder surgery and had to wait almost a year for the next fight which took place in Denver Colorado against American Travis Browne. He lost that fight on points and then lost again on points against fellow Englishman Phil De Freis in November 2011(yet another fight he agreed to at a week's notice – there's a pattern emerging here!) albeit the decision upset and annoyed Rob as he thought he had done enough to win it.

This turned out to be Rob's last fight in the UFC. Problems were setting in: there were injuries, including a broken hand, and frustrations with UFC itself particularly over their lack of support for him in relation to some visa difficulties he was encountering. He was by then also a father, his son Billy having been born during 2011, which meant he had family commitments on top of everything else. For the next few years he worked for a security firm, although he continued to train at the Wolfslair gym in Widnes throughout. In 2015 he made a brief return to the ring (despite being told – again – by his doctor that he should not fight because of cartilage problems in his ankle!) in the ICE Fight Championships, which were promoted by his good friend and fellow MMA competitor Tom Blackledge. Rob won the bout against Marcin Bocian from Poland and was lined up for a rematch against Phil De Freis in November. However persistent injuries finally got the better of him and the fight didn't take place – in fact Rob hasn't appeared in the ring since then (though he claims he hasn't given up hope of one more appearance at some point in the future!)

There has however been plenty to keep Rob occupied since then. He is now teaching all aspects of MMA in gyms in Warrington, St Helens and Liverpool, running his own security business and also doing some bodyguarding work – one imagines he would be pretty effective at all of these!

Rob may not have ended up as a household name and perhaps didn't achieve everything that it seemed at one stage he would in his chosen sport. However he has certainly made his own contribution to the wide and varied sporting success to come out of St Helens over the years – and it may be a long time before we see anyone else from the town do as well as he did in the rough, tough world of mixed martial arts.

Daily Mirror headline in February 2015.

Mick Burke

I have always been envious of mountaineers – not the actual climbing of the mountains but the sense of achievement they must feel, the camaraderie and the thrill of the danger which accompanies so much of what they do. But it is a precarious existence, particularly for those who are "big mountain" men, which was the way that one of his climbing colleagues described Mick Burke. These are men who are driven consistently to challenge themselves in the mountain ranges which make up the world's most difficult arenas. In Mick's case, it was ultimately to cost him his life, in the same way as it has cost the lives of many before and after him.

Mick Burke was actually born in Abram, far too close to Wigan for comfort, in 1941. His redemption came at the age of 11 however when he was despatched to West Park in St Helens for his secondary education, before studying for a degree at Manchester University. He developed his love of climbing in the Langdale area of the Lake District in his mid-teens, reputedly hitching a lift there every Friday evening after school.

Mick took a job teaching physical education at the American School in Leysin, Switzerland in the early 1960s and whilst there, regularly frequented the infamous Club Vagabond, the other regulars of which would make up a *Who's Who* of the British climbing community at the time, notably Dougal Haston, Peter Boardman, John Harlin and Blythe Wright with others such as Chris Bonnington, Martin Boysen and Don Whillan making the occasional visit. It was, by all accounts, a drinking den of some repute and it seems that Mick played a full part in helping the club maintain this reputation. It was also at Club Vagabond that he first met his wife, Beth.

Mick started to gain some prominence in the climbing world around about the same time, when he made a number of ascents in the Alps, notably the north face of the Matterhorn with Dougal Haston. He also scaled the two summits of the Aguille de Dru, a mountain in the Mont

Blanc massif, including only the second ever ascent via the route which became known as the American Direct. This latter climb proved crucial in 1966 when he joined an unofficial rescue party in an audacious attempt to save two German climbers trapped high on the Dru, after he and others concluded that the official rescue party's chances of success were very poor. The whole event became a bit of a media circus, followed live on television by millions. Crucially it was almost certainly Mick's decision to descend via the American Direct which saved the lives of the Germans and on the fifth day of the rescue, all but one climber arrived back safe and sound. Sadly a German who had joined the official rescue party had died of exhaustion after his abseil rope had become stuck in the rocks. The rescued Germans had spent a full ten days on the wall and were unsurprisingly not in good shape; critically however they were alive and the operation rightly achieved iconic status in the history of mountain rescues. The media explosion which followed was not to the liking of any of the climbers and it soon descended into great controversy when one of the successful rescue party, a Frenchman, was expelled from the Chamonix Guides Association for taking part in an unauthorised rescue and allegedly attempting to sabotage the efforts of the official party.

Mick then took himself off to the Americas, initially to Patagonia's Cerro Torre before travelling solo through Latin America and on up to North America where he joined the British mountaineers' invasion of the late 1960s – it seems they livened up the climbing scene quite considerably with their love of music, drinking and bold endeavours, all of which sound to be totally in character. Amongst the climbs completed by Mick at the time, together with Rob Wood, was the first British ascent of El Capitan in Yosemite.

Mick returned to London in 1968 to train as a TV cameraman but still managed over the next few years to fit in trips with Chris Bonington to the Himalayas in 1970 to climb the north face of Annapurna (which was the subject of his first film production *The Hardest Way Up*), to travel with Doug Scott's expedition in 1971 to Baffin Island to scale some of the enormous cliffs on the island and again with Chris Bonington in 1972 to make an unsuccessful attempt on the South West face of Everest (during which expedition Mick's wife, Beth was the official nurse).

After spending some time as a freelance cameraman, Mick joined the BBC and was invited to join Chris Bonington's 1975 attempt to climb

Everest via the South West face, where he doubled up as both cameraman and climber. Mick was paired with Martin Boysen and on the day of their summit attempt, Martin's oxygen set failed and he then lost a crampon making it impossible for him to carry on. Mick apparently had no intention of giving up on the climb. Reporter Christopher Railing, also on the expedition, made the observation that no power on earth would have stopped him continuing. Shortly afterwards Mick met Peter Boardman and Sherpa Pertemba who had made up the second summit party (the first had been Doug Scott and Dougal Haston) on their way back down. Mick was by all accounts in good spirits and asked them if they would return to the summit with him so that he could film them. They declined as they were moving roped and wanted to conserve energy for the descent. Mick asked if they would wait for him on the South summit and as he was only a few hundred metres from the summit, they agreed, thinking it would not delay them long. He then forged on upwards and that was the last time anyone saw him alive. The weather deteriorated and although Boardman and Pertemba waited an hour and a half, Mick did not re-emerge. In horrendous conditions with visibility down to five feet they finally made their way back down to Camp where they met up with Martin Boysen and where they were forced to stay for a whole day and two nights before the storm cleared. Lucky still to be alive, they made their way down the mountain.

The general consensus is that Mick would have reached the summit (and thus made the first ever solo ascent of Everest) but, as with Mallory, we will never know for certain. The body has never been recovered. His death hit all the expedition members very hard and many of them went on to write about the impact Mick's death had upon them. But they were mountaineers and death was an habitual visitor – within two years Dougal Haston was to lose his life in an avalanche in the Alps while Peter Boardman was also to disappear on Everest in 1982.

Mick did not lead a long life but he led a very full life. Virtually all his spare time was devoted to his mountaineering interests; he served on the Alpine Climbing Group as a committee man, secretary and correspondent, he was on the screening committee of the Mount Everest Foundation and he was on the Instructional Committee of the British Mountaineering Council. His film of the 1975 expedition was used for a

BBC 2 documentary *Everest The Hard Way* and the BBC and the Royal Geographical Society jointly founded in his memory the Mick Burke Award, which is awarded biannually, with a view to encouraging "exciting expedition films to be made in the remote parts of the world".

You can't help but be left with the feeling that Mick Burke was a thoroughly decent bloke. There were undoubtedly many flawed characters in the climbing world and in many ways that is understandable given the character traits required to succeed. It does not appear however that Mick was one of them. In none of the mountaineering blogs in which the old guys reminisce about the earlier years, will you find anything negative said about him. A heavy smoker (as were many of the climbers at the time – there are numerous pictures of Mick high up on the terrain with a cigarette dangling from his mouth) and a drinker, he was obviously a social animal, notwithstanding the fierce ambition and determination to succeed which drove him to ever more challenges in the mountains, and he left behind many, many friends who mourned his passing. And amongst those were his wife, Beth and a daughter Sarah who can quite rightly celebrate a life lived to the utmost.

Ex Cowley schoolboy Joseph Siddall took part
in the dogfight in which
Baron von Richthofen ("𝕿𝖍𝖊 𝕽𝖊𝖉 𝕭𝖆𝖗𝖔𝖓")
was finally shot down in 1918.

Sir Bernard Caulfield

"Remember Mary Archer in the witness box. Your vision of her probably will never disappear. Has she elegance? Has she fragrance? Would she have, without the strain of this trial, radiance? Has she been able to enjoy rather than endure her husband Jeffrey? Is she right when she says to you — you may think with delicacy — 'Jeffrey and I lead a full life'? … Is he in need of cold, unloving, rubber-insulated sex in a seedy hotel……. after an evening at the Caprice?"

It is in many ways unfortunate that for all his other achievements, the lasting (and indeed for many, the only) memory of the Lord Justice Caulfield that endures is of his homage to the beauty of Lady Archer at the conclusion of her husband's libel action against the *Sun* newspaper in 1987. As we all now know, he got that one badly wrong. Lady Archer was not, after all, the high watermark of perfection (as one of the newspapers put it) which her charms had led him to believe she was, and in the fullness of time her husband was to end up in prison for perjury.

Quite how Lady Archer managed to bewitch Lord Justice Caulfield so comprehensively that he lost the plot entirely will forever be a mystery. By the time the truth became known, and Jeffrey Archer imprisoned, Lord Justice Caulfield had been dead for nearly seven years. But whilst this incident will forever taint his name, it is important that we should not ignore everything that went before and the quite colourful contribution he made to the legal world during his career.

Bernard Caulfield was born in April 1914 in Peckers Hill Road, which runs at right angles to Robins Lane, not far from St Helens Junction station. He was the son of John and Catherine Caulfield, who had nine children in total. His mother (and later his sister) kept a shop on Mill Lane near the Mill House pub. He was educated initially at St Annes RC Primary School but interestingly, rather than move from there to West Park (or St Helens Catholic Grammar School as it was then known) he attended St Francis Xavier's College in Liverpool, taking the train each day from the Junction station. From there he progressed to the University of Liverpool before embarking upon a career as a solicitor.

As with many young men of the era, his career was interrupted by the Second World War, during which he served in the Royal Army Ordnance Corps before being seconded to the Intelligence Corps in Cairo (alongside my own father, albeit he was some years younger than Bernard). As I understand it, the Intelligence Corps was a sort of counter espionage unit, responsible for gathering, analysing and disseminating military information. Bernard had reached the rank of major before being demobbed in 1947, following which he resumed life in the legal world. He was called to the Bar that same year and was made a Queen's Counsel in 1961. He became Recorder of Coventry in 1963, serving in that post until 1968 when he became a High Court judge. His elevation was notable for two reasons – firstly he was one of the first judges without an Oxbridge background and secondly, he was one of the youngest, at 54, to have reached that level. His achievements were marked that same year with a knighthood.

Sir Bernard was soon to develop something of a reputation, partly for a common sense approach to the law, partly because of his use of colourful language and humour in court (during the Archer trial, prior to the infamous summing up, he had managed to shoehorn into the proceedings references to the six yard box at Anfield, Cardiff Arms Park and the television series Pot Black) and partly because of his activities outside court. By all accounts he startled court officials in 1986 during a Lincoln's Inn charity fundraising event by singing and playing drums with a jazz band. One of the numbers he played that day was "When the Saints Go Marching In" which his son Michael tells me was his favourite song, reflecting his lifelong allegiance to his home town rugby team. *The Daily Telegraph* also reported in its obituary of the judge Sir Edward Eveleigh that he would regularly sing after formal dinners with Sir Bernard Caulfield accompanying him on the piano. In summary, we are dealing here with, if not quite a maverick, certainly someone a little removed from the norm, as was indeed recognised by the *Glasgow Herald* in 1987 which carried an article about him entitled, "The Last of the Characters on the Bench".

After more than 20 years as a judge, Sir Bernard hung up his boots in 1989. He continued to live in Middlesex but maintained his links throughout with his home town, where he still had a number of relatives. He had been President of the Sutton Historic Society from its launch in 1987 and remained in that post until his death in 1994 at the age of 80. In accordance with his own instructions, his remains were transferred to St Helens and after a service conducted by the local priest, he was buried in a simple family plot in St Anne's Church in Sutton.

Most of the broadsheets carried obituaries of Sir Bernard – in a way it was fortunate that these were written before his reputation became tarnished by the imprisonment of Lord Archer, so they focused instead on his career and achievements. That is not to say they do not acknowledge what might be described as his somewhat quirky ways – *The Times* for example referred to his "streak of mischief" and use of "florid language". It did however describe him as a good judge with "an unquenchable thirst for individual justice, sound legal and independent judgment, an equable

Sir Bernard Caulfield's grave at St Anne's Church in Sutton. Image from Sutton Beauty.

temperament and, nearly always, a sure touch in assessing human conduct and evaluating social attitudes." Perhaps that is how we should all remember him.

Sir Bernard was survived by his wife, Sheila, whom he had married in 1953, three sons and a daughter.

Dave "Chizzy" Chisnall

I t is of course mandatory for a professional darts player to have a nickname and whilst "Chizzy" may not be the most inspirational, it has an authenticity in that it almost certainly predates his exploits in the world of darts. It is also unlikely ever to be confused by the public with any other darts player. And although the name may have been reasonably familiar to the darts fraternity, it

Dave Chisnall (left),
Michael Smith (centre, see page 309) and
Martin Murray (right, see page 227)
Photo courtesy of A180 darts.

hit the wider public consciousness big style in 2012 when in his first appearance in the PDC (Professional Darts Corporation) World Championships, he defeated Phil "The Power" Taylor in only the second round of the competition. To put this into some sort of perspective, in the previous 18 championships, The Power had won 13 titles, had appeared in the final on 16 occasions and had never failed to reach the quarter finals. Sadly, Chizzy was unable to maintain the momentum and fell at the next hurdle (which interestingly had also been the fate of the victors on the two other occasions that Phil had not made the final). However, Chizzy had caused a major sensation with his win, one which, regardless of his future achievements, he is unlikely ever to forget.

Not that Chizzy is short of achievements – prior to moving to the PDC at the beginning 2011, he had a number of tournament wins to his name, including the Welsh Masters and the British Open in 2009. In 2010, despite starting the tournament as a 40-1 outsider, he reached the final of the rival BDO World Championship, losing to Martin Adams in an event which attracted a television audience of more than three million viewers. After his defeat, he was interviewed on live television and whilst his responses suggested that he had devoted little time to media training, in his defence he was asked as crass a question as I have ever heard, just moments after his defeat. "What have you learned about yourself during the course of this tournament?" I have fonder recollections of the TV commentary during the competition itself, "We all know St Helens has a great rugby team. Now we know they've got a great darts player as well".

Chizzy was born in Whiston Hospital on 12th September 1980. His father Eric was a warehouse operative and his mother Christine a care assistant. He had four brothers, Lee, Christopher, Jason and Philip, who sadly passed away as a baby. Chizzy attended Parr High School and during his schooldays, darts did not feature at all as he was much more interested in football – in fact he was quite a useful player and had regularly been the top goalscorer for his local team, Ramford, when, at the age of 17 he broke his foot during a match. During his enforced absence from football, he was in a mate's bedroom and scored 100 with the first three darts he had thrown in his life. His mate suggested he came along to play for the local pub team at the Church Tavern in Broad Oak Road. The match was evenly balanced at four apiece when Chizzy was called to the oche. He won that first game to secure the overall match and that is where it all began.

It wasn't long before other members of the pub team were encouraging Chizzy to take up darts seriously. He started playing Super League at the age of 22 for the Bowling Green and when he was 23 he was selected to play for Lancashire B. He won and had one of the highest averages of the day. However he played only that one game, showing little interest in progressing as it seemed at the time nothing more than an expensive hobby. He did continue to play Super League as and when he fancied it and, at the age of 24, was selected again for Lancashire B. Shortly after that he was put into the Lancashire A squad with a number of other St Helens lads and, after just two games, was selected to represent England the following year.

Up to this point, Chizzy had moved from job to job, with the main one being at A180 Darts for Karl and Dawn Holden. However in 2004 he took the plunge and went professional with BDO (the British Darts Organisation). He made his debut in the Welsh Open that year, where he reached the last 32. From there it was onwards and upwards with his first win coming three years later in the 2007 BDO World Cup. Further wins followed in 2008 in the Lancashire Open and the Isle of Man Open whilst 2009 brought wins in the Welsh Masters and the British Open, as a consequence of which he finished top of the BDO International Grand Prix Series. After taking the runner up slot in the BDO World Championship in 2010, he took on a new manager, Roger Schena, who persuaded him to switch to the rival PDC (Professional Darts Corporation). Dave duly attended the Q School in January 2011 and qualified on the very first day he attended. He was now in the big league and his fanbase watched nervously to see how it would all turn out.

In the event, Chizzy went from strength to strength. He was voted PDC Best Newcomer for 2011, won his first PDC event and qualified for the World Matchplay in his debut season. The following year brought the win against Phil Taylor in the World Championships but also wins in a further five PDC events as a consequence of which he was voted PDC Pro Tour Player of the Year. In 2013 he reached his first major final in the World Grand Prix which helped him qualify for the Premier League for the first time in 2014. He retained his place in the Premier League in 2015, when he finished second in the table and lost a tightly fought semi-final 10-9.

2016 however was in many ways the "nearly year". He did win the 10th Players Championship but lost in several other finals, including two majors – so near but yet so far! However Chizzy will have taken great encouragement from the 2017 World Championships, reaching the quarter finals for the first time, where he came up against Gary Anderson. The contest has been described as one of the best ever in a world championship. Chizzy threw 21 maximums of 180 to equal the record for a PDC match (there were 33 in total) yet was edged out by Anderson five sets to three – how different it might have been had Chizzy not missed three darts which would have given him a 4-3 lead!

Despite the fact that he has yet to win a major PDC final – he has now finished runner up on four occasions – at the time of writing he sits at number nine in the world rankings. It can surely only be a matter of time before he adds a major title to his already impressive CV!

Chizzy now lives in Morecambe with his wife Michaela, whom he married in January 2017 and who is also a darts player. They met at the St Annes Darts Open in 2008 and have a daughter, Lexie Rose who was born in 2011. On the tour Chizzy has a reputation of being a pretty laid back character, who rarely gets worked up - indeed he attributes his success at least in part to the fact that he is rarely overawed by an occasion. The big titles still beckon however and it would be great to see him taking some major honours over the next few years.

Shirley Valentine was the name of a class mate of Willy Russell at Rainford High School.

Bernie Clifton

I think it's reasonably well-known that Bernie Clifton is from St Helens though I didn't discover this until many years after I had first become aware of his existence. As a child I used to confuse him with Rod Hull (as did a fair number of people it seems) – after all both of their acts feature to a greater or lesser extent an exotic bird. In the case of Bernie Clifton it was an ostrich whereas Rod Hull had the notorious emu. As far as I am aware, the ostrich never attacked Michael Parkinson although there are many who would take the view that you couldn't have blamed it if it had.

I found out that Bernie was from St Helens because he appeared on *Grandstand* prior to the St Helens v Halifax Cup Final in 1987. The BBC was clearly on the lookout for a larger than life Saints supporter to interview and as these were pre-Johnny Vegas days, Bernie was the obvious choice. I don't recall the content of the interview, other than an observation that the whole of St Helens was there that day and Bernie saying he was looking for someone who owed him "five bob" from when they were at school together.

Bernie was born as Bernard Quinn in Peasley Cross Hospital on 22nd April 1936, son of Dan, a foreman at United Glass, and Margaret. He was the fourth of five boys and the family lived during his early years in Charles Street. The family later moved to Clinkham Wood and then on to Cowley Hill Lane. Bernie was educated at Holy Cross Junior School and then at West Park Grammar, where he recalls being regularly "caned by experts". His only achievement was to be made captain of the cricket 2nd eleven, before he left "by mutual consent" shortly before his GCE O levels. Funnily enough, I don't remember him being lauded as a distinguished former pupil when I was there some 20 years later.

Bernie's showbiz career had begun at the age of 15 in a talent contest at the Theatre Royal (singing "Half as Much") following which he secured for himself a regular slot as vocalist for the Bert Webb Orchestra at the Co-Op Ballroom. Having left school however he was also required to work for a living and after stints as a bread lad (complete with Hovis bike) and TV aerial erector (somewhat ironic given the connection with Rod Hull, who of course died after falling from a roof when fixing his TV aerial), he spent the full five years qualifying as a plumber with St Helens Corporation before National Service intervened. This also killed off his sporting career, as until then he had been playing on the left wing for the St Helens B team.

National service took Bernie to RAF Lindholme near Doncaster where he worked as a radar technician. With Doncaster being very much at the centre of the club world at that time, this gave Bernie the opportunity to continue performing and to supplement his meagre RAF income. It was during this time that he first introduced comedy into his singing routine and he played many pubs and clubs in south Yorkshire. It was there that he met Marjorie – in fact he took to the stage on their first date and sang to her, despite her threatening never to see him again if he embarrassed her. She didn't carry out the threat and the two were married three years later.

Post national service, Bernie spent some time selling vacuum cleaners but then decided to take the gamble and go full-time as a performer. He started to build his reputation on the northern club circuit and was spotted by a television producer at a show in Batley. By the 1970s he was making regular TV appearances, soon to be accompanied by the now famous ostrich, Oswald, adopted at the suggestion of one of his mentors, Les Dawson. He featured in the *Royal Variety Performance*, during which the Queen was reported to be crying with laughter at his antics and from 1978 presented the BBC children's programme *Crackerjack*. Regular appearances on cruise ships, including the QE2, meant that he travelled the world many times over. His repertoire included cabaret, theatre, pantomime and his own radio show.

Bernie has in recent years made other appearances on our TV screens for example in the Peter Kay *Amarillo* video and in the BBC romantic comedy *Love Soup*. And he has not lost his ability to surprise, as evidenced by an appearance on the television show *The Voice* in January 2016 under his real name Bernard Quinn – he had not told any family or friends about his intention to enter in case they talked him out of it! It seems that after the death in 2000 of his wife, Marjorie, to whom Bernie would sing whilst he nursed her through a 12 year battle with dementia, he decided to revive his singing career and enlisted the help of a voice coach at the Royal College of Music in Manchester. He made it through to the live show but on the day none of the judges turned their chairs so that was as far as he got. However it prompted the release of the album *The Impossible Dream* later that year in which Bernie sang 17 of his favourite songs.

At the age of 82 Bernie's career is still going strong. In 2016, as well as a cameo appearance on the *Royal Variety Performance*, he undertook a tour entitled "An evening with Bernard Clifton – from *Crackerjack* to *The Voice*, The Impossible Dream", he hosts a weekly programme on Radio Sheffield and he is working on his autobiography - the odds are that it will be well worth a read!

Also remarkable have been Bernie's spare time interests. He was a permanent member of the England football band in which he played the trombone. The band hit the press with a vengeance when refused entry to England's opening game in Euro 2012 against France in Kiev. Two years earlier, in South Africa for the World Cup, they – or more correctly Bernie – attracted attention of a different kind after a car ran over Bernie's foot, causing a visit to the local hospital, footage of which can be seen on YouTube if you have the perseverance to get through the obligatory Pukka Pies advertising at the beginning of each clip. Thankfully, there was no serious harm done. But whilst many found the various renditions by the band extremely entertaining, there were others who were less favourably inclined and there were mixed feelings when the football authorities decided to ban musical instruments from the grounds at the Rio World Cup in 2014.

Another leisure interest of note is that Bernie flies microlight aircraft and indeed has done so for some 30 years. One assumes he is no longer paying life insurance, as the annual premium might be somewhat prohibitive!

Currently living in Derbyshire, Bernie has four children and four grandchildren – and like every good St Helens expat, still follows the Mighty Saints. "Once a Saint, always a Saint!" as he puts it! And it's hard to disagree with *The Guardian*'s review of an appearance at the Edinburgh Fringe "Bernie Clifton is a certifiable genius!"

Michael Coleman

Michael Coleman is a name that could very easily have slipped under the radar, and indeed in all likelihood it would have done if he had not stuck his head above the parapet a few years ago and become a director and shareholder of St Helens RLFC. As a consequence we can rightly celebrate his success in an arena with which many readers will not be overly familiar – the strange but lucrative world of hedge funds.

Mike was born in Crowther Street, the eldest of four children. His mother was Italian (her maiden name was Vernazza and she belonged to the Vincent's ice cream family, whose

©Copyright Michael Coleman 2018

business is still run by Mike's cousins). His father was from St Helens although like many inhabitants of the town he was of Irish extraction. Mike, his two brothers and his sister attended St Teresa's Primary School in Devon Street. The family then moved to Eccleston Park in the late 1960s which accounts in part for the fact that Michael attended senior school at St Edward's College in Liverpool rather than West Park. He progressed from there to Exeter College, Oxford where he studied geology and then began his working career in 1982 at the London office of Cargill Inc, a large US corporation which traded in a wide range of products. In Mike's case he started as a junior merchant in the natural rubber department.

The move which was to shape Mike's life came in 1984 when he accepted a one year assignment to Singapore from which he has never returned. He stayed in rubber pretty much all of the time he was at Cargill, although he also took charge of Asia Pacific trading in petroleum in 1997. His move away was occasioned by the corporation's decision to sell the rubber business and to transfer management of the Asian petroleum trading to Europe in 2000. Mike initially decided to stay and try to get into the dotcom boom. For once however he got his timing wrong and it didn't work out. As a consequence he left Cargill in 2001 to found a derivatives business with Marubeni, a big Japanese conglomerate. However this didn't work out either and Mike left in 2003 – a good move as Marubeni closed the business down the following year. Instead he decided to follow his dream – to set up his own major commodity fund. This led to him founding Aisling Analytics which became an investment adviser to The Merchant Commodity Fund at its launch in May 2004. Mike was joined at Aisling by an ex-colleague, Doug King and by 2005 Aisling had taken on the role as full manager to the fund.

In 2010 Mike and Doug, together with another Cargill alumnus, Chris Pardey, took control of RCMA Commodities Asia, a global commodity merchant and in March 2014 Aisling changed its name to RCMA Asset Management.

So, success upon success if one looks at the long term, but inevitably it has not been without its hiccups, most notably in 2011 when The Merchant Fund fell 29.6 per cent in value after the team made a wrong call on sugar and petroleum. This was followed by a lesser fall of 7.6 per cent in 2012. But it bounced back in 2013 and then went on to make 59 per cent in 2014! Even at its lowest point it had delivered more than 200 per cent growth to the initial investors in 2004. It does however demonstrate amply the risks which have to be managed on a daily basis for someone running a business such as this.

Mike's involvement at St Helens RLFC began in 2010 and coincided with the move to the new stadium. He had played some amateur rugby league (for Pilkington Recs) as a teenager, and had always maintained an interest in the club, getting to games during visits home to family. With new investment required to take the club to the next stage, this was in his words an opportunity he could not overlook and a "boyhood dream come true". Unsurprisingly Mike, permanently settled in Singapore with his wife Swee Yep and two sons, both of whom were brought up there, gets to only a handful of games each season. He is however now the largest single shareholder so his commitment, albeit from the other side of the globe, is certainly not in doubt. And there cannot be many who would shoehorn into an interview with a hedge fund journalist, as Mike did in August 2014, the following in relation to the two codes of rugby, "As a diehard rugby leaguer, it is manifestly obvious that the 13-a-side game is far superior and only the inherited class biases of the late British Empire have kept it from sweeping all before it!"

It might be the case that we don't see too much of Mike Coleman, but he is nonetheless making a big contribution to the town of his birth.

'I knew a youth who went to the house of
his girlfriend in St Helens where they heartened to the
Rugby League results then turned the wireless off
when the soccer results were about to begin.
His father was astounded to hear of such malpractice and
gravely counselled him to extricate himself.
"You don't want to get mixed up
with that class of folk".'

(Don Haworth)

John Connelly

When he passed away on 25th October 2012, there will have been many football fans to whom the name John Connelly meant very little and it is certainly true that his name does not trip off the tongue in the same way that those of Booby Moore, Geoff Hurst and Bobby Charlton do. However John was so very close to joining those immortals who in 1966 delivered for the one and only time in history the Jules Rimet Trophy, aka the World Cup, to these shores. Indeed John appeared in the very first game of that tournament when England played out a disappointing 0-0 draw

Image supplied by Association of FormerManchester United Players.

with Uruguay. Despite the fact that he hit the post twice in that first match, he was replaced by another winger, Terry Paine of Southampton, for the second and thereafter the England manager, Alf Ramsey famously decided to discard wingers altogether. The wingless wonders did of course go on to lift the trophy and as a consequence, few remember the name John Connelly.

But that is not to say that he was forgotten by those who played with him and by those who watched him play. The former group includes the legends who lined up to form a guard of honour at his funeral: Bobby Charlton, Nobby Stiles, Denis Law, Roger Hunt, Norman Hunter and many others. John Doherty, former Busby Babe, in his definitive *Insider's Guide to Manchester United* describes Connelly as one of Sir Matt Busby's best ever buys and, as a footballer, the complete package. "John was quick, he possessed a fine touch with either foot, he crossed the ball accurately and intelligently and he averaged better than a goal a game which is a fantastic rate for a winger. On top of that, he was brave, he worked his socks off and he was comfortable on either flank". John Doherty was not alone when he describes the decision to transfer him to Blackburn Rovers a couple of months after he played in the World Cup as inexplicable and a great shame for the club.

John Connelly (pronounced with the emphasis on the second rather than the first syllable) was born in Sutton on 18th July 1938 and brought up in Clock Face, where his younger brother Jim still resides. He attended St Theresa's School for whom he played football with some distinction. On leaving school he started to work as an apprentice joiner at Clock Face colliery and was playing football for St Helens Town, when Burnley, then a top flight club with a reputation for unearthing and nurturing young talent, came knocking on his door. After a brief trial he was offered, and signed, a permanent contract in November 1956 and made his debut that same season against Leeds United. By the season 1958/9 John was a fixture in the Burnley side which went on to win the First Division Championship in 1959/60. He was to gain his first international cap that season against Wales in Cardiff. John stayed at Burnley for another three seasons during which they finished fourth, second and third in the league and he also made an appearance in the 1962 Cup Final at Wembley when Burnley lost to Tottenham Hotspur 3-1.

In April 1964 John was transferred to Manchester United for £56,000 and was to spend two seasons at Old Trafford during which time he won a second Championship winner's medal in 1964/5 and played in the European Cup the following year, when United reached the semi-finals. His transfer to Blackburn however signalled the start of a downward trajectory in his career – they had just been relegated to the Second Division team and during the four seasons he was there, John was unable to help them regain their place amongst the elite. He was released in 1970 and then spent three years playing for Bury before hanging up his boots.

In total, John represented England on 20 occasions, scoring seven international goals. His last appearance came in that World Cup opener in 1966. Because he did not actually play in the final, he did not initially receive a World Cup Winner's medal. This was rectified, somewhat belatedly, in 2009 when he was presented with his medal at

10 Downing Street by the then Prime Minister Gordon Brown after a successful campaign persuaded FIFA to recognise players who had played any match in the Finals tournament rather than just those who had played in the World Cup Final itself.

In his post playing career John ran a chip shop in Brierfield, not far from Burnley, where he had settled. It carried the name "Connelly's Plaice" and was a regular meeting place for many Burnley supporters, including BBC Radio 5 Live broadcaster Tony Livesey and politician Alistair Campbell, who would gravitate there to meet one of their heroes. He remains to this day very fondly remembered at Turf Moor where he has a place on the Wall of Legends.

John died at home in Barrowford in October 2012 after battling bone cancer for two years. The flag at Turf Moor flew at half-mast and the Burnley players wore black armbands in their next game to commemorate his passing. He was survived by his wife Sandra, a son and two daughters. He remains St Helens most capped England international football player.

Ray Connolly

I have to confess that Ray Connolly, journalist, author and screenwriter, very nearly slipped through the net, and it was only at the last minute that a journalist friend of mine queried his non-inclusion. I had not, however, appreciated that Ray was from St Helens, nor, given the fact that his name has rarely, if ever, featured in the local press or on any social media in relation to St Helens, does it seem that many other people had either. I hope that this piece can play a part in giving Ray the recognition he richly deserves in his home town.

© Copyright Ray Connolly 2018

Ray was born in St Helens in December 1940. His father, John, was, he believes, a fitter, and his mother, Anne, had previously worked in a dress shop in St Helens. His mother was struck down with thrombosis shortly after Ray's birth and he spent the first few months of his life at his grandparents' house in Lewis Street (where his cot consisted of a drawer, apparently not unusual at the time!) After his mother's recovery, he lived in the family home in Clarke's Crescent, Eccleston, although his father John was rarely there, having joined the Royal Navy early in World War II. Sadly Ray was never to get to know his father, who was lost at sea when his ship went down in a storm in 1944, his body being later washed up on the French coast. Ray and his elder sister Sylvia, were consequently brought up by his mother and grandmother, who moved into the family home. His mother took a job at Triplex to help make ends meet.

Ray attended Windleshaw Primary School and then progressed to West Park, which, he says, didn't really work for him – certainly not in the early years. One of the reasons for this, he suspects, was that the family moved to Ormskirk shortly before he had started secondary school and this meant Ray had to leave home at 7.30 every morning and then take three buses to ensure he arrived at school on time. And there was, of course, the return trip at the end of the day. On top of that, he readily admits, he only ever put effort into the subjects that interested him. The fact that he suffered from a pronounced stammer didn't help matters and he managed to get just 4 GCE O-levels, hardly the sort of return to justify the time and effort he had spent attending the school.

In the sixth form however, Ray achieved a remarkable turnaround. This was in part due to the fact that he could now study subjects he really enjoyed and he managed excellent results in History, English and General Studies (a subject which was a godsend for someone who avidly read the newspaper every day). Still, his poor O level results meant he couldn't get a place at university. He consulted the local education officer in Ormskirk, who in turn talked to Ormskirk Grammar who agreed to supply a place for him. A mixed grammar school (in contrast to West Park which was all boys), was, in Ray's words, like moving "from army camp to holiday camp". He thoroughly enjoyed his time there and, importantly, obtained the right mix of O levels to secure a place at London School of Economics, where he enrolled for a degree in Social Anthropology. It was at LSE that his journalistic career began. Whilst there he was the editor of the *Clare Market Review* (the oldest student journal in the UK) and was also associate editor of the student film magazine, *Motion*.

After completing his degree course in 1963, Ray's preference was to take a job in Fleet Street but nothing was available, so instead – and after completing a road trip across the United States with a friend - he began at the *Liverpool Daily Post* as a graduate trainee. He stayed there for two and a half years during which time he married Elaine ("Plum") Balmforth, whom he had met at Ormskirk Grammar and had later hooked up with again in London. In 1967 they decided to up sticks and move back to the capital with Ray having managed to secure a position at the *London Evening Standard*.

The next six years were something of a rollercoaster. Ray's hobby had been rock 'n' roll and now his job was to write a weekly column on popular culture and music. The list of his interview subjects during this period is endless - it would probably be easier to list those he didn't interview rather than those he did, not just of the music world, but of the 1960s generally! It included the man who had first captivated him at the age of 15 with *Heartbreak Hotel*, Elvis Presley, but most memorably, and on many occasions, The Beatles*. Indeed Ray could have achieved worldwide fame as the man who broke the news of their break up, John Lennon having confided in him but at the same time asking him to keep the information to himself. However Paul then broke ranks, the newspapers got the story anyway and Ray missed out on perhaps the biggest scoop of all! He stayed in touch with Lennon over the following decade and in 1980 was due to fly to New York to interview him on the day of the former Beatle's death – only to find himself writing his obituary instead. It was a 24 hour period he would later dramatise in his BBC radio play *Unimaginable.*

In 1973 Ray left the *Evening Standard* and went freelance. That same year saw the publication of his first novel *The Girl Who Came to Stay* and the release of the film *That'll Be the Day* for which Ray wrote the screenplay. The following year he won a Writers Guild of Great Britain Award for the best screenplay for the follow up film *Stardust.* He was to go on to write some seven novels, a feature-length documentary, *James Dean: The First American Teenager* (which he directed as well), several television drama series, two television films as well as radio plays and short stories. He was a co-writer on the George Martin BBC TV music series *The Rhythm of Life.*

So to say that Ray was prolific in his output would be an understatement of epic proportions, especially when one takes into account that he has continued as a journalist throughout, contributing articles to the *Daily Mail* and all the broadsheets. Having recently published the biography *Being Elvis – A Lonely Life,* he is currently working on radio adaptations of *That'll Be The Day* and *Stardust,* writing a new biography *Being John Lennon,* and trying to coax his screenplay about Dusty Springfield into production – a pet project, as Dusty had, in 1970, many years before it became common knowledge, shared details of her sexuality in an interview with him.

Ray and Plum in 2016 celebrated their 50th wedding anniversary in Venice, having travelled extensively over the years. They live in Fulham and have three children, with two grandchildren now on the scene. Much to Plum's dismay, Ray continues to work seven days a week on his various books and scripts, and writes frequently for the *Daily Mail* (OK, we can't all be perfect!)

It is difficult not to be inspired by Ray's story. Here was a child who was raised in wartime by a single mother, whose initial schooling was hardly successful and whose pronounced stammer from an early age made it difficult for some to envisage him doing any job at all, let alone one in which a major part was conducting interviews. Yet Ray overcame all of these obstacles (he does apparently still stammer in private but describes his success in mastering it when in the spotlight as "having learned to act the part of a man who doesn't stammer"). As a result he succeeded in doing something to which many aspire but few achieve - he has been able to live the dream!

* These interviews are available in *The Ray Connolly Beatles Archive* and *Stardust Memories – Talking About My Generation.*

John Davies V.C.

The first of a quartet of St Helens holders of the greatest military honour, the Victoria Cross, John Davies (known as Jack) also has the distinction of being the only holder of the award to whom it was granted posthumously whilst he was still alive! The award is today on display at the Imperial War Museum in London.

Jack was actually born at Rock Ferry in Tranmere on 29th September 1895, the son of James and Margaret. However the family moved to St Helens whilst Jack was still very young after his father obtained employment at the Sherdley Glass Works of Cannington, Shaw and Company. John went to school in Arthur Street (which used to run between Westfield Street and Liverpool Road) and on leaving school began to work at the Ravenhead Brick and Pipe Works.

The First World War broke out in July 1914 when Jack was 18 years old and he immediately volunteered for action and enlisted with the "St Helens Pals" – officially the 11th Service Battalion of the South Lancashire Regiment. In the event he didn't actually get to France until November 1915, just in time for the carnage that 1916 was to bring. Jack was wounded twice during the battle of the Somme but returned to action each time on the front line. He somehow managed to survive and in early 1918, now a corporal, he was involved in the fighting near Eppeville in northern France. This was at the point when the United States was poised to enter the war. With a view to defeating the Allies before the might of America could be deployed against them, the Germans launched a major offensive on 21st March. Three days later the 11th Battalion was in danger of being outflanked on both sides and received instructions to withdraw. Jack was aware however that any retreat would have to be made via a barbed wire lined stream and, concerned that the men would be mown down whilst trying to negotiate this, decided to launch a rearguard action to keep the enemy at bay. Ignoring his own personal safety, he climbed onto the parapet with his Lewis gun in order to have a better line of fire, and was to stay there until the very last moment, continuing to fire and causing many enemy casualties. As a consequence the majority of his company was able to withdraw safely. Jack however was not so lucky and was presumed by all to have died in action.

Jack's parents, now living in Peasley Cross, were informed by letter of his death, and that "By his very gallant conduct, he no doubt saved the lives of many of his comrades". Later that same year on 23rd May, he was awarded the highest military honour, the Victoria Cross, with the *London Gazette* noting that it was being granted posthumously.

Some two months after the award however a postcard arrived at Jack's parents' home, which he had sent from a prisoner of war camp at Zagan in Silesia (which is now in Poland). One can only begin to wonder how they must have felt, given that news of loved ones having died in battle must have been commonplace at the time and that they would have resigned themselves to his loss. The celebrations were completed when John returned to St Helens on his release after the end of the war and took up his old job at Ravenhead Brick and Pipe Works. On 20th June 1920 he attended a garden party at Buckingham Palace for recipients of the Victoria Cross, one of a number of ceremonial events to which he was invited.

The rest of his life was pretty unremarkable. He married his childhood sweetheart, Beatrice and they had three children. Tragedy did strike however in 1943 when one of their sons, Alan, drowned after an accident on the ice in Taylor Park Lake. John himself died in 1955 at the age of 60 and is buried in St Helens Cemetery.

In 2014 Jack's story was one of those featured in an exhibition which took place at the Manchester Imperial War Museum to commemorate the Great War and the contribution thereto of the people of the North West. On display were various items of memorabilia including the letter informing his parents that he had died in action! Finally, in March 2018, a paving stone in Victoria Square was unveiled in his honour and to mark the 100th anniversary of the award of his Victoria Cross.

Robert Dorning

The name of Robert Dorning may not trip off the tongue for many current television viewers but from the late 1950s through to the end of the 1970s he was a regular feature on our television screens. Indeed he might still be a household name had he taken on a role for which he was at one point identified by the writer Jimmy Perry as the preferred choice – that of Captain Mainwaring in *Dad's Army*, the intention being that Arthur Lowe would play Sergeant Wilson (the two had appeared together already as the boss and his subordinate in the Granada series *Pardon the Expression*). Sadly that did not come to pass, but there is no doubting Robert's place as one of the leading actors the town has produced.

Robert was born 13th May 2013, son of Robert and Mary Dorning. The family lived initially at 108 Croppers Hill (long since demolished) and at some point moved to Pigot Street. Robert Junior attended Cowley School and learned how to play various musical instruments. It was also there that he had his first taste of acting, appearing as counsel for the prosecution in a school play *Trial by Jury*. Identified by the headmaster as someone with an exceptional talent, Robert received plenty of encouragement to pursue a career in acting and after leaving school he went on to study drama and dance in Liverpool. Initially however his objective was to become a ballet dancer and given that his father was a coal miner it is difficult not to envisage this as having been something of a *Billy Elliott* scenario! Whether or not there was family resistance, Robert was clearly undeterred and appeared at one point in the *Nutcracker Ballet* at the Theatre Royal. Around about this time, he was also a member of the St Helens Amateur Operatic Society.

For whatever reason he did not continue his career as a dancer and instead had a short period as a musical comedian in theatre. When World War II broke out, his career in acting had just commenced. His first film role was in *They Came by Night* in 1940 but inevitably everything was put on hold for the duration of the war, during which he served in the

Royal Air Force. Once demobbed however he returned immediately to the big screen and made use of his ballet training as a member of the Corps de Ballet in the ground-breaking film *The Red Shoes* in 1948.

In 1951 Robert married Honor Shepherd, originally from Lancaster, and also an actress. Wikipedia records that she had played the part of one of the dwarfs in the 1937 film *Snow White and the Seven Dwarfs* at the age of 11 although she does not appear in the official credits for the film. Her first recorded appearance was in 1946 in the TV movie *Just William* and she went on to collect 38 credits in total on the IMDb website.

It was towards the end of the 1950s that Robert's television career took off. His first TV series was *Drake's Progress* in 1957 and it seems that thereafter he was in almost constant demand. Among his better known roles were as the tyrannical gentlemen's club secretary in *Bootsie and Snudge* and as a policeman and various other characters in several episodes of *Hancock's Half Hour*. But as well as appearing in classic comedies, he also played two separate characters in *Coronation Street*, appeared in *Emmerdale Farm*, *Emergency Ward 10* and several other TV series. There were appearances in many of the popular television thrillers of the time, including *The Avengers*, *Bergerac*, *No Hiding Place* and *The Professionals*. In fact, to say he made frequent TV appearances would not do him justice - the IMDb website lists over 70 different TV series or programmes in which he made an appearance; we come across his name with such regularity that it might be easier to list the popular TV programmes of the era in which he did not appear rather than those in which he did. His parts ranged from serious roles such as Sir William Lucas in the 1967 series of *Pride and Prejudice* to all manner of comedy roles, including even an appearance on the *Basil Brush Show* in 1978. So whilst he was never likely to be typecast as an actor, his face was a familiar sight to all who watched television during those years.

But Robert's appearances were not restricted to the small screen. His acting career had of course begun in the world of film rather than TV and during the late 1940s and the 1950s he played supporting roles in some 13 films. He continued to make the occasional appearance in the 1960s and 1970s when his main focus had moved away from film to TV work. These appearances included *School for Sex* (1969), *Confessions of a Pop Performer* (1969), *I'm Not Feeling Myself Tonight* (1976), *The Ups and Downs of a Handyman* in

(1976) and a role as the Prime Minister in *Carry on Emmanuelle* (1978). Alert readers might have spotted something of a pattern here, although there were some more serious roles, including one in *Ragtime* (1981) alongside an elderly James Cagney and a youthful Samuel L Jackson, an appearance in *Evil under the Sun* (1982) and finally in *Mona Lisa* (1986).

Robert and Honor had two daughters, Stacy born in 1958 and Kate in 1963. In keeping with the family tradition, both went into the acting profession and indeed there was an occasion in 1979 when Honor and both her daughters appeared in the same episode of *Dick Turpin*.

Robert died in London of diabetes in 1989 at the age of 75. However the family tradition, begun all those years ago at Cowley school, continues with Kate's son, Jack Dorning having completed in 2014 a degree at London's international drama school, the Rose Bruford College

According to the current Earl of Derby,
his family allowed its name to be used
in connection with two sporting occasions:
the annual Derby at Epsom and
the rugby league game between the two
sides at opposite ends of his estate, St Helens and Wigan –
hence the origin of the term "The Derby game".

John William Draper

Photograph by Edward Bierstadt

As we have already noted, Michael E. Arth is referred to in Wikipedia as a polymath. John William Draper is not but it seems to me that anyone who has built a reputation as a scientist, physician, philosopher, chemist, historian, teacher and photographer is equally deserving of the title. As with Michael Arth, John William Draper made his name in America, leading one to ponder whether every expatriate from St Helens living in the USA was very good at lots of things. But whatever the answer to that question, the similarities between Messrs Arth and Draper pretty much end there.

We do not actually know a lot about Draper's early life. He was born in St Helens on 5th May 1811 to John Christopher Draper and Sara Draper (nee Ripley). His father had been born in London and his mother in Whitby, Yorkshire. John's eldest sister, Dorothy (who later became famous as one of the first subjects in his pioneering work in photography) was born in Newcastle upon Tyne in 1807, the next sibling, Elizabeth, in Penrith in 1809 and his younger sister, Sara, in Lincoln in 1813. So the family moved about a bit, an existence no doubt dictated by his father's occupation as a Wesleyan minister.

Exactly when John left St Helens is not clear. He did not initially attend school at all, being home tutored until he was sent to boarding school at Woodhouse Grove in Yorkshire at the age of 11 by which time the family had almost certainly left the town anyway. One might reasonably conclude from all of this that the St Helens influence on his life was fairly limited. But one cannot know for certain and we must anyway include him as his qualifications for entry are beyond challenge.

After leaving Woodhouse Grove, John went through another period of home tuition before attending the newly established University College, where he studied chemistry (his choice of university no doubt influenced by the fact that his father owned some shares in it). Whilst there, he boarded with a Mrs Barker; also living in the house was her niece, Antonia Gardner, daughter of Dr Daniel Gardner, an Englishman who had married into the Portuguese de Piva-Periera family and was at the time physician to Dom Pedro I of Brazil. John went on to marry Antonia in September 1831 and they were to stay together until her death in 1870.

John was not actually awarded a degree from University College as the only educational establishments authorised to award degrees at the time were Oxford and Cambridge – he had to be satisfied with a "Certificate of Honours".

Around about this time John's father died and the whole family – John, his wife, mother and three sisters – decided to move en masse to Mecklenburg in the United States, having been encouraged so to do by maternal relatives who had emigrated there some years earlier to found a Wesleyan community. Initially John had intended teaching at a Wesleyan school but arrived too late to take up the post. In the event, he devoted himself entirely to scientific research and his first independent contribution (he had co-authored some papers in England before emigrating) was published in mid-1834. This was followed by seven more papers which were published in the next two years. At about the same time he enrolled to do a medical degree at the University of Pennsylvania, funded by the earnings of his elder sister, Dorothy, a schoolteacher, who supplemented her income by drawing and painting. She shared John's passion for scientific research and acted as his assistant for the whole of his life as well as caring for his wife after she became ill, and his children. She was also the subject of what may have been the world's first photographic portrait (and certainly the oldest surviving print), taken by John in 1840 when he was only 29.

After graduating and teaching briefly in Virginia, John took a job as head of chemistry at New York University. He then helped found the New York Medical School and was a professor there from 1840 to 1850 at which point he became president, a position he held until 1873, before reverting once again to professor of chemistry.

Whilst John achieved celebrity in the world of photography (as well as the portrait referred to above, he also took the first photograph of the surface of the moon and was one of the first persons to conceive of and execute microphotographs), his advances in this arena actually took place as part of wider research into the chemical effects of radiant energy, which in turn led him to be acclaimed as one of the foremost scientists in the United States in the 19th century. His research left us also with the permanent legacy of the Draper Point (which, simplistically, is the temperature at which almost all solid materials visibly glow red) and Draper's Law (that only absorbed rays produce chemical change).

In the 1850s John involved himself more and more in the area of historical development and in particular the scientific basis of the emergence of dominant nations and cultures in the history of mankind. His views here were closely aligned with those of Darwin and, after the publication of his first work on the subject, *A History of the Intellectual Development of Europe*, he became a valiant defender of science against religion. This culminated in 1874 in the publication of his most famous book, *A History of the Conflict between Religion and Science,* which was notable, inter alia, for its inclusion in the Index Librorum Prohibitorum – the list of publications banned by the Catholic Church as heresy, putting him alongside the likes of Galileo and Copernicus. This was almost certainly also a first for a person from St Helens!

John wrote extensively, his publications ranging from text books on chemistry and natural philosophy on the one hand to a history of the American Civil War on the other. He gave lectures and published numerous papers on an extraordinarily diverse range of scientific subjects. He was awarded membership of many of the learned societies of Europe and the United States, an honorary degree from Princeton and the Rumford Medals for research at the American Academy of Arts and Sciences. He was also the first President of the American Chemical Society. And throughout all of this – indeed for some 45 years from 1836 to just before his death – he did not neglect at all the duties of his occupation as a teacher. This was clearly a most remarkable man.

The achievements of his children might also be described as remarkable. His eldest son, John, became Professor of National History in the College of the City of New York, his second son Henry became a leading astronomer and a pioneer of astrophotography, third son Daniel became Director of the Meteorological Observatory in Central Park, New York and inventor of Draper's Self-Recording Weather Instruments and his granddaughter Antonia Maury another distinguished astronomer. All told, not a bad haul for one family.

So we are talking about someone here who ticks many, many boxes. Any flaws or shortcomings? None, it would seem – perhaps the only observation one might make is that we do not seem to be dealing here with a colourful personality. Although he was said to have a fine personal presence, he was also reported as being mild mannered and quiet with very little self-assertion. According to George Barker in *John William Draper: A Memoir,* he was engaging in conversation and always had attentive listeners but this is contradicted somewhat by Keith Thomson in the *American Scientist*, who described a presentation he made at Oxford University as "long and boring" (this took place at a meeting held only seven months after the publication of Darwin's *Origin of Species*, and which at various times became quite heated). There is not a lot to add – he was certainly a contender for the best scientist that St Helens has produced but "St Helens finest"? Probably a step too far.

Geoff Duke OBE

Geoff Duke has over the years attracted some of the most glowing tributes ever accorded to a motorcycle rider: "the David Beckham of his day", "the original superstar of motorcycle racing", "the first two wheeled superstar", "a sporting icon" and "TT legend" are just a few examples which show the regard in which he was and is held, not just in the world of motorcycling but in the wider

Geoff (right) with his tailor, Frank Barker, also from St Helens, who designed the first ever all-in-one leather racing suit. Image courtesy of Peter Duke.

sporting world. The Isle of Man TT official website comments, "As legends and TT heroes go, they don't come much greater than Geoff Duke". He was Sportsman of the Year in 1951 (three years before it became the BBC Sports Personality of the Year), the only person from St Helens ever to lift the award, and one of only two motor cyclists (the other was John Surtees) to win it, and he was awarded the OBE in 1953. His legend lives on for every current motor cycle rider in the form of the one piece leather riding suit which was his very own invention.

Geoff was born, fittingly, in Duke Street on 29th March 1923, at number 60 above the bakery run by his parents, Tom and Lily. He attended Cowley Prep and Grammar School but was from a very early age besotted with motor cycles, having been seduced at the age of ten by the aroma of Castrol R engine oil and pillion rides on the New Imperial 250cc bike purchased by his elder brother Eric. After Eric was involved in a nasty accident in which he sustained 22 fractures, motorcycles became taboo in the Duke household but this didn't prevent Geoff, together with two friends, secretly purchasing an old Raleigh which they hid in the garden buildings of his friends' house. They secured permission to ride it at a farm in Garswood, pushed it all the way there and spent many enjoyable weekends racing the bike over a self-constructed heavily rutted course. They had even managed to upgrade to a 500cc Triumph before news filtered back to Geoff's parents. In the event, although not happy, they simply pleaded with him to be careful.

As it happened the family was soon on the move, deciding to up sticks and live in Blackpool, as a consequence of his father's arthritis. Geoff was thirteen at the time but it proved to be only a temporary absence and by 1939 the family was back in St Helens, living in Pike Place, Eccleston with Geoff taking up his first job in the Prescot telephone exchange. He saved up every penny he earned and was soon commuting to work on a self-financed (but somewhat decrepit!) 175cc Dot.

Despite the outbreak of war, motorcycling occupied nearly all of Geoff's thoughts until petrol became impossible to purchase. He volunteered for the Royal Signals and managed to secure for himself a position as one of 20 instructors training the despatch riders who were to assist with the D-Day landings and other military communications. During this time he modelled himself on the riding style of a senior instructor, Sergeant Hugh Viney, one of the finest trials riders of the day. Geoff was promoted himself to Sergeant shortly after the end of the war and was demobbed in July 1947. He returned to St Helens, spent his army gratuity on a 350cc BSA trials bike and started to enter – and win – trials in the North West. When the opportunity arose to work in Norton's factory trials department he jumped at the chance and although his trials experience there was not particularly successful, Norton backed his ambition to compete in the Isle of Man Clubman's TT. In his first race on the island in 1948, he was leading the Junior Manx Grand Prix when his bike failed. However he returned the following year and won the Clubman's TT with a record average speed of 82.97mph. A broken leg suffered in Ireland in July did not put him off and he was back riding again in September - indeed he won the Manx Senior Grand Prix that same month.

From then on it was all onwards and upwards. Geoff was invited to join the Norton official road racing team in 1950 and that year came within a single point of winning the World Championship. Already looking to innovate wherever he could, it was in this year that he came up with the idea of the one piece aerodynamic riding suit and he commissioned his tailor in St Helens, Frank Barker, to design it. Frank volunteered immediately not just to design but to make the suit, which when completed weighed less than five pounds and was ready for the 1950TT. Frank also made for Geoff the first close fitting zip up boots in the same lightweight leather. Both items of clothing were to take the motorcycling world by storm and very soon became the standard racewear.

1951 was to bring Geoff's first world championship, not just in the 500cc event but in the 350cc event as well. As well as the Sportsman of the Year award, it was also the year that he married Pat Roberts with whom he was to have two children, Peter and Michael. They set up home in Southport and the following year Geoff left his employment with Norton to become a partner in a motorcycle business in St Helens, but with an arrangement whereby he would

Geoff Duke on the rostrum Swiss GP 1952
Image courtesy of Peter Duke

continue to ride for Norton. As if all this did not keep him busy enough, he was offered the opportunity by Lord Brabazon to race on four wheels as well as two. Geoff accepted and joined up with the Aston Martin racing team, competing in four races in 1952 and by all accounts showing great potential. However he was also trying to retain his world motorcycling title, which was all going pretty well until he dislocated his ankle and broke his leg in a race in Germany. This time the recovery period was in excess of three months which obviously put a stop to all forms of activity in that period.

A big fall out with Norton was to take place at the end of 1952 after Geoff had suggested to the managing director that they needed to develop a machine which could compete with the multi cylinder Italian Gileras. As it happened, he had already been approached by Gilera to see if he was interested in riding for them and although he was initially reluctant to take up with a non-British manufacturer, he decided to accept the offer after what he considered was extremely shabby treatment by Norton. At that stage he was still undecided whether his future lay with two wheels or four. However he soon concluded that he enjoyed car racing much less than motorcycle racing and in addition, the other racing drivers, resenting the publicity he attracted, were not exactly welcoming. He competed in two more races for Aston Martin in 1953, but then went full-time with Gilera. The move paid off handsomely with further World Championships in 1953, 1954 and 1955 – the first World Championship hat-trick!

It might indeed have been more had Geoff not been caught up in a pay dispute involving the private riders, who made up the majority of the grid at grand prix events but were very poorly paid. There was, it seems, fault on both sides and Geoff was caught in the middle and as a result copped a six month ban which forced him to miss the early races in the 1956 championship. Geoff believes also that one of the longer term consequences of this was that Gilera and Moto Guzzi, incensed by the fact that the bans impacted their commercial interests, pulled out of racing altogether at the end of 1957.

Geoff himself had to go through another injury hit campaign in 1957 and after Gilera's withdrawal, rode on his own account in 1958 and in 1959 until September, when, after winning three races at a meeting in Locarno, he concluded the effort was now too great and he announced his retirement from motorcycle racing.

Geoff and his family decided to settle in the Isle of Man where he already owned a hotel and his business interests in future years were wide and varied. He remained involved in motorcycle racing throughout and at one stage worked closely with Gilera (and indeed provided most of the funding) in an attempt to develop a new racing team known as the Scuderia Duke. Unfortunately this was to end in failure. However many of Geoff's other ventures were very successful, particularly in shipping and his son Peter continues to run the very successful Duke Marketing business out of the Isle of Man.

Geoff's first wife Pat died in 1975. His second marriage ended in divorce and on his death in May 2015 he was survived by his third wife Daisy, as well as Peter and Michael, the sons from his first marriage.

There is no doubt that Geoff was an iconic figure in the history of motorcycling. He was instantly recognisable on the track, not just as a consequence of the Lancashire red rose which his helmet bore, but because of his distinctive riding style, which was described on one occasion as "like water flowing from a tap – such smoothness". He became a pin-up in an era when most people associated motorcycles with gangs and violence. He was the public face of Brylcreem and so much in demand that Senior Service, the cigarette brand, agreed he could make clear he was a non-smoker whilst advertising their product ("I don't smoke myself but I always give my friends Senior Service"). He polled over one third of the votes when winning the 1951 Sportsman of the Year Award, despite the fact that the list of other contenders included such household names as Roger Bannister, Denis Compton, Stanley Matthews, Stirling Moss and Billy Wright.

The meticulous approach which Geoff brought to everything in life was perhaps best illustrated by the fact that he was approached before Donald Campbell to attempt the world water speed record on Lake Coniston but, unconvinced by the engineering, turned the opportunity down – a sensible decision as it turned out. Geoff had always wanted to understand every aspect of his machine and if he identified issues he was not happy with, would always insist that they were sorted before he would proceed.

Geoff was laid to rest in the Isle of Man after his funeral cortege, consisting of a number of motor cycles as well as cars, drove one last lap of the 37.73 mile TT circuit where he had made his name. And so concludes the story of arguably the town's greatest sporting superstar of all.

Mark Eccleston

Andrew Quirke, who assisted Mark in writing his autobiography *Pushing the Limits: Succeeding Against the Odds*, posed the question as to why more people had not heard of Mark Eccleston. He lamented the fact that despite having lived in St Helens all his life, he had not even heard the name

until he started work with him. The book was published in 2007 and it is fair to say that the very same question is as valid today as it was then. It would have been a travesty had he not been included in this collection and at one stage that was certainly a possibility. Thankfully, it didn't happen and I hope as a result a few more people will become familiar with both his amazing story and his achievements.

Mark was born in Clock Face on 2nd December 1969, the youngest of three brothers. His dad, Jimmy, worked at Pilkington's and his mum, Pat, was a dinner lady at St Theresa's School which Mark attended for two years before moving to St Mark's in Leach Lane and, in due course to St Cuthbert's for his secondary education. There is little doubt that Mark was a bit of a lad, not averse to getting into all sorts of trouble, interested in girls, and who loved playing sport – initially boxing but then rugby league, which he played at school and then for St Helens Crusaders. Both of his elder brothers had represented the town and there was every indication that Mark would progress even further – by all accounts Saints had him in their sights and given that Mark was a passionate fan, this would have been a dream come true. It was however not to be. Mark left school after his GCE O levels in June 1986 and had a few months to kill before he was due to take up an apprenticeship. He had always been an adventurous boy, fearless and, as he admits himself, at times reckless. But it was in many ways a fairly innocuous incident which was to change his life. In a field at the back of his house, he ran down a steep embankment and somersaulted into a haystack, something he had done on numerous occasions previously. On this occasion however he didn't get his timing right, landed on his head and broke his neck.

The consequences were severe. Not only had he dislocated two vertebrae in the neck, he had severed his spinal cord and as a consequence was left tetraplegic, which means he lost partial or total function of all four limbs. Paralysed from the chest down, he would never walk again. He was to spend seven months in the spinal unit in Southport Hospital and then a further period in a residential home in Birkdale. It is difficult for anyone to know how he or she would respond in this situation but one suspects that Mark's immediate response – resentment, aggression, bitterness – must be fairly standard. Where he differs, however, is the way he turned both himself and his attitude around. There wasn't a thing he could do to change his predicament so he had a stark choice: either wallow in his misery or make the best of it he could. We now know which he chose.

There was some very early evidence of Mark's resolve not to be beaten by his condition. Although the medics were reluctant, he persuaded them to let him try a walking brace. Nobody with his level of injury had ever done it before. Mark stuck at it however and although it was a long process (he blacked out the first time he used it) he was finally able to take it home and used it to walk around each day. At a later seminar involving the world's top specialists in this area, they refused to believe what Mark had managed to achieve with the brace until they had seen the video.

The seeds of Mark's sporting success were actually sown before he returned home. There was a hospital table tennis team which he joined and he soon came to love playing – it provided the release he was looking for. Whilst still at Birkdale he went to the National Wheelchair Games in Stoke Mandeville and won a silver medal. The following year he won gold. And importantly it was at these Games that he had his first introduction to Wheelchair Rugby.

Previously known as "Murderball" because of the full contact nature of the sport, wheelchair rugby is a team event with four players on each side and it immediately appealed to Mark. He played for the Southport team in the National Championships and in 1991 was selected to play for Great Britain in a tournament in Dallas. By the end of 1992 he was the Southport team's player coach, the team had won the National Championship and he had received the "Most Valuable Player" award. He was made captain of Great Britain, toured America with them in early 1993 and then in the International Wheelchair Games in Stoke Mandeville in July that year, captained the team to the final, where they lost to the favourites, the USA. His performances did not go unnoticed and he was approached by the American coach to go to the US and play for Tampa – all costs paid! Mark accepted and acquitted himself sufficiently well to be invited back again the following year. He turned it down although he has reflected often on that decision and is now convinced he made the wrong call.

Mark continued in the sport over the next couple of years and although he was starting to think he needed a new challenge, he first of all had the target of playing in the 1996 Atlanta Paralympics. Mark was again captain but Great Britain lost in the semi-finals, again to the USA, and Mark had had enough. It was time to move on. He became involved with rugby coaching, helping transform Clock Face U15s from no hopers into title challengers. In the meantime however, he had taken up tennis, a sport he had never previously played but which he had encountered at the Wheelchair Games.

Although initially Mark could not even grip the racquet and had to be taught how to tape it to his hand, he was a quick learner and entered his first competition in November 1996. He found a coach based in Wavertree and threw himself into the sport. By May 1998, he had beaten the world number one in his division (the Quad division) in a match in Japan. Later that year he played in the World Team Cup in Barcelona, where Great Britain lost in the final to the USA (yes, them again!) His battle in that tournament against Rick Draney, whom Mark regards as the greatest tetraplegic athlete of all time, is remembered by many as one of the greatest tennis matches of all time – whether able-bodied or wheelchair! In 2001 he was the main man as Great Britain went one better and lifted the World Team Cup, beating Japan in the final, a title which they retained the following year, on this occasion beating the Americans in a closely fought contest.

By the early 2000s, sponsored by Littlewoods, Mark was travelling the world playing tennis and well on his way to becoming number one in the world, something which he achieved in February 2002 and which position he held until April 2003. He was in fact the first British player at any level of tennis to be world number one. Unfortunately by 2003 medical problems were finally kicking in and affecting his performances, but he was determined to stick it out until the Athens Paralympics the following year, the first time that the Quad Division had been admitted. He was knocked out in the quarter finals in the singles but managed a silver medal in the doubles – a big disappointment to him at the time but something he has since come to treasure. By this time, Mark knew that his playing career was nearing its end and he played only two more tournaments after that, retiring in April 2005.

There was however another first in the sport that Mark was destined to achieve. In January 2006 he became the first tetraplegic in the world to become a qualified tennis coach. Having concluded that the problem with British sport was the quality of the coaching, Mark felt he had to walk the walk, obtained the qualification and continues coaching to this day. He is also Disability Sport Development Officer for Halton Borough, teaches PE in a school for children with complex physical and medical needs and is a Mobility and Disability Sports Specialist for Cyclone Technologies. He plies a lucrative trade as a motivational speaker, providing inspiration for anyone faced with what seem to be insurmountable challenges. And he remains a passionate fan of both St Helens RLFC and Liverpool FC.

The narrative above does however represent only the bare bones of a complex but captivating tale. The facts do not convey the hours of practice that Mark put in, the huge determination to succeed and, not least, some of the medical obstacles he encountered along the way. During his rugby career he had to overcome an attack of Automatic Dysreflexia, an extremely painful condition where the blood pressure of a person with a spinal cord injury becomes excessively high. And when playing tennis, he had to deal with the fact that like most tetrapegics, he could not sweat and was therefore very prone to overheating in tournaments held in the warmer climates of the world. He also suffered from a disc protrusion which created a pincer effect on the spinal cord and which caused him to lose permanently some of the movement and strength in his right hand. Finally, the onset of shoulder problems meant that he was unable to perform at anything like his best during his final two years of competition. On the positive side, however, there was the partying, the booze and the girls – one thing that is clear is that the injury did not dampen in any way Mark's sex drive (a huge relief to him when he first realised this) and the travelling and entertainment attaching to both sports he played meant he was never too far away from the action!

Mark was undoubtedly not everybody's favourite person. As a Liverpool supporter, he will not thank me for the comparison but he reminds me in some ways of Roy Keane – he has the same single mindedness and sheer determination to succeed, and like Roy, it did not matter to him if there were a few personality clashes on the way. He certainly did not suffer fools gladly. He had a huge respect for some of his opponents but not others and similarly for some coaches but not others. He hated to be let down by anyone and his frustrations would sometimes get the better of him, certainly on the tennis court. Interestingly whereas Mark regarded his outbursts on the court as part of the process of gaining a psychological advantage over his opponent, his great rival Rick Draney felt it gave him, as his opponent, a boost – his interpretation was that Mark was losing it. Either way, it was an illustration of Mark's passion and his will to win and these attributes played a huge part in his makeup throughout his sporting career.

There were several awards which came his way. He was Dan Maskell's Player's Player of the Year in both 1999 and 2001, the BBC North West Disabled Athlete of the Year in 2002 and the Lawn Tennis Association Disabled Player of the Year in 2002. Many would however regard that as scant recognition for Mark's achievements. His autobiography, although tipped for a place on the shortlist for the William Hill Sports Book of the Year in 2008, had to settle for a nomination as best rugby book in the British Sports Book Awards. But this probably reflects the general disdain the media seems to have for disabled sports. In his autobiography, Mark was himself quite scathing about the BBC's coverage which he saw at the time as restricted to basketball, swimming and the extremely well decorated Baroness Tanni Grey Thompson.

On any objective analysis Mark must qualify as one of the greatest tetraplegic athletes of all time. He is not the type of guy who will appeal to everyone (nor would he want to), but few could question the quality of his achievements, not just in the sporting arena, but in life generally. Let's hope that in the fullness of time he gets the recognition he deserves!

Richard Eltonhead

The name "Eltonhead" will be familiar already to all St Helens readers, Elton Head Road being a well-known thoroughfare linking Rainhill with Sutton Heath. It has a certain added resonance for me as well, on the basis that I built a school there. There were, I concede, others involved in the project (that much can be deduced from my job title of "joiner's labourer's mate") but I like to think that some of the bolts I shot into the structure (in clear contravention of trade union demarcation rules, but we were on a bonus arrangement) have helped keep the edifice in place for over 40 years. But I digress. The name Eltonhead derives from a famous Sutton family of which Richard Eltonhead, born in 1582, was a member. That it is Richard rather than other, more successful members of the family (both earlier and later) about whom I am writing, does have a certain irony but fame and fortune work in mysterious ways.

Richard, together with his second son, also Richard who was born in 1626, backed the wrong horse in the English Civil War and fought for King Charles 1, who was of course soon to part with his head. Their allegiance was apparently something to do with an obligation they had to the royalist Earl of Derby. As a consequence, Richard Snr lost most of his wealth (although not his life) and when he died in 1664 his estate was worth only £63. It seems that the family home, Elton Head Hall, was held in trust for Richard Junior who sold it in 1676 for £2,700. However when Richard Junior died in 1688 his estate was worth only £5. Not a lot for a family with the pedigree of the Eltonheads even in those far away days.

So why then does Richard Eltonhead merit inclusion in this collection? The answer lies in his descendants, not via the unfortunate Richard Junior but via those daughters of his who emigrated to America, and particularly amongst them, Martha Eltonhead (born 1628) and Alice Eltonhead (born in 1630).

The background to their decision to go to America is not entirely clear, but the most likely explanation is provided by Stephen Wainwright, in his work *Sutton's Lords and Masters* who concludes that after his financially disastrous involvement in the Civil War, Richard could no longer afford the dowries for his five daughters. The decision was therefore made to pack them off to Maryland in the United States where Richard's eldest son, William (born 1616) had emigrated in 1640 to take up the position of special envoy to Lord Baltimore, proprietor of the Maryland colony. The expectation was that their youth and the family fertility record would compensate for the lack of a dowry and indeed all of them seemed to find reasonably wealthy, if relatively elderly, husbands with comparative ease in the New World.

It was Martha's betrothal to Edwin Conway Senior in 1643 which was over the years to bequeath to society a staggering list of notable descendants. Her great-great grandson, via her son Edwin, was James Madison, often referred to as the father of the US constitution and who became the fourth president of the United States (and providing a link between St Helens and Madison Square Gardens in New York, which was named after him). But if we track down the line of Martha's daughter (whom she named, interestingly, Eltonhead), we find, remarkably, a second US president, one Barrack Obama. Even that is not all – a separate but equally well researched line of descendants via daughter Eltonhead reveals the name of a certain Brad Pitt. It is fair to say that those in the USA who have done this research have focused more on the fact that Barrack Obama and Brad Pitt are distant relatives rather than the more important fact that they share a common ancestor from St Helens. But for the purpose of this exercise it is of course the St Helens connection that is the more significant.

Martha was not the only one of the Eltonhead sisters to have distinguished descendants. Alice, the youngest of the sisters, can name amongst her issue Richard Henry Lee and Francis Lightfoot Lee, two of the signatories of the Declaration of Independence as well as Robert E Lee, the famous Confederate Army general in the American Civil War. So all in all, not a bad haul for one family.

It is worth noting in passing that the different members of the Eltonhead family were to experience rather varied fortunes. We have seen that both Richard Snr and Richard Jnr died relatively penniless in 1664 and 1688 respectively. William, to whom the five sisters were entrusted on their arrival in America, was to meet a sticky end, being executed by the Puritans following the Battle of Severn in 1655, in which he had fought for his sponsor, Lord Baltimore. On the other hand, Richard Snr's brother, Edward, became Master of Chancery (the English courts set up in America) and also a very large landowner, amassing an estate of some 10,000 acres in Maryland. In other circumstances that might have been enough to warrant a separate entry for him but he was ultimately outgunned by brother Richard, whose legacy to society via daughters Martha and Alice is more than enough to exclude the claims of his brother.

St.Helens Council

Tim Follin

T here is a video on YouTube which carries the title "Tim Follin: The Best Game Composer You Never Heard Of". It tracks Tim's career "and incredible music" until his retirement from game music in 2006. It concludes that Tim was one of the most unfortunate composers of the era in that the quality of his music was never matched by the quality of the games for which he composed and that it was this that led to his early retirement from composing video games music.

Tim was born in 1970 to Vincent, a journalist with the *St Helens Reporter*, and Marjorie, who worked there as a secretary. He was the youngest of three brothers. The family lived in Parr, practically on the roundabout between Derbyshire Hill and Ashtons Green Drive – according to Tim, "like growing up under the Arc de Triomphe but without the culture". Music was part of his life from an early age – on the one hand there was a piano in the house, a legacy from Tim's grandmother and on the other, there was the constant beat of progressive rock to which both his elder brothers listened and to which, by necessity, Tim listened as well. He attended Parr Flat (now Broad Oak) Primary School, where one of the teachers indulged his love of music and played guitar with him. It was there also that he had his first introduction to computers. His secondary education was undertaken at Cowley High but this did not go well. The one dimensional approach to education prevalent at the time did not suit Tim – when the teachers asked what they thought was a simple question and expected a simple answer, that is rarely what they got, not because Tim was deliberately uncooperative but because his mind did not work in the manner the teachers expected. He left at 16 and briefly attended Liverpool's Sandown Music College, an experience he found very worthwhile but that had nothing to do with the education it provided. He left without completing the course.

Prior to leaving college however Tim had been asked by his brother Mike, then a programmer with a small firm in St Helens called Insight, to put some music to the games he was writing on a Spectrum computer. Tim's compositions were the product of much experimentation and some trial and error, but it worked well and several game magazines commented very positively on the quality of the music. After he had abandoned college, Tim went to work for Software Creations in Manchester, again with brother Mike, and this time also with brother Geoff. Many soundtracks followed over the next five years, including Tim's own favourite *Ghouls 'n Ghosts* for the Amiga, an upgraded version of the Commodore 64, for which many of Tim's other soundtracks had been written. This was the most prolific period of Tim's career during which he amassed over 30 credits for his compositions (some of which were co-written with brother Geoff).

Increasingly disillusioned with the working environment (and the level of reward for the work they were putting in), Tim and his brothers decided to move on in 1993 and joined Malibu, the comic company which was trying to get into computer games. They worked out of an office in a run-down business park in Warrington but the whole thing was a bit of a disaster and within a year (during which there had been very little output) it had collapsed.

This was the prompt for Tim to go solo and he was to spend the next 12 years or so as a freelance. During this period he composed some of his best-known works, including *Ecco the Dolphin* and *Starsky and Hutch*. However as many have discovered, freelancing has its advantages but also its worries and frustrations. For Tim one of the frustrations was that game music budgets were never large enough to enable him to hire real musicians and there was the constant concern that he might not generate enough work each year to live on. All of this culminated in his announcement at the end of 2005 that he was retiring from video game music.

During his career, as well as working on games for the Spectrum and the Commodore 64, Tim also composed music for games on Atari ST, Nintendo, Game Boy, Super NES, Dreamcast and PlayStation. His retirement was mourned by many – the website Gamesetwatch carried an article referring to him as the "all-time great video game musician" but at the same time rejoicing that his "legacy of genius music" lived on. Even now, a random google search generates 127,000 hits and perhaps even more remarkably, there are 12,900 Tim Follin videos on YouTube (one of which is a compilation bearing the title "Tim Follin is a God"!)

Tim's intention was to move into graphic design and also into the film world. He had already written, produced and directed two short films, *The Sun Circle* and *Body Counting* which won the Best Short Film award at the Salford Film Festival in 2004. He also became involved in the television industry, and worked for a company in Manchester called Channel M. This led in due course to the setting up in 2013 of his own company Baggy Cat Limited which provides a range of media services, from shooting and lighting, composition of accompanying music, sound mixing and visual effects. His contribution to the world of video games has not been lost entirely however – between 2012 and 2014 he developed the interactive crime drama game Contradiction which was generally well reviewed (indeed 782 reviews for one online store in the US give it an overall score of 10 out of 10). There is, it seems, likely to be more to come in this arena.

Whatever the future holds, we can only hope that Tim finds his current environment more lucrative than the one in which he acquired almost legendary status, and that going forward he is able thrive both in terms of hard cash as well as job satisfaction. He continues to live in the St Helens area with his wife Clare, who worked for the Forensic Science Service (and who was indirectly responsible for Tim's interest in crime and hence the aforementioned video game Contradiction). They have been together almost 30 years (a fact which Tim finds alarming) and have two children, both of whom have apparently inherited the Follin cynical gene (or is that actually a St Helens gene?). Indeed many would regard Tim as a true native of the town in that he refuses to take either himself or, for the most part, life in general, too seriously. But he has certainly played his part in contributing to the wide and diverse fields in which inhabitants of the town have made their mark.

An interesting postscript is that neither of Tim's brothers remained in the games industry either. In both cases they opted for a more dramatic change of scenery – Geoff is now a schoolteacher whilst Mike went into the church and has recently taken up a post with the unlikely title of "Vicar of Werrington and Wetley Rocks (no that isn't something out of *Father Ted!*) – the video games industry clearly affects different people in different ways!

Bill Foulkes

As a one-time leader in the all-time list of appearances for Manchester United (and even now behind only the illustrious names of Sir Bobby Charlton, Ryan Giggs and Paul Scholes), an England international and a survivor of the Munich air crash, there is quite a lot to write about footballer Bill Foulkes. He was not however the first in his family

Bill Foulkes (right) with Sir Matt Busby (left)
Image supplied by Association of
Former Manchester United Players.

to hit the headlines – grandfather William captained St Helens in the very first Rugby League Cup Final, whilst his father also played for St Helens as well as football for New Brighton (then a football league club), as well as being a champion crown green bowler. (As an aside, I played golf with Bill a couple of times and he asked me on one occasion if I knew that his grandfather had won the first rugby league cup final with St Helens.

"They lost, Bill" I told him, "10-4 to Batley".

"Well, I'll be damned," responded Bill. "Are you sure? He always told me that they won".)

Bill was born on 5th January 1932 and raised in Thatto Heath. He attended Nutgrove School (this was some years before its "good" Ofsted rating was challenged by the *Daily Express* because the school's own website was littered with spelling mistakes) and then Whiston Secondary School where he was introduced to football having previously played rugby. It was not long before he started to shine at the round ball sport, although interestingly he played mostly as a goal scoring centre forward at that time.

After leaving school, he did a number of jobs before finally following his father down the pit at Lea Green Colliery. He continued to play football however and was representing Whiston Youth Club when he was spotted by Manchester United. He signed a part-time contract with United in March 1950 and made his first team debut against Liverpool in December 1952 as a full back. More success was to follow as he gained two England Under-23 caps and a full cap against Northern Ireland in Belfast in 1954.

Throughout this period Bill had been doubling up his career as a professional footballer with his job down the mine. At some point his manager, the great Matt Busby, had decreed that all the players should go full-time but Bill wasn't convinced that football would provide him with a long-term career and ignored the instruction. Indeed it was only after his (one and only) international appearance that the manager found out he was still working down the mine and put a stop to it. It seems that Bill had turned up for work in the normal way the day after the game, without realising that even in those days an international cap would carry some publicity! Sir Matt also knocked on the head another potential career option. Bill had taken up golf and within twelve months had reduced his handicap to one, prompting an invitation to turn professional. His manager's advice was to stick with football and whilst there was certainly an element of self-interest there, it is difficult to argue that this was not the right thing for Bill to do.

Bill was a member of the famous Busby Babes team that won the First Division title in 1955/6, at a time when he was also doing his National Service. The team participated in the European Cup the following season, reaching the semi-final, and also successfully defended their Championship title. Tragedy was to strike in the following season however when the aeroplane bringing the United team back from a European fixture crashed at Munich, causing over 20 deaths including eight of the United players. Bill escaped largely unscathed after being thrown from the aircraft but then heroically returned to the wreckage with goalkeeper Harry Gregg to try to pull out other survivors.

Although Bill then took over the captaincy of the team and indeed, together with Harry Gregg, played in a FA Cup tie against Sheffield Wednesday less than two weeks after the disaster he was, unsurprisingly, badly affected by it and for a number of years suffered from sleeplessness, weight loss and lack of appetite. He lost fitness and struggled for form, regularly contemplating giving up football for good. The turning point came when he moved to centre back in 1963, which coincided with United winning the FA Cup at Wembley, their first trophy since Munich. Two more championship titles followed and in 1968 Bill was part of the first English team to win the European Cup. He had scored a critical goal away at Real Madrid in the semi-final (one of only nine he scored in his career – indeed, according to Bobby Charlton, this was the first time he had ever seen Bill cross the half way line!)

Bill stuck around for another couple of years and on retirement in 1970 took up a position as youth coach. He then had a spell in non-league football before spreading his wings and travelling to the USA where he managed teams in Chicago, Tulsa and San Jose before moving to Norway and managing several clubs there in an eight year stint. In 1988 he went to Japan where he managed FC Mazda in Hiroshima until his return to the UK in 1991. His involvement in youth football did however continue until around 2000 when he finally hung up his coaching boots.

Bill passed away in November 2013 at the age of 81 having suffered from Alzheimer's disease for some time. He was survived by his wife Teresa, whom he had married in St Nicholas Church in Whiston in 1955, and their three children. At his funeral, attended by many of his old colleagues, Bobby Charlton gave an address in which he recalled Bill turning up for training in the early days with his face still black from his work down the mine – not a scenario which is remotely imaginable in the present time! Nor is the fact that in his 688 appearances for Manchester United as a full back or centre back, he was never booked on a single occasion. This is even more remarkable when one takes into account his hard man reputation, which led on one occasion to the observation that it appeared he had been hewn from rock in the mine in which he worked.

St Helens may not have produced many footballers but in Bill it certainly produced one who can take his place on the pantheon with the very best!

Chris Foy

When Chris Foy, Premiership football referee, announced his retirement in May 2015, it was no doubt an occasion for celebration for some football fans. Quite why Chris Hoy (not from St Helens!), six time Olympic gold medallist and eleven time world champion cyclist, should regard it as such is not immediately obvious. However his tweet on 19th May explains everything: "Wishing Chris Foy all the best on his retirement from premiership refereeing. My Saturday afternoon twitter feed will never be the same again". In fact it had been quite widely reported over the years that Chris H had received more than his share of twitter abuse, not because he had upset anyone on his bicycle, but because football fans were continually confusing him with Chris F (for whom abuse was of course an occupational hazard).* But then Chris F was never a million miles away from controversy which at times seemed to follow him around. That may well have been a consequence of the fact that he was never afraid to make the difficult decisions that he was regularly called upon to make.

Chris was born in St Helens on 20th November 1962, the eldest of three children. His father was a police officer, his mother a school assistant and the family lived in Sutton. From an early age Chris loved sport and would travel all around with his father watching football, rugby and cricket. It was during this time that he developed a lifelong affiliation with Everton FC and indeed is currently included in the list of "Celebrity Blues" on ToffeeWeb, the independent Everton website. Chris also played football, although he never had realistic expectations of a professional career as a player.

Chris was educated at Sherdley Primary School and then Rivington Road, leaving school at the age of 16 to become an apprentice bricklayer at the now demolished United Glass. It was not a job that he found particularly fulfilling and although he had never previously considered the possibility of following in his father's footsteps, when his father suggested that he might want to try it, Chris decided to give it a go. He knew straight away that he had made the right decision.

At around the same time Chris decided to try refereeing as opposed to playing and on 12th September 1983 he made his inaugural appearance in the less than auspicious setting of the Winwick Hospital playing fields. What struck him more than anything that day was the absence of the camaraderie that you experience as part of a team. As a referee you are out on your own. However whilst he did not think the game had gone particularly well (the manager of one of the teams told him he was "rubbish"!), Chris made the resolve to stick at it, despite the fact that his probationary period in the police made it difficult to fit everything in. His perseverance did of course reap huge dividends in the fullness of time.

It was some 11 years later, when Chris received his first appointment as a Football League official. Initially this was as an assistant referee (known at the time, of course, as a linesman) and he was promoted as such to the Premier League the following year. He did not have to wait long thereafter for his progression to the position of referee, his first game being Hull City against Darlington on 11th August 1996 and for the next five years he refereed in 35 to 40 games a season in the Football League. His big break came in December 2001 with his appointment as a Premier League referee, the first match in which he officiated being a goalless draw between Bolton Wanderers and Charlton Athletic. This did however present Chris with something of a dilemma as he was named as one of the original 24 referees who were expected to perform full-time in the Premier League. Chris already had a full-time job as a policeman and two into one didn't go! However Merseyside Police proved to be an accommodating employer and he was offered the opportunity to work on a part-time basis with responsibility for junior schools in South Liverpool. Chris eagerly accepted this offer as it gave him a chance to get out into the community, to meet and to speak with young people.

From this point on, it was pretty much all systems go and for the next 15 football seasons Chris became, at least in the football world, a household name, respected by the majority of fans as one of the best referees in the game, but inevitably derided by others - there is for example a Facebook page with the title "Chris Foy is a disgrace" albeit that it has hardly gone viral with a mere 5334 "likes" at the time of writing!

The main highlight of Chris's career was the 2010 FA Cup Final at Wembley between Chelsea and Portsmouth but there had been other big games at which he officiated – the League Cup Final in 2009, the Community Shield the same year and the FA Trophy Final in 2007. He also acted as fourth official in two England internationals before his compulsory retirement from international duties at the age of 45 in 2007.

Throughout his career, Chris was rarely away from the headlines. He was the referee during the infamous exchange between John Terry and Anton Ferdinand, he was the referee who sent off Eden Hazard for kicking the ball boy at Swansea and he was the only referee to have had to leave the field after being hit square in the face

© Copyright Chris Foy 2018

by the ball in a Premier League match. And throughout his Premier League career, Chris continued his police work, indeed using his celebrity status to good effect at times when a calming presence was required in a police incident. He was also a prominent figure in many good causes, including "Don't X the Line", "Respect" "Get on with the Game" and "Show Racism the Red Card" and indeed was inducted into the latter's Hall of Fame for his contribution.

By the end of Chris's career, he had refereed over 650 games, had given over 1500 yellow cards and around 100 red. Within the Premier League he had refereed 260 games with 712 yellow and 38 red cards. Of these 38, eight were handed to Chelsea players, leading many Chelsea fans to question his neutrality and Jose Mourinho to suggest that he should not in future officiate at Chelsea games. But it is an irrefutable fact that a referee is in a "no win" position and on the occasion of his last match involving Chelsea (against Hull City) he attracted criticism from both managers. He can however justifiably point out that he is one of the few persons to have cracked Mourinho's inscrutable countenance. It happened at the end of this game when Mourinho was holding a press conference, just as Chris exited the referee's changing room nearby.

"Mr Foy, Mr Foy," called out Mourinho. "Tell the guys please. Diego Costa is crying in the dressing room because you gave him a yellow card. And these guys are asking me why?" Chris, conscious that referees are not permitted to comment, simply dug into his pocket and pulled out a tissue which he handed to Mourinho, with the single word,

"Handkerchief". All those present, including Mourinho, collapsed in laughter.

Outside football Chris has been a prominent supporter of the Knowsley Housing Trust's "Give Rent Arrears the Red Card" movement and has been involved in several fundraising initiatives for the Steve Prescott Foundation. He now lives in Newbold with his wife Beverley and his daughter Melissa and is a Senior Coach at Professional Game Match Officials Limited, looking after the 17 Premier League referees. As well as passing on the benefit of his many years' experience to current referees, he continues to perform his police duties and it can be assumed with some certainty that he will also be involved in the many causes that he has supported – oh yes, and with time to watch both Everton and his beloved Saints as well!

---

*   The confusion did however works both ways as a number of twitter users thought Chris F had announced his retirement in 2013 – it was in fact Chris H.

Ray French MBE

I t is it is difficult to argue with Ray French's credentials for inclusion in this list. He is the only dual code international rugby player to hail from St Helens and he was also for many years, as successor to Eddie Waring, the voice of rugby league on BBC. He continues to do a significant amount of radio work, commenting regularly on BBC Radio Merseyside. On top of this, he did his day job as an English teacher at Cowley School, coached their school rugby teams, wrote some 13 books and spent a period as coach of Liverpool St Helens, the local rugby union side. He is President of the St Helens Past Players

Ray French in action for Saints
Image courtesy of
Saints Heritage Society

Association and also President of Liverpool St Helens Rugby Union Club. What he does with the rest of his time is not recorded.

My first recollection of Ray French was playing for St Helens in the early 1960s. He was not the sort of player to set a game alight, being the type of ball handling forward around whom the runners would buzz, waiting for the offload. One of his early publications *Running Rugby* prompted the observation by Alex Murphy his co-commentator on the BBC, "Running Rugby? Frenchie never ran with the ball in his effing life".

It was during his time playing for St Helens that I recall Mohammed Ali suggesting he might make a good sparring partner. It happened on 22nd May 1966, the day after the Challenge Cup Final win against Wigan at Wembley and the whole of the Saints team, sitting in the front row of the studio audience, was acknowledged by the television show host, the late Eamonn Andrews. His main guest that day happened to be Mohammed

Ali who clearly saw our boys' potential. As far as I am aware, Ray did not take him up on the offer.

Ray was born on 23rd December 1939 in Cowley Hill Hospital, son of Richard (a sorter at United Glass) and Ellen, and they lived with Ray's grandparents in McFarlane Avenue which fittingly, as it turned out, is little more than a stone's throw from Knowsley Road. Ray attended Rivington Road School and then Knowsley Road Junior School before becoming the first family member to attend Cowley Grammar School. Although his early rugby education on the fields by Dodd Avenue near to his home was exclusively league, Cowley of course played rugby union (until then Ray, was not even aware of the existence of another code of rugby!) at which sport he was to excel, gaining four England caps as second row in 1961 when he played every game in what was then the 5 Nations Championship.

Ray was at Leeds University at the time, from where he was to graduate with honours in English, Latin and, somewhat bizarrely, Russian. He did contemplate staying longer in the 15-a-side game and challenging for a place on the following year's Lions Tour, but the temptation of playing rugby league for his home town club, which unsurprisingly was now knocking on his door, was too much. A tax-free signing-on fee of £5,000 (a record for a forward, although Leeds had offered even more) was the icing on the cake.

Ray was to marry local girl Helen Bromilow shortly afterwards so no doubt the signing-on fee came in quite handy. However his decision to go professional caused a potential problem with his prospective teaching career when Loughborough College, which had already offered him a place, then made it virtually impossible for him to attend. However at the last minute he was able to switch to Leeds to obtain his teaching qualification following which he took a job at Fairfield School in Widnes before returning to his old school Cowley in 1965.

In the meantime Ray's career at St Helens was going well, reaching its pinnacle in 1966 when he was an integral member of the legendary four cup winning team. He made in total over 200 appearances before moving on to Widnes in 1967. In 1968 he was selected to play for Great Britain, whom he represented on four occasions, all in the same year, which provides a pleasing symmetry with his rugby union career. He retired from rugby league at the age of 32 in 1971.

It was however after his career had finished that his name became familiar to a much wider audience. He already had a full-time job as he had been teaching at Cowley since 1965 and he started coaching at St Helens Rugby Union Club (now Liverpool St Helens), for whom he had played in his rugby union days. Unfortunately Ray's success as a coach attracted the attention of the Rugby Football Union who did not take kindly to the involvement of an ex-professional in their game. The club was told in no uncertain terms that they had to ditch him, which they dutifully did despite the fact that there were many who took up cudgels on Ray's behalf. Some years later he received a letter of apology from the RFU, albeit somewhat too late for him to resume his coaching career. Thankfully his coaching activities as a schoolmaster at Cowley did continue although he was officially an English rather than a PE or games teacher.

In 1979, Ray wrote his first book, *My Kind of Rugby* and it was as a consequence of this that he was asked by the BBC to do a test commentary when they were looking for a successor to Eddie Waring. Ray got the job and thus began an alternative career which was to last over 30 years until his retirement in 2013.

Ray differed from his predecessor in that he had the respect of the rugby league community as well as those not familiar with the sport. By contrast Eddie Waring had been loathed by many followers of the game, who felt he portrayed the sport as something of a joke, not unlike professional wrestling which also featured on Saturday afternoon television. That is not to say that Ray's commentary did not attract amusement and – perish the thought – even some mild derision. There were undoubtedly some wonderful quotes, which will live long in the memory, for example:

"….and there we see the sad sight of Martin Offiah limping off with a broken finger!"

"He's like a needle in a haystack, he's everywhere".

"Rick Thackray has got a tremendous gash….just above his head."

But with Ray French, it really was a question of what you see is what you get. There were no airs and graces and he didn't try to be somebody he wasn't – in fact he just got on with the job he loved as best he could.

The BBC website contains some glowing accolades from Ray's fellow presenters on his retirement and his contribution to rugby league in particular has been recognised when he received the Mike Gregory Spirit of Rugby League Award in 2010 and an MBE in the 2011 New Year's Honours List. He was a man who has left his indelible mark on the game and gained a legion of admirers in the process.

Ray and Helen, who had two children and now two grandchildren, still live in St Helens and Ray still keeps himself occupied with his radio work, occasional after dinner speaking and responsibilities at Liverpool St Helens. However it might even be that after all these years he is finally getting a little bit of time for himself!

The old St Helens ground at Knowsley Road was used as the backdrop for the film *Best* in the year 2000 as it bore a close resemblance to the Old Trafford of the 1960s and early 1970s.

Sir David Gamble

St Helens can legitimately claim to be the birthplace of a number of major corporations, amongst which are Pilkington, Beechams and the De Vere Group. It would be nice to be able to add the big US multi-national Proctor and Gamble to that list. Sadly that isn't possible but there is indeed a connection. The father of Sir David Gamble, Josias Christopher Gamble, was born in 1775 in Enniskillen in Northern Ireland. A few years later in 1803, James Gamble, co-founder of Proctor and Gamble, was also born in Enniskillen. Josias was university-educated which suggests he came from an affluent background and then went

Photograph taken by Arthur Debenham
© Copyright Debenham Family

on to become involved in the manufacture of chloride which was used to bleach Irish linen. In the *Dictionary of Irish Biography* published in 2009, it is recorded that James Gamble had prosperous relatives who were involved in linen bleaching. The overwhelming likelihood therefore is that the two were related.

Whilst in 1819 James Gamble emigrated to the United States where he was in due course to meet Mr William Proctor, Josias went in the other direction, specifically to St Helens in 1828 at the invitation of a friend of his from Dublin, James Muspratt, who had recently moved to St Helens from Liverpool. His soda making business was falling foul of the authorities in Liverpool because of the extreme pollution it was causing. St Helens, it seems, did not impose any restrictions, probably because its local government was less well established. Josias accepted the invitation and joined as a junior partner. Two years later, however, Muspratt moved on and Josias was forced to bring in new partners, one of whom was Joseph Crosfields from Warrington who was also to go on to become a well-known figure in the chemical industry.

David Gamble had been born in Dublin in 1823 but moved to St Helens with his father in 1828. He was educated privately in the town before spending a year at University College London and then three years at the Andersonian Institute in Glasgow, before returning to St Helens in 1843 at which point he set up a new chemical company, JC Gamble and Son Limited, with his father. Interestingly this was located very close to the original factory and also involved the production of soda and bleaching powders using exactly the same process which suggests that Josias had by then been squeezed out of the business he was running with the Crosfield family. Josias was to pass away in January 1848, aged 72, but with David now in full control, the new business flourished and by 1865 was the same size as the original factory, notwithstanding that this had also grown fourfold in the meantime.

Shortly before the death of his father, David had married Elizabeth Haddock, daughter of the Ravenhead colliery owner, at St Helens parish church. They lived initially in Cowley Vale House (which was on the corner of Dentons Green Lane and Cowley Hill Lane) but then had built an impressive mansion known as Windlehurst (not far from the Pilkington family seat at Windle Hall) into which they moved in the 1860s. David no doubt required the extra space to house his rapidly growing family as they had eleven children in total! The four elder sons all joined their father in the chemical business, which had diversified outside its original activity of soda and bleaching powder into various by-products and also potassium chlorate and bleaching powder. The business did not, like many other chemical businesses, move south into Widnes, preferring the better access to the canal network provided by St Helens. It soon became the town's biggest chemical manufacturer and developed a very healthy export trade to the United States.

Like many businessmen who are committed to free trade, David was at times prepared to dilute his values when it came to the success of his business. In 1883, he was instrumental in the formation of the Lancashire Bleaching Powder Manufacturers Association, one of whose objectives was to maintain profitability within the industry. A particular problem was that Brunner Mond and Co was providing serious competition by using a lower cost ammonia soda process at its plant in Northwich. In due course this led in 1891 to the merger of 48 companies to form the United Alkali Company – ten of these were from St Helens and 16 from the Widnes/Runcorn area, one of which, interestingly, was James Muspratt and Co so it seems he didn't move too far. I can't even begin to think about the logistics of merging 48 companies together but it seems they managed to get the deal done! JC Gamble and Son was valued at £320,000 for the purposes of the merger, considerably higher than any of the other St Helens companies. As an aside, Brunner Mond and the United Alkali Company were two of the four companies which were in 1926 to merge and form Imperial Chemical Industries (later to become ICI).

Outside of his business, David acted as a director of Parr's Bank of Warrington from its incorporation in 1865 until his death. However he devoted the majority of his spare time to local government. As early as 1845, he was appointed as one of the original improvement commissioners (these were local boards, each created by a separate Act of Parliament whose duties were, broadly, to bring about an improvement in facilities such as paving, roads, sewerage and such like, funded by the levy of rates on properties in the borough) and served as its chairman from 1856 to 1862. He was the town's first mayor in 1868 and went on to serve on two more occasions in the 1880s, as well as being Lieutenant Colonel of the local Volunteer Group from 1860 to 1887. His political ambitions however were thwarted when he was narrowly defeated as a Liberal candidate in the 1885 general election.

Education was always high on Sir David's list of priorities – he contributed £1,000 to the newly opened Cowley School in 1892 to ensure that it had laboratory facilities and, together with other chemical manufacturers, made several contributions to the University of Liverpool, the objective being to provide higher educational facilities in the region for present and future employees.

His major legacy to the town however was the gift of £25,000 in 1893 for the construction of a technical institute and a library in the town centre. The Gamble Institute, as it was known, subsequently became St Helens Technical College in 1959 and the building does of course survive to this day.

Outside of work and his activities in the community, David's main interest seems to have been yachting. According to the National Maritime Museum of Cornwall, he began his yachting career in 1858 and went on to own four yachts, the final one of which, Aline, was a 373 ton sailing yacht. He was a member of the Yacht Racing Association and was in 1881 elected as Commodore of the Royal Mersey Yachting Club, a position he held for the rest of his life.

Sir David was made a Companion of the Order of Bath in 1887 and a Knight Commander in 1904. The Gamble Baronetcy of Windlehurst was created in 1897 in recognition of his public services, with Sir David as the first baronet. The current baronet, also Sir David, is the sixth of the Gambles to hold the title.

It was reported that virtually the whole of St Helens came out to pay their respects on the occasion of Sir David's funeral in 1907. The flags of all public buildings flew at half-mast and all business was suspended in the town. He was buried in St Helens Cemetery alongside Lady Gamble and one of his sons, William Gamble, who had died suddenly three weeks earlier.

HANNAH ROSBOTHAM OF
ST HELENS WAS THE FIRST EVER FEMALE RECIPIENT
OF THE ALBERT MEDAL
(SOMETIMES CALLED
THE VICTORIA CROSS FOR CIVILIANS).

Jeffrey Glover

J effrey Glover is another name that may not be familiar to readers despite the fact that he can claim his place on these pages on two separate counts. The first of these is that he was the only prisoner of war captured by the Argentinians in the Falklands War, an experience which, I suspect, not many would choose to feature on their CV. However he later

Jeff Glover in the cockpit.

became the only St Helens man ever to fly in the Red Arrows aerobatics display team, a worthy achievement indeed and one which comfortably ensures his appearance in this collection.

Jeff was born in April 1954 and raised initially in Beaconsfield Road in Dentons Green and then Bleak Hill Road by father John and mother Audrey. He attended Cowley School, where amongst other things he played rugby (I recall playing in an invitation team with him at some point but not much more) touring Argentina and Uruguay with the school in 1972. In the sixth form he started to think about the possibility of becoming a pilot and, whilst studying for a degree in Engineering Sciences at Oxford University, enrolled for an RAF cadetship. During this time he flew Chipmunks and Bulldogs. In 1975 he joined the RAF Future and trained at RAF Cranwell and RAF Valley in Anglesey where he flew Hawks. At the time of the outbreak of the Falklands War he was a Flight Lieutenant based at RAF Wittering. Together with other members of Number 1 Fighter Squadron, he set sail on 25th April 1982 for Ascension Island on the Atlantic Conveyor, a merchant navy ship which was requisitioned by the Ministry of Defence at the start of the Falklands War, arriving 5ᵗʰ May.

Once on Ascension Island Jeff transferred with a number of other pilots to HMS Hermes along with six Harrier jump jets – perhaps quite fortunate for Jeff as the Atlantic Conveyor was later that month hit by two Exocet missiles, which killed twelve members of the crew. HMS Hermes was a Royal Navy aircraft carrier and the intention was that this would be joint operation between the RAF and the Fleet Air Arm, using both the Harrier Jump Jets and the Navy's Sea Harriers. Hermes then set sail for the Falklands and on 21ˢᵗ May – the same day as the first British landings took place – Jeff was due to fly with Air Chief Marshall Sir Peter Squire. Unfortunately the undercarriage on the latter's aircraft didn't open and consequently Jeff flew alone. He was tasked with carrying out armed reconnaissance in the Port Howard area in the West Falklands when he came under enemy fire. Realising that he had lost nearly the whole of a wing, Jeff pressed the eject button and entered hurricane strength winds before landing in the ice-cold ocean. Despite the fact that his arm, shoulder blade and collarbone were all broken, and that he had sustained bad bruising to his face where he had landed in the water, he managed to swim to the surface where he was rescued by Argentinian marines who rowed out in a small boat to collect him. The aircraft crashed on land, unfortunately killing a horse in the process. Jeff's journey to captivity involved a motorcycle pillion ride, a trip in a helicopter and finally a Hercules flight to an Argentinian military hospital where he was treated for his injuries. Throughout these journeys his main concern was that he would not come under fire from the British forces!

Jeff spent about five weeks in the military hospital, before being moved to a hospital in Buenos Aires for a few days and then to Montevideo in Uruguay where he was handed over to the British Consul on 8ᵗʰ July. During his ordeal, he met a number of Argentinian officers (including the pilot who claimed he had shot him down) but experienced no ill treatment. He had been told that there were hundreds of other POWs and it wasn't until he finally got home that he was to discover that the accolade was his and his alone!

After he had recovered from his injuries, Jeff returned to the RAF and joined 216 Squadron at Brize Norton where he flew the Lockheed

Tristars which were used to refuel the Hercules transport aircraft supporting forces in the Falklands, thus enabling Jeff to return to the scene of his capture. In 1985 he was awarded the Queen's Commendation for Valuable Services in the Air. Now a Squadron Leader, he went on to join the Red Arrows and flew as a Red 8 during the 1988 and 1989 display seasons. In the early 1990s he served with NATO during the break-up of the former Yugoslavia before retiring from the RAF in 1996.

Jeff then started to work as a civilian flying instructor based in Stamford, Lincolnshire. In 2007 he hit the headlines again with his decision to sell off his South Atlantic and NATO medals as well as his Queen's Commendation Certificate – according to the auctioneer, none of the medals appeared ever to have been worn! Since then he has flown for Caledonian, Virgin, Easyjet and CTC Aviation. He is currently in Qatar working for Qatar Royal Flight where his duties include flying the royal family – almost certainly another first for St Helens!

In 2002 John Wynn of St Helens,
who had been awarded the
Distinguished Flying Cross 60 years earlier,
became at 85,
the oldest person to carry out a
parachute jump in France.

Greenall Family

During the years in which I grew up in the town, its pubs were dominated by one brewery, Greenall Whitley. However the Greenall name had by then for many years been indelibly associated with Warrington rather than St Helens. Indeed many will recall the advertising campaign of the 1980s for the Vladivar Vodka brand which showed several Soviet officers poring over a map and asking in mock Russian accents the question, "Ver is Varrington?. It was however in St Helens that the founder Thomas Greenall set up his first brewery, an operation which survived for over 200 years until its closure in 1975. Thereafter Greenall Whitley and Company Limited, as it was then known, continued to brew beer at the Wilderspool Brewery in Stockton Heath, Warrington, only for another 16 years, before it ceased brewing entirely to concentrate on its pubs and hotels business (out of which the De Vere Group was to evolve, at one point a member of the FTSE 100 before being sold in 2006 and then becoming one of the casualties of the financial crash of 2009).

Thomas Greenall had actually been born Thomas Greenhalgh in September 1733, into a family, originally from Ashton in Makerfield, which could trace its roots back to Elizabethan times. It was Thomas's great-grandfather who had moved the family seat to Parr. That he went into brewing was initially a consequence of his marriage in 1754 to Mary Turton, daughter of John Turton who had owned and operated the Parr Stocks brewery until his death the previous year. Thomas immediately took over as manager of what was now his mother-in-law's brewery but in 1762 decided to branch out on his own and commenced brewing in Hardshaw. It was in some ways a strange decision as there were already five wholesale breweries in the four townships of St Helens and whilst we do not know the total population, we know from the Militia Return for Parr, the largest of the four townships, that there were only 75 able-bodied men between the ages of 18 and 44 at the time. The more affluent families also tended to brew their own beer so the rest of them must have been a pretty thirsty lot. As it turned out, brewing became by far the most successful of the enterprises in which Thomas was involved, which also included nail making, coal mining and yarn spinning. He went on to buy the Saracen's Head brewery in Wilderspool in 1786, and a further brewery in Liverpool in 1788, both in partnership with William Orrett, who owned several inns in Warrington, and Thomas Lyon, a landowner and partner in the Warrington based Parr's Bank. The Wilderspool brewery was also very successful and they were able to embark upon a major expansion of the operation, spending £4,400 on the construction of a new brewery there which was completed in 1793.

Meanwhile, the St Helens business continued to go well and as early as 1786 had a customer base ranging from Liverpool to Bolton. The firm had even secured business as far afield as Anglesey. By 1800, they were beginning to buy their own pubs and clubs, a move which had the consequence of accelerating the process of eliminating local competitors because, as was customary in the industry, pubs owned by breweries only sold their own beer (this custom did of course evolve into the "tied house" arrangement which was a feature of the brewing industry right up till the end of the 20th century). This is not to say that business was plain sailing as there were major challenges to overcome. The high price of hops following several years of poor crops, grain shortages, poor quality, short measures and bad debts were just some of these. Ironically however, the Napoleonic Wars, which had pushed up the cost of ingredients for the brewing process hugely and thus squeezed profitability everywhere, worked in Greenall's favour in the long run as it made it much more difficult for smaller operations to survive.

There is no doubt as well that Thomas, and indeed his three sons, Edward, William and Peter, all of whom were introduced to the business, were determined and very able businessmen, and were not afraid to address the problems which were facing the industry. In *A Merseyside Town during the Industrial Revolution*, the authors, having examined the letters and ledgers of the firm, were particularly impressed by the attention to detail demonstrated by Thomas during this time. They conclude that the success of the firm reflected not only the organisation and efficiency which characterised the late 19th century but also represented "a moral triumph for perseverance and business integrity".

Thomas and his wife Mary had moved from Parr to Hardshaw Hall, close to his brewery in St Helens which was located on what is now Hall Street. By the time Thomas died in 1805, he owned 350 acres in and around St Helens as well as 14 public houses. An epitaph was erected by his three sons at what subsequently became St Helens Parish Church, which paid tribute to the "unwearied industry" that he had devoted to the family enterprises and his huge contribution to their success.

Although Thomas's death left a big hole (widened further with the demise just a few months later of William Orrett, one of the other founding partners of the Warrington brewery), the succession did in fact look quite assured. As noted above, his three sons were already well versed in the business and after his death, they took over the family interests in the Warrington and St Helens breweries in equal measure. However it was the eldest of the three, Edward, who now became the senior partner and the one, ultimately, upon whose shoulders the future of the operations would rest.

Edward Greenall had been born in 1758, prior to the founding of the brewery, and whilst we do not know a huge amount about his upbringing, he had clearly shown some early business acumen, as he was entrusted with the management of the nail-making business by his father in 1777 when he was only 19 years of age. He was also given responsibility for the Liverpool brewery in 1788 which actually traded under the name "Edward Greenall & Company" and became increasingly involved in managing the St Helens and Wilderspool breweries.

Edward did not marry until 1791, when he was already 33 years old, quite late for the times. His wife was Betty Pratt from Liverpool and it seems at that point, he set up the marital home in the headquarters of the existing brewery in Wilderspool, the decision having just been made to construct alongside it the new enlarged brewery, for which he was given responsibility.

Following his father's death, Edward continued to run the Warrington brewery although in 1807, there was a further change in ownership when Edward and his brothers, together with Thomas Lyon, bought out the one third share of the business which had passed to William Orrett's son. Edward was also heavily involved as senior partner in the St Helens brewery, still in the sole ownership of the Greenall family.

It was, it seems, an exhausting period for the three brothers. Times were still difficult – Britain was almost constantly at war meaning that obtaining adequate and good quality supplies of brewing materials was a permanent challenge. There was in particular a severe shortage of grain, which had an impact not only on every brewing business but also caused extreme hardship for the population at large. However at the same time, the pace of industrialisation was accelerating and this was providing more and more opportunities for the brewing business. All of this clearly took its toll and culminated in the withdrawal from the business of William Greenall in 1812, at a point when he was still only in his mid-fifties. This inevitably ratcheted up the pressure on the other two brothers and three years later, the challenge to the business intensified yet more with the death of Peter, the youngest of the three, in 1815. Edward, the eldest son, now approaching the age of 60, found himself in sole charge of the growing St Helens brewery and the only representative of the family within the Wilderspool partnership.

More disruption was to follow. Edward's brother William, although no longer involved in the business, passed away in 1817 and the following year, Thomas Lyon, the surviving member of the original Wilderspool Partnership and a man upon whose experience Edward had relied greatly, also died. His nephew and heir, also Thomas Lyon, was interested in the brewing business only as an investment, leaving Edward with full responsibility for the whole shooting match – probably not what he had anticipated as he approached his twilight years!

Help was however at hand. After setting up home in Wilderspool, Edward had had five sons and a daughter. The eldest two, Thomas and Peter, were already working in the business and somewhat inevitably, were required to take on more responsibility at an earlier age than they might have expected. Thomas took over management of the Warrington Brewery and Peter was sent to St Helens.

Edward however stuck around and, ever alert to a new business opportunity, in 1819 entered into partnership with Joseph Parr and Thomas Lyon in the Warrington bank previously known as Parr Lyon & Company but which now changed its name to Parr, Lyon and Greenall. It was no surprise either that in 1930, shortly after the Rainhill Trials, and anticipating the rewards it would duly generate, he purchased 45 shares in the new St Helens and Runcorn Gap Railway of which he held 20 for himself with the rest divided equally between his five sons.

In 1935 Edward passed away at the age of 77. He was the last in the family who was St Helens born – his sons who took the business forward from here were all born, raised and educated in Warrington. Edward's role in building the business is often overlooked, with most of the focus being on his father as founder and then the next generation, particularly his youngest son Gilbert, who was the first to live in Walton Hall (Edward had purchased this in 1812 but never lived there) and went on to become a baronet in 1876. But the part played by Edward should not be underestimated. He had been around from the very beginning, initially as his father's right hand man, but then critically, after his father had passed away, followed by the retirement and death of his brothers so soon afterwards, Edward was the one who guided the businesses through difficult times. Most importantly, he helped to ensure the succession by introducing his sons at an early stage into the management of the businesses. As a consequence, he left a business in rude health for the next generation.

Ian Gregson

Ian Gregson is yet another who spent his formative years in St Helens, before moving to the new world and making his mark in multiple areas – in his case as an athlete, actor, musician, author and activist. But it was an event that happened prior to his move that

© Copyright Ian Gregson 2018

arguably shaped his life more than anything else. At the age of 15 he was involved in an accident which resulted in him losing his right leg above the knee. As with others in this collection, his response to this setback was truly inspirational.

Ian was born in Cowley Hill Hospital on 2nd September 1962, son of John and Barbara, both of whom were from St Helens, and brother of Robert. The family lived in Garswood and Ian attended Ashton Grammar School (which has since been renamed Byrchall High School after its founder John Byrchall). Ian excelled in the athletics arena and was a member of Pilkington's track club at Ruskin Drive. Then the accident came – during his school lunch break, Ian attempted to join a moving train at Golborne and miscalculated. However whilst for others this may well have been the end of any sporting ambitions, for Ian it seemed to intensify them. He stayed involved with the Pilkington's club, started to undergo weight training and took up shot putting and discus. After leaving school he continued his studies at Wigan Technical College but in 1981, the family moved lock stock and barrel – including the Jack Russell! - to Vancouver in Canada, the objective being "to get away from Maggie Thatcher", a sentiment with which at the time many in the town would have sympathised.

Although the family found it quite difficult initially to settle in a country where they knew very few people, Ian launched himself straight back into his sporting career. He found that the time he had spent at Pilkington's had left him in good stead when it came to competing in Canada and he first came to the attention of the media in late 1981 when he took part in the first ever Terry Fox run (an annual non-competitive charity run which raises money for cancer research). Ian then went on to represent Canada in the Paralympic Games, competing in the long jump and shot put in 1984 and the discus and shot put in 1988. He took part in the World Championships in Sweden in 1986, finishing in fourth place. Ian received the Chevron Canada Award for Post-Secondary Sports in 1987 and, after he had finished competing, chaired the BC Disability Games for several years.

Athletics was however only one of a number of areas in which Ian was active. He had been studying at the Langara Vancouver Community College and whilst there became the first disabled athlete to win a sports scholarship. He went on to obtain a degree in English and Communications at the Simon Fraser University in Burnaby, British Columbia in 1998. By then he had also kicked off his writing career, writing numerous articles, mainly on disability issues (including a somewhat controversial one on disability and sex which was published in the magazine *Hustler!*) He published his first book in 1998 *Irresistible Force: A History of Disability Sport in Canada.*

Ian had always been interested in politics, had worked with the New Democratic Party in the 1990s and, in 2001 and 2005, stood as a Green Party candidate for election to the British Columbia Legislative Assembly. His radical leanings were further illustrated when he joined the interestingly named Work Less party, standing as a their candidate for the Vancouver elections in 2008, before moving on and standing in the 2011 election for the De-Growth Vancouver Party, which campaigned on environmental and anti-capitalist grounds.

The early 2000s also saw Ian take up a musical career as a guitarist, playing for a while in East Vancouver's well-known Carnival Band, before starting up his own Northern Soul tribute band (well he did grow up in that era!) in 2006. He went on to form a rock band in 2009 before starting his present band the Van City Soul Quartet in 2013.

After obtaining his degree, Ian had worked in the world of post-secondary education but in 2009 he made a quantum leap into an acting career, something with which he had dabbled in the early 1990s. The move was inspired by a chance meeting with Ian McKellen, a childhood hero of his, and since then Ian has appeared on both TV and on the big screen, performing both amputee and non-amputee roles as well as working as an amputee stunt double!

Bearing in mind that Ian managed to raise a family as well as everything else, it is difficult to envisage a fuller life than he has led. He is clearly not a man who likes to settle in a comfort zone and instead is driven constantly to challenge himself. He regards one of his major achievements as having lived without a car for eight years in Vancouver and clearly retains the radical leanings which have featured throughout his life. That said, he remains a *Coronation Street* addict, so it seems he has never been totally divorced from the mainstream!

Ian currently lives with his partner, actress Lisa Peterson. He still has many relatives in St Helens and lots of friends in the Garswood area – indeed he runs both the Garswood Remembers and Byrchall High School Former Pupils pages on Facebook.

It is obvious to all that St Helens has produced an extremely wide range of interesting and diverse characters over the years, and it has to be concluded that Ian is definitely up there with the best of them.

George Groves

George Groves is possibly the best-known of our exports to the United States and is, depending upon your view of the legitimacy of Colin Welland's appearance in this list (see later), either our only Oscar winner or one of only two Oscar winners from the town. It was however only through the efforts of his sister Hilda, already in her 90s, that there was any official recognition in this country of his pioneering work in developing the technology that

Image reproduced by courtesy of Stephen Wainwright.

brought sound to the silent film screen. In 1996 however two British film industry plaques were finally unveiled to commemorate his achievements, one at his birthplace in Duke Street and the other at the prestigious Warner Bros. cinema in the West End.

George was born on 13th December 1901 and was educated at Ravenhead School in Nutgrove and then Cowley Grammar. He helped out in his father's barber shops and also learned to play a number of musical instruments, his father having founded the first brass band in St Helens. The family moved from Duke Street to Owen Street in 1906, then to Speakman Road in 1911 and finally to King Edward Road in 1913. Although George excelled at school, he was also from the age of 14 playing the cornet in an orchestra. The school objected to him taking Monday afternoons off to play in the matinee performance at the Theatre Royal and, as a consequence, he left school early and the family hired a private tutor from the Gamble Institute. This didn't seem to hinder his academic progress as he went on to win a scholarship to Liverpool University where he obtained a degree in Engineering and Telephony in

1922. His first job after completing his studies was in Coventry with a division of GEC, where his work involved developing early wireless receivers. His life took a critical turn however when he met Olga, a dancer with the Tiller Girls (a dance troupe which began in the 1900s but which had its heyday in the 1950s and 1960s) whilst back in St Helens for a weekend. Olga was about to embark on a lengthy engagement in New York and George resolved to follow her there. On 1st December 1923 he set sail from Liverpool for New York, with no guaranteed employment and an expectation, according to the immigration documents, of staying in the United States for just two years.

In the event, George found employment relatively easily with the research team at Bell Laboratories (part of the legacy of Alexander Graham Bell), which was developing film sound technology and from that point on he never really looked back. Settling in was facilitated by the fact that George had brought with him his French horn and he played in a number of orchestras during his early years in New York. George soon became an important member of the Bell research team and when Warner Bros. bought the technology, George was seconded to Los Angeles. Whilst there, he played a key part in synchronising the musical soundtrack, provided by a 107 strong orchestra, for *Don Juan* – the first full-length film ever to have done this. The film was a success, others with musical accompaniments followed and in 1927, the whole operation, including George, was moved lock, stock and barrel from New York to Hollywood. That same year he was responsible for the sound on *The Jazz Singer*, the first ever film with synchronised dialogue and the one generally regarded as heralding the end of the silent film era.

George went on to pursue a career in film which was to last a further 44 years and during which he was to pioneer many more techniques and practices which are today commonplace. He played a critical part in many landmark films, winning Oscars for best sound on *Yankee Doodle Dandy* in 1942, *Sayonara* in 1957 and most famously, *My Fair Lady* in 1964 – a film which has been described as George's pride and joy. In total he worked on 32 films that received nominations for best sound, one of which was *Woodstock,* the 1970 film chronicling the famous music festival which, according to George, gave him more enjoyment than any other film.

With the exception of a spell in the RAF during the Second World War (when George had been responsible, inter alia, for the sound in over 400 training and educational films which were made for the armed forces), he worked for Warner Bros. from his initial secondment in 1926 until his retirement in 1972. He spent the great majority of his time in Hollywood, although there were spells with Warner Bros. UK operation between 1931 and 1933 and for a few months in 1947. One of George's dreams as he approached the end of his career was for a purpose-built modern scoring and dubbing complex. His dream was realised shortly before he retired with the opening of the Groves-Rice Complex at the Burbank Studios in Hollywood, the design, engineering and construction of which he supervised.

On 23rd October 1972 George was awarded the prestigious Samuel L Warner Memorial Award by the Society of Motion Picture and Television Engineers which was presented to him by Jack Warner, for whom he had worked for so long and whom George regarded as more of a father than a boss.

On the personal front, the relationship with Olga did not last – she had been captivated by somebody else and returned the engagement ring to a heartbroken George. In due course he was to find love again and in 1930 married Clemence Apperson, a contralto singer, in Los Angeles. The event attracted the attention of the *St Helens Reporter* which stated that it was a spectacular affair attended by many leading figures in the film industry. They had two children together but the marriage ended in divorce. In 1951, George married for the second time, on this occasion to Jane Blackman, and they went on to have one child together.

George's retirement sadly did not last long. He had been suffering from heart problems for some time and in 1976 he died of a heart attack and was buried at the Forest Lawn cemetery in Hollywood Hills, his coffin draped with both the Union flag and the Stars and Stripes.

As noted earlier, it was only through the untiring efforts of George's sister, Hilda, valiantly supported by the St Helens Film Society, that his achievements were belatedly recognised in this country. Hilda passed away in 1998 but the legacy was now in place and as part of the Liverpool City of Culture celebrations in 2008, the world premiere of *The Quiet Little Englishman,* a play chronicling George's life, was held at the Park Palace Theatre. The title of the play was inspired by the name by which the star of the *Jazz Singer,* Al Jolson, referred to the man who became his lifelong friend, and who more than anyone else, was the pioneer of sound in the world of film.

Milton Grundy

Neither the name of Milton Grundy nor the subject of cross border tax planning, in which he developed his expertise, is likely to excite the average inhabitant of St Helens (or indeed of anywhere else). But he is indeed a remarkable man who has certainly made his mark in the legal world, as well as making a significant contribution to the world of arts.

Milton was not a name which featured frequently when I went to school in St Helens – actually it didn't feature at all - but Milton Grundy, who was admittedly born nearly 30 years before me in 1926, was raised in Bleak

Hill, only a stone's throw from my family home in Millbrook Lane. He later moved to, as he puts it, a rather grander house in Cowley Hill Lane where he may well have encountered a young Bernie Clifton. They may or may not have been soulmates!

Son of Edward and May, and elder brother of Eleanor, Milton was educated initially at Cowley Prep school and then at Cowley Grammar. He describes his childhood as uneventful but nonetheless enjoyable. At the age of 14 however he was packed off to Sedbergh School, where he played rugby and also learned to play the piano. After school, he did military service in the Middle East (adding Hebrew and a rather rustic Arabic to the French, German and Italian he had learned at school) before taking his degree in English at Cambridge. Although he resolved to make a career in law, he had a great love of the arts which he never gave up. Indeed, whilst studying for his Bar exams, he was simultaneously teaching at RADA. He was called to the Bar in 1954 and worked in the Chambers of Sir John Foster before founding Gray's Inn Tax Chambers in 1965. It went on to become, and is still today, one of the leading Tax Chambers in the country, housing several of the country's leading tax QCs. Milton himself, at the time of writing and at the ripe old age of 91, still attends on a regular basis!

In 1975 Milton co-founded the International Tax Planning Association, an organisation of which he is currently President and whose annual conference he still chairs. He is the author of numerous tax books and publications, mainly focussing on cross border transactions and international tax planning, and he was for many years regarded as one of the UK's leading experts on offshore tax havens.

The passage of time has not in any way dulled Milton's passion for the arts. His London home for a number of years was 33 Warwick Square, a Grade II listed property which includes a grand staircase with domed ceiling, a ballroom and a huge conservatory. In the late 1970s he set up the Warwick Arts Trust, of which he is still Chairman, in the house to help young artists. The galleries and conservatory were also home to his own art collection.

In 1958, he purchased some land in Chipping Norton and in 1964 erected a house designed by the architect Patrick Lichfield. The surrounding Japanese garden was designed by the artist Viacheslav Artoshenko, with whom Milton had co-authored *Mediterranean Vernacular: A Vanishing Architectural Tradition* and with whom he had travelled to Kyoto, whence some of the inspiration for the garden had come. The pool was designed and constructed by a team of Japanese gardeners whilst Artoshenko and Milton together took responsibility for the planting. The garden was used for one of the scenes in the 1971 film *A Clockwork Orange*.

Milton was also author of a number of other books, most notably *Venice: An Anthology*, a classic travel guide to the city which is in its sixth edition.

It is safe to say that Milton has come a long way from Bleak Hill and that his current surroundings do not probably bear much resemblance to those of his youth. He is unlikely ever to become a household name in his home town (and indeed has had little connection to it since his schooldays) but that doesn't mean that we should not acknowledge and respect his many achievements since then.

Liam Hackett

It has to be conceded that St Helens is not a hot bed of diversity. Indeed, this collection features a depressingly small number of women, there is no ethnic community worth talking about and the LGBT+ community is pretty non-existent. Liam Hackett however bucks the trend big style – openly gay and a regular spokesperson on diversity issues, he was recently rated by the internet platform Richtopia at number 51 in a list of the world's 500 most influential

© Copyright Liam Hackett 2018.

Chief Executive Officers, well ahead of many household names and the CEOs of some of the largest organisations in the world!

Liam was born in Whiston Hospital in January 1991, has one brother and was raised in Clock Face by his mother. He was educated at St Aidan's Primary School in Lindsay Street, Sutton Manor Community School and then at Sutton High Sports College (now Sutton Academy). His schooldays were not a happy time for him – he committed the cardinal sin of being different and, like many before him, suffered the consequences. He was bullied from a very early age for over ten years, being subjected to homophobic abuse even before he even understood what being gay was. It caused him to have to move primary schools but this did little to alleviate the problem and once at Sutton High, things got steadily worse, particularly during the period when he was coming to terms with his sexuality. This coincided with a period of self-loathing, prompted by the conditioning that being gay was intrinsically a bad thing and by a festering inner resentment that he was not like all the other boys.

Liam's first attempt to come out could not have gone worse. His messages to a school friend who had assured him that he felt the same way about Liam, were printed off and shared around the entire school. This resulted in a severe beating which caused him to be sent home from school. Other beatings followed – on one occasion Liam was hospitalised and had to have stitches in his face. Liam's lowest point was when a blogging website was set up to discuss his sexuality and to which people could contribute anonymously. However, this turned out inadvertently to be something of a turning point – a distraught Liam confided in his mother who unhesitatingly promised him her unconditional love and support whatever his sexuality. And when his high school days finally came to an end, despite all the trauma he had undergone, he came away with a raft of A and A* grades at GCSE and moved across town to Carmel Sixth Form College for his A levels.

From this point on Liam's career started to blossom. He grew in confidence, entered into his first relationship and came out completely with his family. He went on to study Business and Management with Marketing at Sussex University and in May 2012, on the day after his graduation, he set up two organisations, a digital marketing agency called Hackett and Tiger and the anti-bullying charity Ditch the Label, which attempts to address the bullying problem by empowering young people, and by persuading them that there is absolutely nothing wrong with being different. It avoids labelling anyone as "bully" or "victim", terms which it believes only drain confidence from young people and looks to provide support for both those who bully and those who are bullied in order to solve the root issues. In 2016 alone the charity supported over 540,000 young people.

The honours have since arrived thick and fast. Liam is now a Fellow of the Royal Society of Arts, sits on the advisory board of the Anti-Bullying Alliance, is a member of the 5Rights Initiative and sat on the Growing Up Digital task force headed by The Children's Commissioner for England.

He is a visiting lecturer at the University of Sussex and was awarded Notable Alumni status in 2015. He has given evidence in the European and UK Parliaments, debated at the Cambridge Union Society and

Oxford Union, spoken at many academic and sector conferences and has made numerous television appearances on both news and feature programmes.

Internationally throughout 2016 he represented the UK and Ditch the Label in the White House, wrote for USA government on lessons learned from the UK and was invited to contribute an article for the *United Nations Chronicle*. In February 2017 Liam was invited to speak as an expert on a panel at the United Nations in New York – Media and Information Literacy: Educational Strategies for the Prevention of Violent Extremism. He regularly speaks on a range of issues surrounding bullying, cyberbullying, equality, discrimination, gender, self-esteem, masculinity, digital technology and young people to audiences up to 12,000.

Still only 27 years old, Liam's appearance on the Richtopia list and the international launch of Ditch the Label in 2016 suggest that this may only be the beginning.

Frederick Hall V.C.

Frederick William Hall has the distinction of being the very first St Helens holder of the Victoria Cross, although sadly, having died in the heat of battle, he was no longer around to receive it. He was in fact born in Kilkenny in Ireland on 21st February 1885 (where his father Bombardier Frederick Hall was stationed) but the family moved to St Helens at some point when Frederick was still very young. Most reports indicate that they arrived in 1891 when he was just six years old, but the 1891 census reveals that his younger brother Augustine, who was then two years old, had been born in St Helens which would suggest they had been there since at least 1889. At that time Frederick had two elder sisters and two younger brothers with two further brothers arriving in the next few years. The family lived at 81 Ormskirk Street before moving to 56 Dentons Green Lane.

In February 1901, Frederick Junior joined the army, enlisting with the Cameronians (Royal Scottish Rifles) a couple of weeks before his 16th birthday. No doubt there was an expectation that he would sign up – it was not only his father who had been in the military, his grandfather had served in the Crimean War and his uncle in the Boer War. Frederick was initially stationed at Chatham Barracks in Kent, his occupation being listed as "Boy Infantry (Line)" in the 1901 Census. In November 1902 he was appointed bandsman but in 1905 stepped down from this position at his own request. He was appointed lance corporal in 1905 and corporal in 1909. There does not seem to be much information on his whereabouts in these years but according to the 1911 census he was stationed in Bloemfontain in South Africa. He was promoted to sergeant in March 1913 but was discharged just two months later. We can only surmise that this was because his mother and at least three of his brothers had emigrated to Canada (his father had died in 1905) and that Frederick wished to join them. When he arrived he took up a job as a clerk in Winnipeg, where the family had settled.

Frederick's time in civvy street did not however last long. In July 1914 the First World War broke out and Frederick enlisted initially with the Winnipeg Light Infantry but was then transferred to the Winnipeg Rifles. By 15th October he was back in England for a 16 week training regime on Salisbury Plain during which time he was promoted first to sergeant and then to colour sergeant. In February 2010 he set sail for France with the rest of his battalion, their first destination being Strazeele, a small village in northern France where they were introduced to trench warfare. By April they had moved to a position near Ypres in Belgium and on the night of 23rd April, Frederick's platoon was located about 1,500 yards behind the front line. Heavy German bombardment (which included poison gas) had caused major casualties and the platoon was called forward to hold a position in the early hours of the morning. The commanding officer was killed and Frederick took charge. The platoon managed to advance to the front line where they took up a position under severe fire. Frederick and two other soldiers then went back part of the way to rescue two wounded soldiers. Having brought them in successfully, they heard the cries of a third soldier who was only 15 yards behind the front line but on an exposed bank. Frederick and his two colleagues attempted a rescue but both his colleagues were wounded in the attempt. Frederick then made a further attempt on his own, reached the wounded man and hauled him onto his shoulders. However he then raised his head slightly to check his direction and suffered a fatal hit by a single bullet in the head. The wounded man also died shortly afterwards.

The award of the Victoria Cross was announced on 22nd June 1915 in the *London Gazette* and it was presented to his mother in Winnipeg in August 1915. Frederick's body was never found and he is one of the missing who were commemorated in 1927 on the Menin Gate Memorial in Ypres (the register shows his mother at this stage living in Leytonstone, England so she presumably moved back sometime after 1915).

Frederick's father's headstone in St Helens Cemetery bears a dedication to his son and a stone was laid at the St Helens Cenotaph on 22nd April 2015 to mark the centenary of his heroic act. The road in which he lived in Winnipeg was renamed Valour Road in 1925 to honour Frederick and two other recipients of the Victoria Cross all of whom had lived there.

Thus the story of the first Victoria Cross to be awarded to a St Helens man (and the only one to a soldier who did not survive the war) comes to an end.

Barry Halpin (aka Barry the Banjo Player)

When Barry Halpin died in Goa on 3rd January 1996, it is unlikely that he would have expected to appear in even such a modest compilation as this one. Let us fast forward seven years however to the publication of a book by retired Scotland Yard detective Duncan MacLaughlin entitled *Dead Lucky – Lord Lucan: The Final Truth* in which he finally reveals what happened to Lord Lucan. But the picture on the front cover is not Lord Lucan at all – it is unmistakeably Barry the Banjo Player from St Helens!

Unsurprisingly, this case of mistaken identity received huge press coverage. In a letter to *The Guardian* the folk singer and comedian, Mike Harding, told how he laughed until he cried when he saw a picture in *The Sunday Telegraph* of the missing Lord Lucan, purportedly tracked down to Goa in India. "To think that anybody could mistake my old pal Barry Halpin for Lord Lucan," he said. By all accounts Barry always addressed friends as "old cock" and although few of us can claim to be conversant with Lord Lucan's vocabulary I think it a pretty fair bet that this particular expression would not have featured too often.

Barry was born on 11th March 1938, the son of van driver William Halpin and raised in Hawes Avenue, Carr Mill. He attended Cowley

School and went on to train as a teacher. According to *The Daily Telegraph* who tracked down two of the teachers at Allanson Street Primary School where he taught, he was a somewhat unconventional teacher, who always walked to school and whose teaching methods were "different". With long hair, a dark beard and moustache on the one hand, but always wearing a jacket (with leather elbow patches) and tie, he was no doubt an unmistakable figure around and about the school.

Given his vintage, Barry did of course have to do national service and there are plenty of references to him on the RAF Mountain Rescue website although it has to be said, more relate to his drinking than to any particularly heroic rescues!

It seems Barry always had a passion for music, drink and travel. Whilst he was teaching by day, his evenings were spent in the folk clubs of the North West, which was no doubt where he encountered Mike Harding who became a good friend. According to Harding, Barry was a talented musician who as well as the banjo could also play concertina, guitar, mandolin and tin whistle. There is no doubt as well that Barry was a heavy drinker, something to which pretty much everyone who knew him testifies. But it was the travel bug that finally took over Barry's life and was responsible for the posthumous fame that he has since secured.

During his teaching days, Barry had taken time off and travelled extensively in Ireland, learning Gaelic music and in 1968, according to a friend of his from Cumbria, John Baynham, he had taken himself off to India with Baynham's brother and two other friends. It was not until 1971 that he finally made the break with the UK, moving permanently to Australia whence it was reported that he became head teacher of a school in the bush near Alice Springs, working with aboriginal children. The trail becomes a little murky after that but it seems that he then spent some time in Goa before returning to Australia in 1976 and spending some three years or so in Perth, supposedly trying to earn enough money busking to open a small business in Goa or a hotel near the beach. There is little evidence that he was successful in this objective but there is no doubt that he did make his way back to Goa circa 1979 (one report claims that he was fleeing the Australian tax authorities which sounds possible given that he was unlikely to have filled out full details of his busking earnings on an Australian tax return).

Once back, Barry appears to have settled in Goa for good (with the exception of two trips home to St Helens, the first in 1986 for a family funeral and the second in 1995, shortly before he died of liver failure, to say his goodbyes). He apparently ran jungle tours which no doubt contributed to the nickname "Jungle Barry" (though this morphed at times into "Jungly Barry" or "Mountain Barry"). There are a number of pictures of Barry circulating which attest to the continued existence of the hippy lifestyle, the long hair and the (by now) very long beard. Interestingly, the age enhanced Scotland Yard computer image of Lord Lucan at the age of 68 suggests that if he had survived he would have been bald but it seems that Duncan MacLaughlin either did not consult this or did not believe it.

Barry's death in January 1996 was marked by a death notice in a local Goan newspaper which ran as follows:

> "Barry Thomas Halpin (Jungle Barry).
> Dearly loved and sadly missed by all of us.
> Goodbye old cock."

A death notice, placed by his sisters Rita and Mildred, appeared in the *St Helens Reporter.*

It is worth noting that Mr MacLaughlin stood by his Lord Lucan story. "I expected this to happen. There is no way someone would go on the run and not assume someone else's identity. But I say to people, please produce photographic evidence that your Barry Halpin is my Barry Halpin"

The book's publisher, John Blake, went further: "I 100 per cent stand totally by the book. Lord Lucan may have taken on Barry Halpin's identity when he died". But then, after all the time and trouble that went into publishing the book what choice did they really have?

Barry may not have been the most famous person from St Helens but if there were a short list for the most colourful, he would certainly make the cut.

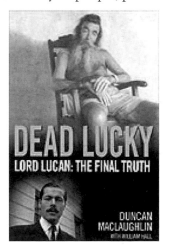

*Front book cover which
claimed he was Lord Lucan.*

Professor John Harris

J ohn Harris was a fairly late inclusion in this list. I had been aware of him only in his capacity as co-author with Professor Theo Barker of their masterpiece *A Merseyside Town in the Industrial Revolution: St Helens,* but that was about it. However it has since been made clear to me that, although John Harris did not perhaps achieve quite the same profile as his friend and

Image provided by Paul Harris.
Reproduced courtesy of
Birmingham University.

fellow academic in St Helens itself, within the academic world he achieved equal if not even greater prominence as one of the foremost authorities on the Industrial Revolution. I have mentioned my own (somewhat sparse!) credentials as an economic historian elsewhere and it might be inferred that I should have known this already but I would justify my ignorance on the basis that my own involvement in this world terminated when John's career was barely at the half way stage!

John was born on 14th May 1923 in St Helens. His father John Seddon Harris* was a joiner and his mother Mary had been a milliner. The family lived in Martin Avenue (near Bishop Road) and John attended Cowley Prep, the funding for which was in part provided by his father's sisters, both of whom were teachers. It was there that he first encountered Theo Barker, who was to become his lifelong friend. The two moved on together to Cowley Grammar School which is where their common interest in economic history was cemented.

On leaving Cowley, John went initially to Manchester University but as with many of his generation, the war disrupted his academic progress. He served in India with the Royal Corps of Signals and then moved to

South East Asia with the Royal Army Education Corps. After being demobbed in 1947, he resurfaced at Manchester University to complete his degree and the following year was reunited with his old school friend, Theo Barker, who had moved to Manchester to do his Masters. Much of the research for the book *A Merseyside Town in the Industrial Revolution,* which we have noted elsewhere is generally acknowledged as having broken new ground in urban history studies, was carried out at this time – indeed the university took the unusual step of allowing the two men to do parallel theses for their Masters Degrees, John on St Helens in the 18th century and Theo on St Helens in the 19th century, both of which were largely incorporated into the text of the book.

Both men went on to complete their doctorates in Manchester, following which John took a job as a lecturer in 1953 at Liverpool University. That same year he married Thelma Knockton, also from St Helens, and the couple set up home in Mitchell Road in Toll Bar before later moving to Forest Grove in Eccleston Park. Following publication of the above book in 1954, John gave a series of lectures in St Helens which resulted in the founding of the St Helens Historical Society in 1959. He then went on to convert some of the research that he had done for his PhD thesis into another book, *The Copper King,* a study of Welsh solicitor, Thomas Williams, one of the country's wealthiest men in the 18th century, who was responsible, inter alia, for bringing Welsh copper to Ravenhead.

Whilst at Liverpool John conducted research into Prescot's watch-making industry, which included a short appearance in a TV documentary, and also into Liverpool's maritime history, for which he received many acknowledgements in books and publications by others. He was however able to find enough time for other extra-curricular work, being involved in the founding of the Prescot Museum, the formation of North West Society for Industrial Archaeology and History (which survives to this day under the name of the Merseyside Industrial Heritage Society) and the setting up of the journal *Business History.*

John was no less active after moving to Birmingham in 1970 to become Professor of Economic History at Birmingham University, a prestigious position as the oldest chair of economic history in the country. His interest in industrial archaeology led him to play a large part in the transformation into industrial museums of areas such as Ironbridge

143

(where he was responsible for establishing the Ironbridge Institute for postgraduate studies into industrial heritage, the first of its kind). He was also for many years a Council Member of the Economic History Society and, between 1981 and 1984, was Chairman of the International Committee for the Conservation of the Industrial Heritage.

Throughout his time in Birmingham, John continued to maintain close contact with his home town, returning on many occasions to give lectures and to take part in day schools. On his final visit in September 1996 to attend the celebration of the centenary of the Gamble Institute, he was once again in the company of his old friend, Professor Theo Barker, and both spoke about the rich industrial history of the town, with John in particular stressing the critical importance of the Ravenhead area in the Industrial Revolution.

John had been devoted to his wife Thelma – indeed she was an almost constant companion at conferences at home and abroad. Her death from a brain tumour in 1994 – by which time John was Emeritus Professor but nonetheless still very active in University life – was a major blow to him and it was just three years later in March 1997 that he suffered a major heart attack and died.

This was not however the last that historians were to hear from John Harris, nor from the Harris family. Shortly after his death, the mammoth volume *Industrial Espionage and the Transfer of Technology: Britain and France in the 18th Century*, the product of some 30 years' painstaking research into the efforts of the French government to steal the secrets of British technology was published (indeed in recognition of his work in this area, the French government had some years earlier awarded John the title of Chevalier de l'Ordre Des Arts et Lettres, a considerable honour and one rarely bestowed on a foreigner). And one of his two sons, Paul, also brought up in St Helens, is a senior lecturer in War Studies at Royal Military Academy in Sandhurst, the author of four books on military history and a Fellow of the Royal Historical Society.

It is fair to say that reading any biography of John Harris, or indeed his great friend Theo Barker, is unlikely to set the pulse racing. Nor would either feature in any shortlist of the great adventurers that St Helens has produced. That should not however detract in any way from their achievements in the academic world, esoteric as that may be to many readers. Both showed characteristics in their careers that we would like to think are typical of the townsfolk generally – in John's case, these included a reputation for integrity, common sense and a great respect for others alongside a healthy dislike of pomposity and mild disdain for certain aspects of the academic world. And unlike others who have flown the nest, rarely to return, he retained his links and devotion to the town of St Helens until the very last.

*   The family was related to the Seddon family (see section on Richard Seddon).

Squadron Leader Jeff Glover
from St Helens was the only Prisoner of War
captured by the Argentinians
in the Falklands War.

Paul Harris

I feel I ought to start this short biography by saying that until I started to look at Paul's career, I knew what choreography was in the same way that I knew what art was. However, whereas with a painting I could envisage the process between the blank piece of paper with which one starts and the work of art which appears at the end, I was totally unable to say the same about choreography. I now know a little bit more but all that has done is to reinforce the fact that I still know very little. However, like everyone else, I feel qualified to evaluate and indeed enjoy the finished product and my education has certainly been enhanced by looking at the career and achievements of Paul Harris.

Paul was born in Haydock on 1959, the elder son of Tom, a sales manager, and Renée, an occupational therapist at Rainhill Hospital. The family lived on Fosters Road and they were joined a few years later by Paul's younger brother, Geoffrey. Paul attended Richard Evans Infant and Junior Schools and began dancing (and entered his first competition) at the age of eight – his idea rather than his parents' but this was by no means a *Billy Elliott* scenario as his parents were more than happy for their son to take part in any form of exercise. In any case it wasn't as if Paul was throwing all his eggs in one basket. Whilst at Ashton Grammar School, to which he moved for his secondary education, he revealed himself to be a decent goal keeper, appearing regularly for the school team, as well as showing early promise as a runner – he took part in the Lancashire Championships at 800 and 1500 metres and was a member at Pilkington Harriers Athletics Club. He also played some rugby league as a scrum-half. But it was ballroom dancing that got the vote and Paul formed a successful partnership with Denise Byrom from Millbrook Lane in Eccleston, with whom he toured all over Europe and collected a host of trophies. At the age of 15 Paul became Junior Champion at the British Open Championship in Blackpool (still the world's most famous annual ballroom dance competition). He went on to achieve numerous awards in the dance world, most notably UK and West European Champion, as well as winning the English National Championships on three occasions and becoming number one in the world in both ballroom and Latin American dancing.

By his late teens Paul had become a professional dancer and in 1978, after leaving school, moved to London. Over the next few years he explored many other forms of dance, including ballet, jazz and tap. He retired from competition in 1983 and briefly performed shows with his partner on big cruise liners, but it was soon time to move on. He enrolled to study at the Academy of Live and Recorded Arts in London with a view to kicking off a career in the acting profession, and graduated in 1987.

Throughout the 1990s he plied his trade both in theatre, where he starred in three major national productions and television, where he played a number of leading roles. It was in fact a television programme that provided the link to the next stage of his career. Paul was playing a part as a Latin American dancer in *Casualty*, in which he had choreographed the dance sequences himself. The owner of the Pineapple dance agency got in touch and asked him to look at a script for a production set in the 19th century. The film was *The Tichborne Claimant*, the first feature film of director David Yates (also from St Helens and with whom Paul was to link up again with great success in the *Harry Potter* series). Paul impressed him sufficiently that he was asked to do the choreography and as soon as he went into the rehearsal room, he knew he had found what he was looking for – working with the actors was, in his own words, "like an epiphany". He now knew that what he wanted to do in life was to contextualise his dance and acting backgrounds and he has never deviated from that since.

And thus began a stellar career as one of the world's leading and best-known choreographers. Paul's list of credits is too lengthy to record here but they include numerous television series, including the BAFTA winning *Bleak House* and *The Way We Live Now*, many well-known films and a whole host of theatre productions, the best-known of which was probably John Osborne's 50th anniversary revival of *The Entertainer* at London's Old Vic. The list of actors whom he has coached reads like a *Who's Who* of current day Hollywood. Ironically however neither of the two best-known works in which he has been involved actually contained any dancing! These were the wand fight sequences in

Harry Potter and the Order of the Phoenix (as a result of which there is now a permanent interactive hologram of Paul in the Warner Brothers Studio in Leavesden) and the laser scenes for Catherine Zeta Jones in the Hollywood blockbuster *Entrapment*. In 2008 Paul won the Carl Alan Award for Choreography in recognition of his significant contribution to the dance in the theatre industry.

Alongside his work as a choreographer, Paul has pursued a complementary and equally successful career as a dance teacher. He has contributed to the syllabus for the both the Honours and Masters degrees at four London drama schools and wrote the course guide for drama schools in 19th and 20th century social dance. He is a dance tutor at several universities and was the main dance coach in the BAFTA winning episode of *Faking it* entitled "Kick Boxer to Ballroom Dancer". He has taught widely overseas, notably in South East Asia, and has been an adjudicator at many international dance championships, including the Blackpool Dance Festival which of course, he won as a junior.

In the late 1990s Paul founded (and he remains Artistic Director of) the London Theatre of Ballroom the purpose of which is to help preserve ballroom dancing as one of the performing arts, thus again enabling Paul to combine his two backgrounds of dancing and acting. This is Britain's only ballroom-based theatre company.

Somehow amongst all the above activities, Paul found the time to write a book *Salsa and Merengue – The Essential Step by Step Guide*, which is to all intents and purposes the text book for the professional examinations in salsa, merengue and mambo for three British Dance Council teaching organisations.

Paul currently lives in London. He has two daughters, Lara and Ava, with the former model Anna Luong. Lara has already hit the headlines in the St Helens local press when in 2014, at the age of eight and on a visit to her grandmother, she auditioned successfully for a role as a munchkin in the *Wizard of Oz* at the Theatre Royal, where her father had performed all those years ago! One gets the feeling that we might be seeing more of her in the future. And one suspects there is plenty of mileage still left in her father and that we have not yet heard the last of him!

We have seen that St Helens has produced stars in an extraordinary range of occupations and industries. Paul has however blazed a trail that stands him out as being without equal in his chosen field.

Norman Harvey V.C.

Norman Harvey was born in Bull Cottages, Newton-le-Willows on 6th April 1899 to father Charles, a railway plate layer, and mother Mary. He had five brothers and three sisters and the family lived at 6 Golborne Dale Road. Norman was educated at St Peter's C of E School and on leaving took up employment firstly with a firm called Randall's and then Caulfield's which is where he was when the First World War broke out. Although only 15, it seems he volunteered and enlisted in the 4th Battalion South Lancashire Regiment in November 1914. One can only assume that he lied about his age, as did so many young recruits at the time.

Norman was sent to France and wounded in action on two occasions. The first injury in 1916 was only slight but the second, over a year later, was more serious and when he returned to England for treatment, his correct age was discovered. Although by then 18, he was still officially too young to be sent overseas to fight so instead he was sent on a course in bayonet and physical training, which he passed with excellent qualifications and was then posted to Portsmouth. However with the Allies losing so many men, there was inevitably pressure for him to go overseas again. In April 1918, almost as soon as he was 19 (which was the official age at which a soldier could be sent overseas) he was transferred to the 1st Battalion, Royal Inniskilling Fusiliers and sent to Belgium.

It was there, just 17 days before the armistice, in Ingoyhem, not far from the French border, that Norman won his Victoria Cross. His battalion was being held up near a farm by machine gun fire and was suffering severe casualties. According to his commanding officer, Norman took it upon himself to charge the enemy singlehandedly, running around the left of the farm. Gunfire could be heard and when Norman re-emerged he had killed two men, wounded another (using the bayonet so the course he had done came in quite handy!) and captured twelve men and two guns. And if that wasn't enough, later in the day he charged another enemy strongpoint in which a machine gun was hidden and put the enemy to flight. That night after darkness had fallen, he went out alone to make a reconnaissance and gather important information. He did all of this moreover with a badly sprained ankle. When his sergeant observed that, "He seemed to live a charmed life" it is unlikely that there would be many who would have disagreed!

Norman's citation in the *London Gazette* appeared on 6th January 1919, although by then the number of Germans he had faced at the farmhouse had somehow risen to 20! He came home to Newton to a rousing reception of more than 2,000 people and received his Victoria Cross from the King at Buckingham Palace on 15th May 1919.

By now a lance corporal, he was demobbed later in the year and returned to Newton to work on the railways. The family was then living at Parkside Old Station Buildings, near the train line to Manchester. However before the year was out he had married Nora Osmond, who had served in the Queen Mary Army Auxiliary Corps and they went on to have two daughters and a son together.

During the inter-war years, Norman attended the House of Lords VC dinner in 1929 and was one of the guests at the official opening of the Mersey Tunnel in July 1934.

Norman had not considered himself too young to enlist in the First World War and, conversely, at the age of 40 did not consider himself too old to enlist in the Second World War. He joined the Royal Engineers and became a sort of father figure for the younger troops. He would allegedly reply when called to attention on parade, "Sergeant Harvey VC Sir!!" after which the commanding officer would salute him and continue with the roll call. Norman was promoted to Company Quartermaster Sergeant and was posted to Palestine. Sadly his supposedly charmed life came to an end on 16th February 1942 when he was killed by a single rifle shot. Although he is recorded as having died in action, it is likely that the shot actually came from his own gun.

Norman was buried in the Khayat Beach War Cemetery in Haifa (now in Israel) thus bringing to an end the quite colourful story of one of St Helens genuine heroes. There will however soon be a permanent reminder as the Newton and Earlestown Community Group is raising funds to build a statue in 2018 to commemorate the centenary of his deeds.

Jack Heaton

It speaks volumes for the regard in which the town of St Helens holds the sport of rugby union that the name of Jack Heaton is known to very few and indeed information about him was difficult to come by. Yet this was a man, who, as retirement approached in 1949, was described by *The Guardian* as one of those rare players who would achieve "permanent renown" for "changing the whole tendency of the game". And not only did Jack play for England on nine occasions, he actually captained his country in his final two international appearances. Had not the Second World War intervened,

Image provided by Vikkie Birt,
Original by Jordan and Metcalfe, St Helens.

causing the suspension of international matches from 1939 to 1947, there is little doubt that he would have represented his country on many more occasions than he did. The word "icon" featured regularly when those who knew him spoke of his impact on the rugby world yet his name has all but disappeared from the town's public consciousness.

Jack was born in St Helens on 30th August 1912, son of Robert, a master pavior and owner of a haulage business (Robert's cousin, Charles, owned the Heaton's removal business). Jack's mother, Sarah, ran a pie shop in Baldwin Street. Jack's elder brother, Bob, played for St Helens Recs and he had a younger sister, Marjorie, who in the fullness of time took over the pie shop. The family lived in Dentons Green Lane before moving to Bleak Hill. Jack attended Cowley School from the age of 11, where he performed well in his studies, and at the same time excelled at most sports, captaining the school rugby team.

After leaving school he studied architecture at Liverpool University, and, whilst still in his teens, also captained the university rugby team. He played many times for (and captained) Lancashire, gaining his first three international caps for England in 1935 whilst still a student. Although he had links (via the Cowley connection) with St Helens RUFC, it was to the higher profile Waterloo Club that Jack gravitated after he had concluded his studies. There he linked up with his cousin and classmate from Cowley, Dickie Guest, who also went on to gain international honours in 1939 on the wing, with Jack inside him at centre. During this time the two of them maintained their contact with St Helens RUFC and would turn out in the annual Old Boys game against the school team.

Jack was now working as an architect in Liverpool (as a consequence of which he had to decline the invitation to tour South Africa with the British Lions in 1938) and in 1939 he married Nancy Clarke in St Helens who was well-known locally as a dancer and singer and performed a number of times alongside Robert Dorning. National service required him to move to Nottingham and whilst there he played for (and indeed captained – there is a theme developing here!) Nottingham RUFC and the Barbarians invitation side.

After the war, he returned to St Helens and set up home with Nancy and newly born Vikkie at 9 Elm Grove in Eccleston Park, which he designed himself. He worked in Liverpool, having founded the architectural partnership of Heaton and Crawford in Dale Street and it was back to Waterloo for his club rugby. He resumed his responsibilities as captain of Lancashire, representing the county until the end of the 1940s and leading them to two successive County Championships in 1947 and 1948 (indeed it would have been three had he not missed the 1949 final through a shoulder injury). International honours were to return in 1947 when Jack and his cousin Dickie were two of only three players who had represented England pre-war to be selected again after the war had finished. Jack's final international game came when he captained his country against France in April 1947.

Jack was to maintain his links with Waterloo after his retirement from the game, becoming President of the Club and also of the Lancashire Rugby Union. He also regularly brought a Jack Heaton XV to play against St Helens RUFC at Moss Lane at the end of each season, which was for a number of years a very valuable fundraising opportunity for the club. He went on to found the Liverpool Sportsman's Association and, demonstrating that he was also something of a visionary, wrote a coaching manual decades before the RFU produced its own version. He would also regularly persuade other leading players to accompany him on visits to schools to help with the coaching of young players.

There were however many more strings to his bow than his architectural work and his rugby. He was an excellent cricketer, having played for St Helens Cricket Club in his early days and later captaining Northern Cricket Club as well as turning out for the Lancashire Second Team. He was by all accounts a pretty decent golfer as well.

Away from the sporting world he was very active in the world of the Masons, at various times acting as Secretary of the Masonic Lodge in St Helens, Chairman of the Committee of the Prescot Masonic Hall and Grand Officer of the United Grand Lodge of English Freemasonry. On top of all of this, he was a magistrate on the Liverpool Bench for many years. So all in all, Jack had a pretty active life on every front.

After retiring as an architect in 1983, Jack and his wife Nancy went to live in Llandbedrog on the Lleyn Peninsula, which is where they were to stay for the rest of their days. Jack died on 25th October 1998 and the accolades he received from players past and present are a fair indication of the regard and warmth in which he was held in the rugby world, not just for his ability on the field but also because of his many personal qualities off it. He was survived by Nancy, the wife to whom he was devoted, Vikkie and two grandchildren, Rachel and Hannah.

Jack Hill (aka Eawr Nell's Jack)

Billingers are a funny lot. That much is indisputable and as such this statement is unlikely to give rise to much controversy. The species has of course been watered down in recent years with the influx of residents from Liverpool and elsewhere but that does not make it any easier to classify old Billingers. Some have attempted this over the years – the writer, WN Lockie, allegedly wrote that Billinge was, "a Yorkshire village in Lancashire with the manners of Yorkshiremen…". I suspect this was not intended as a compliment but Billingers could perhaps take reassurance that their belief that they were a special breed was shared by an outsider.

It is certainly the case that most inhabitants were indeed fiercely independent and saw themselves as Billingers first and foremost. At the same time many had leanings towards either St Helens or Wigan, particularly when it came to rugby league. The popular belief was always that the Chapel Enders were St Helens supporters, whilst those from Higher End would support Wigan. This may have been broadly true but it was never quite as clear cut as that. However, albeit probably not with rugby league affiliation in mind, the politicians did go some way to formalising this when, following the Local Government Act of 1974, Chapel End and some parts of Winstanley became part of the Metropolitan Borough of St Helens with the rest going to the dark side.

This leaves us with the dilemma of who to include in this collection and who to leave out. On any objective analysis, Richard D Lewis would make the cut – a linguist who speaks 11 languages, founder of the Berlitz Language School, one-time tutor to the wife of the Emperor of Japan, writer and author of nine books, his credentials are beyond challenge. However, notwithstanding the fact that he wrote in *The Billingers* that he was fortunate to be raised in such a special place, in his own memoirs (which he named *The Road From Wigan Pier*, for goodness sake) there is just a single reference to Billinge in over 400 pages and that was in a list of what he describes as "Wigan villages". Technically, he does qualify for inclusion as he was raised in Slack Farm, at the bottom of Main Street and very much in Chapel End. However, given his claim that Billinge is a special place, we should clearly adopt special rules governing the inclusion of Billingers. And he doesn't make it!

All that said, I am nonetheless indebted to Richard Lewis as I have drawn much of the information I have regarding Jack Hill, who is included, from his book *The Billingers*. Jack too was a Chapel Ender and whilst we have no information regarding any affiliation outside Billinge, Carr Mill Dam, indisputably part of St Helens, plays a very large part in his story and that is enough to secure his place.

Jack was born John Hill on 20th October 1860, son of Thomas, a miner, and Ellen. Jack had two older and two younger sisters, and the family lived initially in Chadwick Green, Chapel End. At some point in the next few years they moved to Billinge Rant, which was off Rainford Road and which was renamed Red Barn Road some time at the end of the 19th century. We don't know a lot about Jack's childhood other than that he followed his father down the mine, but we do know that during the cold winters he would spend his leisure time ice-skating on the northern shallow waters of Carr Mill Dam.

It was during the winter of 1879 that Jack's reputation started to spread. That winter was known as The Big Frost and Carr Mill Dam was frozen over for weeks on end. During this period skating contests there would attract huge crowds of spectators and, still aged only 19, Jack started to win consistently, taking on allcomers, not just locally but from around the country. Each victory provided a welcome boost to the normal earnings of the Billingers as they wagered more and more on each contest and, for every victory, Jack collected a trophy which would go on display at the Brown Cow on Rainford Road. Soon he had notched up 22 successive victories and he and his supporters proclaimed him as the champion of all Lancashire.

The main centre for speed skating at that time was the Cambridgeshire Fens where the low lying terrain and wet landscape would quickly freeze over in cold winters. Speed skating had been held there for many years but its golden age was in the second half of the 19th century when crowds numbered in their thousands would regularly turn out to watch the races. The National Skating Championship was set up in Cambridge in 1879 and indeed some international matches against Holland took place. George "Fish" Smart won the first British Professional Championship that same year but news of Jack Hill's exploits filtered through. It is not clear who made the challenge but once accepted, the only choice of venue was Carr Mill Dam as the ice was by then melting in the Fens.

And so, on 27th December 1879, Fish Smart and his entourage arrived in Billinge, were hosted at the Brown Cow and the following day the big challenge took place at Carr Mill Dam in front of an enormous crowd – estimated by some at more than 20,000. The contest was close and as it drew to an end it looked as if Fish Smart was going to edge it but somehow Jack managed to dig deep and produce one last lung bursting effort which right at the last propelled him past Smart. Jack had won, albeit by just a few inches, and Billinge proclaimed one of its own as Champion Ice Skater of Britain.

There followed a period of warmer winters which meant that Jack was unable to repeat his triumphs over the next few years. The story in *The Billingers* finishes there but it is alleged elsewhere that Jack travelled to the Fens for a return match against Fish Smart which Smart won. Certainly the contest at Carr Mill was the only defeat which Smart suffered in that or the following winter and he later went on to skate in the international matches against Holland and won his final British Championship in 1887.

By this time Jack was universally known as Eawr ("Our") Nell's Jack. It seems that his mother's brother, from Sims Lane End in Garswood, asked one day who this Jack Hill was, about whom all the fuss was being made, "It's Owd Hill's lad, you know, him that wed a wench called Nell from Sims Lane End," he was advised. "That'd be Eawr Nell's Jack then," responded Nell's brother and the name stuck.

Jack married local girl Mary Frodsham in 1881 and they went on to have six children together. They didn't move far, living initially on The Rant and later moving to the Brown Cow where Jack took over as landlord. He died in 1823 aged 63 and it is possible that, to this day, he is Billinge's only national sporting champion.*

*   Records for these events are understandably not comprehensive but it is worth noting that a Thomas Chadwick wrote to the *St Helens Star* some years ago ("Whalley's World") claiming that his father, Bill Chadwick (although apparently known as Billy Greenhall) from Haydock, took on and beat Eawr Nell's Jack on several occasions.

David Hitchen

Cycling has of course experienced a huge increase in popularity in recent years, although St Helens already had a proud cycling history, being home in the late 19th century to the largest cycling club outside of London. Without doubt, however, our most famous cyclist was David Hitchen, whose life was so tragically cut short in a road accident on 21st September 2014.

Photograph supplied by Greg Lunt
© Copyright Peter Jones 2018

Dave was born on 15th December 1971 to father David and mother Barbara. He had a younger sister Lisa and the family lived initially in Parr before moving to Haydock. Dave was educated at Parr Flat and then Legh Vale primary schools before starting his secondary education at Haydock High. Following another family move, this time to Billinge, Dave switched to Rainford High. His introduction to cycling came at a very early age. He had been the proud owner of a chopper and a BMX bike as a child and needed little persuasion when his friend suggested they joined St Helens Cycle Racing Club, of which Dave was to stay as a member for several years.

After leaving school, Dave initially flirted with the idea of becoming a policeman but in the end settled for a job at Pilkington. However, pretty much all his spare time (and savings!) was devoted to cycling and he set himself the target of becoming full-time and securing an Olympic place. He was trained by the legendary Harold Nelson in Salford and these years were arguably the high point of Dave's career. In the early 1990s he won a stream of club competitions (he was St Helens club champion in the ten mile time trial three years running) and started to enter international events.

It was around this time that he decided to move on from the St Helens Club and joined New Brighton. This seemed to be paying early dividends when Dave was selected to represent Great Britain in a team road race in Southern France which took in the Pyrenees. He also became "King of the Mountains" after winning the Tour of the North, a five-day stage race in Northern Ireland that same year (although he never actually got to take his prize home – Dave may have been first to the finishing line but the trophy had mysteriously disappeared by the time the presentation came!)

Unfortunately, just as it seemed that Dave's career was starting to take off, his progress was unexpectedly halted – he started to suffer from chronic fatigue syndrome (known also as M.E.) which unsurprisingly had a major impact on his performances. The condition was to last for several years and, although we will never know for certain, probably cost Dave his Olympic place. Thankfully it did not stay long term and Dave was able to race competitively again although he never quite reached the previous levels of performance. He continued to ride for New Brighton and latterly for the coveryourcar.co.uk racing team run by his old friend from the St Helens Cycle Club, Greg Lunt.

Dave had been employed in a number of jobs over the years but in the year 2001, at the age of 29, he enrolled at the University of Salford for a three year degree course in Sports Science, Psychology and Therapy. He duly graduated and subsequently worked for St Helens Council, The National Health Partnership and latterly for the Chamber of Commerce. Around about this time, Dave was asked to help train Nicola, a South African who was doing a triathlon. They struck up a relationship together, married in 2009 and had a daughter, Izzy, whom Dave adored and took with him on his bike at the every opportunity!

A big fan of St Helens RFC, Dave was more than willing to provide help and support with the various cycling challenges which Steve Prescott and others were undertaking to raise money for the Steve Prescott Foundation. Indeed he had intended taking part in what was probably the biggest challenge of all (running the Paris Marathon, cycling to Calais, kayaking to Dover, cycling to London and then running the London Marathon). Unfortunately he was not permitted time off work, which seems rather mean-spirited of his employers, but there was nothing he could do about it.

As well as his love for cycling, Dave had by now discovered another love, one for the mountains, valleys and pubs of the Lake District and he would spend much of his leisure time there with family and friends.

The end, as noted earlier, came in September 2014, when Dave was taking part in the Bolton Bash event. He had been providing support services to the riders in the event, was hit by a motorcyclist and died. His death stunned the cycling community. At his funeral at St Aidan's in Billinge, where he still lived, his friends and colleagues turned out in great numbers and over 100 cyclists followed the hearse in pouring rain for the five mile journey from church to crematorium. He is remembered fondly by the whole of the cycling community and in June 2015 a Dave Hitchen two-day event was introduced by the British Cycling Federation to be held each year in Dave's memory.

Dave was clearly an extremely successful cyclist who won international honours. He may not have fulfilled his dream of making it into the Olympic team, but it is entirely possible that this might have happened had things panned out a little differently. But to think of him just as a cyclist who won races is not really doing him justice – he was in fact a legend in the cycling community, someone with no respect for reputations (by all accounts on a training run with Sir Bradley Wiggins shortly after the latter had won the Tour de France in 2012, he told him to, "Keep up, you've just been on a seven week holiday in France") and somebody who put back as much into cycling as he had taken out. It did not matter to him that he had suffered a broken pelvis, a broken thumb and a scaphoid fracture of the wrist whilst on his bike, nor that he had been knocked off by a car at the end of a race. This was someone who was prepared to advise, support and mentor anyone who wanted to get on a bike, someone for whom cycling was an integral part of his life but someone whose contribution to life generally was so much more than his achievements on a bicycle.

Tommy Horton MBE

Professional golfer Tommy Horton, born on 16th June 1941, is another sportsman from St Helens who has been honoured by the Queen, this time by an MBE in the year 2000. It is unlikely that he actually picked up a golf club before he left St Helens to live in Jersey in 1947, but, as we have established elsewhere, the influence of one's early upbringing simply cannot be ignored. And Tommy retained throughout his life a very clear recollection of the cobbled streets of the town and also of the townsfolk discussing Pilkington's glass!

© Copyright Philip Inglis 2018

Tommy's father, also Thomas, was from Gillingham in Kent and was serving in the armed forces at the time of Tommy Junior's birth. His mother, Germaine (known as Mimi), was originally from Jersey but had been evacuated to St Helens along with a significant number of Channel Islanders. She was accompanied by her daughter Rosie when she arrived and shortly afterwards gave birth to Tommy. She later had a third child, Peter. When they arrived they lived briefly with John Kelly in Frederick Street before moving in with a Mrs Guest (whose relatives still live in the town) initially in Hoghton Road and then round the corner in Elizabeth Street. In 1947 after Thomas Senior was demobbed the family moved to Jersey where Thomas Snr had the opportunity to work on a farm.

Tommy Junior was educated in Jersey but when he was given the opportunity to join Royal Jersey Golf Club as assistant professional at the age of 15 he jumped at the chance. He stayed there for three years before moving to take up the role of assistant professional at Ham Manor Golf Club in Angmering near Worthing. Although he won a couple of Sussex county events, he was little known outside the county until he entered the British Assistant Professional Championship in 1963. It was here that an opportunity came his way in the form of Mr Ernest Butten, a successful London businessman, who conceived the idea of sponsoring and training a group of the best of Britain's young golfers in an attempt to find a potential Open Champion and with a view to regaining the Ryder Cup. He had decided to interview the top five players in the Championship and fortunately Tommy finished fourth. The group – which included two future Ryder Cup players in Tommy himself and Brian Barnes – became known as the Butten Boys.

Tommy believes he was privileged to take part in what was a revolutionary training programme – not only were they coached by an ex-Open champion at a new state-of-the-art golf centre developed by Butten at Sunridge Park in Bromley, they were also given fitness training, medical advice, access to dental care and physiotherapy, as well as assistance on everything from personal finance to public speaking. In the second year Butten promised the boys that if they finished in the top twelve in the Order of Merit, he would pay for them to spend the winter in South Africa. In the event Tommy (who finished 11th) was the only one to qualify and Butten withdrew the offer. Tommy decided therefore to leave the Butten Boys and went to South Africa anyway, funded by a whip-round by 20 members at Ham Manor who put in £50 each. Tommy won £800 whilst there and used this to repay the members most of what they had put in!

Tommy returned to Ham Manor in 1967, this time as the professional, staying there until 1974 when he returned to take up the role of professional at Royal Jersey. During this time however he became an established player in the professional arena, clocking up a number of wins, including the South African Open in 1970. In 1972 he joined the newly formed European Tour and went on to win eight tour events, as well as two tournaments which were later to become European Tour events. He was a member of the Ryder Cup teams in both 1975 and 1977, played in the Open on 20 occasions (with four top ten finishes) and the Masters on four occasions – not a bad career record to date. But the best was yet to come!

The advent of the European Senior Tour, which by happy coincidence was launched in 1992 just a year after Tommy reached the qualifying age of 50, saw a dramatic change in his fortunes. He was to win no less than 23 tournaments on the Tour, as well as the Tour Order of Merit a record five times (in 1993, 1996, 1997, 1998 and 1999). Until 2007 he stood at the top of the list of all-time Senior Tour career earnings. In addition he won the British Senior Club Professional Championship in each of 1995, 1996, 1997 and 1998. He continued playing on the Tour, albeit intermittently until 2011 although he retired as professional at Royal Jersey in 1999.

Tommy's golfing legacy was not restricted to his on course performances. Off the course, he made a huge contribution – his own short game clinics were legendary and he played a major part in the setting up of the European Annual Tour's Training Week, leading a team of coaches who were to provide instruction and support to many of the stars of the future. His commitment to the junior game was enormous and he acted as Honorary Captain of the Junior Ryder Cup team on four occasions. On the administration side, he was a member of the Board of Directors of the European Tour from 1984 until 1993. At this time he was already on the committee of the Seniors Tour and in 1996 he was elected as its Chairman, and in that capacity became once again a Member of the Board. He resigned in 2006, around about the time he was reducing his playing commitments.

Unsurprisingly his dedication to golf did not go unnoticed, hence the MBE in 2000 for his services to golf. In 2012 he was made an Honorary Life Member of the European Tour.

Tommy married his wife, Helen, whom he had met whilst she was working for Ernest Butten, in 1967 and they had two children and five grandchildren. He continued to live on Jersey, and retained his involvement at Royal Jersey Golf Club until he sadly passed away on 8th December 2017. And notwithstanding that he had lived away from the town of his birth for some 70 years, he followed closely the fortunes of St Helens RLFC throughout the whole of his life.

Barry Houghton MBE

Barry Houghton might so easily have been the sort of businessman who sold up, made a bit of money and retired into oblivion. Not so. In fact Barry has become far more notable in retirement than he ever was running the Rainford Group, an electronics company which he founded in 1971 and which was merged into the US group Reltec in 1994 at a reported value of £80m.

The reason why Barry subsequently become so much more newsworthy? Firstly, in 1995, he bought a village in Gloucestershire which carries the name of Salperton. This is not just any old village however. Some 900 years old, it boasted at the time a magnificent mansion, 33 Cotswold-stone cottages, 1,650 acres of land, a Norman church and a working farm with 170 cattle and 600 sheep. And all for what these days would seem a fairly paltry sum of £8m. Other potential buyers were reported by *The Independent* to include the Sultan of Brunei and Sir Paul McCartney.

This was however only a staging post in the grand plan. Barry turned his attention to sailing which had been a lifelong passion. In 1998 he made the first of his yacht purchases which he named – what else? – Salperton. And so began the strategy of buying increasingly grander yachts, each with a three to four year design and build cycle, and each bearing the name Salperton.

Barry was born in St Helens on 29th February 1948, son of Bill, who worked at Pilkington and Elsie. He was educated at Cowley Grammar. After his GCE A levels, he hitchhiked to the South of France and took a job as a crewman on a yacht, which then sailed around the Mediterranean. He was totally seduced by the experience but came back, he says, only because he wanted to see his girlfriend. Once back home he took a couple of short-term jobs before going to work for Alcan Aluminium in London. At the age of 22 however, with capital of just £1,500 he set up his own business, Rainford Group, back in St Helens. Over the next 28 years he built Rainford into an extremely successful telecommunications business.

In 1992 Granville Private Equity took a 25 per cent shareholding in the company, a deal which helped fund the purchase of substantial UK assets from Marconi Telecommunications and then to provide mobile telephone base stations for Nokia, Siemens, Motorola, Ericcson and Lucent. The company was listed on the London Stock Exchange in 1995 and Barry retained a 48.5 per cent shareholding. It was not long however before the company was taken private again. KKR, the US private equity giant, had recently purchased a division of Rockwell Corporation in the USA, which it renamed Reltec. This entity was then merged into Rainford in 1996 and the combined entity was floated on the New York Stock Exchange in 1997.

Barry had always said that he would retire at the age of 50 and he was as good as his word. The listing of Reltec was the point at which he retired from the company. This enabled him to move on and to start to live his dream.

Barry's lifestyle now underwent a fundamental change. He spent a brief period of time in Switzerland dealing in high-end property but then threw himself lock, stock and barrel into the sailing world. He bought his first yacht in 1998, but within a year was designing his second. Salperton II was a 53 metre ketch, which was notable as the biggest boat ever designed in New Zealand – it was even featured on a postage stamp. Barry decided however it was a little too big so downsized to the 44 metre Salperton III, also built in New Zealand. The 46 metre Salperton IV came along in June 2009, this time not just with cruising in the Pacific in mind but also something a little bit more exciting – Barry wanted to get involved in the superyacht racing circuit.

For the next few years, Salperton IV was regularly to be seen in regattas all around the world. There were collaborations with Olympic Gold Medallist Shirley Robertson and New Zealand's Cameron Appleton, wins in both Europe and the Caribbean and the founding of the Super Yacht Racing Association after a near fatal accident to the first mate in a regatta in Sardinia. This resulted in the introduction of a number of safety measure in superyacht racing.

In 2014 Barry pulled out of competitive racing having planned an epic trip for Salperton IV from Panama to the Galapagos, on to the Pacific Islands of Tahiti, Tonga, Fiji and the Marquesas and then New Zealand, before turning back and sailing through the Southern Ocean around the tip of South America, then to the Falklands and Brazil before heading back over to the Mediterranean.

Barry is currently planning to build another 47 metre yacht and as a consequence Salperton IV is, at time of writing, on the market with a sale price of €15,850,000 – appealing, yes, but probably slightly out of the price range of most readers!

Barry has homes in Mere in Cheshire, in Verbier in Switzerland and also has a house under construction in Mallorca (where he has a smaller boat, a Sunseeker Superhawk). He currently spends 12-14 weeks per year sailing, much of the winter skiing in Verbier and divides the rest of his time between his other homes. He and his wife Susan have been married for 45 years and they have a son Jason (who is now in charge at the Salperton Estate in Gloucestershire), a daughter Lisa and four grandchildren. Still only 70, there are no doubt many more experiences to come.

THE BEATLES

APPEARED AT
THE PLAZA, DUKE STREET
FIVE TIMES IN 1962 AND 1963

Ian Lenagan

I an Lenagan was born in Wigan in 1946 and is now Chairman and owner of Wigan Warriors. Prima facie, therefore, he has no place in this compilation. But Ian was a Roman Catholic and, at that time, there was no Catholic grammar school in Wigan. Hence, he was despatched to St Helens Catholic Grammar School - later to be renamed West Park - in Prescot Road to complete his education. If I am to maintain consistency regarding the criteria for entry, he has to be included.

Son of Bill, a fitter, and Winefride, a bookkeeper, Ian was raised in Scholes with an elder brother Tony – another West Park student - and younger sister Ann. He attended St Patrick's Primary School before moving to West Park Grammar in 1957 (where he was a classmate of Pete Postlethwaite – both played in the same school rugby team under the legendary Joe Coan, who was later to achieve fame as coach to the all-conquering 1966 Saints team). Ian also excelled in athletics and was St Helens Schools High Jump Champion in 1962.

From West Park, he went to the University of Manchester where he obtained a BSc (Hons) in Mathematics in 1967 and then to Liverpool University where he gained his Masters Degree in Magnetohydrodynamics in 1968 (doesn't mean a lot to me either but sounds pretty impressive!)

Ian married in 1969 at St Oswald's, Ashton-in-Makerfield to Sandra Gee whose family came from Haydock. Ian is somewhat coy about her rugby affiliation merely making the observation that Haydock is a mixed hotbed of both Wigan and St Helens supporters. First son, Simon was born at St Helens Hospital in 1970 and second son, Adrian, in Wycombe in 1975.

After leaving university, Ian's first job was as a programmer at the CEGB in London at Bankside Power Station – now the Tate Modern Museum – before moving to Liverpool, back to London and then to Leeds working for Burroughs Corporation (now Unisys) in sales, marketing and branch management.

It has to be remembered that Wigan RLFC was in the doldrums at this time and Ian confesses to having strayed a little during these years. In one interview, he admits to having gone to watch Leeds against St Helens at Wembley in 1978, and it seems he also had a dalliance with Leeds United until the uniquely frightening atmosphere of Elland Road put paid to that. He drifted to other sports as well and recalls having attended the North of England's Rugby Union victory over the All Blacks at Otley in 1978 and watching Bob Willis's heroics on the famous last day of the test match against Australia at Headingley in 1981.

Ian's next move was to Oxfordshire where he worked as Managing Director of a technology company before setting up Workplace Systems, his own computer software company in Milton Keynes. This proved to be very successful worldwide, and was listed on the London Stock Exchange in the year 2000 which was a nice little earner for Ian who picked up £29m from the flotation. He stayed on as Chairman until the final exit in 2011, when he pocketed a further £17 million which, no doubt, provided some consolation for finally severing his connection with the business he had founded all those years earlier.

After his initial financial success at WorkPlace, Ian started to extend his business interests into theatre production (his son Simon is an actor). Ian produced more than 40 plays, musicals and revues in the West End, regional theatres and at the Edinburgh Festival, his most successful being *One Flew Over the Cuckoo's Nest* starring Christian Slater. He is still a full Producing Member of the Society of London Theatres.

His passion for sport led Ian to become involved in the professional sports club sector in 2005 when he acquired 89 per cent of Oxford United FC, at the time playing in League 2, and 66 per cent of London Broncos (about to become Harlequins RL) playing in Super League. He operated as Chairman of Broncos for over two years until, in 2007, the chance of a lifetime came his way – the opportunity to buy hometown club Wigan Warriors from Dave Whelan who at the time owned both the football and rugby clubs in Wigan. Ian jumped at the chance and remains in situ as Chairman and owner to this day, having collected three Super League titles, two Challenge Cups, two League Leaders trophies and a World Club Challenge trophy (ouch!!) during his ten years of his ownership. (Ian takes pleasure in pointing out that this eclipses the St Helens performance over the same period under his friend and West Park compatriot, Eamonn McManus, albeit he has some way to go before he can overtake Eamonn's total haul!)

Ian's involvement in football was instigated by his two sons as sometime supporters of Oxford United since the family had moved to Woodstock in Oxfordshire in 1982 (which Ian had represented as Mayor in 2000 and 2001). Operating as Chairman and CEO of Oxford United, Ian was elected to the Football League Board in 2013 and to the FA Council and then to the FA Board in 2014.

His ultimate accolade in football was to be appointed Chairman of the newly-titled English Football League (EFL) in 2016 for a three-year period, one of the responsibilities of the post being to present the League Cup to Wayne Rooney at Wembley in early 2017 after the Manchester United victory over Southampton.

Ian did not disappear from the technology world either. He set up and is now Chairman of three software businesses – InnovEd, Animalates and The Sports Office, which operate in the education, kids' exercise and player performance management sectors.

Ian is, by all accounts, a pretty decent bloke, something which we will attribute at least in part to the influence of the environment in which was schooled! Certainly, it is the case that relations between the St Helens and Wigan clubs improved markedly after he became owner (albeit that they were probably at an all-time low in the Whelan/Lindsay era immediately prior to that!)

An entry into this collection was probably not on Ian's bucket list, nor will he probably count his appearance on these pages amongst his greatest achievements. But, for our part, we must acknowledge that his story is evidence that there has also been the occasional success story coming out of Wigan. However, we can justifiably claim that Ian's education in St Helens - which Ian himself admits was first class - played a not inconsiderable role in helping him achieve what he has!

Rachael Letsche

There are, to the best of my knowledge, only two sports in which St Helens can boast an official world champion, and one of these is the somewhat unlikely sport of tumbling.* For those who have not come across it previously, it is described on the British Gymnastics website as "a truly breath-taking type of gymnastics" which is all about "somersaults, twists and flips and linking them all together". It all happened in November 2014, when Rachael Letsche won the gold medal in the women's individual tumbling final during the World Championships in Daytona Florida. It was indeed Britain's only gold and one of only two medals in total won by British athletes at these championships.

Rachael (centre) celebrates her world title
© Copyright FIG 2018.

Rachael was born in St Helens on 1st November 1991, daughter of William and Catherine, and younger sister of Zoe and Steven. The family lived in Sutton and Rachael attended Willow Tree Primary School before moving on to Sutton High at the age of eleven. It was at this age that she entered the world of tumbling, although she had been doing artistic gymnastics since the age of five. She trained at Warrington Gymnastics Club and in 2001 made her competitive debut at the Cheshire and Merseyside Competition in the Novice under-10s category.

It was not until 2005 however that Rachael started to turn heads. She was selected to represent Great Britain that year in the World Age Group Championships in Holland and in November was crowned British Tumbling Champion in the 14-15 year group. The following year she was part of the GB team that won gold at the Junior Tumbling Championships in France but she had to settle for second place in both the French Open in May and at the British Open in December in the Under-16 category.

In 2007 Rachael moved with her friend Jenny Dawes to the Wakefield Gymnasium Club (this meant her parents had to drive her to Wakefield four times a week, not an insignificant commitment!) and the success just kept coming. She became Portuguese Junior Champion and again won gold at the British Tumbling Championships. The European Tumbling individual gold medal in Copenhagen in 2008 was next on the list, with a second gold medal in the team event at the same games. However disaster then struck – after competing in the 2009 World Games in China, Rachael then suffered a major foot injury in the 2009 World Championships in London which effectively ruled her out for the best part of the next two years.

Thankfully, this signified no more than a prolonged setback to Rachael's career. Now in the Senior Category she tied for gold in the European Tumbling Championships in St Petersburg in 2012 and took a runner's up medal in the team event. The following year she competed in the World Games in Colombia and came away with a silver medal. Then came the big one. In November 2014 at Daytona Florida, after qualifying for the final in 8th position, she took the gold medal in the World Championships and overnight achieved something of celebrity status in the North West, with television and other appearances now having to be added to the daily schedule. Her achievement also attracted national recognition, with Rachael being named as Sky Sportswoman of the Month in December 2014.

The following year more brought more accolades, notably the Sportswoman of the Year at the Pride of St Helens Awards, which coincided with Rachael announcing her retirement from the sport. At the time she was studying at St Helens College for cabin crew qualifications and also had in mind joining the Cirque de Soleil, with whom she had spent two months in 2013. She currently works as an instructor at Warrington Gymnastics Club and already has seen two of her young protégés compete in the British Championships. Let's hope that she is soon able to help someone else achieve the same success that she had!

* The other sport is of course motor cycling as set out elsewhere in these pages.

Kellie Ann Leyland

Whilst in the Lily Parr era, women's football was extremely popular in St Helens (the St Helens Ladies team was indeed one of the strongest in the country), it is fair to say that there is not an abundance of women international footballers in the modern era who have originated from St Helens. Actually there is only the one. Kellie Ann Leyland ticks that box, having represented Northern Ireland on 38 occasions. However when one looks at Kellie's background it is hardly surprising that her sporting career focused on the round ball.

Kellie (in green) in action for Northern Ireland.
Image supplied by Jenny Leyland.

Her mother, Jenny Leyland, was awarded an MBE in the 2011 New Year's Honours list for services to grassroots football. Jenny, a qualified physiotherapist, had also played football as a teenager before going into coaching where she was active in both Laffak and Newton–le-Willows over the years. Her biggest challenge however came when she set up a football academy in Sutton Manor from scratch in early 2008 and within three years had two teams in the Warrington League, as well as a thriving section for the very young children. At the time of writing she is sending out four teams per week at different age groups.

Kellie was born on 5th November 1986, daughter of Jenny and brother of Kristian. She showed little interest in what might normally be regarded as a young girl's activities, started playing football at the age of seven and played for her first team at nine. She was educated at Newton-le-Willows High

School and played for the school team. Representative honours soon came – she was selected for Merseyside U16s and, whilst still a 15-year-old, was selected to play centre back for England U17s. She played club football as well, turning out at various times for Huyton and Garswood Saints. After her GCSEs she was accepted for a scholarship in the women's international academy in Durham, where she did her A levels. During this time, she switched allegiance to Northern Ireland and after impressing in a couple of friendlies, was selected in the U19s squad for the European Championships in Lithuania in 2003. The following year she was handed the captaincy of the U19s side and her full international debut came in 2005 when she was selected to play against England in a tournament in the Algarve.

During this time, Kellie was playing her club football for Everton Ladies. She then managed to secure a place at Hartford University in Connecticut to do a four-year PhD course. Women's football is of course far more popular in the United States than it is here and once there, the awards for Kellie started to flow thick and fast. She represented the university team and was America's East Coast Defender of the Year in 2006. Her team, the Hawks, won both the Conference League and the Conference Tournament, with Kellie being named in the Dream Team for both. Finally she was selected to play for her regional team – not bad for the only British girl in the set up! Throughout Kellie's stay, she would jet back and forth for the Northern Ireland internationals and was regarded by her coaches as exceptionally fit – but then she was training five times and playing three times each week so that was hardly surprising!

After obtaining her PhD in Communications, Kellie spent a season playing for Ottawa Fury before returning to the UK in 2009 to play for Curzon Ashton Ladies in the FA Women's Premier League Northern Division. Sadly, injury was to intervene – Kellie had to undergo an operation on her knee at Thameside Hospital which did not go well and then required further surgery which was carried out at Wrightington Hospital. This effectively brought her career at top level to an end.

Kellie took up a job as a prison officer in 2014 and had recovered sufficiently to be able to represent the National Women's Prison Team in 2015. But while her playing days at the elite level are probably behind her, for the foreseeable future she stands head and shoulders above any other St Helens female footballer of the modern era.

Owen Livesey

The dedication which athletes routinely show to their sport and the time commitment they are prepared to make in order to increase their performance levels is often cited as the difference between glory and failure. It seems to me however that it must be far easier to be dedicated when one is either earning a significant amount from the sport or at least has the prospect of earning such an amount. I have a much greater admiration for those who have to make great financial sacrifices to fund their participation in a sport when there is no pot of gold at the end of the rainbow. Into that category I would include the 2014 Commonwealth Games judo gold medallist, Owen Livesey – someone who consistently had to seek financial support and sponsorship simply to keep going, notwithstanding what he had already achieved in his chosen sport.

Owen was born on 3rd August 1991 in St Helens. His father, John, was a bus driver and his mother, Joanne, a prison officer. Owen had two younger sisters and the family lived on Allan Road in Haresfinch. He attended St Peter and Paul Primary School, then on to Haydock High for his secondary education before finally moving to Carmel College to do his A levels. It was in the sports arena however that Owen made his mark from a very early age. Whilst still at primary school, he was playing rugby league regularly and it was to help with the rugby that his dad, himself a bodybuilder, took Owen along to the judo club at the age of eight.

For many years Owen was able to balance the demands of both sports. In rugby he was a powerful centre and it wasn't long before he was snapped up by Saints as a promising junior. He was to stay there for five years, touring Australia with the Academy in 2006, but there came a point, inevitably, when he was forced to choose between the two. Saints were concerned at the time commitment required by the judo and made it clear that now was decision time. Owen elected to stick with the judo, his thinking being that as an individual sport, he and he alone was responsible for results. He did not however give up rugby entirely at that stage, moving to Pilkington Recs where he played for the U18s until it became impossible to combine the two sports.

In the meantime, Owen's judo career was going from strength to strength. He trained at the SKK Judo Club in Earlestown and in 2007 was chosen to represent Great Britain in the European Cadet Championships in Malta and also in the European Youth Olympics in Belgrade. A series of medals was to follow – competing at 73 kilos he won gold at the British Cadet Championships in both October 2007 and October 2008, as well as gold at the Junior National Championships in January 2009. His first medal as a senior, also a gold, came in the Scottish Open Championship, again in October 2008. With an

Owen Livesey in action
© Copyright Mike Varey of Elitepix.

Olympic place in London 2012 as his goal, Owen started to train full-time at the elite judo institute which was set up in Dartford and other medals followed – two golds in the Northern Ireland Opens of 2010 and 2011 and a silver in the 2010 Welsh Open. In 2011 he was also picked for the GB team for the Junior World Cup. His world however came crashing down when he missed out on selection for the London games – fed up and disillusioned, he came back to St Helens vowing never to return to judo, and revived his rugby career, firstly with the Widnes Vikings Academy and then back to Pilkington Recs. At this stage his judo career seemed to be over for good.

The break was however only to last for 18 months. After a defeat by Blackbrook, Owen realised how much he was missing judo and resolved to give it another go. He uprooted again and went to train full-time at Camberley in Surrey. It turned out to be a dream comeback as success followed success. It began at the end of 2013 when, now competing in the 81 kilo section, he won the Welsh Senior Open in November as well as taking the silver medal at the European Open in the same month. He finished the year with gold in the British Championships before launching into 2014 with gold in January in the Scottish Open. March brought two silvers in the Pan American Open in South America as well as gold in the English Senior Open and in May he took bronze in the European Open. The big one came in July with a gold medal in the Commonwealth Games in Glasgow, which Owen won by defeating his compatriot Tom Reed in the final. His achievements were recognised by the town when he won Sportsperson of the Year in the 2014 Pride of St Helens Awards.

Owen then turned his attention to qualification for the 2016 Rio Olympics. Again based in Camberley he worked as a security guard at weekend and saved everything he could to devote to his judo career. Supported by the club, by Talenttracker and by personal sponsors he threw himself into the qualification process competing all over the world for the next two years. His medal tally was as impressive as the air miles he clocked up – four golds, two silvers and two bronzes in World Cup events, as well as golds in the European Cup, the British Championships and the Scottish Open. Sadly it was not quite enough to get him on the plane to Rio and it left Owen once again at a crossroads in his sporting career. As things stand, he has returned to amateur rugby league and has set himself up as a personal trainer. But whichever path he chooses in life from here, he has left some indelible memories and can state without fear of contradiction that he is St Helens greatest ever judo star!

This short biography would not however be complete without mention of Owen's two younger sisters, both very accomplished judokas in their own right who have each amassed their own medal haul. Like Owen, both Amy and Bekky came through the ranks at the SKK Club in Earlestown – they now train at the British Judo Centre of Excellence in Walsall. With their sights set on qualification for the 2020 Olympics, there is every chance that we will be seeing a lot more from the Livesey family.

Walter "Scruffy" Longton, DFC and Two Bars, AFC, 1915 Star

Walter Hunt Longton was born on 10th September 1992 in Whiston, the son of Walter Henry and Mary. Hunt appears to have been his mother's maiden name. Walter Junior was the eldest of four brothers and he also had one sister. The family were farmers at the time of the 1901 census, the address being given as Whiston Hall Farm but by the time 1911 came along they were living in West Street, Prescot, with Walter Snr apparently being in employment as a "motor carrier". A few years later the family moved to "Inglewood" in Derby Street, Prescot.

Walter in uniform. Photograph reproduced courtesy of Kit Syder.

Walter Junior attended school initially in Prescot but then went on to Cowley Grammar which qualifies him for entry into this collection. On leaving school he was apprenticed as an engineer at the Wire Works in Prescot (later to become BICC). He then moved to Birmingham to work as a tester for Alldays and Onions Matchless Motorcycles and also the Sunbeam Motor Car Company, which was based in Wolverhampton. He clearly had an adventurous spirit as he spent his spare time racing the early motorcycles, amassing some 25 medals as well as appearing in Isle of Man TT races in 1913.

After the outbreak of the First World War, Walter joined the Queen's Own Worcestershire Regiment in August 1914 and in April the following year sailed from Avonmouth to Egypt where his duties included escorting Turkish POWs to Cairo. From August to December he took part in the infamous Gallipolli campaign. He was injured and returned to the UK to recover, during which time he transferred to the Royal Flying Corps and took his flying certificate at Hall School in Hendon. In April 1916 he was appointed temporary Second Lieutenant and the following July was promoted to flying officer. His job at this time was a test pilot, but his work also included developing training programmes and encouraging recruitment to the Royal Flying Corps. In June 1918 he was awarded the Air Force Cross for devotion to duty in a non-combat role.

Around about the same time, Walter was transferred to France with the 85th Squadron and on 7th July he secured his first "victory", bringing down a Fokker DVII, which he followed up that same month by downing three more enemy aircraft. August was to bring another two victories, the second of which was part of an action in which Walter led a formation of six aircraft which downed an equal number of German machines. It was in recognition of this that he was awarded in November the Distinguished Flying Cross, the citation for which referred to "a brilliant performance, reflecting great credit on [Walter] as leader" of the formation.

Somehow during the midst of this activity, Walter found the time on 3rd September to marry Lily Eleanor Miller, an ambulance driver, in London. That same month a promotion to Flight Commander came his way, as did a transfer to the 24th Squadron where he was employed on air reconnaissance duties. He was back in the air on 29th September and over the next ten or so days carried out twelve tactical air reconnaissance trips – it was these which led to the first Bar to his DFC (denoting an additional award), announced on 8th February 1919, the citation for which included "bringing back valuable information and gallantry in attacking enemy troops on the ground". During the rest of October he notched up another five victories to bring his total haul to eleven. A second bar was added to the DFC on 3rd June in general recognition of distinguished service during the war, permitting Walter membership of an elite group of only three airmen who were awarded a DFC with Two Bars. Walter was also awarded the 1915 Star for his service in Egypt and Gallipoli.

After the war had finished Walter re-enlisted with the newly created Royal Air Force as a Flight Lieutenant on 1st November 1919. He carried out Air Staff Duties and then worked at the Directorate of Training until 1924 when he was promoted to Squadron Leader (taking joint control of

58 Squadron with a young Arthur Harris, who later became better known as "Bomber" Harris) at Worthy Down. His final posting was in October 1926 to the Flying School at Netheravon.

Throughout the post-war period, Walter was regularly involved in the extremely popular Aerial Pageants, where the experienced pilots would race, perform acrobatics and on occasion play out fake aerial combats. Walter indeed became quite a celebrity on this scene. He also participated in Air Races organised by the Royal Aero Club, tying for first place in the Daily Mail Light Aeroplane Prize in 1923, winning the inaugural Grosvenor Cup in 1923 and then again in 1926. This was however still very early days in the history of air travel and the death toll inevitably bears witness to this. It is somewhat chilling to note that after the 1923 Grosvenor Cup, in which Walter beat the favourite Major Ernest Foot, the local paper reported that a good day's sport was rather ruined when Major Foot was later burned to death after crashing whilst flying home.

Sadly, Walter could not cheat death either. The end came when he was one of three pilots who died in a disastrous event at Ensbury Park in Bournemouth in June 1927. It was the first race of the day and each of the twelve aircraft involved was handicapped with Walter starting off second. The aircraft were bunching, a collision took place and that was the end of that.

Walter was described in his obituary as one of the best-loved and most valuable men in British aviation. He was buried with full military honours at St Mary's Church in Upavon with 500 men from the RAF present. His wife provided the headstone for the grave and his colleagues a plaque which was erected in his memory.

What seems to have disappeared with the passage of time is the origin of his nickname "Scruffy". It is possible that the obvious explanation is the correct one, but given that he is impeccably turned out in every single picture which exists of him, it may be that the opposite is true.

One final postscript to the story is provided by the auction of his medals which took place in London in December 2011. They were bought for £36,000 by a private collector.

Harold D'Acre Robinson Lowe

There are not many in this life, from St Helens or indeed anywhere else, who can boast that a dinosaur has been named in their honour. This distinction was however conferred on Harold D'Acre Robinson Lowe, after whom the dinosaur Monoclonius Lowei was named, by Charles M. Sternberg, the famous American-born fossil collector and palaeontologist. Harold Lowe had worked as a field assistant to Mr. Sternberg, eventually becoming his right-hand man, working alongside him in the field each summer for the

Harold on one of his field trips.
Photograph courtesy of Darren Tanke
(Canadian Museum of Nature)

best part of a decade. He was not therefore a completely random choice when it came to naming the dinosaur but I don't think that detracts in any way from the unusual nature of the accolade – Sternberg was responsible for naming some 37 newly discovered species of Canadian dinosaur in his career and Harold Lowe was the only civilian upon whom the honour was bestowed.

Harold Lowe was born into a St Helens family on 1st February 1886 and appears initially to have lived at 114 Robins Lane before moving at some stage before the 1901 census to 260 Boundary Road. By this time Harold was 15 and working as a carter (which means, I think, that he either owned or drove a cart, probably of the two-wheeled variety). Harold's father was initially listed as a farmer but by 1901 had morphed into a cattle dealer. In 1905 however, when Harold was 19, the whole family appear to have upped sticks and moved to Canada, initially to Ontario before moving west to Alberta in 1908.

Harold's life in Canada was chronicled in great detail in the March 2008 edition of the *Alberta Palaeontological Society Bulletin*, although one assumes that this publication is not widely read over here (and possibly not even in Alberta although I may be doing it a grave injustice by indulging in such speculation). Harold is described therein as "a forgotten name in early Albertan palaeontology history" and the author, Darren H. Tanke, of the Royal Tyrell Museum of Palaeontology in Drumheller, makes prodigious efforts to put this right. Two things become clear very quickly from this work.

The first relates to the hardships that early settlers farming in west Canada had to endure. Disastrous harvests, prairie fires which destroyed homesteads, ranches and devoured animal feed, bitterly cold winters spent under canvas whilst new homes were erected – all of these and more were suffered by the Lowe family as it attempted to establish itself in what was a sparsely settled and at times extremely inhospitable place (quite a change from Boundary Road, one imagines).

The second is the entrepreneurial spirit and determination not to be beaten shown by Harold and his three brothers as they attempted, not just to survive, but at the same time to prosper in their new homeland. In the years up to 1925, they were engaged not only in farming but also as agents in the coal business. In addition, they ran a threshing mill, a haulage and excavation business, sold and hired horses, whilst their mother ran a boarding house. Clearly at times they did prosper, as was evidenced by the purchase of a Ford Model T car in 1916, the previous two years having yielded plenty of rain and a bountiful supply of crops. Harold then went on to form his own carting or haulage company, became involved in garden tilling and at the same time broke and trained horses for the Canadian military overseas. By 1919 however he had moved into the taxi and livery business before moving from Youngstown to Drumheller, a new and bustling coal town, where he and his brothers continued to operate a taxi business as well as starting their own local bus line.

What can be safely concluded however is that neither Harold nor his brothers were able to make their fortunes from any of the various businesses that they conducted. In 1920 Harold married Daisy Maude Woodford (from Key Haven in Hampshire, though it is not recorded how and where they met) but, after selling the taxi and bus business, in 1923 he spent the summer away from home in Waterton Lakes, presumably doing seasonal work. Harold then worked as a taxi driver before, in 1925 and at the age of 39, finally becoming involved in the activity which was to assure his place in history, that of fossil collecting.

It seems that Harold commenced work for Charles Sternberg on the basis of a personal recommendation of a team member who had decided to leave. Harold was in many ways the perfect field man, partly because of his strong, wiry build but also because of his background with horses, vehicles, haulage and excavation, all of which stood him in excellent stead for the work he was now doing. It is also likely that Sternberg valued having an older man on board with more life experience than many of the other workers. The initial period of work was three and a half months, during which time Harold created a good enough impression that he was to go on and become a key member of Sternberg's team in Alberta throughout that and the following summer – valued so much that he was the only person ever recorded as being allowed to leave camp to go home when his daughter was ill. All other persons wanting to leave camp for personal or any other reason were required to hand in their notice. Harold worked with Sternberg again in 1928 (after which there was a break for some years in field work in Alberta), and in 1929, when Sternberg drafted in Harold to work with him in Saskatchewan, rather than take the cheaper option of employing local men.

The schedule of summer work was a perfect fit for Harold as he was now working as a coal miner in the winter, when the demand for coal was at its peak. When the workers were laid off in the early summer he had the field work to fall back on. However there followed a lengthy break in the summer work after 1929 during which time Harold became involved locally in Drumheller in palaeontology. Some of the fossils found whilst he had been doing field work had been attributed to him and he had clearly developed a great interest in the subject. He helped organise some local day trips for the public to collect fossils, gave some of his own collection to a public display in the town and was prominent in campaigning for a local museum to be set up. It was 1935 before he worked with Sternberg again, this time in Manitoba, again being preferred to local men, with the work extending through the summers of 1936 and 1937. From time to time these expeditions resulted in very significant finds which would be chronicled in scientific journals, sometimes decades after the event – and one as late as 2016! But whilst 1937 was the last occasion during which Harold would work with Sternberg, he had clearly left his mark, hence the naming of Monoclonius lowei in 1940 "in honour of Harold D R Lowe who worked as field assistant for many years".

Harold saw out the rest of his life by taking on various jobs but retained his interest locally in fossils, continuing to help push for, albeit unsuccessfully, the museum - the onset of the Great Depression followed by outbreak of the Second World War effectively put paid to any chance of that happening. Shortly before the end of the war, the family, which now included two daughters and a son, moved to British Columbia and by all accounts loved the pleasant climate, mountains, trees and fresh air. Harold worked there as a janitor, a maintenance man at a local restaurant and then finally for an automotive company right up to the date of his death in 1952 at the age of 66 from a heart attack.

Harold's son Don, who has himself now passed away, told me that Harold never returned to the UK after he left (nor interestingly had Don ever been to the UK, despite the fact that both his parents hailed from there). He did not moreover know the origin of his father's middle name, "D'acre" which I suspect was not commonplace in St Helens (nor in British Columbia for what it's worth!) at the time. He did however speak with great affection of his father and clearly admired him greatly. He believed his father was a man whose views were respected, was hard working and industrious and stayed fit and agile throughout his whole life. It is rather sad however that someone such as this, whose name would live on for generations, never achieved financial comfort in his lifetime.

Peter McCarthy

Pete McCarthy falls into the same category as Pete Postlethwaite, a Warringtonian who was lucky enough to be educated in St Helens, albeit Pete McCarthy was some five years younger than his fellow townsman. I knew him at school as Peter Charles Robinson, born on 9th November 1951, son of an English father and Irish mother. He had two younger sisters, Catherine and Patricia, and a younger brother Paul.

Pete attended West Park Grammar School, an education he later described as "carrot and stick without the carrot". Like Peter P, he also dabbled with the idea of joining the priesthood but interestingly was talked out of it by his own parish priest. His summers were invariably spent on a farm in his mother's childhood home on a farm in Drimoleague in Cork, something which was to provide much inspiration for his future writings. Pete went on to gain a first class degree in English Literature at Leicester University following which he spent a year travelling in the United States and Mexico, this being in an era well before the gap year became common currency.

Once back in the UK, Pete qualified as a teacher and taught briefly at a comprehensive school in Suffolk. However this was really only a temporary sojourn as Pete's intention was to build a career in television and comedy. This led him to move to Brighton in 1975 (which he presumably considered to be more of a centre for the performing arts than Warrington or St Helens) initially taking a job at a community arts project. There he co-founded the Cliff Hanger Theatre Group, a sort of travelling outfit which put on shows in pubs, initially just for beer money. Its first production was *The Featherstone Flyer*, inspired by co-founder Steve McNicholas, a Yorkshireman who went on to create the blockbuster *Stomp*. Pete had now started to live the life he wanted to live and thrived on both writing and performing. There was however already a Peter Robinson on Equity's register, so it was at this point that he adopted his mother's maiden name of McCarthy. Tours followed, including one of the Liverpool pubs, and over the next few years there were several more productions, one of which, *Gymslip Vicar*, was nominated for a Laurence Olivier Award.

The next stage of Pete's career saw him move into the comedy world, both as a stand-up (he was a compere at London's Comedy Store) and a writer. He wrote scripts for, inter alia, Mel Smith and Griff Rhys Jones, and also wrote a stage show which he performed at Edinburgh, and then on tour in both Britain and Australia, with poet Roger McGough.

Much of Pete's work was inspired by his Irish Catholic upbringing and, unsurprisingly perhaps, alcohol featured quite heavily. Indeed his solo effort *Hangover Show* won the 1990 Critic's Award for Best Comedy at the Edinburgh Festival and was nominated for a Perrier Award (it is still available to view on YouTube, if anyone is interested). It was also broadcast on BBC Radio 4 and it was this which led to the offer by Channel 4 to host their new travel programme *Travelog*, which attempted to break new ground in travel series and enabled Pete to indulge in his other passion, travel at someone's else's expense! He went to places which at that time were way off the beaten tourist track – Zanzibar, Laos, Costa Rica and Vanuatu were just a few of the places from which the show was broadcast. Pete went on to present a number of television and radio programmes over the next few years.

It was not his broadcasting work however which propelled Pete into the public consciousness but his first book *McCarthy's Bar* published in 2001, a travel book which involved exploring his mother's homeland whilst searching for his identity and the answer to the question, "What exactly does being Irish mean?" Throughout the book he follows his own maxim, "never pass a bar with your name on it without having a drink". Given that there are many McCarthy's Bars in south west Ireland this makes for a somewhat entertaining journey. The book turned out to be a huge bestseller and an international success, with over a million sales. He followed this up with *The Road to McCarthy* in which he travels the world tracing the history of the McCarthy clan. Pete was working on a third book about the six counties of Northern Ireland when, sadly, he was diagnosed with cancer in February 2004. He died in Brighton in October that year.

Pete's writing was in a very easy to read, conversational style, not unlike Bill Bryson, and is infused throughout with examples of deadpan humour much of which, one suspects, has its origin a long way back and almost certainly covering his schooldays in St Helens. The regular stream of visitors to the McCarthy's Bar in Castletownbere, whose frontage appears on the cover of his first book, shows no sign of abating, even 13 years after Pete's death. He is further remembered by visitors to Brighton because, in keeping with the tradition whereby buses there are named after notable deceased persons with a connection to the area, his name adorns bus number 913.

Pete was survived by his wife Irene. He came to parenthood quite late in life but made up for lost time with the births of daughters Alice, Isabella, and Coral between 1988 and 1997 — by all accounts, and not unlike others who arrive there a little late in life, he embraced parenthood as a magical experience. And he never forgot his origins, as illustrated by the announcement at his memorial service that they would be playing the Rugby League hymn, "Abide with Me" to reference his support of Warrington Rugby League Club — wrong club of course but he got the sport right!

"I've never seen a woman with a beard. And I've been to St Helens".

(John Bishop)

Eamonn McManus

Everybody in St Helens now knows of Eamonn McManus. The reason for this of course is that he has been a major shareholder and chairman of St Helens RLFC for the best part of two decades, his involvement having commenced when he took early retirement from HSBC in the year 2000. Prior to that however, his business was conducted on the world stage rather than within the confines of St Helens Borough and his name was far more likely to attract recognition in the world of international finance than it was in his home town.

Eamonn was born in Haydock in May 1956, the youngest of four children, having three elder sisters. He attended St Mary's Primary School in Blackbrook and went on to attend West Park Grammar School before studying law at St John's College, Cambridge. He did his articles at Norton Rose, a major London legal practice, but just at the point when his expectation had been to return to the North West and work for one of the major commercial law firms in the region, he was intrigued by an advertisement in *The Financial Times* for trainee executives in merchant banking. He attended an interview which was conducted, rather fortuitously as it turned out, by the son and namesake of the founder of the Chindits*, Major General Orde Wingate. Eamonn's father had himself been a Japanese prisoner of war who had survived the infamous Thailand to Burma Death Railway. The interview consisted mainly of a discussion around their shared family histories, which could not have done any harm to his prospects as within a week Eamonn was on a flight to the other side of the world. And so it came about that in 1982 Eamonn kicked off a career in Hong Kong working for HSBC as an investment banker, rather than pursuing what might have been a more mundane career as a solicitor in Manchester.

It turned out that Eamonn was rather good at investment banking. He was appointed head of Asian Corporate Finance in 1993 and then became Divisional Chief Executive Officer. He became a member of the firm's Global Investment Banking Committee in 1997 and advised on many of Asia's largest mergers and acquisitions, including HSBC's takeover of Midland Bank in 1994. He also advised on many of the largest equity capital market transactions in the region, notably the privatisation programme in the People's Republic of China. It was during this period that Eamonn was named as one of the top 100 finance professionals in the world by *Global Finance Magazine*. So all in all, he did pretty well – so much so that he had filled his boots sufficiently to be able to retire from the world of banking at the ripe old age of 44 in the year 2000.

Whilst in Hong Kong it had not been a case of all work and no play. Eamonn had previously played Rugby Union for Cambridge and, whilst in London, for Saracens (although in his own words, they played on an open field in those days, rather than at their current home, the slightly more palatial Allianz Park). Having moved to the Far East, he went on to accumulate 30 caps for Hong Kong, several as captain, as well as appearing in the Hong Kong International Sevens tournament for five consecutive years and in one World Sevens tournament in Sydney. There were certainly some high points, with wins against Japan, the USA and Samoa but the size of some of the defeats against the All Blacks and Fiji is probably best glossed over. The experience however certainly provided Eamonn with something colourful to add to his CV! During his time over there he also met and married Betty, a colleague at the bank who came from a Hong Kong Chinese family, and they went on to have two children, Anne and Shaun.

It was the children in fact and the decision that they should be educated in the UK which prompted the return to this country in 2000. But Eamonn had no idea

Eamonn watching the Derby game against Wigan with Ryan Giggs.
Photograph courtesy of St Helens Star.

at the time of the rollercoaster which was awaiting him in his home town. This was certainly no retirement in the normal sense of the word.

The seeds of his involvement at Saints were sown during the 1997 World Club Challenge, a tournament which pitched the Super League Clubs against the top NRL sides. It wasn't a particularly successful venture for Saints - they lost every group game, progressed nonetheless to the knock-out stages (courtesy of a somewhat contrived format), but then exited the competition after a heavy beating at Brisbane Broncos. On the way to Australia however they had stopped over in Hong Kong and were entertained by Eamonn at the HSBC headquarters. The directors invited him to invest in the club and he agreed, albeit not thinking that he would ever be anything but a passive investor.

Once back in the UK however, he was invited to join the board, which he did, despite the fact that, having had a look at the finances, had concluded that the club was in fact a basket case. But one thing led to another and he then became Chairman, mapping out a strategy for the future, the key constituent of which was the construction of a new stadium – it simply was not financially viable to run the club if it were to stay at its historic ground in Knowsley Road. He thus embarked upon a project which took ten years to complete (he had originally estimated two to three!), which involved him taking control of the club, bringing in wealthy investors from outside, and project managing a process so tortuous that investment banking started to feel like a walk in the park in comparison. But as we all know he got there in the end, St Helens ended up with a brand new, state-of-the-art stadium and the club was for the first time in many years back on a firm financial footing. We can only speculate as to what would have happened if that stop off in Hong Kong had never taken place.

However it was not just off the field that Eamonn can boast of an impressive performance. Since his initial involvement, the club has amassed five Challenge Cups, six League Leader Shields, two World Club Challenges as well as wins in four Grand Finals – not bad by any standards and comfortably maintaining the club's position as having the largest haul of major trophies in the Super League era!

Eamonn's current intention is to spend more of the close season each year in Hong Kong, where Betty's family still live and where, somewhat ironically given that they were the reason for returning to the UK in the first place, both his children have gone to work. For the foreseeable future however he will still be at the helm at the Langtree Stadium so it would be nice to think that the performances on field will match the impressive off field performance of the last few years!

*   The Chindits were the largest of the Allied Special Forces in the Second World War. They operated deep behind enemy lines in Burma and were reliant totally on airdrops for their supplies. General Wingate himself lost his life in the campaign.

The St Helens V Wigan 1966 RL Cup Final
at Wembley attracted a bigger crowd
than the World Cup Final between
England and West Germany
at Wembley a few weeks later.

Bill McMinnis

As is evident from these pages, St Helens has produced many sporting heroes over the years. Who is the greatest of them all? It is unlikely that there would ever be a consensus on this, but one candidate who would certainly have his supporters is a name which will actually be unfamiliar to many others. That name is Robert William ("Bill") McMinnis, and in the view of Tom Hackett, a fellow Sutton Harrier and himself a county runner, Bill "could credibly claim to be the St Helens athlete of the century,

Bill entering Anfield Stadium at the end of the Liverpool Marathon. Supplied by Allan Moore.

despite the "men of steel" who have graced Knowsley Road".

Bill was born in 1915 and lived on Bronte Street in Newtown. His father, also Robert William, was a glass worker, and Bill was the second of nine children and the eldest of five boys, born to mother Ada. He was educated at Rivington Road School where he took part in many sports. In addition, the family all attended Newtown Congregational Church, whose Sunday School ran a whole series of sporting activities throughout the week and Bill was an enthusiastic participant in these as well. It seems that he made a decent fist of every sport he engaged in but it was running at which he excelled and also which he enjoyed the most. Indeed he took every chance to run that he could – from delivering his father's lunch each day by running to the Sheet Works from Newtown on the one hand to long runs to Billinge and back propelling a hoop along traffic-free roads on the other.

The first job Bill had involved delivering groceries and this provided yet more opportunities to run and, as the alternative was public transport, to save money as well. After leaving Rivington Road School at 14, he joined the family window cleaning business and in the evenings would run at Ruskin Drive under the watchful eye of William Worsley, a senior Northern Counties Official. In 1936, inspired by Ernie Harper, British marathon runner who finished second in the Berlin Olympics, Bill joined Sutton Harriers, the town's premier athletic club. He was very quickly promoted to the first team and honours started to accumulate. He was part of the Sutton team that won the West Lancs Senior Championships in 1937, 1938 and 1939, the Northern Senior Championships in 1937 and 1939 and which took third place in the National Senior Championships in 1937*. It is rumoured that Bill's stamina in part derived from the fact that he did not like the cold, harsh hands of Walter Massey, the club's masseur, so deliberately continued to train later than his team mates, waiting for Walter to go home!

The outbreak of war in September 1939 inevitably meant the end of his early running career. Bill volunteered for the RAF and, short periods of home leave apart, it wasn't until he was posted to Skegness in 1941 that he was able to run competitively again, winning a silver cup in the RAF Championship as part of the unit's track team. However overseas duty was next and, now a flight sergeant, Bill was to spend the rest of the war as part of a medical mobile unit in the Far East, initially in India and then moving southwards through Burma, as the Japanese retreated, and finally to Malaysia just as the war ended.

Back in the UK, Bill elected to stay in the RAF as a Physical Training Instructor and was stationed at Padgate. However, he was soon struck down by a ferocious attack of gastroenteritis, no doubt a legacy of life in the jungle, and although he recovered after a period of sick leave, he decided it was too late to revive his running career. Fortunately an old team-mate nagged him into returning to Sutton and, although it took a short while before he was back to his best, he went on to help the team win the National Cross Country Championships in 1947, 1949, 1950 and 1951 (they were second in 1948!) as well as making a clean sweep of the

West Lancs and Northern Championships in those years. There was no shortage of individual honours either for Bill, who was selected to represent Lancashire in 1947, 1948, 1950, 1951 and 1953, the Northern Counties in 1949 and finally England at cross country in 1953.

In addition to his Sutton Harrier obligations Bill also took part in cross country, road, and track events with the RAF, again with great success, becoming RAF and Inter-Services Cross Country Champion in 1951. In 1953, after he married Doreen and they had set up home in Pewfall, Bill had yet another opportunity to run and indeed for many years he treated his daily twelve mile round trip to Padgate as a valuable training opportunity.

It was in the early fifties however that Bill started to focus more and more on marathon running and he was to achieve even greater success at this distance. He had won the Liverpool City Marathon in 1951, his first ever attempt at that distance, went on to win the Northern Counties Marathon in record time in 1953 and notched up a number of other successes before having his best ever year in the open age events in 1955, winning the Polytechnic Marathon (from Windsor to Chiswick) and, four weeks later, the AAA Marathon at Reading. As a consequence he was selected to represent Great Britain and Northern Ireland later that year at an international event in Prague, the first Sutton Harrier ever to gain such an honour – and he was 40 years old at the time!

One might be forgiven for thinking that by this time Bill had done enough running for several lifetimes and it is true that he did ease off for a while. However in 1974, at the age of 59, he completed two legs in the Sutton Harriers 75th Anniversary St Helens to London relay and was then persuaded to recommence competitive running. Arguably the next few years were even more remarkable than the earlier years. In 1975 at the first Veterans World Athletic Championships in Toronto, Bill won the over sixties 5000m and 10000m track events and the 1000m cross country event. Over the next five years he travelled the world and competed in the World Championships in Gothenburg 1977, Hanover 1979 and finally Christchurch in 1981, notching up a total of seven veteran World Championships, before finally hanging up his boots for good in 1982.

That didn't mean of course that Bill was severing his ties completely with the running world. He continued to be involved in a number of capacities at Sutton Harriers and played a large part in the production of the 2007 history of the club *From Acorn to Oak*. He served as Club President there (and, after its merger with the St Helens Athletic Club in 1990, at the newly named St Helens Sutton AC) until his death in 2013 at the ripe old age of 98. He was active till the very end – indeed to mark his 90th birthday he went jet skiing!

He was survived by his wife Doreen and his two daughters, Carol and Elizabeth. His contribution to the town has been permanently recognised by the naming of McMinnis Avenue in Parr in his memory.

*   By 1939, Bill had been joined in the senior team by brother Fred, himself an excellent athlete, a representative of Lancashire and England at cross country and a stalwart of Sutton Harriers for many years.

The St Helens YMCA Scout Group, which is still in existence, can lay claim to being the world's first scout group, having been formed in February 1908 after a visit to the town by the founder of Scouting, Robert Baden Powell, who had come to the town to share and promote his ideas.

Jim Manley

History is littered with examples of artists who did not find their calling until late in life – Van Gogh and Monet are two of the most famous of these. Albeit not quite in the same league (well not yet anyway), St Helens can nonetheless contribute one of its own to this august club, artist and painter, Jim Manley, who was born in St Helens on 17th January 1934 but did not sell his first painting until well into the third decade of his existence!

Photo courtesy of Jim Manley.

Jim started life in Bronte Street, off Rivington Road in Newtown, son of Jack, a plate glass cutter at Pilkington's and grandson of "Big Paddy" who ran a tobacconist shop on Duke Street. His mother, Mary was a box maker at the timber yard. Jim had two brothers, Jack and Ralph, and was educated initially at Windleshaw Primary School before moving to West Park in 1945. He left in 1951 with A levels in History and English and, with National Service next on the agenda, somehow persuaded the RAF that his schoolboy knowledge of Latin meant he could work as a Russian translator. I haven't worked that one out either, but it did mean his two years of service passed relatively comfortably.

After being demobbed in 1954, he drifted initially from job to job, working in forestry, down one of the coal mines, at UGB and in work study before enrolling in 1957 at the De La Salle Teachers Training College in Middleton (more commonly known as Hopwood Hall). It was there that he was introduced to the world of art by one of his lecturers, and the art students' tales of Bohemian life in late 19th century Paris were enough to give birth to an obsession which was to last the rest of Jim's life.

He still had the rather more pressing matter of earning a living however and his first teaching job was at St Michael's School Widnes, where he stayed for five years until 1964. It was there that he helped launch several youngsters into professional rugby as well as becoming involved for the first time with children with learning difficulties. By then married to Margaret Barnes, also from St Helens, and with two sons, Joe and Peter, they moved to a bigger house and a new working environment in Millom, Cumbria where Jim taught at St James School. Soon afterwards, the final member of the family, John, arrived on the scene. Whilst there Jim obtained his Certificate in Special Education and moved in 1968 to Baliol School in Sedbergh – not an experience he remembers fondly (he describes it as akin to a military regime) but whilst there he did sell his first painting at Abbot Hall Gallery in Kendal. In 1970, he made the final move of his teaching career, to Ardmore House, a residential special school in Downpatrick, Northern Ireland. It wasn't the sort of move that would have appealed to everyone as these were the early years of the Troubles which were to haunt Northern Ireland for much of the next 30 years. It did however work out perfectly for Jim. The school had a liberal, caring atmosphere and he was to stay there until his retirement from teaching. At the same time his painting career was about to take off. He had found his spiritual home.

Jim's first exhibition took place at Down Cathedral, shortly after his move to Ireland and this was followed over the years by many more throughout the whole of the British Isles. Plenty of awards have come his way, including the Royal Ulster Academy's Landscape prize in 1997, the Watercolour Prize in 2005, and, possibly his most prestigious, the Patron's Prize at the EVA (Exhibition of Visual Art) International Annual Exhibition in Limerick in 1984 (the cash prize of £1,000 subsidised quite a lot of Guinness in those days!) Many of his paintings have been purchased by public collections, including the Walker Art Gallery in Liverpool and Stormont Castle in Belfast, as well as a number which have been purchased for private collections. In 1995 he achieved the art equivalent of an international cap when he represented the United Kingdom at a watercolour symposium in Latvia and he achieved top status in Irish art when in 2013 he was invited to present a piece to the National Self-Portrait Collection which is on permanent display at

Limerick University. And in 2016, he was accorded the greatest accolade of all when he was elevated to the exalted level of full member of the Royal Ulster Academy!

Jim describes his style of painting as "a thoroughly mixed media incorporating water, acrylic, pastel and collage" and the themes as "the interaction between the landscape, humans and wildlife". Commentators have observed that his paintings combine the best of Irish and English traditions "playing on the cusp of the traditional and innovative". His methods originated in part at least from the fact that Jim had little spare time and so had to produce instantaneous results. Over the years however little has changed, notwithstanding the fact that his retirement from teaching in 1988 means that he is no longer pressed for time as he used to be.

Jim's life in Ireland was not just a whirlwind of teaching and art. He played rugby for Ballynahinch as well as setting up his own side, Manley's Marauders, made up primarily of ex-Gaelic footballers (a pretty scary thought). He travelled the length and breadth of Ireland and developed a passion for mountaineering which culminated in him conquering the 4061m summit of Gran Paradiso in Italy in 1980!

It is probably not unreasonable to conclude that Jim is now in the twilight of his career as an artist (and indeed as a mountaineer) but it is nice to think that for some people everything in life can at some point come together. And whilst Jim may not be the most famous person to come from St Helens, there is every chance that he is the best artist the town has ever produced!

Kym Marsh

A ctress and singer Kym Marsh, was born on 13th June 1976 in Whiston Hospital, daughter of David, a joiner and Pauline. She had an elder sister Tracey and two elder brothers, David and Jonathan. Kym was raised in Garswood, which, for anyone not familiar with the area (or who is under the mistaken impression that Garswood is part of Wigan) is a village within the Metropolitan Borough of St Helens. The family lived in Kinross Avenue and Kym attended Garswood Primary School.

By the age of ten she had already persuaded her father to let her sing in the local Labour Club, suggesting she had her sights on a show business career from an early age! Her experience at secondary school was not a positive one however – Kym was bullied and ended up leaving and attending the Elliott-Clarke Theatre School in Liverpool. This was not a particularly good experience either and Kym took solace in her singing, releasing a single entitled "One Kiss" at the age of 13 in 1990 under the name of Kimberley on a small record label, Jelly Street Records. Three years later she released a second single, "One More Chance". She also provided the vocals for a number of dance bands, did some session work and somewhere along the way entered the *St Helens Star*'s Young Star talent competition.

In 1994 Kym had her first child, David, with her then fiancé, also David, a local builder. Two years later they had a second child together, Emily, but the relationship broke up in 1999. In 2001 Kym decided to give up hope of a career in show business and enrolled at a Beauty College. However just two weeks in, she was persuaded by her mother to audition for *Popstars* and ended up as a member of the newly formed Hear'Say, which went on to record two number one singles, the first of which, "Pure and Simple" was the fastest selling debut single of all time. Famously, Kim did not disclose during the auditions that she had two children and when the news later broke, it provided her first taste of the publicity which was to accompany her career from that point on.

In 2002 the group broke up somewhat acrimoniously (inevitably, according to Kym, when you put three young feisty women together!) Kym immediately launched a solo career and signed a recording contract with Island Records. Things went well initially – she had two top ten hits but her third signal flopped as did her album. Island did not extend the contract and Kym had a decision to make about her future. She decided that it did not, after all, lie in the music world but that she would forge a successful acting career instead.

In 2001, Kym had started a relationship with Jack Ryder who was at the time playing Jamie Mitchell in *EastEnders*. In 2003 they married (and sold the wedding pictures to *OK* magazine) but things didn't go to plan. They split, reconciled and after Jack left *EastEnders*, they moved to Manchester, with Kym hoping to secure North West based acting roles. She made brief appearances in BBC's *Doctors* and then *Hollyoaks,* but her big break came in April 2006 when she was offered the opportunity to appear in *Coronation Street*. The initial intention was that she would be involved in only four episodes, but her character was an immediate success and she was offered a permanent role. Kym grabbed the opportunity with both hands - she was voted Best Newcomer at the National Television Awards in 2007 - and has never looked back. Indeed having been on set now for more than ten years she can justifiably claim to have joined those *Coronation Street* legends who have become national institutions!

Kym's personal life has however not had the stability that she managed to achieve in her professional life. She split from Jack and they were later divorced. In the meantime, she had started a relationship with *Hollyoaks* actor Jamie Lomas. Tragically their son, Archie, was born prematurely in 2009 and died shortly after birth. Two years later however, they had another child together, Polly, and then tied the knot in 2012. Once again however, it was not to last and the couple split in 2013. Since then, Kym has provided regular material for the tabloids and celebrity magazines all of which seem eager to follow every liaison she has had. At the time of writing she is dating personal trainer Matt Baker (who obviously knows how to get results in every way, as Kim also released her own workout DVD in 2015, with the title *Power Sculpt*). Unsurprisingly, speculation regarding the future of the relationship has taken up many lines of newsprint!

Whilst she cannot claim to be the best actor nor the best musician to come from St Helens, Kym's life story, her profile and celebrity status certainly mark her out as one of the most colourful of the many successful characters that the town has produced. And one suspects that the tabloids will not be short of material for a few years yet!

Pauline Yates of St Helens
turned down the role in
THE AVENGERS
which went to
Honor Blackman.

Adam Martindale

I have never quite been able to work out in which category I should place Adam Martindale. There is no doubting his qualifications for a place in this roll of honour. It is surely a major achievement when someone from a present day humble upbringing manages to secure a place at Oxford; to come within a hair's breadth of a similar achievement (and to fail through no fault of his own) as the son of a struggling yeoman from St Helens in the 17th century, is no less than remarkable. On top of that he went on to become a prominent Presbyterian minister, wrote several books and other publications on subjects as wide-ranging as theology, mathematics, agriculture, sailing and the discovery of rock salt in Cheshire and finally in 1685, a year before his death, published his autobiography, *The Life of Adam Martindale* in which he displays a remarkable memory for the detail of his eventful life (albeit one that few of us would actually have chosen!) So this was no ordinary yeoman's son!

Born in Moss Bank in September 1623, Adam was fortunate in that his father, Henry, who had fallen upon hard times financially, was still prepared to use what little money he had to indulge Adam's passion for learning. From the age of six when he encountered his first book and was taught to read by his brothers and sisters, he claims he could have read all day "without play or meat" and then, of his own accord, took to reading the Bible and any other book he could get his hands on. The following year he was sent to the free school in St Helens and cheerfully travelled the two miles each way. However he is scathing about the quality of the teachers ("a simpleton and a tipler", a "silly and unconstant man") and his fellow pupils ("Dullards in the same classe with me having power to confine me to their pace") – not what we would today regard as very Christian sentiments! Adam's complaints to his father did result in a move to a fee-paying school in Rainford. The schoolmaster there was more to his liking (academically that is, he wasn't so keen on his fondness for corporal punishment) and when the teacher moved to a school in St Helens, Adam duly followed him.

Things weren't going well at home however. One of his brothers had married an unsuitable young girl, against the wishes of the family (it seems she did in fact turn out to be a good wife, but Adam attributed that to God's goodness and certainly not any prudent choice of his brother!) His sister (who had moved to London, also against the family will, and then married) lost her own child, and shortly afterwards Adam's beloved mother died of pleurisy. The sister in London resolved to return with her husband to be near her father, but she contracted smallpox on the journey back and ended up dying herself just four months after her mother. Adam himself then suffered a bout of smallpox and indeed went blind for several days, but ultimately went on to survive the disease. To cap it all, another brother married a Papist and disappeared to Ireland, never to be seen by the family again.

Adam's father was then persuaded by relatives and friends that Adam would be better off learning a trade than staying at school and as a consequence Adam abandoned his studies and started to work for his father. This didn't last long – one senses that Adam's heart would not have been in it - and he was soon back at school, firstly in St Helens, where he discovered his old teacher had become a drunkard, then to Rainford again, where he finally found "an eminently able and diligent master". However the merry-go-round continued when this teacher also moved to St Helens*, with Adam duly following, and in 1639, when he was 16, his teacher advised him that he was now proficient enough in Latin and Greek to go to Oxford!

Unfortunately, it was by then abundantly clear that war was brewing, so Henry advised Adam to put Oxford on hold till everything had blown over. In the meantime Adam took a series of jobs including one as a teacher at his old school in Rainford. At the point of the outbreak of hostilities in Liverpool in the spring of 1644, he was employed by Colonel John Moore, MP for Liverpool, as a clerk to the quartermaster of his regiment (a position he took as part of a strategy to avoid soldiering if at all possible) but ended up nonetheless taking part in the defence of the city against the forces of the Prince Rupert and the Earl of Derby. In due course the Royalists took the city and Adam ended up in prison, albeit this was a far better outcome than for many of his fellow parliamentarians!

Adam was released from prison during the following summer and had little appetite to continue as a soldier. Instead he went back into teaching and had high hopes of reviving his university aspirations. However, possibly as insurance against any future calls to arms, he began to prepare for the ministry and almost immediately found himself accepting an appointment as a preacher in Gorton, east of Manchester. His congregation was made up of several squabbling religious factions, with none of which he was totally comfortable, so it was in many ways a difficult time for him. On the positive side, whilst there he met Elizabeth Hall from Droylsden and in 1646 they married in Manchester Church. Some 15 months later, Elizabeth gave birth to their first child, also Elizabeth.

Notwithstanding the difficulties he had faced in Gorton, he must have done something right as he was invited to accept appointments in six parishes in Yorkshire and five in Cheshire. His preference was to go to Yorkshire, where he felt he would more likely be in the company of likeminded puritans, but Royalist victories there made that a bit too problematic. Instead, in 1648, he took a position at Rostherne in Cheshire and shortly afterwards applied for ordination as a minister in Manchester. However a small group of Rostherne parishioners objected, which suggests that his arrival there had not met with everybody's approval. Adam managed to sidestep these objections by applying instead in London and he was duly ordained in July 1649. At the same time he published his first book *Divinity Knots Unbound* which either impressed or reassured the local population as the opposition within the parish pretty much disappeared with its publication.

Adam's tenure in Rostherne was to last some 14 years but that did not mean that any element of stability had entered his life, whether from a personal perspective or otherwise. Three of his six children born in that time died as infants, and Adam also had to deal with the deaths of his elder brother and his father. And whilst his faith was clearly important in helping him deal with these tragedies, times were very difficult for religious men and Adam's position made it impossible for him to escape the endless controversy. The turmoil troubled him greatly and he worried endlessly about the rights and wrongs of various argument and beliefs. Nevertheless, notwithstanding a short period in prison in Chester, he managed to stay in place until the restoration of the monarchy signified the return of the Anglican prayer book and its enforced use in every church in the land. Adam did not conform, as a result of which he was indicted and decided to resign his position. On 17th August 1662 he preached his last sermon in Rostherne Parish Church.

Adam and his family continued to hang around Rostherne, albeit in less salubrious accommodation, and he attended church and farmed a small holding in nearby Tatton. However he also threw himself into the study of mathematics and quickly acquired quite a reputation as a maths teacher. He was soon able to make a decent living as such, and indeed was employed by Anglican as well as non-conformist gentry. But times changed yet again, with the magistrates starting to turn a blind eye to breaches of the law during the late 1660s. Adam started to preach again, mainly in Manchester but also to various congregations in Lancashire and the Pennine Valleys. He also accepted an appointment as Lord Delamere's chaplain at Dunham Massey. The ability of nonconformists to preach was briefly formalised by the enactment of the Declaration of Indulgence (which Adam welcomed only grudgingly, as in his view tolerance should clearly extend to Presbyterians but not to "Papists, Quakers and all the other wicked sects"). In 1673 however the Test Act withdrew all such licences so Adam was back to square one.

Although he could no longer preach, Adam stayed in situ as Lord Delamere's chaplain but it was far from a full-time occupation. It did therefore give him far more time to write and indeed most of his books and publications were completed around this time, including his main mathematical work *The Countrey Survey Book: or Land-Meters' Vade Mecum*, a guide to methods of land measuring, and another book on theology *Truth and Peace Promoted*. Unfortunately his private life continued to be dogged by sadness and tragedy. His youngest son, who had been born in 1660, died in 1663, his eldest Elizabeth died of a fever at the age of 25 in 1673, and Thomas, a teacher who Adam had at one stage hoped would attend Oxford, died in 1680, also after contracting a fever. This left only Hannah, who suffered from polio, and Martha, of the eight children Thomas and Elizabeth had together.

In 1674 Adam moved his family to Millington, which was much closer to Dunham and in 1681 they moved to Mere. However three years later Lord Delamere died and the family moved out to Leigh, where they purchased their own home. Adam was briefly jailed again in 1685 on suspicion of being involved in the Monmouth Rebellion (he wasn't) and then he was required to travel to Lancaster to give evidence as a witness in a civil action. His health was already failing and the round trip on horseback did not help. He did however manage to complete his autobiography, but passed away in September 1686 at his home in Leigh. He was buried that same month in his old parish of Rostherne.

In his book *Lancashire Diarists*, the author JJ Bagley concludes that there is little doubt that Adam enjoyed his life but one cannot help but feel that there was a great lack of fulfilment. Certainly from a religious perspective it was a time of great strife and his personal life was permanently touched by grief and sadness. Still, it was a remarkable life for one of humble origins and represents another colourful example of a St Helens person who made his mark on the wider world.

*   Adam comments that this particular teacher was the only one in his period of observation who left St Helens a sober man, which paints a quite interesting picture of education at the time!

Lew Martindale (aka Lew Yates)

Lew Yates is someone that I have no wish to upset, for reasons which will very quickly become clear. Anyone known as "Wild Thing" with a CV that includes the occupations of boxer, doorman, unlicensed fighter and all round hard man is someone you want to keep onside if at all possible.

Wild Thing in fact is the title of Lew's autobiography which was published in 2007. The sub title *The True Story of Britain's Rightful Guv'nor* hints at the nature of much of the content and it is indeed a fascinating, if at times somewhat disturbing, insight into the nether world of violence occupied by Lew for much of his adult life.

The story began around the end of the Second World War, on 3rd June 1945 with the birth of Lewis Martindale in Edgeworth Street in Sutton Oak. This was, as Lew puts it in his autobiography, the commencement of a new war, one in which Lew takes on the rest of the world and in particular anyone who stood in his way. Lew had an elder brother and two younger sisters and began his education at St Anne's Primary on Monastery Lane. He didn't last long there as a result of a particularly brutal beating by the nuns after Lew had been apprehended by one of them whilst in a school playground fight. His mother, appalled by the injuries inflicted upon him, moved him to Robins Lane School immediately. Whether this incident had a lasting impact on Lew we will never know for sure, but his schooling could certainly not be regarded as a success and he describes the day he finally left as one of the happiest of his life.

Lew had by then already embarked on what might have been a glittering boxing career. From the age of six he had attended a boxing club over the Roundhouse pub, moving in due course to the Britannia Boxing Club in Peasley Cross and finally to Lowe House. Whilst there, he was trained by the legendary George Gilbody, who taught him, inter alia, all the dirty tricks of the trade. Outside the ring, he took a series of jobs as a trainee mechanic but after a number of misdemeanours was to lose each of them. Finally, on the basis that he had looked pretty useful when involved in fights there as a punter, he was taken on as a doorman at the Plaza in Duke Street, thus setting in train a life which was to include manning the doors of some of the most famous (and indeed violent) clubs in the country.

In the meantime, Lew had married his girlfriend Jean and they had had their first child. Desperate to kick start his career as a professional boxer he moved the family to Preston where an ex-pro boxer was appealing for top amateurs to join him with a view to turning professional. Before this could happen, Lew managed to secure for himself a place in the ABA North West Championship and came up against Billie Aird, northern champion for the last three years. It didn't go well – not so much the fight itself as the outcome. Lew was given a public warning for head butting (George Gilbody may have taught him the tricks of the trade but not how to avoid being caught) and promptly picked up the referee and threw him across the ring. This was probably not the best course of action for someone who wanted to make a career out of boxing and indeed the resultant ban pretty much killed off any chances Lew had of succeeding in this particular career ambition.

Lew had obtained employment initially as a doorman in some of the clubs in Preston and Blackburn and after a while Jean set herself up as a hairdresser in Burnley. Two further children had arrived by this time and Lew decided to take a day job with a view to introducing a semblance of normality into their lives. However after losing a job at a building site following a slight altercation which left the other guy in hospital, Lew found it difficult to obtain steady work and made the decision to go to London. He had a specific objective in mind. He had heard the boast of Roy "Pretty Boy" Shaw, Britain's unofficial "guvnor" (i.e. champion unlicensed fighter), ex-criminal and indeed mental patient at Broadmoor, that he would wager £10,000 that he could beat anybody in a fight. Lew did not need a second invitation and moved down to London in 1976 to make the challenge.

Things started to unravel pretty soon after Lew arrived. Shaw managed to avoid fighting him for some five years, during which time Lew worked the doors in a number of Essex and London clubs (he was advised early on that nobody used his own name in this line of work so Lew adopted the surname "Yates", his nickname as a child having been "Rowdy Yates", the cowboy played by Clint Eastwood in the *Rawhide* series who had always been getting into fights!) His family life unfortunately did not survive the disruption – on his first visit back north, he discovered that his wife had been having an affair and that was the end of that. Jean did a disappearing act and Lew, after a period in which he stayed in the family home with the children, made the decision to take them with him back to London. He had started training at the gym owned by Terry Lawless (one of the most successful managers in British Boxing history) but that had to give way once the children were living with him. His job however continued to provide a fairly regular cycle of violence, his reputation was growing and his contact list started to read like an *A to Z* of the London criminal underworld.

The fight with Shaw finally took place in October 1981 although the timing of Shaw's acceptance of the challenge was not ideal for Lew, who was suffering from an umbilical hernia, recovering from a stab wound in his back and had only six weeks to get himself into shape before the fight was to take place. On the basis that he might never get the chance again and that he had waited five years for the opportunity, Lew agreed to the fight which was to take place at the Ilford Palais nightclub.

On the night everybody who was anybody in the unlicensed fight game was there – spectators were standing on chairs, tables, even the bar, to get a view of the ring. What Lew had not realised, however, was that the outcome of the fight was a foregone conclusion – Shaw's financial backers made sure of that. That Lew was clearly winning the bout seems to be accepted by pretty much everyone – well, everyone not in Shaw's camp that is. But with one minute and twelve seconds of the second round still to go, and Shaw dead on his feet, the bell rang to end the round. At the end of the third with Lew comfortably hammering home his advantage, the referee stopped the fight, alleging that Lew's eye, which had suffered only a minor injury when they had clashed heads, was too badly damaged for him to continue. The crowd went wild shouting "Fix! Fix!" but to no avail. The story was put about that Lew had been unable to see out of either eye and all film of the fight mysteriously disappeared (there is video footage available of nearly all of Shaw's other fights). And that was the end of that.

Shortly before all of this took place, Lew had married again and his wife Margaret soon gave birth to a son. She began to put pressure on Lew to give up his lifestyle and after an attempt on his life late one night, Lew agreed. They moved to a village called Manea in Cambridge and although Lew did continue to work the doors for a while, he finally gave them up and started a business as a dog breeder. Three more children arrived over the next few years but it was all too good to last. Margaret was missing London, Lew had no intention of going back and in the end divorce was the only answer. Lew maintained his contacts in London (indeed during a difficult financial period he ran a burger van in East London) but today lives alone in Cambridge where he coaches boxing and is a personal trainer. Sadly violence has followed the family around – Billy, Lew's youngest child from his first marriage (who also wrote a book entitled *My Life on the Run*) was murdered in 2013 and a few years earlier, the girlfriend of the first child of his second marriage, Lewis (and the mother of Lewis's two children) was convicted of murder after coming to Lewis's assistance during the course of a fight.

It would be very easy on the basis of the above to come to the conclusion that the Lew Yates was nothing more than a mindless thug, but the evidence of those who knew him certainly suggests otherwise. In one of the testimonials at the end of his book he is described as "funny and personable, nothing like any bouncer I had ever met….sharp and witty and with a huge personality". Another makes particular mention of how, after knocking a troublemaker out at a club, Lew would always check that he was not seriously hurt and then organise a cab to take him home. Bernard O'Mahony, who assisted him with the autobiography, describes him as always polite and good humoured and a very decent man, a real genuine guy. He points out that despite his lifestyle, Lew never spent a day in prison, never took nor sold drugs and was one of the few to emerge unscathed after rising to the top in the murky business in which he was involved.

We know from Lew himself that his temper was his Achilles heel and there is a suggestion as well that a dark side could emerge when he was under the influence of alcohol. And one suspects that Kate Kray (widow of Ronnie) knew what she was doing when she included Lew in her book *Hard Bastards 2*. However it is interesting to speculate as to what might have been if things had turned out differently – if he had not been banned from professional boxing at such an early stage in his career for instance. Jimmy Sheridan, a well-known East End entrepreneur, is also of the firm belief that had Lew been born a cockney, the guys with the right connections would have made sure that he reached the very top. In Lew's case however, that was never to be – but he has certainly left his mark on many of those who encountered him, in more ways than one!

The first fatal railway accident took place in St Helens in 1830 when William Huskisson MP was run over by George Stephenson's Rocket.

Thomas Melling

An engine driver is not generally regarded as a glamorous occupation. Or more correctly, it is no longer regarded as a glamorous occupation. But if we go back to the 19th century and the advent of the railway in this country, the situation was very different indeed. Because of the Rainhill Trials, described by some as the most remarkable event of the Industrial Age, St Helens already holds pride of place in the history of rail travel. But in the person of Thomas Melling it also produced a character who carved out his own niche in that world and whose journey began in Sutton Locomotive Sheds and ended transporting the Egyptian Royal family across the Sahara desert!

Thomas was born in 1818, son of Thomas (whose occupation is described as a "nailor") and Elizabeth (known as Betty). He was baptised on 12th July that year in St Mary's Chapel, as St Helen's Church was then known. There was also a younger brother, William, born in 1822. Although we do not know a lot about his early life, Thomas was always referred to as a native of Moss Bank and it seems his working life started as an engineering apprentice in Sutton on the St Helens and Runcorn Gap Railway. He clearly did pretty well at his job as it did not take too long for him to progress to the sought after position of engine driver.

At some point in or around 1840 Thomas married – his wife's name was Mary and her birthplace was Bold. Their first child, John, was born in Sutton but their second, Thomas, in Liverpool which suggests that Thomas Snr may perhaps have moved to work on the Liverpool and Manchester Railway at some point. Around 1847 the family moved to Birmingham, where Thomas took up a position with the London and Birmingham Railway (which had recently merged with several other companies to become part of the London and North West Railway). Thomas was to stay there for six years, during which time he reputedly drove the first express train between London and Birmingham. The family, which now included two more children, Mary and Edward, lived in Duddeston Row together with three lodgers and a domestic servant.

In 1853 Thomas moved on, having secured a more senior position with the Great Western Railway. He was to stay there for three years although it is not clear whether or not the family moved from Birmingham to the West Country. The big move came in 1856 however when Thomas entered the service of Allcard, Buddicom and Co, a British company whose contracts included not just supplying the locomotives for, but also managing and operating, the train line between Paris and Rouen. Thomas duly acquired a certificate as a "driver of the first class" on this line, known as the Chemin de Fer de L'Ouest. It is possible that the move to France was prompted by the death of Mary, Thomas's first wife. Certainly whilst in France, Thomas had another daughter – she was born in 1858 and was named Elizabeth, the same name as her mother, another Englishwoman, although it is not clear whether or not Thomas remarried at this point. We do not know either what happened to the children of the first marriage, other than John who was sent to be educated at Cheltenham Grammar School as a boarder (suggesting that the family may perhaps have moved to the West Country), before joining his father in France and serving his own apprenticeship in engineering.

In 1858, Thomas spread his wings yet further and took a position in Egypt which was, somewhat bizarrely, the second country after the United Kingdom to construct a rail network (the engineer was a certain Robert Stephenson!) Thomas's duties were to drive the trains between Cairo, Alexandria and Suez and he was to stay for some 20 years. During his time there, he transported Dr Livingstone across the desert in 1859 and then in 1863 he received great praise from the Egyptian government for driving the English mail through the country during a destructive plague. In 1867, he was presented with the first of two gold watches for conveying an officer who had arrived from Constantinople with urgent despatches 131 miles across the desert from Alexandria to Cairo in just two hours twenty minutes without a single stoppage, described at the time as the "most extraordinary run ever performed by a locomotive". Thomas's duties also included the carriage of the Egyptian royal family and his second gold watch was awarded after he had transported the mother of the Viceroy of Egypt (or the "Khedive" by which term she was known) to prayers at Tanta. She was apparently delighted at the manner in which he had performed this duty (but then, given that she had previously travelled on the back of a camel, one assumes that pretty much anything would have been an improvement!) Thomas was joined in Egypt by his son John after completion of his apprenticeship in France. John in due course became a Chief Engineer in the Egyptian Navy and whilst there married Elizabeth who was originally from Northumberland, which was where his family settled on their return to England.

On his own return, Thomas went back to his roots and set up home in Thatto Heath (Cairo Square and Cairo Street were so named to mark his return) and where a grateful Egyptian government erected a plaque to commemorate his achievements. It seems likely that he lived in one of the terraced houses there before moving the family in 1879 to Suez Lodge on Portico Lane which he had built for himself and which also bears a plaque which was later erected in his memory.

Around about this time, he remarried, this time to Elizabeth (yes, another one!), who was some 31 years younger than him and whose birthplace was recorded as Windle. They went on to have several children – Anne who was born in 1879 (but who sadly died in 1885), Thomas in 1881, William in 1883 and another Anne who was born in 1887 (Thomas by then was 69 years old so clearly still had some energy left!) By all accounts the house was full of mementoes from his time in Egypt including some beautiful sea shells and two Egyptian mummies! He loved horse riding and the children were all very well educated, so it sounds like he had a bit of money to spend as well.

Thomas passed away on 17th November 1896 and is interred in the graveyard at Christ Church Eccleston alongside his brother William and his daughter Ann both of whom had died in 1885. They were later to be joined by his son William who perished when *HMS Active* went down in 1901 and his widow Elizabeth in 1929. Thomas's grave bears the epitaph:

"FROM CAIRO TO SUEZ HE DROVE THE FIRST TRAIN
AND IF HE WERE ABLE HE WOULD DO IT AGAIN
HE LOVED TO RUN THROUGH EGYPT'S SANDY SOIL
AND VIEW THE ANCIENT RUINS OF JOSEPH'S TOIL"

That Thomas, who we can assume was a man of humble birth given his father's occupation as a nailer, should have achieved so much is clearly a testament to both his ambition and his sense of adventure. He was truly one of the unsung heroes of the town of St Helens and, alongside Sir James Sexton, perhaps its greatest adventurer.

*   Interestingly Thomas's occupation is recorded in the 1851 census as a "Retail Brewer" which I originally thought was an error. However Thomas's great-great granddaughter, Val Woodward, a resident at Reeve Court Retirement Village in St Helens, possesses a vase which is inscribed "T. Melling, Engine Tavern, Birmingham" which suggests there may indeed have been some involvement in the brewing industry as well as the world of railways.

St Helens is the birthplace of both
the railways (the Rainhill Trials)
and modern canals
(the Sankey / St Helens Canal)

John Molyneux V.C.

The final member of the quartet of Victoria Cross holders, John Molyneux (like John Davies, always known as Jack) was born on 22nd September 1890 at home in Marshalls Cross Road. He was the eldest child of Joseph, a coal miner at Sherdley Colliery, and Minnie Jane. John had four younger sisters and no brothers. He was educated at Holy Trinity School in Parr but like many of his generation, left at the age of twelve to work, initially at Pilkington's and then at Cannington Shaw before joining his father down the pit at Sherdley. His interests included bird watching and he was a nature lover, hobbies which may, one suspects, have set him apart from some of his fellow pupils at school.

Photograph courtesy of Stephen Wainwright of Sutton Beauty

However given that he grew to 6 ft 5 inches in an era when the average height was 5ft 6 in, and that his other hobby was boxing, it seems unlikely that anyone would have teased him too much about it. He also joined the Peasley Cross concertina band, where his father was the conductor.

Jack continued to live with the family who had by now moved to Sherdley Road. His occupation as a miner might well have been a life sentence if war had not broken out in 1914. Jack volunteered immediately and enlisted with the 2nd Battalion of the Royal Fusiliers (St Helens). His initial training was at Dover and he was then sent in April 1915 to fight in the infamous and ultimately disastrous campaign in Gallipoli against the Turkish forces of the Ottoman Empire. Jack was present for most of the fighting but after suffering a minor injury and then frostbite, was probably relieved to escape the carnage when he was evacuated in November to Malta to recover.

He was next posted to Egypt before coming back briefly to England. It was however only a brief respite and by March 1916 he was in France with the rest of his unit, where he was involved in the Battle of the Somme. Again, he managed to survive but suffered two wounds and was taken back to England for treatment at hospitals in Leicester and Burton. After a home visit to St Helens in April 1917, he returned to the fray at some point during the summer and in October was involved in fighting near Langemarck in Belgium. It seems that he was inspired (or perhaps enraged is a better description) by the death of one his friends and when an attack by the British was being repelled by machine gun fire, despite being up to his waist in mud, he organised and led a bombing party to capture the trench whence the fire was coming. To add to the danger, the trench was in front of a strongly held house occupied by snipers and immediately after he had secured the position, Jack jumped out of the trench and charged another enemy position in front of the house, calling for others to follow. By the time reinforcements arrived, he was involved in hand-to-hand fighting with such fury that the Germans who had escaped death – more than 20 of them – were more than happy to surrender.

It did not take long for the decision to be made to award the Victoria Cross. The announcement was made in the *London Gazette* the following month and Jack was back in England on 12th December to receive the award at Buckingham Palace from King George V. He was soon back in St Helens where he was transported in an open carriage from his home to the Town Hall. He received several awards, one of which was a concertina from his old band in Peasley Cross and he apparently performed the "Blue Bells of Scotland" on the Town Hall steps in front of a cheering crowd of several thousand. The following February he was awarded the Croix de Guerre, a Belgian military honour.

After being demobbed in January 1919, Jack went back to Sherdley Colliery and shortly afterwards married Mary Agnes Lyne (she was known as Agnes) who was originally from a village called Clifford Chambers near Stratford-upon-Avon but had been working in Southport which is where Jack met her. They had two children, Joyce born in 1920 and Joseph in 1921. In 1925 he started to work at Pilkington's and when the Second

World War came along, he served as a sergeant major in the Pilkington's Home Guard. On VE day, according to the *St Helens Reporter*, he once again performed with the concertina alongside his son who played the trombone.

Jack attended numerous dinners for holders of the Victoria Cross in London as well as a garden party in Buckingham Palace to which he brought both of his children. He died on 25th March 1972 in Ashtons Green Home in Parr aged 81 and shortly afterwards, his son, Joseph, sold all his medals at auction through Sotheby's, quite a controversial move at the time but defended by Joseph on the grounds that his father had told him to do it. In the event, they were purchased by his old regiment, the Royal Fusiliers and are now on display at the Tower of London museum.

St Helens Council decided in July 2017 to name a new street in Sutton "John Molyneux VC Close" and later in the year a commemorative paving stone was laid next to the St Helens Cenotaph to mark the centenary of the presentation of the Victoria Cross at an event attended by many of Jack's descendants and their families.

It was said of Jack by the superintendent of the nursing home that he was one of the old brigade, who never complained, even when he started to lose his eyesight. Certainly he regarded himself as having been lucky in life, reflecting once that he was the only one of the sergeants in his unit who had gone out to France with him who had survived the war. And he will always be remembered as the first St Helens holder of the Victoria Cross.

Herbert Mundin

Herbert showing off his facial dexterity!
Photograph courtesy of Stephen Wainwright.

Herbert Mundin, who was to become a renowned Hollywood actor, was born in St Helens on 21st August 1898. Like John William Draper before him, he had Methodist connections, was to leave St Helens early in his life and ultimately achieved fame in the United States rather than this country.

Once again, I am indebted to the meticulous research carried out by Stephen Wainwright for many of the details of Herbert's life and background. It seems his father, William Mundin, was a member of the Primitive Methodists, a strain with which I was not previously familiar and which in due course was subsumed back into the mainstream movement in this country at least (it apparently survives in the United States, though not, as far as I am aware, courtesy of young Herbert). Primitive Methodism seems to have been a sort of working class version of the main thing and also seems to have been a bit more fun, involving jolly hymn singing and the like. Whether Primitive Methodism had anything to do with the fact that William had four wives and 19 children I know not.

At the time of Herbert's birth on 21st August 1898 to William's fourth wife, Jane, the family lived at 206 Windleshaw Road but moved to St Albans shortly after his birth. It is not entirely clear why they made the decision to leave. William was an ex-labourer and reformed alcoholic whose job at the time was described as a "Police Court Missionary". He provided social and pastoral care to persons in trouble, representing them in court when necessary. It seems he carried on the same role in St Albans, initially at least, though he later became Hertfordshire's first probation officer. That there was an attachment to the town in which William had met Jane is clear from the decision to name their house in Paxton Road, St Albans "St Helens Villa" (and although originally from Boston in Lincolnshire, William was to return to the North West after he had been diagnosed with cancer and, following his death in 1924, was buried in St Helens Cemetery).

Herbert attended the prestigious St Alban's Grammar School and on leaving school started to train as an electrical engineer before joining the Royal Navy after the outbreak of World War One. It seems during his four years at sea he served on three minesweepers as a wireless operator, two of which sank, leaving his elder sister Clara to describe him as having a "charmed life". A permanent legacy of his time at sea however was a realisation that he had a funny face, that he had enjoyed performing and that he had the ability to make his colleagues laugh with his impersonations and his story telling. He now knew what he wanted to do with his life.

After he was demobbed, all Herbert's efforts were focused on creating a life in theatre. His first stage appearance took place in 1919 and for the next couple of years he pleaded and pestered his way into roles in touring repertoire companies. Ironically his break came at a performance in Eastbourne in 1921 when he was standing in for the main comedian, whom Andre Charlot, a French impresario, had come to watch. Andre was sufficiently impressed by Herbert to engage him for his revues and Herbert made his first performance for him later that year in the Prince of Wales Theatre in London. This was the start of a seven year relationship with Charlot which would see Herbert performing in New York as early as December 1923.

The remainder of the 1920s was a whirlwind of performances mainly in the UK and the United States, although in 1928 he travelled to and appeared throughout Australia and New Zealand. He was almost always cast as a comedian or a comic character but could also sing and dance – indeed in 1927 he featured on two gramophone records released by Columbia which were the first ever live recordings of a theatrical performance.

In 1926 Herbert appeared in a very early live broadcast made by the BBC and in 1928 made his first film appearance in a "talkie" called the

Bulldog Breed, although little is known of this. However there was clearly something about "talkies" that appealed to him. He began in 1930 to focus all his time and efforts on a career in film, despite having previously expressed doubts as to whether talking pictures would ever take over from the theatre. He appeared in the film *Ashes* in which he played a cricketer who was taking part in a game of cricket which lasted for 60 years. This was the first of seven British films in which he was to appear over the next 18 months. By the end of this period he was a well-known figure in Britain, with advertisements for his films regularly portraying him as "England's greatest comedian". Notwithstanding this success he made the decision to seek his fortune in the heart of the movie-making industry in Hollywood and accordingly set sail for America on 16th May 1931 – he was to return to his homeland on only one occasion before his untimely demise.

Herbert's move to the United States was in many ways a brave one as he was largely unknown there and unsurprisingly he struggled initially to find work. However after securing relatively small roles in a succession of minor films the work started to flow in on a regular basis. By the end of 1933 he had appeared in no less than 19 films with his most notable part as George, the cockney pub landlord in *Sherlock Holmes* (in which he was billed ahead of Dr Watson!) By now he was firmly established in America and appeared in a further nine films in 1934 and then eight in 1935, including, most famously, a role as the incompetent cook in *Mutiny on the Bounty* with Charles Bligh and Clark Gable. Indeed he was so busy in this period that one of the film magazines ran an article explaining how a radio communication system had been set up to direct him from film set to film set so that he was able to work on four films at a single time!

Over the next few years Herbert appeared in a further 14 films, the best-known of which were *Tarzan Escapes*, in which he provided the light relief by playing the adventurer Rawlins, and *The Adventures of Robin Hood*, in which he played Much the Miller's son, a role which is regarded by some as his career highlight. He was contracted to appear in a number of other films when on 4th March 1939, as a passenger in a car driven by his friend on the way to a dinner party in Van Nuys, California, he suffered fatal injuries following a collision with another vehicle. He was buried four days later in Inglenook Cemetery in California and his funeral attracted over 400 mourners.

Herbert's mother Jane, now living in Wallasey, was heartbroken at the news as she had not seen him in person for eight years, whilst the wider family, which included relatives still living in St Helens, were reported as being in shock. Herbert had no children although he had been married twice. He met and married his first wife Hilda in 1921 when they were performing at a concert party, but this did not last long. In 1924 he remarried, this time to an Australian-born actress Kathleen Reed, herself already a widow, who occasionally made minor appearances in Herbert's films. This relationship was also doomed to fail – they separated in 1934 and after Herbert's death, Kathleen devoted her life to charity fundraising, organising many balls at top New York hotels which were attended by a host of celebrities.

Notwithstanding the premature end to his life at the age of only 40, Herbert will certainly be remembered as one of the very earliest character actors, his trademark role being as a maverick or eccentric, usually with the cockney accent he had learned during his days with the navy. He was known as "the scene stealer" as he often deflected the attention away from the lead actors and also as "the man with a thousand faces" because of his remarkable facial dexterity.

St Helens has produced many actors but Herbert Mundin stands unchallenged as the greatest Hollywood star amongst them.

Alex Murphy OBE

Notwithstanding my intention to keep the number of rugby league players to a minimum, there are one or two without whom the collection would be very obviously incomplete. Alexander James Murphy is one of these. If there is such a thing as a rugby league legend, whether from St Helens or elsewhere, then I would suggest that Alex fits the bill better than anyone. His was undoubtedly one of the few names which genuinely transcended the sport itself and which was for a long time instantly recognisable even to those who had little or no interest in the game. What is quite remarkable is that he managed to achieve this in an era when there were no television chat shows, guest appearances on quiz shows and the like and with no involvement or profile outside rugby league itself.

Of course to be renowned does not always equate to being loved and Alex Murphy, always a hugely controversial character, has as many detractors as he has admirers. He acknowledged as much himself by naming his 2000 autobiography *Saint and Sinner*. However not even his greatest detractor could argue against Alex's inclusion at the top of any list of the best rugby players (of either code) that Britain has produced.

Murph was a prodigious talent from a very early age. Born on 22nd May 1939, he lived on Sunbury Street, Thatto Heath with his three sisters and elder brother. His dad worked at Rainhill Hospital and his mother at Pilkington's. He was educated at St Austins School and it wasn't long before his sporting talents were spotted. He enjoyed an outstanding schoolboy rugby career but also shone at football with Everton at one stage interested in signing him. In the event he was to sign for Saints at midnight on his 16th birthday, in what has been described as something close to a military operation, with Saints only too aware of interest from other clubs.

Alex did not have to wait long for his first team debut which came against Whitehaven on 11th April 1956 whilst he was still a few weeks short

Another try for Alex Murphy in his prime.
Photograph courtesy of Saints Heritage Society.

of his 17th birthday. This also marked his first request for a transfer as Alex thought he had done well enough to retain a first team place whilst coach Jim Sullivan thought otherwise. However it wasn't long before he had made the scrum-half spot his own nor indeed was it long before the international selectors came calling, with Alex being the youngest ever tourist when selected to go on the British Lions tour of Australia in 1958.

Thus a glittering career at both club and international level had begun but it was never to be plain sailing. Indeed it was at the pinnacle of Alex's success with St Helens that the first big fallout took place, at the end of the 1966 season which had seen Saints sweep the trophy board with four cups. The dispute revolved around the purchase by St Helens of Tommy Bishop, also an international scrum-half and the decision to play Murphy in the centre. It culminated in Alex making the move to unfashionable Leigh where he was installed as player-coach at the ripe old age of 27! He was also at the time the highest paid coach in the rugby league – not bad for someone with no previous coaching experience.

It wasn't however just Saints that Alex fell out with. He had been first choice scrum-half ever since the 1958 tour of Australia when he had broken into the test side and indeed been one of the heroes of the Battle of Brisbane when Great Britain had beaten the Aussies with only nine fit men on the field. By the time 1966 came round Murph, now captain of the all-conquering Saints side of that year, confidently expected to be appointed captain of that year's touring party to Australia. The selectors however preferred Harry Poole of Leeds and as a consequence Murph spat out his dummy and refused to tour – something he has said he now bitterly regrets.

The Murphy magic was soon in evidence at Leigh. As player-coach Alex was able to put together a pretty decent side and the first silverware arrived in 1969/70 when Leigh won the BBC Floodlit Trophy. However the unthinkable was to happen the following year - not only did they beat St Helens in the Lancashire Cup Final but went on to win the Challenge Cup at Wembley against the mighty Leeds, who had been huge favourites to lift the trophy. The final was not without controversy and Alex, as ever, was right at the centre of this. The Leeds captain Syd Hynes became the first man to be sent off at Wembley, his offence having been an alleged head butt on Murphy who was stretchered from the field but later recovered sufficiently to collect the trophy as well as the Lance Todd award for the man of the match. The story persists that Murphy had winked at his team mates from the stretcher (and Syd Hynes has to this day maintained his innocence) but Alex has always denied this. Either way, the Cup win was a massive achievement with Leigh's only other Cup win, before or after, having taken place in 1921!

Alex did not hang around at Leigh for long after that. He moved to Warrington, again as player-coach, at the start of the 1971/2 season and was soon working his miracles there. In 1972/3 Warrington won the League Leaders Trophy and then the following year it was once again back to Wembley where Alex captained his third different club to Challenge Cup success.

1975 marked Alex's retirement as a player but he continued in the coaching position until 1978, by which time his trophy haul at Warrington had reached six. His next move was to take him to Salford, who had been known in the mid-1970s as the Quality Street Gang because of their expensive signings but who by then were struggling to put together quality performances on the field. Alex's time there was not a success, the blame for which he laid fairly and squarely at the door of the Board (or more correctly the owner) for not backing him financially. He didn't stick around and in 1980, it was back to Leigh where the magic was to resurface with a Lancashire Cup win against Widnes in 1981, followed by, arguably, Alex's greatest coaching achievement of all, the championship in the same season – Leigh's first since 1906!

It was no surprise therefore that the bigger clubs were knocking on Alex's door and Wigan, at the time a sleeping giant, was his next port of call. Alex was to deliver some success – third in the First Division in 1982/3 and the first silverware for 18 years when they won the John Player Trophy against Leeds. Indeed the following year there was a Wembley trip, albeit Wigan were soundly beaten by a strong Widnes team. The scene was set however for the biggest bust-up even in Murphy's career when in July 1984 he flattened Maurice Lindsay, the Wigan Chairman (and an extremely controversial figure himself) in his own office, after a dispute over money. Murphy reckons to this day that Lindsay wanted him out so deliberately provoked him (Lindsay had called him a "money grabbing little bastard" so there may be some truth in this). Either way, Alex was gone, Wigan turned to antipodean coaches, started to throw huge amounts of money around, bought all the best players and inevitably began to win trophies. To what extent Alex can take credit for laying the groundwork for all this is a big question. Alex certainly believes he played a big part and there is no doubt that there was more of a winning mentality at the club after his period in charge and the crowds had also returned. But we will never know the answer to the "what if" question – would Wigan have had the same success with him in charge?

With almost inevitable predictability, Alex returned to Leigh, who had fallen upon hard times in his absence, but this time there was no magic wand as Leigh were relegated from the old First Division. By the following November he had led them to the top of the Second Division, but was not destined to be around when they bounced back to the First Division at the end of the season – he was back where it all began as coach to St Helens, his arrival being celebrated in some parts as the "return of the Messiah". Certainly there were high expectations but overall his stay did not live up to them. The only silverware to arrive was the John Player Trophy after a stirring win against Leeds at Wigan in 1988. There were admittedly two Wembley appearances but a performance lacking any structure whatsoever led to a 19-18 loss against Halifax in 1987 in a game that all logic suggested Saints should win, and a 27-0 humiliation against Wigan two years later meant Murphy had now coached losing teams in his last four Wembley appearances. There were rumours throughout of player discontent and indeed Saints lost one of their home-grown superstars, Andy Platt, to Wigan during this time, supposedly after he had become disillusioned with the club. It was no surprise when the board decided in January 1990 to dispense with his services and that was the end for Murph and his home town club.

Yet another brief spell followed at Leigh followed by a stint at Huddersfield, another club in the doldrums despite a rich history, but the glory days of Murphy the super coach were now gone. With the exception of a brief period as Director of Rugby at Warrington in the mid-1990s and another spell in the same capacity at Leigh (where else?) in 2003 his formal involvement with the game was now over.

That is not to say that Murph disappeared from our lives. He was a commentator on BBC alongside Ray French for a number of years, regularly penned articles about the game in the press and became a well-known speaker on the after dinner circuit. If his coaching services were no longer in demand, his opinions certainly were. And even now, he is ever visible in and around the game, and took part at the ripe old age of 75 in the Rugby League Founder's Walk (looking a lot more sprightly than some other far more recently retired players!)

Alex was awarded the OBE in 1988, was voted the Player of the Millennium in a poll at the turn of the century and has been inducted into the Halls of Fame at both St Helens and Warrington Wolves. Anecdotes involving him are legion, many of these being great examples of Alex's quick wit. Outraged to hear that Tom Van Vollenhoven, the great Springbok whom Saints had signed from rugby union, was being paid throughout the year rather than just during the rugby season, Alex apparently challenged the Board and asked why he could not also be paid on a similar basis:

"Do you really think you are as good a player as Tom Van Vollenhoven?" asked the chairman.

"I am in effing summer!" responded Alex.

Ray French tells the story of Alex's introduction to the game of golf.

"Just hit the ball onto the green," Alex was told and he proceeded to do just that.

"What do I do now?" he asked.

"You hit the ball into that hole," he was told.

"Why didn't you tell me that the first time?" quipped Alex.

There is no doubt that Alex was one of the greatest players ever and in the view of many the greatest scrum-half the world has ever seen. His performances as fly-half for the RAF during his spell in National Service suggest that he would also have been a superstar in the other code. Playing against MJK Smith, the England Rugby Union international and future England cricket captain, Murphy apparently tackled him on more than one occasion so comprehensively that his captain is reported as having advised,

"Hey, Murph old chap. Go a bit easy on Smithy, he has to play at Twickers on Saturday". Murphy's reply,

"He won't be playing effing dominoes on Saturday if he tries to jink past me like that again!" was perfectly in character.

It is clear from the above that Murphy was one of the great characters of the game. He will never be wholly loved, not even by the Saints fans for whom he could do no wrong as a player – his admission for instance that he turned down the St Helens coaching job in 1982 because Wigan was the biggest rugby league club in the world, not only demonstrates how misguided he could be, but also alienated many of his biggest fans. And his detractors would also argue that as a coach he was quick to take credit for winning teams and equally quick to blame the players when things went wrong. But as he freely admits, he tells it as he sees it, there is never a hidden agenda and he has been big enough to accept that he got some things wrong, a good example being his refusal to tour in 1966 as noted above.

By contrast to his life in the public eye, Alex's personal life has been more stable. Married for more than 50 years to Alice, a former teacher at Holy Cross and St Alban's (and who never craved the limelight), Alex is now a grandfather. His role as a family man however is not what has interested the press for the best part of his 75 years! We wait with interest to see if there are more headlines yet to come!

Martin Murray

S t Helens has never been able to boast a world champion boxer but there is one man who has come closer than any other and that is Martin Murray. On four separate occasions he has fought for the world title but sadly, and indeed at times controversially, he has fallen on each occasion at this last hurdle. The bare facts however betray nothing of the story behind his achievements or indeed his life in general.

Although Martin achieved success in boxing at a very early age, his progress through life was not without its challenges. He was born on 27th September 1982 in St Helens, son of Derek and Carol, and grew up in Fingerpost with his two brothers and a sister. He attended Merton Bank Primary School and then St Augustine's before moving to Cowley for his secondary education. Although Martin can recall wearing a pair of boxing gloves as a toddler, his real introduction to the sport came at the tender age of just seven at a taster session with St Helens Town Amateur Boxing Club, then run by the legendary local trainer John Chisnall. Martin was also playing football and rugby league at the time but at the age of ten, boxing really started to take over. He had his first amateur fight the following year and success soon followed. Schoolboy titles came his way and he also gained international honours, representing England in Ireland, Cyprus and Uzbekistan.

Throughout his schooldays Martin showed all the dedication that was required to succeed, working hard and resisting the temptations of alcohol. His ambition had been to join the army boxing team when he left school but he didn't get through the medical at first time of asking because of a skin problem and he was asked to get a clearance from his doctor. Unfortunately in the meantime, things started to go wrong – the dedication he had previously shown did a disappearing act as Martin began drinking and succumbing to the attractions of a less disciplined lifestyle. He was employed in a series of dead-end jobs and soon started to find himself in trouble. A series of prison sentences was to follow, including one in Cyprus. Martin readily admits that his life could easily have continued in a downward spiral. He went back to boxing and even managed to win the ABA welterweight title in 2004 but another prison sentence followed. However two things were to change his life irrevocably. The first was the news he received in prison that his long-time mentor John Chisnall had died and not being able to attend to funeral hit Martin hard. The second took place in Panama Jacks Bar in Warrington at the end of 2005, when he met his wife Gemma. It was at this point that he resolved to knuckle down and sort his life out.

Martin returned to the ring as an amateur at the end of 2006 and the following year made the decision to turn professional. His career could not have had a better start – he won his first 23 fights and earned a shot at the world middleweight title against Felix Sturm on his own territory in Germany in December 2011. It was the first of a number of controversial decisions that Martin was to experience when the fight was adjudged to have been a draw. Still, he had something to look forward to, as it was straight off to Barbados for his wedding to Gemma and there was every likelihood that he would get another chance at the world title.

Two further wins in 2012 did indeed earn Martin a second chance when he agreed to take on Sergio Martinez on his home territory in Argentina for the WBC middleweight title in April 2013. The lead up to the fight was dominated by references to the Falklands although Martin sensibly refused to get involved. In front of a hostile screaming crowd of 40,000, Martin had Martinez on the canvas twice although one was deemed a slip by the referee so did not count. In the end it took a late rally by Martinez to secure a unanimous points victory although many, including Martin's promoter Ricky Hatton, thought Martin had done enough to win.

His third attempt at a world title, after another four wins, was against Gennady Golovkin in Monaco in February 2015. On this occasion Martin could have no argument with the result. Despite a battling performance which drew plaudits from many, he was stopped for the first time in his career in the 11th round. Martin was back in the ring just four months later however and after three comfortable wins, secured his fourth attempt in November the same year against Arthur Abraham. The fight took place in Germany (which Abraham rarely left) and once again controversy surrounded the result which went the way of Abrahams with the all-American judging panel split two to one. Martin himself thought he had won the fight and his camp made very clear that they were up for a rematch, but that was never going to happen. Instead, after one further win, he fought a world title super middleweight eliminator against another British opponent, George Groves, in June 2016 and suffered his first defeat in a non-world title fight.

Some fans were of the view that Martin should call it a day but he has soldiered on, clocking up two more wins so it would be a brave man who tries to predict where it will all end. So that leaves his professional record at the time of writing as 35 wins, 4 losses and one draw, during which time he was at various points British, Commonwealth, WBC Silver and WBA Interim Middleweight Champion – mightily impressive, even if it hasn't delivered the world title he wanted so much. His battling style has been praised by many of boxing's greats, including Lennox Lewis and Roberto Duran, and he has shown time and again that he is a true warrior in the ring. His fans currently face the dilemma experienced by so many boxers in the past, wanting on the one hand to see Martin fight again and on the other, hoping he does not outstay his natural time in the ring, the choice many have unfortunately made before him.

But it is arguably not Martin's career as a boxer that defines him. As someone who has turned his life around completely, he is in many ways the perfect role model for young people. He never tried to hide his past, but on the other hand has not sought to glorify it in any way. When he says that the best thing to happen to him was meeting his wife Gemma and that his family (they have three young children, Archie, Amelia and Aisla) is the most important thing in his life, it is abundantly clear that he is not just saying this because it is expected of him, but that he genuinely means it. He is a qualified youth worker, working with the council, going into schools and prisons and sharing his own experience with those who have also gone off the rails. He has recently opened a Health Food Restaurant in St Helens, is an ambassador for the Steve Prescott Foundation and a passionate Saints supporter as is evidenced by the club badge which has adorned his shorts in every one of his professional contests. One cannot help but admire the way he has got to grips with his life and he has certainly done the town proud both inside the ring and out! His autobiography, due to be published in 2018, will certainly be a compelling read!

Charles Nevin

Readers will have noted my occasional references to the journalist, author and humorist Charles Nevin. Charles, more than anyone else, has done his bit over the years to promote the town of St Helens, and particularly the rugby league team, in both his press articles and books.

His articles have appeared in the most unlikely of places - for example, he wrote an article in the *New Statesman* in 2005 in which he expressed total bemusement at the club's decision to dispense with the services of their coach, Ian Millward, albeit that it was clear from his prose that he was inwardly pleased that the club's reputation for the unorthodox was being maintained.

Charles has also used his books as a medium to impart the same messages. In *Lancashire – Where Women Die of Love* (to which he refers, with more than a little tongue-in-cheek, as his "minor, possibly cult, classic"), he devoted a full chapter, entitled "The Greatest Game", to his own relationship with the town and the rugby league team that he loves. Joanna Lumley described the book in her *Times* review as "an absolute joy" although it is not clear whether it was the chapter on rugby league and St Helens which most fired her enthusiasm. What I did rather like was the fact that the book was published in 2004 but updated as early as 2006 since Charles clearly felt he needed to include reference to the 75-0 defeat of Wigan in a Challenge Cup match which took place in the previous year (OK, he may have made other changes as well but this was the one which, for me anyway, stands out).

To my mind however, the *coup de grace* however was an article in the *New York Times* in which he posed the question whether or not 2016 was the worst year ever but concluded that for him at least this was eclipsed by 1989 because of Saints humbling loss by 27-0 to the old enemy at Wembley that year! Quite what the American readership made of that, I know not.

Many from St Helens will be familiar with the family business, Nevins, a chain of grocers founded by Charles's grandfather in the 1920s, with branches dotted around the St Helens area until it was taken over by the Co-op in 1998. Charles himself was born in 1951, son of Jack and Jean, at a time when the family home was on Prescot Road, backing on to Grange Park Golf course. However after spending his early schooldays at the preparatory school for the St Helens Catholic Grammar School Charles was, as befits the son of a local wealthy grocer, despatched to boarding school, albeit not one that was a household name – initially to Barlborough Hall near Chesterfield, followed by Mount St Mary's College, just a couple of miles from there, both of which were Jesuit institutions.

Charles emerged as sane as one can be after such an education and went on to study at University College Oxford before embarking on a career in law. However in the mid-1970s he decided to kick off an alternative career and made his move into journalism. The coming years were to see him report from many different parts of the world for pretty much every broadsheet that you may care to name. He has also written regular humorous columns and diaries for the *Sunday Telegraph, The Times, The Guardian, The Independent* and *The Independent on Sunday*. I recall some particularly amusing rugby league related articles he penned for *The Guardian* in the 1990s, though he did lose the plot at one point. This was after an especially heavy home defeat to Wigan in 1997 and the main thrust of his article seemed to be that he had been forced to go through the pain of watching this match in his local pub in London solely for the benefit of his readers. But I guess this was understandable in the circumstances as I also remember being emotionally scarred by that game.

Charles has written three other books. There was *The Book of Jacks*, a history of the popular name (and the name of both Charles's father and one of his sons). This was not a commercial success and led to the rueful observation by his publisher a month after publication that, "It may be, Charles, that you and I are the only two people in the world who think this book is a good idea". Charles was on safer ground – in St Helens anyway – with *So Long Our Home,* a 232 page history of St Helens RLFC published at the time of leaving Knowsley Road in 2010 and co-authored by Alex Service. His latest offering represents his first foray into the world of fiction; a collection of quirky short stories with the intriguing title

Lost in the Wash – with Other Things - not exactly mainstream stuff but for that very reason, definitely worth a read!

Charles lived for a number of years in London before moving to Somerset where he lives with his wife, Liv. He would make – and continues to make - regular journeys back north, initially to Knowsley Road and latterly to Langtree Park (I can't bring myself yet to call it The Totally Wicked Stadium), the new home of his heroes. He has two sons, the aforementioned Jack, and William. Interestingly, his entry in *Debrett's People of Today* lists his clubs as Berkshire Press and the St Helens Bowling Club (which for those who do not know, is located on Regents Road, between Prescot Road and Taylor Park) – I may be wrong but I suspect *Debrett's* does not include amongst its other entries too many members of this august establishment!

The changing rooms at Cowley School
and the track at Ruskin Drive
featured in the film
CHARIOTS OF FIRE.

Brendan O'Neill

Brendan O'Neill may not be a name which is familiar to everyone but his legacy will certainly not have gone unnoticed. Whilst Chief Executive of Guinness Brewing Worldwide, Brendan was responsible for the introduction of the Guinness Irish Pub Concept. This in turn led to the proliferation of Irish bars across the globe as he sought to market his product with the selling point that wherever you were in the world, the Guinness you bought would be exactly the same as the Guinness you bought at home. In a way, it was a strange marketing strategy as the majority of people I knew who drank Guinness always used to claim that the Guinness they drank at home was not a patch on the Guinness you could buy in Dublin. However regardless of the rights and wrongs of this debate, it is undoubtedly the case that Brendan's time at Guinness was a major success. At least he left there on a high, moving seamlessly to the even more prestigious post of Chief Executive at ICI.

Brendan was born on 6th December 1948, son of John, a doctor, and Doris. He was raised with his two younger twin brothers in Denton's Green and attended West Park Grammar School, where he was one of my prefects. He spent his final year there as head boy and even at the time one sensed that he saw great things in prospect for himself. From there Brendan went to Churchill College, Cambridge where he studied Natural Sciences before moving on to the University of East Anglia to do a PhD in Chemistry. It seems his experience there had the consequence of turning him away from his intended career as a scientist and into the somewhat less esoteric world of industry.

Following completion of his studies Brendan resurfaced in the North West for a few years, working as a financial analyst initially with Ford and then with the late but not so lamented vehicle manufacturer British Leyland. He jumped ship in 1981, possibly recognising that it didn't have too bright a future, and moved to London where he worked briefly for BICC and then Midland Bank (arguably another basket case at the time as it had just embarked on a disastrous attempt to penetrate the US market) before settling down in 1987 (well for eleven years anyway) in a variety of roles at Guinness. It should be borne in mind that Guinness was only just emerging from the Distillers debacle which led to the imprisonment of the "Guinness Four" so Brendan was clearly not afraid of a challenge. However this move clearly worked for him and in 1993 he was appointed to the main board and given the top job within the brewing business. His success in that role no doubt tempted ICI who recruited him in May 1998, initially as Chief Operating Officer, with Brendan stepping up to take on the Chief Executive role the following year.

ICI was of course yet another multinational group in transition, this time away from the old bulk chemicals business founded on heavy industry into what Brendan saw as the vibrant, new age, specialty market. He was naturally under great scrutiny in the role and certainly didn't shy away from the publicity, giving a number of interviews promoting the new business model. He was not afraid to take difficult decisions either, whether it was the job cuts which inevitably came with the transformation or the move away from the iconic headquarters at Millfield in London to somewhat more modern accommodation behind Selfridges on Oxford Street. Sadly, there was no happy ending to his time at ICI. After publishing disappointing results at the beginning of 2003 (which led to the share price falling to a ten-year low), a profits warning in March (caused in part by a software failure which led to raspberry flavours going into strawberry yoghurts!) proved to be the last straw. Brendan had lost the support of the investors and fund managers with the financial press reporting that he "had fallen on his sword".

Brendan's reputation was not entirely tarnished and he retained a string of non-executive appointments, most notably at Tyco the troubled US manufacturer. He did however pretty much disappear from the public profile when he stepped down from the ICI job.

It would not be unfair to make the observation that Brendan's biggest successes were probably in the area of marketing. He also knew how to market himself – a profile in the *Daily Mail,* as part of a series entitled "How I got where I am", contained the quote: "Basically I am a people person" which prompted the wry observation from a school friend of mine that this could not be the same Brendan O'Neill who used to regard the rest of the human race as a sub-species. On another occasion *The Financial Times* described him as a "six foot three rugby playing giant" and whilst it is undoubtedly correct that Brendan was six foot three, rugby was certainly not on his CV at school, nor indeed in his later years when he once confided in us that he had given up hope of finding a sport in which his performance was mediocre rather than shocking. But there were other areas which he promoted which did have more basis in truth. He liked to share with journalists the contrast between his musical tastes (which were very much rooted in the 1960s hippy era and included the likes of The Grateful Dead as well as Bob Dylan) and the musical tastes of other FTSE 100 Chief Executives. And despite his academic background at Cambridge University, he never tried to hide his upbringing nor change an accent which the press would from time to time highlight as evidence of his relatively humble roots.

Brendan's family life has been somewhat more stable than his career in industry. Married for many years to Margaret, whom he first met during his schooldays, he has one son and two daughters. He may not be the best-known of our exports nor can he claim to have been as successful as other industrialists such as John Rylands or Sir Michael Smurfit, but he is certainly another who would make the shortlist of the most colourful characters the town as produced.

Between 1917 and 1957 chemical warfare and nerve agents were manufactured at a site in Sutton Oak.

Lily Parr

Lily Parr is arguably the town's most under-exploited brand but that probably reflects the esteem in which women's football is generally regarded in this country. In the United States, by contrast, where the women's game is huge, one suspects she would have legendary status. There was a time in this country however when women's football was attracting crowds which were at times comparable to those watching the men's game. This state of affairs was shamefully brought to an unseemly end by the Football Association in 1921, when it issued an edict banning women from playing on any football league ground on the basis that "the game is quite unsuitable for females and should not be encouraged". The women's game has never really recovered from this body blow.*

Lily was born on 26th April 1905 and lived in Union Street, near Lowe House Church. Her parents were George, a glass worker, and Sarah. Lily was the fourth child of seven and it seems from a very early age that she had no interest whatsoever in what were at the time regarded as standard female pursuits, instead playing both football and rugby with her elder brothers. As a result of her large and robust build she was able to hold her own in most sports. It was football however which appealed to her most and she would spend many hours on her own perfecting her technique. At the age of 14 she started to play for St Helens Ladies, who were at the time a pretty decent team in women's football which had been undergoing something of a boom in the post-war years.

One of Lily's very early games was against the strongest team in the country, the Dick, Kerr Ladies from Preston, named after the munitions factory in which they worked. The team had formed in the First World War and had raised significant amounts of money for charity. The St Helens Ladies were their closest rivals but it seems nearly always lost when they played against them. However it was in this match that Lily came to the attention of the Albert Frankland, the Dick, Kerr Ladies team boss. He persuaded her and a teammate, Alice Woods, to move to Preston to play for his team whilst at the same time providing them with a job in the factory for which they were paid ten shillings a week. It is said that Lily asked to be paid in part in Woodbine cigarettes – whether this was true or not, it was certainly the case that Lily was a lifelong heavy smoker and Woodbines were her cigarette of choice.

In Lily's first season for the Dick, Kerr Ladies – and let's remember that for the major part of the season she is still only 14 years old – she scored a staggering 43 goals and earned the reputation of being able to score from anywhere on the pitch. Already nearly six feet tall and with a shot supposedly as hard as any male footballer, Lily attracted the attention of the press far and wide. Her willingness to get stuck in, her competitive spirit and her tough approach set her aside from other women footballers, but observers were also enthralled by her speed and excellent ball control. A local newspaper suggested at the time that "There is probably no greater football prodigy in the whole country".

The Dick, Kerr, Ladies with Lily at the front holding the ball.
Photograph courtesy of Gail Newsham

During that season Albert Frankland invited the Societies Feminine Sportives de France to come to England to play a series of international matches against the Dick, Kerr Ladies. Lily played in these games, the first of which was at Deepdale, home of Preston North End and which attracted a crowd of 25,000. Three more games followed in this country followed by a tour of France in which the Ladies played another four games. England won five of the games, France one and there were two draws. On their return to England, the Ladies began a series of fundraising games for ex-servicemen, the first at Deepdale (when floodlighting was provided by two anti-aircraft searchlights) and then on Boxing Day 1920 at Goodison Park against Lily's old club, the St Helens Ladies, which was watched by a crowd of over 50,000. Two weeks after that they played another charity game, this time against Bath Ladies, at Old Trafford in front of 35,000 spectators, a game in which Lily scored four goals.

In 1921 the Dick, Kerr Ladies played a total of 67 matches in front of more than 900,000 spectators. Two matches which stood out were a game against the Best of Britain which they won 9-1, with Lily pitching in for five goals and then, with the team representing England against the French national side, Lily scored all five goals in a 5-1 victory. Most of their games were covered on *Pathe* newsreels and Lily was fast becoming a national hero. However that was as good as it got – a bombshell was about to drop.

One of the main problems was that most of the players came from working class backgrounds and much of the money now raised by the team was going to causes not popular with the establishment. For example, help was being provided to many miners who were in dispute with the mine owners over pay cuts. On top of this there was a general resentment of the fact that many women were now doing jobs that had traditionally been done by men (a legacy of the First World War) yet there was large unemployment amongst the male population. Add to this a major concern within the Football Association that the popularity of the women's game was now so great that it might conceivably overtake the men's and one can perhaps see why the FA felt under great pressure. And so, on 5th December 1921, the FA issued the above mentioned edict and thereby dealt a permanent and fatal blow to women's football.

Albert Frankland made valiant efforts to keep the Dick, Kerr Ladies alive, taking them initially on a tour to Canada only to find that the Canadian football authorities would not let them play there. They then went to the United States where they encountered no such problems – indeed they were permitted to play not only against the US women but also against many men's teams there. On this tour the Dick, Kerr Ladies also competed in a challenge race against the American ladies sprint Olympic relay team and actually beat them, with Lily the second of the British quartet to run.

On their return to the UK, the team managed to stay alive through a combination of sheer determination and a never-say-die spirit. They played whenever and wherever they could, ranging from Ashton Park in Preston to various rugby grounds (including Cardiff Arm's Park) and would even practise on a ploughed field if that were the only place available. Problems continued to arise however, particularly after Dick, Kerr and Company Limited was taken over by English Electric, which signalled an end to the team's funding and the loss of many of the girls' jobs.

Lily was one of those who lost her job and she along with some of her teammates was provided with alternative employment and accommodation at Whittingham Hospital and Lunatic Asylum, an organisation for which the Dick, Kerr Ladies had raised a lot of money. As always, Frankland had a hand in this – it seems his sister worked there – but there was in fact a strong basis for employing the girls, which was that the work was difficult and involved long hours, hence employing fit and healthy athletes did make sense. In her first few days Lily was to meet a co-worker, Mary, with whom she fell in love and they became lifelong partners. Characteristically, Lily was very open about the relationship (unusual of course in that era) and few dared to challenge the relationship, at least to her face. In due course the couple bought a house and were to stay together for the rest of their lives.

Despite the severing of the link with Dick, Kerr and Company, Frankland was determined that the team should continue (his motives may not have been squeaky clean here as there were over the years rumours of financial irregularities involving gate receipts and a strong suspicion that he was lining his own pocket, albeit nothing was ever proved) and he rebranded them as Preston Ladies, the name under which they played until their final game in August 1965. Unlike many of the other girls, Lily continued to play, even though the game had a much lower profile and certainly in the war years was difficult to maintain. In 1946 she was made captain and continued to score a plentiful number of goals, despite now playing at full back and even, on occasion, goalkeeper!. She played her last game in 1951, by which time she had a total of 967 goals to her name and since signing for the Dick, Kerr Ladies had missed only five games.

Lily continued to work at Whittington Hospital, concentrating now on her nursing career, eventually reaching the post of Ward Sister, until her retirement in the mid-1960s. In 1967 she developed breast cancer and underwent a double mastectomy (despite which she refused to give up smoking the Woodbines). She fought on for another eleven years but the cancer finally defeated her and she died on 24th May 1978 in Goosnargh. She was laid to rest in St Helens Cemetery, where she was later joined in her resting place by her younger sister Doris.

Lily was without doubt an iconic figure who had almost faded into obscurity and indeed would probably have done so had it not been for the sterling efforts of Gail Newsham, author of *In a League of Their Own* and the person responsible for the website (www.dickkerrladies.com), both of which track the history of the Dick, Kerr Ladies team and are the product of a mountain of research. Her work almost certainly led to Lily receiving posthumous recognition in 2002 by becoming the first female to be inducted into the Football Hall of Fame. Lily has also in recent years become a key figure in lesbian and gay history, such that between 2007 and 2009, the Lily Parr Exhibition Trophy was played for by LGBT teams from England, France and the USA, to commemorate those early games by the Dick, Kerr Ladies.

There is no doubt that Lily was a larger than life character. Although in public, she came over as shy and reserved (she could never manage more than a single sentence when called upon to speak at a post-match reception) she was well-known for her dressing room banter and a dry sense of humour. She also had a reputation of never turning down the opportunity to make a bit of money on the side, often secreting the match ball which she would then sell to supplement her wages. But she also had a softer side, which no doubt helped make a success of her nursing career, and her kindness and generosity were recognised by many. She is truly a worthy contender for the title of "St Helens Finest!"

---

* The ban was not lifted until 1971 and it was not until February 2008 the FA finally issued an apology of sorts.

Michael Parr

St Helens has never been short of actors and indeed the production line of soap stars over the years has been extremely prolific. The question then, is all around who should be included in this collection – in the same way as we are spoilt for choice with rugby league players, so it is undoubtedly the case that we punch above our weight in the soap world. But one man who has arguably achieved that little

Photograph courtesy of St Helens Star.

bit extra is Michael Parr, star of *Emmerdale,* who in 2015 took home no less than four awards at the annual Inside Soap Awards.

Michael was born on 6th August 1986 and was brought up on Hard Lane. He had three younger sisters and because their mother, Glenda Rogers, is American, the children all have dual nationality. Michael went to St Teresa's primary school before moving on to De La Salle College at the age of eleven and finally to Mount Carmel Sixth Form College. Michael's academic career wasn't a particular success however – he was dyslexic and by his own admission not ready to learn. He was more interested in martial arts and he secured brown belts in both Thai and kickboxing. However from very early days there was an element of the showman in his character and it was the acting bug which bit deepest. After having been asked by a teacher to sell tickets for a play in which he wasn't appearing, he resolved, in his own words, "to steal the show!" and thereafter he put himself forward for all the school plays. Conveniently, the Elizabeth Hill School of Dance and Drama was just around the corner in Greenfield Road and after studying there, Michael went to the East 15 Acting School at the University of Essex, from which he graduated with a degree in drama.

Post-graduation, Michael's first roles in theatre were playing a male prostitute in *The Back Room* and an artist's muse in *Studies for A Portrait*. He also managed occasional slots on television, with brief appearances in *Hollyoaks, Casualty* and *Doctors* as well as a few small film roles. However in between acting jobs, he still needed to pay the bills – living in Camden doesn't come cheap. Initially he worked as a barman but then applied for and was taken on as a learning assistant in a special needs school in Essex – a role which he has described as both the most difficult and the most rewarding of any he has ever done.

The big break came in 2013 when he was offered the role of bad boy Ross Barton in *Emmerdale*. Michael admits to almost having a panic attack at the prospect of uprooting himself from London and moving to Leeds where all the filming is done. However it was an opportunity he could not turn down and *Emmerdale* has of course propelled him dramatically into the public consciousness with a nomination as early as the following year for Best Newcomer in the National Television Awards. And then of course came 2015 with the Inside Soap Awards for Best Actor, Best Bad Boy and Sexiest Male, whilst *Emmerdale* itself won the award for Best Soap.

Now an established television star, Michael's life has changed somewhat – not least because his appearances in the tabloid newspapers have become commonplace. It did appear at one stage that his *Emmerdale* career was over after his on-screen character had apparently been murdered. But it turned out that he survived the attack and was soon back on our screens – and it would seem he is likely to be there for the foreseeable future!

Away from filming Michael has been heavily involved in the Steve Prescott Foundation and in October 2016 he completed the hike to Kala Pattar via the Everest Base Camp – a journey which took him to a finishing height of 5,645 metres above sea level and enabled him to raise the best part of £10,000 for the charity.

Michael Pennington (aka Johnny Vegas)

I t is not immediately obvious to me why, but I have on several occasions, including in the national press, seen Johnny Vegas referred to as "St Helens finest". I am never quite sure how I should interpret this piece of information. Should I simply take it as the ultimate compliment to Johnny with no hidden agenda present? Or was there a subtext? Was this a subversive way of saying to the folk of St Helens "and that's the best you can manage?" It goes without saying that I will assume that it is the former which is the correct interpretation, in which case we

Photograph courtesy of Johnny Vegas.

should warmly applaud his contribution to the national image of the town.

It is certainly the case that if one casually drops into conversation the words "famous people from St Helens", a fairly frequent response will be on the lines, "Who is there? Apart from Johnny Vegas?" This is perhaps not surprising since he is certainly a larger-than-life character and he makes frequent appearances on our television screens, as well as being quoted on a whole range of subjects in the press. Not too long ago I came across a report in *The Guardian* education supplement of a session he ran at the "What's the point of art school?" conference in which he expressed some typically forthright views. Moreover he has never made a secret of his origins nor his affiliation to the rugby club, frequently being photographed wearing a Saints baseball cap perhaps most famously when dining with Johnny Depp, though sadly, the rumours that Depp accompanied him to Knowsley Road which abounded at the time, do not appear to have any basis in fact. His autobiography even includes, in the acknowledgements at the end, the following tribute:

> "To St Helens, for the honest to goodness decent folk who populate it and for having the greatest Rugby League team on the face of the planet. For being the town that makes me sad to leave, proud to preach about whilst away and eternally glad to come home to! I'm SAINTS until I die, I'm SAINTS until I die, I know I am, I'm sure I am, I'm SAINTS until I die".

I think we can safely conclude that his attachment to the place is genuine!

It was however his autobiography, titled *Becoming Johnny Vegas* and published in 2013, which revealed a character that very few knew existed. That character is not Johnny Vegas but Michael Pennington. This is the Michael Pennington who was born on 5th September 1970 to Laurence and Pat, with two elder brothers, Robert and Mark and an elder sister, Catherine.

The family lived in Thatto Heath and Michael was raised as a devout Catholic. After attending St Austin's Primary School, he chose to enter the seminary at Upholland to train as a priest at the age of eleven – there was even an angelic picture of Michael in the *St Helens Reporter*, accompanied by an article entitled "Three for the Priesthood". The book tells of the emotional scars which that experience left, his desperation to leave but the impossibility of sharing this desperation with the family. He tells how he felt he had missed out on childhood, how he returned from the seminary as a 30-year-old but in a child's body. We then learn about the self-loathing he endured during his time at West Park Grammar School and later at Carmel College, the beatings he suffered at the hands of his elder brothers and the embarrassment which came from his lack of sexual experience. We find out all about his paranoia that he had cancer but felt totally unable to share this with anyone. His decision to study pottery follows (he has a degree in Art and Ceramics), the reaction at home ("But you're from Thatto Heath!"), his time as a barman at the Brown Edge and finally his resolve to carve out a career in comedy. But it wasn't

Michael Pennington who was to have the career in comedy. This is where Johnny Vegas enters the story.

The decision to go into comedy did not signal, by any means, the end of Michael's torments. He (as opposed to Johnny) was terrified of going on stage. To appear on stage, he had to summon up Johnny and to summon up Johnny meant downing copious amounts of alcohol. Even that was not straightforward. He could not afford to overdo it, at least not until after the performance. And he also had to manage very carefully the pace at which he would drink – too quickly and he would end up vomiting with nerves before he went on to the stage. When Johnny (or Michael?) died on stage at the Edinburgh Festival in 1995 final of the "So You Think You're Funny?" competition, despite being the odds on favourite having wiped the floor with the competition in the qualifying round, this was wholly attributable to the fact that he could not afford any alcohol beforehand. It was, as he puts it, "an unholy and unmitigated disaster….the unimaginable prospect of going on stage sober".

Alcohol, unsurprisingly, is a constant theme in the life of Michael and is essential to the persona of Johnny Vegas. The autobiography ends when Michael gives in to Johnny and lets him take over completely. In his own words he was now "a much-lauded, highly-functioning professional drunk riding high behind the wheel of an 18 stone monster truck of inevitable tragedy". One suspects Part II of the autobiography will cover the subsequent years of trying to become Michael Pennington again.

Johnny won the Festival Critics award in 1997 and was nominated for a Perrier award. He has won a host of other awards, including Best Newcomer at the British Comedy Awards in 2001, Comedian of the Year at the *GQ* awards in 2003, the Les Dawson Award for Comedy in 2005 as well as several awards from the Royal Television Society and a nomination for the Golden Rose of Montreux.

It is fair to say that Johnny broke new ground in comedy. He would always introduce himself as an entertainer and not a stand-up. Much of his early material – in so far as he had material – was of the "you don't know what it's like to be me" variety in which he laid his soul bare to the world. He would lay into other comics, not realising that this was a cardinal sin in stand-up. Nobody had ever seen anyone ranting at audiences in the way Johnny did, doing his pottery on stage whilst conducting wild singalongs with the audience, overrunning with total abandon and finishing the evening in crazy alcohol-fuelled parties. It certainly ruffled a few feathers and wasn't everyone's cup of tea by a long way. But Johnny Vegas had arrived with a very loud bang

But it is not only on the stage that you will see or hear Johnny Vegas. He has been on our screens for many years, most notably in the PG Tips advert (with the monkey) but he has also appeared in a string of television programmes including three series of the sitcom *Benidorm* and seven series of *Ideal*, a dark comedy series in which Johnny plays the lead character, Moz, who is a drug dealer in Salford. His roles however have not been limited to comedy – there were many plaudits for the serious role he played in the Andrew Davies 2005 adaptation of the Charles Dickens classic *Bleak House*. He takes the part of Krook, a rather unpleasant character, who owns a bottle shop and seems to spend most of his life drinking its contents – perhaps appropriate given Johnny's long-time relationship with alcohol. In the same year he also played Bottom in the BBC production of *A Midsummer Night's Dream* although as far as I am aware there was no drink connection in that one.

Johnny has appeared in film although it has not really been a highlight of his career – well not so far at least. *The Sex Lives of Potato Men* was universally panned and indeed described in a number of reviews as possibly the worst film ever made. Some accolade. *The Libertine* (with Johnny Depp) had at best mixed reviews as did Mel Smith's *Blackball*, although it has to be said that making an entertaining film around the game of bowls was always going to be a challenge.

More recently, Johnny has moved into the director's chair and in 2013 directed two episodes in Jimmy McGovern's *Moving On* series as well as *Ragged*, a Sky Arts drama and a feature-length radio version of the 1963 classic *This Sporting Life* in which he recruited several St Helens players to bring the noises of the rugby field to life.

Johnny's personal life has not been without its ups and downs. He married Kitty Donnelly in San Francisco in 2002 after a whirlwind romance and sold the wedding pictures to *Viz* for £1. They had one child, Michael, but the marriage didn't last and they separated in 2004. Although there were attempts at reconciliation, it was to no avail and a messy divorce followed in 2008. In 2011 Johnny married Maia Dunphy, the Irish television producer, in a private ceremony in Seville and in 2015 they welcomed their first child, Tom Laurence, into the world.

I have the distinct feeling that anything I write about Johnny Vegas (or his alter ego Michael) is nothing more than work in progress. There is clearly much more to come. But for the time being, the only place to finish is with the name of Johnny's company – who else but he would use the name "Woolyback Productions Limited"? Pure class and it would be nice to think that it will make the big time at some point in the future.

So, the key question – is he indeed St Helens finest? If not, then he is certainly up there with any other contenders for that title!

Pilkington Family

I t is not difficult to work out where to start with the Pilkington family – WILLIAM, born in 1800, and his elder brother RICHARD, born in 1795, were the two founder partners and they must take pride of place. The difficulty however is where to stop. William for example had 14 children (albeit two died as infants) whilst Richard had a mere six (well he didn't marry until he was 42 so hadn't left himself much time!) Of course not all went to work in the family business but even the most cursory reading of the history of the company will throw up a legion of names, all connected with the Pilkington family and a great number of whom were involved at some stage with the business. Professor Theo Barker in his definitive work *The Glassmakers: Pilkington 1826–1976* identifies 29 direct descendants of William and Richard who served as directors of the company and most of these would qualify for inclusion in this collection as for many years it was a requirement that Pilkington directors must live in or close to St Helens. Education however was another matter entirely, as pretty much all were educated elsewhere: Eton, Harrow, Shrewsbury, Ampleforth, Dulwich, Rugby and Winchester are just some of the schools which feature on the CVs of the family directors.

The Pilkington family (or this branch at least) had originated in Horwich. The move to St Helens came about because William Pilkington (father of the William and Richard referred to above) became apprenticed to a doctor in St Helens in 1781. He then had a spell at St George's Hospital in London, before returning to the town as a partner in a medical practice. Quite how much medicine was administered is questionable, unless one includes the administration of alcoholic drinks in that classification. Like many doctors at the time, he ran a wines and spirits business, and indeed one which was so successful that in 1813 Dr Pilkington decided to abandon his medical practice and move full-time into the wines and spirits world. This business was based in Church Street in the town centre and it seems the family lived on the premises. Dr Pilkington retired in 1826 and went to live in Windle

Hall with its large surrounding estate. Richard, still unmarried, moved with him whilst William, his wife and already large family, stayed on.

It was in that same year that the glass business began, initially as the St Helens Crown Glass Company, when William Jnr agreed to provide capital to fund two glassmakers with technical knowhow, John William Bell and Thomas Bell. Peter Greenall of the brewing family (who was William's brother-in-law) also invested as did another local family, the Bromilows. The business started production at the end of 1827 but very soon started to encounter difficulties, notably with the Commissioners of Excise. Court proceedings ensued which apparently cost John William Bell so much money that in 1828 both Bells had to sell their share of the partnership to the other investors, which seems a bit unfair given that they actually won the case. However this led to William taking charge and he made his mark at an early stage, dismissing James Bromilow, who was the bookkeeper, for incompetence. This led to the Bromilows also leaving the partnership and at this point William's elder brother Richard came in to look after the books. So almost by accident, the two brothers were thrust into a position where they had to run the business. In 1829 the company was renamed Greenall and Pilkington.

It is fairly clear that it was William, who was the driving force behind the business. Chairman from the beginning and a wonderful salesman, it was he rather than the elder Richard, who was responsible for nursing the early business through the trials and tribulations which it encountered and then to go on to build it into a leading British glassmaker. But it was a marriage made in heaven in that the quiet, religious and totally trustworthy Richard was the perfect foil to his much more active brother and exactly the right person to look after the shop while William was away. Together they built the foundations for the multinational corporation which was to emerge in the future.

By 1837 the business was flourishing sufficiently that the decision was made to dispense with the family wines and spirits business. The equipment was sold and the premises let out as a shop, which meant that William's family had to move out. They removed to Millbrook House in Eccleston which they rented from the Greenall family – all very incestuous. However in 1845, shortly before his death, Peter Greenall withdrew from the partnership. The reason for his withdrawal is not entirely clear but may have had something to do with his involvement as a Member of Parliament in pushing through the St Helens Improvement Bill despite local opposition from landowners and industry. In 1849 the business was renamed Pilkington Brothers.

The business went from strength to strength, partly because of the early decision to move away from the production of crown glass into the manufacture of sheet glass and by 1860, Pilkington and two other glass making firms were responsible for 75 per cent of all the window glass made in this country.

Richard passed away in 1869 and William retired that same year. At this point he was living in Eccleston Hall but then moved to North Wales to see out his retirement. He lasted only another three years however and died in 1872.

At the time at which William and Richard moved on, four of their sons were already involved in the business and they now took up the reins. We are told these were very much men on a mission, but driven not by a desire to make profit for themselves but simply the urge to develop and grow the business. Moreover they were prepared to back this up with their own money and invest heavily to make things happen.

It was, by all accounts, William son of Richard (known as WILLIAM WINDLE) who was the outstanding partner of the second generation. Born in 1839 and educated at Bruce Castle in Tottenham (there are no clues as to why this establishment was chosen), he was actively involved in the business until the year of his death, 1914, at the age of 74. He has been described as the person responsible for making Pilkington one of the most technically advanced glass companies in the world – not as an inventor but as someone who would exploit and develop the technical advances made by others. He became a mayor of St Helens (as did his brother Richard) and was well-known for his benevolence. Like his father he was a committed member of the congregational church whereas his uncle William and his cousins had abandoned the non-conformist traditions of the family and attended Christ Church in Eccleston, a relatively new Anglican place of worship.

William Windle had married Louise Salter in 1867 and it fell to two of their children, brothers AUSTIN AND CECIL PILKINGTON to be the main movers and shakers within the third Pilkington generation.

Austin was the elder of the two - born as a twin in 1871, he had been educated at Shrewsbury and Oxford before joining Pilkington in 1894. He did however suffer from ill-health, having contracted tuberculosis (his twin brother, a strong athlete, had died five years earlier from lung problems) and, almost as a last resort, in 1907 moved with his wife and family to Colorado on the basis that the air there was particularly dry and thin. He had a house built between Colorado Springs and Denver which he named Windle Springs and whilst there continued to stay in close touch with the Pilkington business, both in the UK and North America. The climate seemed to have the desired effect and in 1914 he was able to return to St Helens with his family, taking up residence in Eccleston Grange on Prescot Road and resuming a full-time directorship. After the war years, in which he served with the 5th South Lancashire Battalion, he became chairman unexpectedly in 1921 following the death of the then chairman Arthur Pilkington at the age of 50.

Austin was undoubtedly very able and also exceptionally active but it seems he did have his faults, one being unpredictability and, more seriously as it turned out, a total inability to delegate. A nonconformist like his father and grandfather before him, totally honest and dedicated, he was nonetheless somewhat idiosyncratic – he would often be seen for example wandering around St Helens in an old raincoat and scruffy hat, sometimes with important documents stuffed into the pockets. One gets the impression that he was somewhat aloof and possibly disconnected from the workforce.

Cecil was born in 1875 and also educated at Shrewsbury and Oxford, before joining the family firm in 1897. Unlike his elder brother, he was very hands on; he worked well with the employees and would sometimes work with them throughout the night, leading a team of engineers. He was a master of the technical side, with a huge practical knowledge of the glassmaking process. Unfortunately his personal life was also blighted by ill health, not his own but that of his wife and son. It was his wife's desire to live in a healthier place than St Helens (!) which prompted the Board of Directors to agree in 1929, for the first time, that a director could live elsewhere. The deal was that Cecil would work in St Helens from Monday to Thursday afternoon and to reflect his reduced involvement his salary would be halved. Following this agreement he moved permanently to Oxford where he based himself for the rest of his days. He passed away in 1966.

Both brothers were intelligent, active and enthusiastic and once again, they complemented each other perfectly. Austin was a complete master of the commercial side of the business whilst Cecil's knowledge of the technical side was second to none. The advancement of both had been accelerated by a combination of death and early retirement of other members of the Pilkington family. Their period of stewardship was also not without its challenges which included, inter alia, a world recession. They did however deliver to the next generation a business built on much firmer foundations than the one which they themselves had inherited, not least because of the advances it had made in the rapidly growing safety glass industry.

The two brothers epitomised in many ways the paternalistic nature of the business. Following a redundancy programme in the mid-1920s, they personally set up and funded a displaced glassmakers' compensation fund. It was also under their watch that the staff superannuation and employee pension schemes were set up, well ahead of their introduction by much better known major UK companies. The brothers did not become national figures in the way that many other industrialists of the time, such as Samuel Courtauld or Seebohm Rowntree, did. It was as if they felt they had a duty to work hard for both the company and the community and the less anybody else knew about their business, so much the better. But it was their resistance to change which proved, in part at least, their undoing. The management structure, to the extent that it existed at all, had changed little since the partnership days of the 19th century. Austin and Cecil, together with the other main directors of the time, all got on with their own thing, had little interest in delegation or co-ordination and did not appear to perform any of the oversight that one would expect directors in their position to do.

The end came as a consequence of a combination of events: the introduction into the business during the late 1920s and early 1930s of further members of the fourth generation of Pilkingtons (there had only been one up to that point) followed by some poor trading results in the period to 31st March 1931. There appears to have been a bit of a bust up around that time between Austin and Cecil which prompted both to proffer their resignations as executive directors. In Austin's case, the exchange of correspondence with the Board makes it clear that running the business without any delegation of authority had taken a great toll on his health and he was offered a six month leave of absence by the Board.

Whilst it was unfortunate that their period at the helm should end in this manner, both brothers did continue as non-executive directors for many years. Austin continued to live in Eccleston Grange and remained on the board until his 80th birthday in 1951. He did not however have long to enjoy his retirement as he died later that year. Cecil by contrast retired earlier – he travelled regularly from Oxford to St Helens for board meetings until his retirement at the age of 75 in 1950 but was then able to spend his final 16 years enjoying life on his farm until his death in 1966 at the age of 91.

I noted earlier the introduction of members of the fourth generation of the Pilkington dynasty to the firm in the late 1920s and it was one of these who became perhaps the best-known of all the Pilkingtons – he was certainly the first to buck the trend and become a national figure. This was WILLIAM HENRY PILKINGTON, eldest son of Austin, who was in the fullness of time to become Sir Harry and then Lord Pilkington.

Lord Harry was born in 1905 and made the move to Colorado with the family at the age of two. Following his return in 1914, he was educated at Rugby and Magdalene College, Cambridge. He joined the company in 1927 and immediately became involved in the sales side of the business.

Lord Harry's generation was the first to have to undergo a rigorous period of training before being accepted into the hierarchy – this was one of the far reaching changes to the managerial structure pushed through by Lord Cozens Hardy after the resignations of Austin and Cecil. Not all of the newcomers made the cut but Harry, who had been made a sub-director in 1930, was, together with another family member, Douglas Phelps, the first to be appointed to the Executive in June 1934. By the following year, at the tender age of 30 and following some unexpected retirements, he became the most senior executive on the commercial side of the business and after progressing steadily within the firm he became Chairman in 1949 with Douglas Phelps as his right hand man.

As Chairman, Lord Harry was content to leave Douglas Phelps in charge of the day-to-day running of the business whilst he was able to stand back and look at the bigger picture. He was a compulsive traveller, flying thousands of miles around the globe each year. He would also represent the firm in its dealings with government and with business organisations such that his name became one of the best-known in industry at the time.

He remained as Chairman until 1973 during which time he oversaw the most remarkable period of growth in the company's history to date. This included the transformation of the company into a huge international concern, primarily on the back of the development of the float glass process. This was by some distance the most significant leap forward in technology that the manufacturing world of glass had ever seen. He also presided over the landmark strike in 1970 and the decision taken around the same time finally to abandon the private company status which it had treasured for so long and to list its shares on the London Stock Exchange. The company he left in 1973 was in many ways unrecognisable from the one he joined in 1927 but there can be little doubt that he played a very major part in Pilkington becoming the giant that it then was: a company with important manufacturing or processing operations in Europe, across both American continents, the Indian sub-continent and Australasia. It had over 32,000 direct employees, 12,000 of whom worked overseas and many more if one also counted the employees of all the associated companies in which Pilkington had a major interest. Group turnover in 1976 was in excess of £300 million with profit before tax of £34.5 million – not a bad little earner at the time!

As noted above, Lord Harry was the first member of the family to become a public figure, in stark contrast to his predecessors. He became President of the Federation of British Industries in 1953 and was appointed a Director of the Bank of England in 1955, remaining there until 1972. Indeed the list of his outside appointments is endless – he was the president of several trade bodies and federations, a member of many others, Chancellor of Loughborough University, a Director of the New York based Business International Corporation and Chairman of the National Council on Education for Industry and Commerce. He also accepted a number of appointments from government; these included reports into education, medical remuneration, fuel efficiency and broadcasting. Interestingly he was in part responsible for the proliferation of pirate radio stations in the 1960s after the Pilkington Committee which he chaired between 1960 and 1962 concluded that the British public did not want commercial radio and as a consequence applications for broadcasting licences from around 100 commercial radio stations were refused. Not quite the outcome he anticipated!

It was not just in the national realm that Lord Harry was active. He was a Justice of the Peace from 1937, President of the South Lancashire Magistrates Association, the St Helens YMCA, St Helens Rugby League Football Club, St Helens Amateur Operatic Society and Grange Park Golf Club as well as being a governor of St Helens Technical College.

Multiple honours found their way to his door. He was awarded honorary degrees from the Universities of Manchester, Liverpool, Loughborough and Kent, and he was made a Freeman of St Helens, Deputy Lieutenant of Lancashire and Vice Lord Lieutenant of Merseyside. Fellowships at the Royal Society of Arts, the British Institute of Management and the Institute of Building were bestowed upon him. And of course he received his knighthood in 1953 and became a Life Peer in the New Year's Honours of 1968. It was as if he was making up for all those years and generations of Pilkingtons who had elected to stay under the radar.

It is a wonder Lord Harry was ever able to find time for his day job. That he was able to do this as successfully as he did and at the same time incorporate into his schedule all his other engagements and responsibilities, led his successor, on the occasion of Lord Harry's retirement to comment that he had set both a good and bad example – good because he was so active, creative and buoyant, but bad because to try and follow in his footsteps would kill off most people.

Lord Harry remained based in St Helens all of his life, having moved into Windle Hall, still a Pilkington family residence in 1930, on the occasion of his marriage to his first wife, Margaret ("Peggy") Rowan, with whom he had one son and two daughters. Peggy died in 1953 and in 1961 Lord Harry married Mavis Wilding. He passed away in 1983.

And so we move onward to the fifth and final generation of the Pilkington family. The first, and by a long way the most notable, member of this

generation to join the group was ANTONY RICHARD PILKINGTON
– later Sir Antony. Born in 1935 and a great-great-grandson of founder
Richard Pilkington, Antony was educated at Ampleforth and Trinity
College Cambridge. He was unusual in that he was a Roman Catholic, as
had been his father Arthur Cope Pilkington who had been advised when
he joined the firm that "the question of his religion would not prejudice
your interests so long as it does not interfere with the business". Antony
attained the rank of Lieutenant in the Coldstream Guards before joining
Pilkington in 1959 as a trainee working in UK and export sales. He did,
in due course, progress to become chairman of the group and has the
distinction of being the last family member to hold this position.

Antony's initial advancement came with his promotion to marketing
manager of the flat glass division in 1959 and he joined the board in 1973.
He became deputy chairman in 1979 to the founder of the float glass
process, Sir Alastair Pilkington*. It was the float glass process, developed
in the mid-1950s which had catapulted the company into world leadership
and had created a handsome stream of royalties which had in turn
underpinned Pilkington's earnings for many years. However by the
time Antony came to the helm in 1980 the golden days had long gone
and he was instead facing the onslaught of the industrial recession of
the early 1980s from which the UK's manufacturing industry has
arguably never recovered.

Antony did therefore preside over difficult times. The 1980s recession
hit the company hard and the workforce was reduced dramatically as a
consequence – of the 11,500 workers in St Helens in 1981 only 6,500
remained by 1986. However under his leadership the company was accorded
much credit for the manner in which it dealt with the redundancies. Terms
were generous and help was provided for those who had been made
redundant via the pioneering Community of St Helens Trust which had been
set up in 1978. Antony was the first chairman of the trust which was in turn
the first local enterprise agency in the UK and provided the model for many
others which were set up throughout the UK during the 1980s.

During the 1980s Antony also oversaw the Pilkington involvement
in Ravenhead Renaissance, a ground breaking partnership between the
private and public sectors – Pilkington, British Gas and Milverny
Properties (now the Greenbank Partnership) represented the private

sector with St Helens Council representing the public. Ravenhead Renaissance went on to deliver over £500m of infrastructure and property development projects into the town.

There were other challenges Sir Antony had to face whilst at the helm. In 1986 the predatory BTR, an industrial conglomerate which had grown by acquisition followed by ruthless cost cutting, made a hostile bid to take over Pilkington. Politicians, including government ministers, the local council, the employees, the trade unions, just about the whole of St Helens joined the board in its attempt to maintain its independence. The strapline of "Pilkington, the world's leading glassmaker – let's keep it that way" was to be seen everywhere in the town and the local media. The defence was successful and after an arduous nine week battle, BTR was forced to withdraw with its tail between its legs. The contrast with the rather meek surrender to Nippon glass in 2006 could not have been greater.

During his time in charge Antony Pilkington was praised for the transparency he brought to bear – he was quoted in February 1987 as saying, "A company is not just pieces of paper. You have strategy, people, a community and an effect on a nation's economy". But not everything that he touched turned to gold. His attempt to broaden the Pilkington business into spectacle and contact lenses by acquisition in 1987 presented the group with a multitude of problems leading ultimately to their divestment between 1993 and 1995. And he was faced with yet another industrial recession in the early 1990s, just when Japanese and US glassmakers were entering the European market place and when competition from the French glassmaker Saint Gobain was intensifying. However he was not afraid to take the first steps on the path which he thought would be required to take Pilkington's into the 21st century: he commenced the reform of Pilkington's old fashioned hierarchical management system, placed great emphasis on the importance of salesmanship and was forever searching for new ways to reshape the group to help it respond to market conditions. His contribution was recognised by a knighthood in the Queen's Birthday Honours of 1990.

In 1995 Sir Antony retired and was replaced by the first non-family chairman, Nigel Rudd. He continued to pursue his other interests – he was, at various times, a Director of GKN, National Westminster Bank and ICI, he was a Governor of Liverpool John Moores University, a member of the Court of Manchester University, a Deputy Lieutenant of Merseyside and High Sheriff of Cheshire. Sadly he did not live to enjoy his retirement for very long, passing away at the age of 60 in the year 2000.

Sir Antony has been described as a gentleman of the old school, not necessarily comfortable in City circles. He was a somewhat reserved character who could come across as slightly diffident. By contrast, he was renowned for his love of fast cars and motor racing. He would drive to work in a 1956 Maserati and was an enthusiastic collector of prestigious cars. His interest was said to stem from a car purchased for him by his parents to entice him away from motor bikes. This was a HRG Sports two-seater in 1951 and he went on from there to build up a collection described as "wonderful" by the chairman of the auctioneers Bonhams. He competed personally in the Mille Liglia, a gruelling 100 mile race through Italy in one of his cars, a Maserati 300s. In 2012, some years after his death, the auction of his remaining five cars created quite a stir in the classic car community. Interestingly, a random google generates more references to the posthumous auction of his cars than it does to his lifetime's work

Sir Antony had married in 1960 into the Dundas dynasty which dates back to Sir Lawrence Dundas, a Scottish businessman, landowner and politician in the 18th century. His wife, Kirsty Dundas, by whom he had three sons and a daughter, was herself awarded an MBE in 2010 and in 2012 was made an honorary freeman of St Helens in recognition of her services in the voluntary sector and her support of local arts.

This brings to an end the Pilkington story. The company lives on, albeit as a subsidiary of a Japanese company, whilst the family itself continues without any direct link to the company it founded all those years ago. But for 180 years the fortunes of the family, the company and the town were inextricably linked and together they elevated St Helens to a position on the world map rarely occupied by a town of similar size and population.

*   Sir Alistair Pilkington was not actually from St Helens and was at best a distant relative of the St Helens Pilkington family – see the chapter "Not From St Helens".

Robert Rodney Porter

It may come as a surprise to many but St Helens can count amongst its ranks a Nobel Prize winner. This momentous event took place in 1972 when the somewhat unheralded Rodney Robert Porter took the Nobel Prize in Physiology or Medicine together with his colleague Gerald Edelman, for their work in determining the chemical structure of an antibody – not an area I am familiar with nor one which, even having read in more detail the nature of the discovery, I could even begin to understand. What does seem to be clear however is that the work of the duo was ground-breaking in its field.

Rodney Robert was actually born as Robert Rodney Porter on 8th October 1917 in Newton-le-Willows. Interestingly his birth seems to have been registered three times on the same page in the Warrington register of births, once as Robert R, once as Robert RP and once as Robert S, unless by an amazing coincidence three women with the maiden name of Reese and the married name of Porter all gave birth to a son which they named Robert in the same quarter. Born to Joseph, a railway clerk, and Isobel, Rodney was an only child.

It is recorded that he was fascinated by science from an early age and after leaving Ashton-in-Makerfield Grammar School in 1935, studied Biochemistry at the University of Liverpool, graduating with first class honours in 1939. He started to study for his PhD but the Second World War put paid to that. Rodney served in the Royal Artillery, the Royal Engineers and the Royal Army Service Corps, reaching the rank of Major. He was involved in the invasions of Algeria, Sicily and Italy so it seems this was active service in its fullest meaning. He remained in the Mediterranean until he was demobbed in 1946.

At Liverpool University, Rodney had met and befriended Sam Perry, who was later also to become an eminent biochemist as well as a rugby international. After the war they decided they would enrol together at Cambridge University to complete their PhDs. Rodney worked under the supervision of Fred Sanger, who was also a Nobel Prize winner (and indeed the only Briton ever to have won the Nobel Prize twice) and completed his PhD in 1948. He stayed one more year at Cambridge and then spent the next eleven years at the National Institute for Medical Research at Mill Hill before moving to St Mary's Hospital Medical School as Professor of Immunology. His final move took place in 1967 when he moved to Oxford University as Professor of Biochemistry.

It seems that pretty much all of his career was devoted to the study of antibodies, which certainly sounds an awful lot of time on just one subject but clearly it paid off when he made his breakthrough in 1969. By then he had been elected a Fellow of the Royal Society in 1964, received the Gairdner Foundation International Award for his outstanding contribution to medical science in 1967. After the Nobel Prize in 1972, he received the Royal Medal the following year and, ten years later, the Copley Medal in recognition of his work on the structure of immunoglobulins (which I think is another word for antibodies). His final award was when he was named in the Order of Companions of Honour by the Queen in June 1985.

Rodney married Julia New in Surrey in 1948 and together they had two sons and three daughters. He was to continue working at Oxford University until his untimely death in September 1985 in a road accident in Winchester.

As a final postscript, in 1991 the home of the newly-founded Oxford Glycobiology Institute at the University of Oxford was named the Rodney Porter Building in his memory.

The first place in the world where one railway crossed another was in Sutton Leach in St Helens.

Peter Postlethwaite OBE

Peter Postlethwaite was not born in St Helens, nor did he ever actually live there. Indeed he mentions frequently in his autobiography, *A Spectacle of Dust* published posthumously in 2011, that he hails from Warrington. However he also covers at some length his education at West Park Grammar School and on the basis that it was at school where he first encountered the joys of theatre and where he experienced his introduction to the world of drama, I think we can safely say that St Helens played an integral part in his upbringing. Indeed fired up by the visits he was making to the Everyman Theatre, which was later also to play an important part in his life, he became involved in staging a number of productions at West Park, with one of the De La Salle Christian Brothers, Brother Dominic, acting as producer – *The Importance of Being Earnest* and *A Man for All Seasons* were just two of these. Pete records that it was around this time that he realised that the acting profession was for him, as it would give him an opportunity to be creative whilst at the same time allowing him to make statements on life in general. Theatre became, as he puts it, his abiding passion. That said, it could easily have been the case that neither St Helens nor the wider world would have encountered Pete Postlethwaite as he actually entered the seminary at Upholland as an eleven-year-old with a view to becoming a priest.

He had been born on 7th February 1946 to William and Mary in Warrington and was the youngest of four children. Both of his parents were devout Catholics and he had attended St Benedict's Roman Catholic Primary School. The decision to become a priest was however his own. As with Johnny Vegas, it never happened but Pete seems to have taken it in his stride – certainly in his case there do not seem to have been the emotional scars which contributed so much to the shape of Johnny's life. I think however I am in no fear of contradiction when I say that in Pete's case, the acting profession would have been a poorer place had the priesthood turned out to be his true vocation.

Pete was to become well-known in the acting world as both a smoker and a drinker. St Helens cannot be blamed for the former as it seems that he started smoking at the age of ten, presumably when he was still at St Benedict's Roman Catholic Primary School in Warrington. However it is highly likely that the St Helens influence was at least in part responsible for his fondness for a few beers. He records how he spent a not inconsiderable amount of time in The Bird i'th Hand on Prescot Road (West Park School being in those days located very close by) and also in the Sefton, where the landlord was the father of one of his schoolmates. Much later in life, Pete would commonly be found drinking with his brother Mike in St Oswald's Club in Warrington, causing not a little amusement once he had established his place amongst the Hollywood glitterati.

On leaving school, Pete moved initially to St Mary's teacher training college in Twickenham, choosing to study PE, as he was quite athletic and had in mind to become a PE teacher, with drama as his second subject. It was drama however to which he devoted nearly all his time and effort. After qualifying and spending a brief period at an approved school in Formby, he moved to Loreto College in Manchester to teach English and drama. His passion for the latter however led to a major falling out with the headmistress and he decided to enrol on a two year course at the Bristol Old Vic Theatre School.

From there Pete never really looked back. His acting career began in earnest when he was invited to appear at the Everyman Theatre in Liverpool and he stuck around there for some four years. Colleagues at the time included Julie Walters, with whom Pete was to have a lengthy relationship, Bill Nighy, Matthew Kelly, Jonathan Pryce and many others. From there it was a fairly itinerant existence for the next few years, with appearances pretty much all over the place, including a stint back in Bristol. He was then provided with a gateway into television by Alan Bleasdale as the lead in *The Muscle Market*, following which there were several other TV appearances including *Coronation Street, Last of the Summer Wine* and *Minder* alongside his theatre work until his movie debut in *A Private Function* in 1984.

And it was of course the world of film that was to make him famous – *Distant Voices, Still Lives* in 1988 caused everyone to sit up and take notice, and then his performance as Guiseppe Conlon, one of the wrongly accused Guildford Four, in the 1993 film *In the Name of the Father* secured him his only Oscar nomination and propelled him to worldwide stardom. Pete tells the story of turning up at the Oscar ceremony and initially not being allowed in, on the basis apparently that the security men did not recognise him. It took the intervention of Gregory Peck who happened to be passing at the time and who did recognise Pete from the film, to secure him entry. Given that they had to move one of the "fillers" – those who are hired to sit in empty seats - from his place at the ceremony, one wonders whether or not he may have indulged in a spot of pre-event celebration. This is pure surmise of course but the fact that he does admit that his visit to the US for the Oscars was essentially a week of partying and that a party is no good if you can remember too much about it (and he can't), would suggest that I may not be too far from the mark.

Further performances in films such as *Brassed Off* in 1996 secured for Pete his place as a national institution and he was famously described by none other than Steven Spielberg as the greatest actor in the world following his performance in *The Lost World: Jurassic Park*. IMDb lists in total more than 100 television and film credits, the last of which was in *Killing Bono* in 2011, which was filmed after he was diagnosed as suffering from pancreatic cancer in 2011.

Pete's home was in Shropshire, a county he had come to love and in which he had settled with his partner Jacqui Morrish in the late 1980s. They had two children together, Will in 1989 and Lily in 1996, and had married in 2003. Pete was to spend his final days there with his wife and children, working on his autobiography which was published posthumously later in 2011.

A Spectacle of Dust is certainly worth reading as one is left in no doubt about Pete's passion for acting and his complete and utter dedication to the quality of his performance, regardless of whether it was for theatre, television or film. Indeed, passionate is probably the word that describes him best, whether in the context of acting or one of the many causes, mostly radical, which he espoused. But it is slightly disappointing in other ways – too many of the actors (or actresses) which he encountered during his life were "great guys, we hit it off straight away" for it to have real credibility (the nearest he comes to slagging anyone off was a brief snipe at Bono). And for all his passion, his politics, particularly in relation to Thatcher and the miners' strike, are somewhat simplistic. But then again, when you have achieved in life as much as he did, these are pretty insignificant criticisms and in any case, we cannot know for certain what the book would have been like had he survived to read and, one assumes, edit the final product. One thing that is very clear from his writing is that this is not a man with an ego – the humility comes through loud and clear.

Pete was awarded the OBE in 2004 and received an honorary degree from Liverpool University in 2006. But what is perhaps most striking about his career is that he does not seem to have any detractors. On the contrary, he is almost universally regarded as one of the best British actors ever and did not seem to attract adverse criticism of any sort. I suspect that a major reason for this is the humility that he conveyed in life, whether in his acting or his writing. This is a man who had been told by the head of Bristol Theatre School that he had "a face like a f**king stone archway" and who had been advised on several occasions that to succeed in the acting world he would have to change his name. But it is perhaps the measure of the man that he took the first piece of advice as a compliment and ignored the second.

Steve Prescott MBE

Steve Prescott made 117 appearances for St Helens, scoring 52 tries and kicking 66 goals. He moved to Hull FC where he also made 117 appearances, scoring 56 tries and kicking 197 goals. He spent a season at Wakefield, appearing on 25 occasions, scoring three tries and kicking 13 goals. He played for Great Britain Under 21s, England (for whom he was at one stage the record points scorer in a game with 22 points) and Ireland. He also toured Papua New Guinea and New Zealand with the British Lions. It is clear therefore that by any standards he was an

Steve at the London Marathon
Photograph courtesy of
Saints Heritage Society

excellent rugby player. But what marks him out from the crowd was not his rugby but his response to being diagnosed on 8th September 2006 (the day his second son, Koby, was born) as having a rare form of terminal cancer and being advised that he had only months to live. There was to be no happy ending but the story from there on was to reveal what a truly remarkable man Steve was. The title of his autobiography, *One in a Million*, which was intended to reflect the odds of contracting the cancer from which he suffered, is in fact the most appropriate badge that one could pin on Steve himself.

Steve was born on 26th December 1973, son of Eric and Pat. He was raised in Wingate Avenue, Nutgrove, alongside his elder brother Neil and his younger sister Suzanne. He was educated at St John Vianney on Eltonhead Road, followed by De La Salle School and then briefly Carmel Sixth Form College. It is fair to say he never set his sights on academic success but he was notable from an early age for his sporting prowess, not just on the rugby field but also in athletics and football. But it was no real surprise that he was to end up as a rugby league player – the pedigree was certainly there with his father, Eric, having played for St Helens, Widnes and Salford in a lengthy professional career and his great uncle, Alan, who made over 400 appearances for Saints, having achieved legendary status in the history of rugby league by playing almost the whole of a test match as a prop forward against Australia with a broken arm. So Steve had some big boots to fill when he signed for St Helens in November 1992.

Steve's rugby career, glittering as it was, was littered with, and ultimately ended by, injury. Most of his success arose at St Helens, with cup winning appearances at Wembley in 1996 and 1997 and a championship medal in the first Super League competition in 1996. He recalls fondly however his days at Hull, where he made many friends and where the family settled prior to the career-ending knee injury he suffered playing for Lancashire in 2003. It was not until the following year however that it became clear that he would never play again and although there was some discussion about a legal case against the surgeon who had initially operated on what had seemed to be a straightforward knee injury it all came to nothing.

Steve stayed on in Humberside and started to pursue a career in sporting education as a teaching assistant at Hull College Sports Department. He also played a little bit of rugby union for Hull Ionians. He married his long-time girlfriend Linzi whom he had known since his days at De la Salle College (they already had their first child, Taylor, who was born in 2001) but it was not long before Steve started to think there was something wrong with him – he was suffering from constant bloating and indigestion and was losing strength and fitness. Several visits to the doctor did not pinpoint the problem and it was only when he paid to see a specialist privately that he was given the devastating news.

Steve's initial response was, unsurprisingly, one of complete despair and, in his own mind, an inability to come to terms with the situation. He attributes his turnaround to a visit by his old coach Steve Crooks who inspired him to take the view that however long he had left, he had to spend that time fighting the disease for all he was worth. But not even he could have expected Steve to respond in the truly inspiring fashion which he did.

Together, Steve and Linzi left no stone unturned in their search for some light at the end of the tunnel. They researched the disease (pseudomyxoma peritonei) as best they could, and they consulted far and wide. This involved not just Castle Hill Hospital in Hull, where he was being treated and The Christie in Manchester, to which he was referred, but also a specialist whom they identified in Basingstoke and even a consultant in Washington DC at a world-renowned centre for the disease. Steve underwent an operation in Basingstoke to "debulk" – essentially to remove tumour from the body, although he was advised in advance that they would not be able to remove it all. In the event, they removed ten kilos of tumour, the colon, the spleen, some of the small bowel and some of the stomach. This had a number of consequences – the loss of the spleen meant a big reduction in the effectiveness of the immune system, thus rendering Steve far more likely to pick up infections and the removal of the colon meant that Steve was left with an ileostomy. However, importantly the surgeons were pleased with the results of the operation as it meant that he would have an extended, and a better quality of, life than had first been feared.

Life of course was never going to be the same. Steve now had to undergo chemotherapy, change his diet (despite which change he would suffer a number of extremely painful bowel obstructions) as well as deal with other consequences such as the mucin produced by the tumours which would periodically force itself out through the skin. But undeterred by all of this, the next phase of Steve's life saw him undertake a series of challenges which it would be difficult for the great majority of fit and able persons even to contemplate.

It all began with the Rugby League community rallying around, as it always seems to do in tragic circumstances, and organising a boxing event to raise money for Steve and his family. Steve was initially slightly embarrassed by the whole thing but Lee Radford of Hull fought Stuart Fielden, then of Wigan, at the Hull Ice Arena ("The Rumble by the Humber") in front of 2,000 spectators and the night was a huge success. Other events were organised, including a "Legends" game between the St Helens 1996 Challenge Cup winning side and a team of All Stars which took place at Knowsley Road with nearly 6,000 attending. It was events such as these which led to Steve making the decision that he had to do something himself to inspire others whilst he still could – thus came into being the Steve Prescott Foundation, the purpose of which was to raise money for two charities very close to Steve's heart, The Christie Cancer Hospital in Manchester and the Rugby League Benevolent Fund.

A number of events organised by the Foundation were boxing shows, one at the Reebok stadium in Bolton, one at Batley Frontier and a final one at Sutton High Leisure Centre in St Helens. Together these raised almost £70,000 for the foundation. But it was Steve's own involvement which will inevitably remain most in the memory.

The first of these, which took place in October 2007, was a 199 mile walk from Hull to the Super League Grand Final at Old Trafford via Liverpool. Steve had only just finished a course of chemotherapy so inevitably found it extremely tough, both mentally and physically. He made it however and although he attributed that to others getting him through the ordeal, his resolve to continue and take on more difficult challenges was a direct result of the sense of achievement and, as he put it, the urge "to show people that you can still do things despite being diagnosed with terminal cancer".

More and more challenges followed. Steve ran the London Marathon in April 2008, completed a second Trans-Pennine walk to the Grand Final the following year and then the London Marathon again in April 2009. The barriers were really pushed for the next challenge, a cycle across the length of France from Perpignan to Calais, then from Dover to Uxbridge followed by a 24-mile trip along the Thames in a dragon boat before completing a half-marathon to arrive at Wembley for the Challenge Cup Final. Tougher still was the decision later that year to run from Hull to the Grand Final over a period of four days – the equivalent of four back to back marathons. This challenge was not straightforward for Steve as during the first day he suffered from a bowel obstruction – the sort that would normally have required him to spend a few days in hospital. Despite spending the night on the bathroom floor in agony and not sleeping at all, Steve managed to re-join the runners for the last five miles of the following day which he completed despite an extremely inflamed bowel and a distended and tender abdomen. Day three was then completed in full and day four saw him arrive at Old Trafford with yet another gruelling challenge under his belt.

By now, Steve's mind-set was that he wanted to challenge himself more and more. Next up was a cycle ride from Land's End to John O'Groats over a period of nine days – tough enough in itself – but when you graft on to that the decision to climb Snowdon, Scafell Pike and Ben Nevis on the way, it starts to look positively insane! Then came the idea of running the Paris Marathon, cycling to Calais, kayaking across the English Channel, cycling from Dover to London and then completing the London Marathon. Apart from the kayaking across the English Channel everything went to plan. Initially the challenge had involved just Steve and his old team mate Paul Sculthorpe, but when told that weather conditions meant kayaking was impossible and that the only option was a five-man rowing boat they had to call for reinforcements. Ex-Saints colleagues Chris Joynt, Bernard Dwyer and Steve Hall obliged. They all arrived at short notice late on the Friday night and had to be at the dock for 5.00am – the only window in the weather conditions under which even a rowing boat would be permitted. Nobody had any experience of rowing yet seven and half hours later they had made it. An indication of how rough the waters were can be gleaned from the fact that Martin Blondel (who was in many ways the driving force behind the foundation and most of the challenges) broke two vertebrae after falling over in the support boat.

The last challenge undertaken by Steve was arguably the toughest of the lot. The 48-Hour Challenge involved first of all swimming for one mile and then a 13-hour overnight cycle from the Humber Bridge to Liverpool. Steve did not finish until 7.00am, after enduring torrential rain and nearly gale force winds during the last seven hours of the trip. After a brief rest it was a swim across the Mersey which took place despite dire warnings that it was not safe and that anyone attempting the swim would be risking his life and then a half marathon to the Runcorn Bridge.

The next morning involved kayaking 27 miles along the Bridgewater Canal starting at 6.30am – this part of the trip included a number of unscheduled stops in canal-side pubs but Steve and his colleagues made it to the Grand Final with 15 minutes to spare, just in time to do the coin toss with the Warrington and Leeds captains who were contesting the 2012 Grand Final.

Aside from the challenges, and something that is longer lasting in that it has survived Steve's passing, he and the Foundation were also responsible for the setting up of the St Helens 10k, the sporty fun days in Taylor Park and the Pride of St Helens Awards, all of which have now become regular fixtures in the annual calendar.

All good things must come to an end however and late in 2012 Steve's health started to deteriorate markedly. More chemotherapy was undertaken but the side effects were now getting worse. Steve was admitted to hospital, initially because of a bowel obstruction but he was kept in and his condition continued to worsen. He was transferred from Whiston Hospital to Salford Royal, having lost two stone in weight. After four weeks in Salford Royal, Steve was discharged but by this point his bowel was no longer functioning which meant he had to be fed intravenously and had to enter a nasal-gastro tube up his nose to enable him to aspirate.

It was in July 2013 that Steve received a call out of the blue asking if he could attend a meeting with a surgeon from Oxford to discuss the possibility of a small bowel transplant – something he had always been told was impossible. It was at this meeting that it was suggested to Steve that it might indeed be possible to undertake pioneering surgery and in effect bring about a permanent cure. Unsurprisingly, and despite the obvious risks, Steve grabbed the opportunity with both hands. There was still a lot to go through, notably several operations, one to deal with a kidney obstruction and which required the insertion of ureteral stents, another to deal with an abscess caused by a perforated bowel (which led to a scare that the major surgery might not, after all, be possible) and then an alarming dip in oxygen levels which prompted a short spell in intensive care. He was however finally approved for a transplant and put onto the list. There was then the inevitable wait for suitable organs.

The call finally came on 15th October 2013. From then on everything was a bit of a whirlwind for Steve and Linzi. All the preparatory procedures were put in place, family members rushed down to Oxford and, after what seemed like an interminable wait for the organs to arrive, Steve went under the surgeon's knife. After 32 hours of surgery, the operation was pronounced a success. Steve had finally defeated the cancer that had transformed his life.

Sadly, this did not turn out to be the happy ending we all craved. Complications were to set in and the new organs rejected Steve's body – the converse of a transplant rejection, this is known as Graft Versus Host Disease. Steve passed away at 3.00am on 9th November 2013 at the age of 39.

During his relatively short life there were many accolades which went Steve's way. He was awarded in 2009 the Mike Gregory Spirit of Rugby League Award and in the same year the Arthur Brooks Memorial Award for services to rugby league. An MBE was to follow in 2010. He was guest of honour in the same year at the Challenge Cup Final, presenting the trophy to the winning Warrington team and in 2011 was awarded an honorary degree by the University of Hull. He was also selected that year by the *Independent on Sunday* as one of the top 100 people who make Britain a happier place to live. This apparently caused much amusement amongst friends and family, some of whom, by Steve's own admission, were more likely to categorise him as Mr Grumpy rather than Mr Happy! In the concourse of the new Saints stadium at Langtree Park, he is depicted in one of the murals which pay tribute to the greats who have played for the club throughout its illustrious history and there is a silhouette of him sitting on a park bench next to Johnny Vegas and a glass blower in Sherdley Park.

Since Steve died, we have seen the renaming of the annual Man of Steel Award for the sport's outstanding player as the Steve Prescott Man of Steel Award. St. Helens and Hull FC now play each year for the Steve Prescott Cup and the walkway linking St Helens town centre with Langtree Stadium bears the title of the Steve Prescott Bridge.

Where does all of this leave Steve in the pantheon of St Helens all-time greats? It is difficult to argue that he should be anywhere other than near the very top – indeed it is fitting in many ways that he should have been involved in founding the Pride of St Helens Awards as that is precisely the title that many would apply to him. And this short biography would not be complete without a special mention of Steve's wife Linzi who was at his side and provided invaluable support during a period when together, they defied all the odds and lived by the mantra which Steve adopted, "What the mind believes, the body achieves".

Ray Ranson

Ray Ranson was a footballer who made 233 first team appearances for Manchester City and eleven appearances for the England Under 21 side. He also played professionally for Birmingham City, Newcastle United and Reading, notching up in total some 445 professional league appearances. There were, in the course of these 445 games, only two goals to which he can attach his name, but he was a defender so stopping rather than scoring goals was the job he was employed to do. However it was not just his playing career which prompted his inclusion in this collection, as arguably it is not the football he played that has made his name as widely recognised as it is. It was for his subsequent dealings in the world of football finance for which he became more famous – or as some would prefer to name it, infamous!

Ray was born on 12th September 1960, son of Ray Snr and Margaret. He had a younger brother Paul and was brought up in Manville Street in Peasley Cross. He attended Sutton High School where he did not excel academically but certainly did at football, and indeed was selected to represent England Schoolboys. Unsurprisingly he was soon attracting the attention of professional clubs and was offered terms by Manchester City for whom he signed as an apprentice in 1976. He made his first team debut against Nottingham Forest on 23rd December 1978, a game which ended in a 0-0 draw. The following year he was selected to play for England Under-21s and made eleven appearances between 1979 and 1982. The highlight of his career at City was an appearance in the 1981 FA Cup Final against Tottenham Hotspur and then again in the replay, also at Wembley, which City lost 3-2. In 1984 he moved to Birmingham City and then in 1988 to Newcastle United.

It was during his playing days at Newcastle that Ray first became involved in the world of insurance. He got together with an old friend from the North West and in 1991 they formed a company called Coversport which dealt in sports-related insurances, for example, a personal accident scheme for footballers which he introduced to Gordon Taylor at the Professional Footballers Association. This clearly turned out to be quite lucrative as Ray, who was playing at Newcastle in 1992 at the time of the return of the messiah, Kevin Keegan, felt able to turn down Keegan's offer of a player/coach role. By then, he was sufficiently confident his future lay outside the managerial or coaching world.

Instead, Ray returned briefly to City before finishing his career at Reading in 1995. However by then he had already come into contact, via his insurance business, with Matthew Harding, the Chelsea Vice-Chairman and part owner. Harding was the largest shareholder in the Benfield Group (which was to become one of the world's largest reinsurance groups) and shortly before his untimely death in a helicopter crash in 1996, he entered into a joint venture with Ray and acquired 50 per cent of Coversport. It was at this point that Ray first started to attract attention (and some would say notoriety) by developing novel schemes to facilitate football transfers, most notably a "sale and leaseback" system, used extensively by Leeds United to fund the purchase of players at a time when Leeds were riding high in the Premier League and reaching the semi-finals of both the Champions' League and the UEFA Cup (now the Europa League). It did of course all end in tears for Leeds and fingers were pointed at Ray, although he vigorously defends the financing he put in place and lays the blame on subsequent transactions which Leeds entered into and which had nothing to do with him – as he puts it, "they rolled the dice again and this time they lost".

In 2002 Ray sold the balance of his company to Benfield and when Benfield itself floated on the stock market the following year with a market capitalisation of £750m, Ray cashed in again having invested in a small shareholding in the company. He then took twelve months off before plunging back into the sports world with the purchase in 2004 of Prozone, a sports analysis business which tracks players' movements and performance data. Ray had big ideas for the business, stating at the time he wanted to make it the equivalent of Bloomberg for football and whilst it would be difficult to say he achieved that goal, he did turn it into a profit-making business before selling in 2011.

In the meantime however Ray had not been idle. As early as 2002 he had shown interest in buying a football club, initially Aston Villa and then his old club Manchester City (a long time before Sheikh Mansour arrived on the scene!)   An abortive attempt to buy Southampton followed but he was finally successful in 2007 when, alongside hedge funds managed by SISU Capital, he acquired Coventry City just in time to prevent them going into administration.

Unfortunately Ray's time at Coventry did not go smoothly. Performance neither on nor off the field was good and in 2011 Ray resigned as Chairman around about the same time as the Football League announced an investigation into a loan made to Cardiff City by Sport Asset Capital, a company which he controlled. At the time Ray owned around 16 per cent of the shares in Coventry, presumably worthless given the parlous state of the club's finances, and which Ray gave up at the time of his resignation. There is no doubt however that Ray felt badly let down by SISU and his supporters on the Board were very clear that his resignation had been prompted by the fact that SISU would not back him financially and had indeed sold players against his advice.

This was not the end of Ray's involvement in football however. Through his company R2 Asset Management, he became involved in what some would regard as the murky world of football transfers but which Ray would describe as simply providing access to funds for smaller clubs who might want to bank some of the value of their assets (i.e. their promising players) before they were actually transferred. Ray's business might, for example, buy 50 per cent of the rights to a transfer fee for a player valued at £6m for which he will pay £3m. If that player is subsequently sold for £10m, then Ray's business has made a £2m profit. But Ray was never one to stand still and, ever the innovator, after several years of planning, R2 Asset Management was renamed The London Sports Exchange, which is an internet trading platform, launched in May 2015. It enables, on the one hand, sports clubs and stars to securitise their future earnings and on the other asset managers and other professional investors to trade in a new class of assets. Ray envisages football, golf and motor racing being three of the main sports which will take advantage of it.

Ray is still North West based and lives with his second wife in Bowdon in Cheshire. He is a father of five and describes himself as a "half decent golfer" when he gets the chance. However given his track record so far, there seems little likelihood that he will be finding much time to devote to his leisure activities at any time in the near future!

Andy Reid

Some years ago I listened to a motivational speaker the main thrust of whose presentation was that we cannot control the circumstances in which we find ourselves but that we are defined by the way we respond to them*. I was immediately reminded of this when I heard the story of Andy Reid. One can only speculate as to how one might react to losing both legs and an arm at the age of 33 but this is exactly what happened to Andy after he was blown up by a Taliban IED (improvised explosive device) just days before his tour of duty in Afghanistan was due to end. In Andy's case however, we can only marvel at the truly inspirational way that he responded to a situation which many would have found unbearable.

Andy was actually born in Birkenhead on 21ˢᵗ September 1976, son of William and Barbara, but came to St Helens after his father took a job as a projectionist at the Savoy Cinema. William was a keen motorcyclist and this led indirectly to the first family tragedy after an accident in which Andy's mother, a passenger in the sidecar, suffered serious leg injuries. The injury came to dominate the childhood of Andy and his three sisters and, somewhat presciently, after a series of painful operations, the decision was made to amputate the leg below the knee. It was her ability to come to terms with her situation and overcome the obstacles which it inevitably generated, that was to provide a major source of inspiration for Andy later in his life.

As a schoolboy, Andy also loved motorbikes as well as playing sport, particularly rugby league, a passion which has stayed with him for the whole of his life. He was educated initially at Rainford High before finishing his schooling at Broadway High. Andy openly admits that he was hardly a model pupil, having resolved at a very early stage that he wanted a career as a soldier. Although he tried to sign up at 16, he was turned down on more than one occasion for being underweight and had to wait until he was 21 (and thoroughly fed up with his day job of driving forklift trucks), before the military would accept him.

Training followed as did his first tour of duty in Northern Ireland where in 1988 he was to witness the consequences of the Omagh bombing and the death and destruction which that event wreaked upon the community – sights which he describes as still sticking like a screensaver at the back of his mind. But other, more positive experiences were around the corner: as well as training in the Lake District and the Brecon Beacons, there were also two spells in Canada, one in the Grand Canyon (incorporating a trip to Las Vegas) and a trip to Kenya and Tanzania in which he climbed Mount Kilimanjaro.

Although Andy had started army life in the Queen's Lancashire Regiment, he volunteered to join the Duke of Wellington's Regiment (later known as the 3rd Yorkshire battalion) and served in Kosova and Iraq before being deployed as a section commander in Helmand Province in Afghanistan in July 2009. This was certainly his most difficult posting to date and, as the tour approached its end, he was counting the days to his return to the UK. The explosion which was to transform his life took place ironically whilst he was conducting a handover to the replacement platoon commander. Andy's life was saved by the prompt action of his colleagues and after his initial treatment back at camp he was then immediately flown to Selly Oak Hospital in Birmingham where he underwent six weeks of intensive treatment. This was a long, long way from the return to the UK to which he had been so looking forward.

Andy's response to his situation in many ways mirrors that of Steve Prescott – initial anger and despair, and a difficulty in coming to terms with the fact that he had always been proud of his self-sufficiency but was now unable to complete a simple task himself. However out of the despair slowly rose a steely resolve to make the absolute best that he could of the position he was in and in the same way that Steve had the invaluable support of his wife Linzi, Andy was fortified by the constant presence of his girlfriend Claire despite the fact that at the time she was herself going through a major cancer scare. Claire was indeed to become Andy's wife in 2011 and they now have a son William, born in 2013 and most recently a daughter Scarlett, born in early 2018.

The first target Andy set himself was Remembrance Day 2009, a mere 29 days after the accident. He was told that he would have to be able to get out of his wheelchair himself and then back into it if he wished to attend. Having been given the challenge, Andy took it up successfully and as a consequence was permitted to join his old unit at Warminster for what was inevitably a very moving and emotional day. Andy was now on the road to recovery and although there would be many setbacks on the way (an infection in his stumps caused by dirt from the explosion being one of them), a determination to succeed in all the targets he set himself was now the overriding emotion.

Rehab took place at Headley Court in Surrey and by February he had started taking driving lessons. His next target was to be able to walk on his artificial limbs in time to take part in the medals parade in July 2010. It was in his own words, touch and go, but he made it and marched with the other members of his section to receive his Afghan campaign medal from the Duke of Wellington himself.

Andy's charity work started around the same time, after he was approached by a member of the Army Benevolent Fund. Without really thinking it through Andy volunteered to do a sky dive. This attracted a significant amount of interest which turned out to be a good thing as once the realisation of what he had agreed to do kicked in, he became utterly terrified at the prospect but felt that he couldn't possibly let everyone down by pulling out. In the event it all passed off in a very straightforward manner and the buzz gave Andy a real taste for charity work.

Several more events were to follow, including a five-day charity-fundraising motorbike ride from Land's End to John O'Groats (via St Helens!), the Washington marathon on a bike, a charity single with a St Helens group Titors Insignia, and more sky diving. He has also taken up a career of motivational speaking, prompted by an impromptu request by the captain to speak to the passengers (over 800 of them) whilst on a cruise, and has opened The Cinema Bar in St Helens in the old Plaza on Duke Street.

Andy has received widespread recognition for his achievements, the first award coming as early as December 2010 when he was nominated for, and won, the Overcoming Adversity Award at the *Sun's* Millie Awards. He was also a double winner at the inaugural Pride of St Helens Awards in 2012, winning the Award for Courage as well as the overall Pride of St Helens Award. His autobiography *Standing Tall* (a "must read") was published in 2014 and he remains an ambassador for both the Army Benevolent Fund and the Steve Prescott Foundation. It would be difficult to write a more inspiring story and it certainly elevates Andy into the list of heroes the town has produced.

*   The speaker was Debra Searle – whilst the name may not mean much, readers may well recall the situation which led to her becoming, albeit briefly, a household name in 2002. She was the wife part of the husband and wife team which set off to row the Atlantic in a 23-foot plywood boat. However shortly into the trip, her husband, a six foot five top-level oarsman for whom rowing was a passion, became so spooked by the endless ocean, the pitch black nights and the constant sound of the waves, that he had to be rescued by helicopter. Debra, who, by contrast, had previously only ever rowed in Poole Harbour, continued the journey alone and finally made it to Barbados after 111 days at sea, in which she had encountered 30-foot waves, force 8 storms, sharks and dodged huge tankers, all the time dealing with the loneliness which was, inevitably, ever present.

Isabel Robey

I sabel Robey was born sometime around 1540 and reputedly lived in a cottage on Crank Road near Windle Island. She had the misfortune to be denounced as a witch in an era when, unlike the world of Harry Potter, the Muggles were clearly in the ascendancy.

The somewhat precarious nature of existence in those days is illustrated by the circumstances which led to her ultimate demise. It is not at all uncommon for someone to disapprove of a relative's choice of spouse but in Isabel's case it turned out to be a grave mistake which was to have disastrous consequences. After she made her displeasure known when her goddaughter decided to marry a certain Peter Chaddock, the said gentleman proceeded to denounce her, complaining that she had wished aches and pains upon him and caused him physical discomfort.

On 16th July 1612 she was hauled before Sir Thomas Gerrard, who was a Roman Catholic who had been appointed by the Protestant King James 1, who was in turn a firm believer in witchcraft). It did not help Isabel's case that she was not popular with her neighbours who appear to have come out in force to denounce her. The result of all this was that Isabel was sent to Lancaster for trial and was listed with the Pendle and Samlesbury witches at Lancaster Assizes on 18th August 1612. Sir Edward Bromley presided, which was again somewhat unfortunate for Isabel as he was apparently keen to secure promotion to a circuit near London and given that the head of the judiciary was the aforementioned King James, he would not have wanted to preside over the wrong result. If there were a betting industry at the time, it is likely that you would have got pretty long odds on Isabel being found not guilty.

Sue Gerrard, in her book *Isabel Robey – The Windle Witch* details how the neighbours' complaints were repeated before the courts. Jane Wilkinson, for example, complained she had become "so pained that she could not stand" after she had turned Isabel Robey away when she was begging for milk. Margaret Lyon asserted that she had heard Isabel Robey boasting that Peter Chaddock would never recover until he begged for forgiveness. She also gave evidence that a wise man whom Peter had consulted had declared that Isabel was no witch and that Peter Chaddock had accepted this – however unfortunately for Isabel this was conveniently ignored. A third neighbour, Margaret Parre stated that she had heard Isabel Robey claim that she had bewitched the aforementioned Jane Wilkinson. None of this of course constitutes the sort of evidence that we would put in the category of "compelling" but it requires only a cursory reading of the proceedings at the time to realise that evidence generally was fairly peripheral to this sort of judicial process. Isabel, who was not permitted a defence counsel, appeared on the second day of the trial and was unsurprisingly found guilty. The 1604 Witchcraft Act gave the judge no option other than to hand down the death penalty. Together with the remaining nine of the Pendle witches she was permitted one last drink in the Golden Lion in Lancaster before being taken to the moors above the town and hanged on 20th August 1612.

Isabel clearly paid the price for being a cantankerous old woman who was not afraid to utter curses which others either took at face value or simply chose to use against her at the trial. She was a victim not just of the times but also of the fact that Thomas Gerrard likely saw an opportunity to ingratiate himself with the witch-fearing Protestant King James and of the ambitions of Sir Edward Bromley. Whatever the circumstances however, Isabel Robey has become an integral part of the history of St Helens.

The Gerrard Arms in Dentons Green Lane commemorates the Gerrard family. It is a great shame that nobody has yet thought to name a public house after Isabel Robey, the Windle Witch.

Hannah Rosbotham

Photograph courtesy of Stephen Wainwright from Sutton Beauty

Hannah Rosbotham was born in Sutton in 1858, the daughter of glass cutter Peter and his wife Elizabeth. She had two sisters and one brother and lived at 8 New Street in Sutton.

Hannah attended the nearby Sutton National School (known as "Sutton Nash") which had been founded by a local clergyman, the Reverend Henry Vallancy. It was located on a stretch of New Street known at the time as Workhouse Lane (because, unsurprisingly, a workhouse had been located there until 1843). Hannah went on in due course to join the school as an assistant mistress and on 14th October 1881, at the age of 23, she was in charge of the infant school as the headmistress was absent due to ill health.

This turned out to be the day of one of the worst storms ever to hit the United Kingdom. It was the day of the famous Eyemouth fishing disaster in Scotland when a total of 189 fishermen lost their lives. Throughout the country there was a trail of death and destruction. But another disaster could so easily have happened in St Helens had it not been for the actions of Hannah Rosbotham.

School was taking place as normal, or as normal as anything can be when a furious gale is raging outside. There were some 200 children in total crammed into the school. Hannah was teaching some of the elder children, whilst the younger ones – about 40 in total - sat upstairs in a gallery at the far end of the large room where Hannah was.

Above the gallery was a belfry and at about 11.00am, a loud rumbling noise could be heard, followed immediately by a huge crash as a large stone from the belfry, weighing well over a ton, came down through the roof and shattered all around the children in the gallery. As one might expect, a stampede ensued with all the children desperate to get out of the building. James Plews, the headmaster of the adjacent boys junior school, made his way over to the infant school, having heard the loud crash and encountered a mass of children blocking the door with some trying to climb over others. He set about clearing the area and passing out the uninjured children. However in the meantime, Hannah had made her way through the thick dust-filled air to the gallery staircase which was littered with debris. She managed to ascend the staircase and there found one small child, Harriet Bradbury, who had died instantly, eight who had suffered injury, some severe, but miraculously a large number who were terror-stricken but unhurt. These she helped evacuate from the building before setting about freeing the injured, many of whom were covered in rubble. One young girl in particular was reported as having been completely buried and in grave danger of suffocation. Quickly and unaided, Hannah tore away at the stones, plaster and timber whilst all the while further debris continued to fall around her. James Plews, on entering the area where Hannah was working away and coming to her assistance, reported that there was an imminent danger that the storm would take the whole roof away and that the gable wall would fall in its entirety into the gallery. However despite the fact that her life was in great danger, Hannah continued until every one of the children had been freed, carrying the badly injured herself before finally emerging into the playground where she broke down in tears. Later, having gathered herself together, she went about visiting at their homes all the children whom she had saved.

The local people of Sutton thanked Hannah for her bravery by holding a collection which raised £13 (nearly £1,000 in today's money). More widespread recognition was to come however with the award of the Albert Medal by Queen Victoria on 16th December 1881, an award which was sometimes described as the Victoria Cross for civilians. Hannah was the first-ever female recipient of the award and was for some years the only female to have received it. When it was finally replaced by the George Medal in 1940, there were still only 16 female recipients.

Hannah went on to marry James Parr, a local glassworks clerk, in 1887. They lived in Peckers Hill Road and then New Street so didn't move very far – in fact Hannah was to continue working at the school for 41 years, and at some point became headmistress. It is not believed that the couple had any children. Hannah died in 1934 at the age of 77 and is buried in Sutton Parish Churchyard.

The monthly magazine *Strand* (famous as the first publisher of Arthur Conan Doyle's *Sherlock Holmes* stories) carried an article in 1896 describing in detail Hannah's act of bravery and she also features in Henry Charles Moore's collection *Noble Deeds of the World's Heroines*.

Willy Russell

St Helens has always been a bit ambivalent when it comes to its relationship with its close neighbour, the city of Liverpool. There is certainly a shared identity which derives from geography, strong Irish roots, sporting affiliations and similar political leanings. But against that St Helens has always valued and cherished both its accent and its independence and for many there is still a lingering resentment that our heritage, which was always more Lancashire than Merseyside, was ignored in the Local Government Act of 1972 which heralded the 1974 boundary changes.

The purpose of this preamble is to put into context the inclusion in this collection of Willy Russell. After all, surely he is far more closely identified with Liverpool than St Helens? On what basis can his inclusion be justified? Well, he does in fact qualify on two separate counts – not only did he live in Rainhill for the first five years of his life but his secondary education took place in Rainford. And given that he is one of the many Liverpool people widely admired and respected in the town, it is perhaps reassuring to know that we played more than a bit part in his life story.

Willy's father, also William and originally from Upholland, had married Marjorie Baldwin in Knowsley in 1946 and they initially took up residence in Dee Lane in Rainhill. Willy was born the following year on 23rd August 1947 and brought up as an only child. His father was extremely resourceful, always on the lookout for opportunities to make money and at various times worked as a miner, printer's clerk and labourer as well as running a number of businesses of his own, including a fish and chip shop, an insurance agency, even a mobile library! Willy did not have an easy relationship with his father however and spent more time with his mother who had been a nurse but went on to run a draper's business. Willy describes her as aspirational and attributes his later ability to create convincing female characters at least in part to the time he spent as a child in female company.

At the age of five Willy's family moved to Knowsley Village and Willy attended Maypole Primary School. However a combination of the fact that he was one of the youngest in his year plus several bouts of sickness meant that he did not progress well. His secondary education commenced at Woolfall Secondary School in Huyton but this didn't work out well for him either and at the age of 15 he was despatched to Rainford County Secondary (now Rainford High School).

Willy cannot be described as an academic success at school (he left with one GCE O level in English Language) but there was an important legacy from his time at Rainford which played a major part in defining his subsequent career. He had always enjoyed reading and storytelling but it was during the silent reading sessions at the school, that he learned what he describes as "the power of words" and developed a longing to use words to convey his feelings to others. More specifically, one of his classmates at Rainford was called Shirley Valentine, a name which was of course to resurface much later in Willy's life!

The expectation for many of the pupils at Rainford was that they would obtain employment in one of the glass factories in St Helens and Willy recalls being taken on a school trip to one of the bottle plants so they could see what was in store for them. That didn't appeal to him however and instead, at the suggestion of his mother, he became a ladies' hairdresser in a salon in St Helens town centre. The urge to write was already present however and initially it was music which provided him with an outlet. Like many of his generation he was inspired by the Beatles whom he had seen perform at the Cavern Club in their pre-fame days and he started to write his own songs as well as running a folk group at a local café. It was there that he met Annie, later to become his wife and who, together with her family, played a large part in creating the person he was to become. It was Annie's mother who talked Willy into studying at night school to secure the 5 GCE O levels he needed to get into teachers' training college. Willy did exactly that and after attending St Katharine's College in Liverpool, spent a year teaching in Toxteth. His teaching career didn't last long either but this time it was for the right reasons.

He had started to write plays whilst at St Katharine's and in 1972 took his work to the Edinburgh Festival where it impressed writer John McGrath who recommended him to the Everyman Theatre in Liverpool.

His first major success was *John, Paul, George, Ringo......and Bert,* a stage production which premiered at the Everyman in early 1974 and later that year transferred to the West End, winning Best Musical in the *London Evening Standard*'s Theatre Awards.

Willy continued to write and play music, but it was his scriptwriting that was to flourish over the next few years. He did not restrict himself to stage productions however, venturing also into the world of screenwriting for television films. He was propelled into the international limelight by a production commissioned by the Royal Shakespeare Company, *Educating Rita,* which certainly had some parallels with Willy's own return to education as an adult. It premiered in the West End in 1980 and went on to be shown in New York and many other places around the world, before being adapted for the 1983 film which was nominated for two Oscars and a major success at the Box Office. Its enduring quality was further emphasised when, some 16 years later, it was made into a radio play.

The next big one was *Blood Brothers,* a play which was notable also for the fact that Willy wrote the music and the lyrics as well as the script. First shown in Liverpool in 1983, it won the Laurence Olivier Award for Best New Musical and went on to become the third longest production in West End history, as well as long stints on Broadway and many other parts of the globe.

It was 1986 before his erstwhile school friend from Rainford, Shirley Valentine, was to re-emerge (or, more correctly, her name rather than Shirley herself!) in a play which was again first shown in Liverpool before transferring to the West End and in due course to Broadway. Both Willy and Pauline Collins, its lead star, were to win Olivier Awards whilst Pauline went on to win a Tony Award for best actress. The film version was released in 1989, also with Pauline Collins who won a BAFTA award for best actress as well as being nominated for an Oscar.

These are of course only the highlights of a career which was prolific in every way. The plays, films and musical scores for which Willy has been responsible over the years are too numerous to detail here. But remarkably, Willy has yet more strings to his bow, including the publication of a novel in 2000, the release of an album in 2004 and more recently an exhibition of his artwork at Kirkby Art Gallery.

In 2013 the John Moores University in Liverpool recognised his enormous contribution to the Arts by establishing the Willy Russell

Archive, a comprehensive collection of material produced during the course of his career.

Willy has stayed close to his roots, living in a 1790 cottage in Woolton with his wife Annie. He has three children and four grandchildren, to all of whom he is devoted. He still travels regularly into Liverpool to work in his office there, a Georgian House which he bought in 1999. He describes his interests now as more exploratory and experimental than in the past which suggests that there may be even more arenas in which his name might surface at some time in the future!

Willy Russell is undoubtedly one of the most celebrated playwrights that this country has produced and it is fair to say that much of his work derives from events and experiences in his own life – and it is good to know that, whilst it is probably a step too far to describe him as one of us, a number of those life experiences certainly took place in the town of St Helens!

John Rylands

John Rylands is certainly a name which many will recognise although not all will make the St Helens connection. This is hardly surprising when one considers that he was widely known as "John Rylands of Manchester" (also the title of the most comprehensive biography of his life, written by D.A Farnie, who was, as it happens, one of my tutors at the University of Manchester in the early 1970s and whose work I have drawn upon greatly in this synopsis).

Statue in the John Rylands Library in Manchester.
Photograph courtesy of Brian Leyland

John Rylands has also been referred to on many occasions as Manchester's first multi-millionaire, and as the embodiment of what came to be known as "the Manchester man" (often contrasted with "the Liverpool gentleman"). Thomas Southcliffe Ashton, the eminent historian of the industrial revolution, wrote in 1934 that when the authoritative history of the Manchester merchant is compiled, "the name of Rylands will appear large on its pages". The *Manchester City News* even went as far as to refer to Manchester as his "native city" in an article in April 1865. And to top it all, the sarcophagus which marks his place of burial in the Southern Cemetery, Manchester, bears the inscription "John Rylands of Manchester". The reality however is that for the 19th century owner of the largest textile manufacturing concern in the United Kingdom, St Helens is where it all started.

Rylands was born in Parr on 7th February 1801 and is at the time of writing the only famous resident of that parish listed in Wikipedia (surely some mistake?) His mother, interestingly, was Elizabeth Pilkington, aunt of Richard and William Pilkington, founders of Pilkington Brothers. His father, Joseph was a weaver and then a hand loom manufacturer, as well as running a draper's shop in Hardshaw. John was the fifth and youngest child, born when his mother was already 40, but was the child who at a very early age displayed a real aptitude for life in commerce. He was educated at Cowley School but by the age of 16 had already started his own business as a hand loom manufacturer. It was not long in fact before his three elder brothers joined him and together they started to build up a successful wholesale trade – so successful in fact that his father abandoned his own business and also joined him to form Rylands and Sons. It was this business which was in due course to become what was described in 1879 by a local journalist as "the largest and most important manufacturing and mercantile operation in the world".

The move to Manchester took place in 1823 and whilst he was not well-received by the Manchester wholesalers with whom he was in competition, the timing could hardly have been better. The 1820s were boom times for the city of Manchester or Cottonopolis, the name by which it became known. In that decade alone the population of the city grew by 45 per cent and Rylands and Sons made the most of the opportunities which the move opened up for the business.

It continually extended its operations, right through from manufacturing to the finishing trades and it also started to sell goods of other manufacturers as part of its wholesale trade. Initially it dealt mainly in linen but in the 1830s cotton was to take over as the main product. The first cotton spinning mill was acquired in Wigan in 1830, the second in 1839 in Ainsworth near Bolton (the first in which power looms were installed, which used coal from a nearly colliery to create the steam power) and the third in 1843 in Manchester itself, which, in his own words, marked the beginning of a "new era in my existence". The wholesale trade meanwhile continued to thrive and in 1849 the first London warehouse was opened, thus permitting access to the biggest single market in the country. By the early 1850s John Rylands was the largest textile merchant in Manchester and the first native of Lancashire to achieve millionaire status. By 1860 he was regarded as the most successful textile merchant in the country.

The following decade brought with it the challenges of the cotton famine of 1861–1865 but Rylands and Sons not only survived but from 1864 expanded its manufacturing operations still further with the acquisition of three more establishments, all of them in Manchester, and with the construction of a model mill at Gidlow in Wigan. By 1865 the firm had 4,500 employees. Yet further expansion followed, into Liverpool, Yorkshire and Cheshire and a bleaching operation acquired in Chorley was turned into the largest bleaching and finishing works in Europe. The drive to grow was relentless. The London office became a major branch of the firm in 1874-5 and at the same time the overseas operations, until then relatively modest, became the new focus. Offices were opened in Paris and Montreal, whilst agencies were established throughout the globe – from Constantinople to Rio, from Genoa to Barbados and from Madras to Port Elizabeth. And throughout this period, the firm continued to grow at home with a second Gidlow mill opening in Wigan in 1880 as well as the extension of manufacturing operations to London.

By the time of his death at the age of 87 in December 1888, the firm had 12,000 employees, it operated 200,000 spindles and 5,000 looms and had an annual income well in excess of many sovereign states. John Rylands had created the biggest operation within the textile industry of any single entrepreneur and was referred to in various publications of the time as "the monarch of the cotton industry", "the Wellington of commerce", "the cotton king" and "the greatest merchant prince the world has ever seen". His estate was valued at £2,574,922 – a huge sum at the time but which was arguably dwarfed by the size of his lifetime contribution to the world of trade and commerce.

So what does all of this tell us about the man himself? One thing which is clear for all to see is the drive and ambition which seems to have pervaded everything he did. He may have been small and unimpressive in appearance and reticent in manner but that belied a fierce determination to succeed which was all-embracing. He was a workaholic, never missing a single day at work, regularly arriving in the office at 8.00am whilst in his seventies. He was certainly not afraid to take on any opposition to achieve his goals. From his early days in Manchester when he encountered the hostility of the existing wholesalers, he showed that he was prepared to defy tradition, for example by keeping his warehouse open for buyers at the midday break. He broke the monopoly of the Manchester linen houses in the Scottish and Irish market, he refused to follow the customary practices of other merchants in Manchester and, as a commercial traveller in his early days, had declined to socialise with his fellow travellers in the evenings. If he felt too reliant on other suppliers, he would move into that area of business himself. He was also a man who clearly did not want to share power with others and who found the concept of partnership uncomfortable.

His eldest brother Joseph left the business as early as 1836 and in 1842 his father, Joseph senior, agreed to dissolve the partnership leaving John in sole control. His second son, William did join him briefly as a partner in 1859 (two years before his untimely death in 1861), and he also seems to have relented a little in the 1860s, firstly by entering into a partnership with his nephew, John Cross (son of his sister Eleanor), in the new Gidlow works in Wigan and a few years later when, in 1867, he permitted his associate Reuben Spencer to join him as a partner in Rylands and Sons. By 1872 however he had once again secured full control by buying out his nephew from the Wigan business and terminating his partnership with Reuben Spencer. Even after the incorporation of the business into the limited company Rylands and Sons Limited, the style of management did not change. He made sure that the articles of association of the company entrusted him personally with supreme power. Meetings of the Board of Directors could at best be described as infrequent – in fact none at all took place between March 1877 and March 1883! So this was most definitely a man accustomed to getting his own way and he made sure things stayed that way.

One could be forgiven, in the light of the above, for picturing John Rylands as a driven but dour individual, puritanical in his beliefs and for whom the pursuit of power and wealth was everything. But it seems there was a lot more to John Rylands than such a picture would paint. He was a connoisseur of fine wine for example and ensured his cellars were always fully stocked. He owned a handsome 30-ton yacht which was moored at Hoylake on the River Dee and on which he entertained his senior employees. He loved to play chess, billiards, bowls and croquet. And his puritanical beliefs did not prevent him adorning his houses with books, water colours and bronze and marble sculptures.

Moreover to think of him as uncaring would also be to do him a grave injustice. He maintained a complete and absolute integrity in all his dealings and had a great concern for the welfare his employees, building libraries and schools for their benefit. Employees benefited for the most part from a job for life and, although wary of trade unions, he was generally able to avoid bad industrial relations by overseeing the establishment of employee associations such as benevolent societies, recreational clubs, brass bands, dramatic societies and the like. Outside the business he became one of the great philanthropists of his age – he made great provision for orphans and widows, both at home and in Italy, a country for which he had a great religious fascination and in which he became a Knight of the Order of the Crown as a consequence of his liberal benefactions there to the poor. He built the Stretford Town Hall with a gymnasium and public hall, he established a free public library there, a public baths, and several institutes with bowling greens, tennis courts and children's playgrounds.

It is difficult however not to reach the conclusion that it was the tragedies which continually beset him in his personal life which influenced much of what he did. He had married Dinah Raby in Manchester in 1825 and she gave birth to two sons, John Garthwaite in 1826 and William in 1828. However in 1829 his mother, Elizabeth, to whom he had been very close, died at the age of 68. This by all accounts caused him deep distress and worse was to come – during the next five years, Dinah gave birth to five more children, none of whom survived his or her first birthday. On top of all of this Dinah herself died in 1843 at the age of 40.

One might have expected that such a catalogue of tragedy would have led a person to question his religious beliefs but in John's case it seems to have intensified them. He was baptised as a Baptist in 1830 and attended Baptist chapel regularly before moving to a Congregational church in 1842. He even arranged for, and financed, the compilation of a Rylands Bible which contained 5,810 numbered paragraphs for ease of reference. Interestingly however, his beliefs were not at all sectarian and he avoided as far as possible any denominational associations, his belief being that all churches should be broken up in order to create a new harmony in which all religious men could participate. So in religion, as in many other aspects of his life, John Rylands was ahead of his time, promoting an ecumenical approach that was certainly not in keeping with the mood of the times.

John Rylands remarried in 1848, his new wife Martha having also been brought up in Parr where she and John had been childhood friends. His personal life did not become any easier however as he had a major bust up with his elder son around about that time, as a result of which John Garthwaite left the firm permanently. The marriage to Martha did not produce any further children and tragedy struck yet again, when his second son, William, upon whom all of John's hopes were now focused and who had recently become a business partner of his father, died at the age of 33 in 1861. John was devastated by this event, more than any other – it created a huge void in his life and, critically, left no heir to the empire he had created. Finally, his elder son, although estranged for some years, died in 1872, leaving John completely childless, followed by Martha's death in 1876 which left John once again a widower.

This chain of events may perversely have been responsible in part for the continuing success of the business. Careers within Rylands and Sons were open to all and were based wholly on merit rather than family connections. This meant that once John had finally taken his foot off the pedal, there was a very able Board of Directors who could assume effective control. Many already had a stake in the business as John had taken the relatively unusual step of making shares available to principal employees and clients. All of this conspired to ensure that the business would survive his death in December 1888 and that its future was, in the medium term at least, secure.

John Rylands was not a national figure during his lifetime, being relatively unknown outside Lancashire and Cheshire. He did not aspire to join the landed gentry, possibly because the death of his son would have made this somewhat pointless but also, one suspects, because that was not what he was about. He showed no interest in politics and declined the offer of a nomination as the Sheriff of London (prompted by the City becoming aware of his considerable wealth) as this would have meant moving away from Manchester. The only outside commercial venture with which he did become involved was the construction of the Manchester Ship Canal. This was however more likely than not prompted not by vanity but by the prospect of reducing transport costs, so important for his own business (and possibly also to distance himself once again from the other Manchester merchants who generally declined to risk their capital in what was clearly a very high-risk venture).

After his move to Manchester, John lived in seven different places before finally settling in Stretford, purchasing the extensive Longford Hall estate. This was where he first established his own library, a love of books having been instilled in him by the mother to whom he was devoted. The library was dispersed some years later and we actually know very little of its true extent but a catalogue compiled in 1881 listed nearly 1,800 titles. He also had a smaller library in the London house which he had purchased in 1875 and which contained 325 titles when sold in 1908, was a shareholder in the Portico Library in Manchester and donated 500 books to a public library that was set up as part of the Longford Institute in Ryde on the Isle of Wight where he had purchased a property in 1882.

John did marry for a third time in 1875 and the fact that his name is now far more widely known than it had been in his lifetime is in part a consequence of this. His new wife was Enriqueta Augustina Tennant, who had been born in Havana in 1843 and who was therefore some 42 years his junior. They had met when Enriqueta had been a companion of Martha in her later years. Whether such an association raised eyebrows at the time is not recorded but Enriqueta did become the chief legatee in his will and consequently did not do too badly when John passed away 13 years later. But to be fair to her, she devoted a good part of the rest of her life to preserving his memory to the public, initially by the construction of the Rylands memorial in Southern Cemetery but most notably by the founding of the world-famous John Rylands Library in Manchester. She proved also to be a worthy steward of her husband's fortunes and when she herself died in 1908, her estate was worth £3,448,692 notwithstanding the fact that during the period since his death she had made charitable gifts totalling £473,000.

The story of the John Rylands Library is amply recorded elsewhere but it is worth noting that the name of John Rylands survives elsewhere to this day – many streets, sports teams, clubs and other organisations bear the Rylands name. Longford Estate is now a public park in the Borough of Trafford. And the business itself? After flourishing for many years after John's death, it suffered a decline after the Second World War, in common with most of Lancashire's cotton businesses, and in 1953 was subsumed into Great Universal Stores Limited. The name did survive for a while but was finally removed from the register of companies in 1989, some 170 years after it all began in very humble circumstances in St Helens.

Richard Seddon

We regularly hear that current politicians are a pretty boring lot (well until quite recently we did!) and that the colourful characters of yesteryear have disappeared, to be replaced by a bunch of automatons. If that is indeed the case then it is unlikely that had Richard Seddon been born in such an era, he would have entered politics. He may have been accused of a lot of things but being boring was not one of them – as is evident from the nickname King Dick, by which he was known during his time as Prime Minister of New Zealand.

There is no shortage of material chronicling Richard's life. David Hamer is perhaps his most recent biographer, having contributed to the biography section of the *Dictionary of New Zealand,* but as long ago as 1906, the year of Seddon's death, J. Drummond wrote the first, which was entitled *The Life and Works of Richard John Seddon, Premier of New Zealand 1893–1906.* And visitors to Wellington cannot have failed to notice the huge statue in the Parliament grounds, sculpted by Sir Thomas Brock, with the inscription:

RICHARD JOHN SEDDON
BORN ECCLESTON, NEAR ST. HELENS, LANCASHIRE,
ENGLAND, 1845

ARRIVED IN NEW ZEALAND 1866
MEMBER OF PARLIAMENT FOR
HOKITIKA (1879-1881)
KUMARA (1881-1890)
WESTLAND (1890-1906)

PRIME MINISTER 1893-1906

DIED 10 JUNE 1906 ON BOARD OSWESTRY GRANGE
WHILE RETURNING TO NEW ZEALAND FROM SYDNEY

Richard's birth on 22nd June 1845 is reported as having taken place in what was then School Brow, but is now Eccleston Hill on Prescot Road. He was the third of eight children. His father, Thomas Seddon was a headmaster at Eccleston Grammar School (believed to have been part of his house in Eccleston Hill) and his mother Jane was also a teacher although it seems that the school at which she taught, Eccleston Denominational School, closed when she married. However notwithstanding the family background in education and his father's reported desire to turn his son into a Latin scholar, it seems that young Richard was far from a model pupil. He certainly did not extend his education beyond the age of twelve at which point he was removed from the school apparently on the basis that he was a difficult and unpromising pupil. So not an auspicious start for the future politician.

His first job after leaving school was helping out at his grandfather's farm in Barrow Nook (near Bickerstaffe) but things do not seem to have worked out any better there. This was followed by spells at the Daglish foundry in St Helens and then the Vauxhall foundry in Liverpool, neither of which, for one reason or another, seem to have been particularly successful so perhaps it was no surprise that in 1863, at the age of 18, he decided to work his passage to Melbourne in Australia on the *Star of England*.

Initially things didn't go much better Down Under. Richard spent some time prospecting in the goldfields and the rest of his time labouring in railway workshops. He had certainly not amassed sufficient wealth to impress the parents of Louisa Jane Spotswood to whom he became engaged at the turn of the year 1865/6. Possibly as a response to their refusal of permission for Richard to marry their daughter, he decided to make his way to New Zealand in February 1866 and it was there that things started to take a turn for the better. He joined his uncle, Nathan Seddon, and seems to have made a considerable amount of money from his activities in the Waimea gold mines on the South Island – enough at least to return to Melbourne just short of three years after he left to marry Louisa, who rather helpfully was still single and available. Now accompanied by his new bride, Richard returned to New Zealand and the roller-coaster began.

Richard's activities were wide and varied. Initially based in Stafford, he opened and ran stores, obtained licences to sell alcohol and generally seems to have had his fingers in lots of pies. He also started to represent miners in court, acting as a non-legally qualified litigant. He then moved to Kumara and opened a hotel, stores and a butchery there. In 1877 he was elected as mayor and the following year narrowly avoided going bust after filing for bankruptcy but then managing to avert that state by reaching an agreement with his creditors. Bankruptcy would most probably have signalled the end of his political aspirations but in the event he was able to stand as a candidate for parliament in 1879 and was elected as representative for Hokitika. He stood again in 1881 as a candidate for the newly created seat of Kumara and was again successful. He remained as their representative until 1890 when he was elected to represent Westland, which position he was to retain until his death in 1906.

Initially Richard's focus was very much on local issues, identifying very strongly with the miners. However as time went on, his ambition grew and he made himself an expert in parliamentary procedure. He was also a very accomplished political strategist and, after aligning himself with the Liberal Party, completely outmanoeuvred his main rival for the premiership when the Liberal Premier, John Ballance, died in 1893.

As Prime Minister, Richard was something of a control freak and, rather than risk having independent-minded ministers in charge of various departments, he had a tendency to appoint himself. At one stage during his premiership he was also Minister of Labour, Colonial Treasurer, Minister for Public Works and Minister of Defence. Later in his prime ministerial career he took on the roles of Minister of Education and Minister of Immigration. All of this inevitably meant a rather long working day and no doubt contributed to the reputation he developed as an autocrat. He was also accused of surrounding himself with "yes men" of rather limited ability rather than more skilful operators who could not be trusted always to agree with him.

It will come as no surprise that Richard made a number of enemies but he was generally able to get the better of them and he managed to stay in post for the 13 years until his death in 2006, making him New Zealand's longest serving prime minister. A number of major reforms were enacted under his watch, including the Government Advances to Settlers Act and the Industrial Conciliation and Arbitration Act, both in 1894. However he is remembered mainly for the Old Age Pensions Act of 1898 which he pushed through despite great opposition, driven by a long-standing concern over the fate of the miners whom he had represented in court. He was also one of the architects of the Workers Dwellings Act of 1905 as well as helping introduce a superannuation scheme for teachers shortly before his death, possibly an indication of the regard in which he came to hold his own parents.

Richard was a committed imperialist and was often critical of Britain's caution; his major achievement in this area was persuading Britain to allow New Zealand to annex the Cook Islands in 1901. He was less successful in his aspirations to take control of Samoa, Fiji and Hawaii.

Many felt that Richard had passed his sell

Photograph by Herman John Schmidt

buy date in the early 1900s as the consequences of his long hours of work and travel started to take their toll on his health, and there was a lot of pressure on him to resign. However although he did indicate that he might step down in 1907, he never actually got that far, dying on board the ship that was returning him from a visit to Australia on 10th June 1906. He was buried on Observatory Hill, adjacent to the Botanic Garden in Wellington.

Richard Seddon is without doubt a huge figure in the history of New Zealand politics and his name was to be invoked many times by the labour movement. He certainly liked to be regarded as a man of the people – it seemed not to bother him that his enemies made fun of his accent, which they described as uncouth (a St Helens accent uncouth? Surely not!), and for which he was known to apologise. He was a man who was relentless in pursuit of his objectives and who had the capacity to carry out the work necessary to see them fulfilled. He was a big drinker and a big eater, which no doubt explains how he came to weigh in at some 20 stone in his later years. He liked to promote an image of geniality when handling crowds and big meetings, which he did with ease. Most of all he wanted the populace to see him as the representative of the common people, standing up to the wealthy classes and large commercial interests.

Richard remained married to Louisa with whom he had six daughters and three sons. They had initially stayed in Kumara but moved to Wellington in 1895. He was also followed to New Zealand by two of his sisters and two of his brothers.

The statue in the Parliament grounds is not the only monument erected in his memory – there is a further statue in Hokitika and also an inscription in St Paul's Cathedral in London. The town of Seddon in New Zealand and the Melbourne suburb of Seddon were also named after him. And in St Helens itself, his birthplace on Eccleston Hill has a commemorative plaque above the front door. But perhaps the legacy which sums him up best is the stuffed lion in the Wellington museum, which had been presented to Richard whilst he was Prime Minister and which was the first animal to take up residence in the newly created Wellington Zoo. It was later given the name of King Dick in his honour.

The only VC ever awarded posthumously to someone still alive was to Jack Davies, a St Helens man.

Sir James Sexton CBE

Included in this collection are a number of rags to riches stories, there are many which feature extremely colourful and adventurous characters and of course there are also those persons who achieved a certain eminence in their chosen field. However there are a very few who qualify under each of the above headings. One of these is most certainly Sir James Sexton.

Although actually born in Newcastle upon Tyne on 13th April 1856, James moved to St Helens as a very young child and

so can quite properly be regarded as a native of the town – indeed he himself described it as his spiritual home, notwithstanding his deep Irish roots on the one hand and a life which took him to many far-flung spots around the globe on the other. His father, also James, had migrated to England after the family had been thrown off their farm in County Wicklow by an absentee English landlord, leading to the death of his own parents. James's mother, Ann, although born in Warrington, was also of Irish stock and her family too had suffered grievously at the hands of the English. All in all therefore, a certain animosity towards the British was probably understandable.

That the family settled in St Helens was quite accidental – their lifestyle was quite itinerant and whilst on their way to Birkenhead looking for work in the docks, James's mother had fallen ill and could not travel further. They decided to stay for a few months and his father acquired a small "mush faking" business (something to do with repairing umbrellas, I'm told) in Tontine Street, where they also lived (this was at the bottom of Bridge Street, where Chalon Way now runs). Their stall in the market was next to the one used by a certain Thomas Beecham Senior who was selling the pills that were to make his family famous. James's mother also knitted and sold colourful women's woollen caps.

The umbrella business actually turned out to generate enough for the family to earn a respectable living, although they had to supplement its earnings by taking in lodgers, meaning every spare inch of accommodation was fully utilised. The family continued to grow as well; James was the eldest, but another six were to arrive over the next few years, so every penny came in useful. The household diet was enriched by the pheasants regularly poached by father and son from Lord Derby's estate. (Many years later, after Lord Derby had sent him a haunch of venison, James disclosed that this was not the first time he had enjoyed game from the Knowsley estate – apparently Lord Derby laughed heartily and the King, who was in attendance at the time, was also greatly amused).

James's father was also a prominent member of the Irish Republican Brotherhood and their house was regularly used to store firearms – somehow they managed to escape detection, even when the local police searched their premises (the family had been tipped off in advance by the local police chief, himself a member of the Brotherhood!) James also recalled a late night visit to the house by a young Michael Davitt, who went on to become one of the leaders of the Irish republican movement.

James attended Lowe House Primary School but his earning potential was important to the family so he left at the age of nine, initially to take up employment in clog manufacture(!) but very quickly moving on to a job at Pilkington's. By the age of 13 however he could contain no longer the adventurer in him and after an abortive attempt to get to London, he ran away to sea, initially as a stowaway on a ship bound from Liverpool, but after revealing himself on the second day, for the rest of the journey as a member of the crew on a four month voyage to San Francisco! He was not to return home for some ten years, during which period he was shanghaied (effectively kidnapped after being drugged and forced to join the crew of a ship which had sailed by the time he regained consciousness), involved in life-threatening rescues at sea, witnessed shark attacks and, during a period after he had jumped ship in London, worked in a chemical factory. Quite what might have become of him had his father not died at the age of 43, leaving his mother to bring up the rest of the family, we will never know. As it was James felt he had no choice other than return home.

Although he worked briefly in St Helens, his seafaring experience soon led James to work on the docks at Liverpool and it was here, appalled by the working conditions and the corrupt practices which prevailed at the time, that he started to gain a reputation as an agitator. As a consequence, work became hard to come by and his situation was worsened still further when he was the victim of a terrible accident at work, which resulted in him suffering a broken cheekbone, a right eye forced out of its socket and a partially fractured skull. A period in hospital of several months ensued. Despite the recently enacted Employers' Liability Act, his employer denied any liability although he did offer James some light work once he was back on his feet at a reduced wage (and to rub salt in the wound, deducted two shillings and sixpence from James's first wage packet to cover the cost of the cab to the hospital!)

In 1881 during his early days at the docks James had married Christina Boyle in West Derby. Christina was born in Liverpool but we know nothing about the circumstances in which they met. They did not have any children and appear to have separated at some point in the early 1900s. At this point however she was indirectly responsible for the next setback which James faced. After she had one day brought his dinner down to the dockside, an insulting reference to her by, in James's words, "one of the brutes in human shape amongst the bosses" prompted James to knock the said gentleman unconscious. His employment did not of course survive this incident and he was lucky to escape prosecution. And it naturally reduced even further his opportunities for work on the docks. After a period working as a painter on a shipping line, he set up a small business operating a coal yard with a donkey and cart. But his resolve to improve the conditions of the working men on the docks had not gone away – on the contrary, it had intensified.

Although James had been involved for several years in trying to organise the working men (and indeed had instigated a strike in 1885 which was, in his own words "a lamentable, woeful, total failure"), the trade union movement started to kick off seriously after the founders of the dockers' union in Glasgow decided that Liverpool should be their next port of call. James was one of the first card-carrying members and the union grew in Liverpool very quickly indeed. The employers, frightened by what was happening, may have themselves instigated the 1889 strike with a view to smashing the union before it could get any stronger. The strike ended with only some small concessions and for James personally it meant bankruptcy, as he had allowed his customers all their usual supplies on credit. Critically however, although numbers fell, the union survived and its national headquarters were moved from Glasgow to Liverpool. James, now more determined than ever, was in 1893 appointed as General Secretary of the National Union of Dock Labour.

Nothing in this job was easy – apart from the animosity of the employers, James also had to deal in the early days with the fact that the dockers themselves were split in all sorts of ways and he also had to weed out corruption which had quickly become endemic within the organisation. But perseverance was clearly one of his strong suits and after overcoming these difficulties, he was in due course able to devote substantially all his efforts to improving the welfare of the dockers, for example by successfully lobbying to have them brought within the terms of the Factory and Notice of Accident Acts which had previously not applied to them. He was to remain General Secretary of the NUDL until its merger with the Transport and General Workers' Union in 1922, a combination which he played an active part in bringing about. Thereafter he became National Supervisor of the Docks Trade Group within the new union and stayed in this post till 1928. During his period at the helm, he gained a reputation for both integrity and competence and was in large part responsible for dockers' union's success in gaining recognition by the employers, the agreement of a minimum wage and the setting up of the National Joint Council of Port Labour in 1920. He also sat upon the parliamentary committee of the TUC from 1900 to 1921 and was its president in 1905.

Throughout all of this, James did not neglect his political activities. He was quite heavily involved in the early discussions around the formation of an independent Labour Party and first stood for Parliament, unsuccessfully, as candidate for Ashton-under-Lyne in 1895. He had to wait however until 1918, when he came full circle by being elected as Member of Parliament for St Helens, a seat which he was to hold until 1931. He was also very active in local politics, having had a seat on the Liverpool City Council from 1905 and becoming an alderman in 1930. He had been awarded a CBE in 1917 and was knighted in 1931. In 1934 he was granted the Freedom of the City of Liverpool.

After losing his seat in Parliament, James retired and went to live with his niece in Wavertree, where he spent his time writing his autobiography and otherwise working in the garden. He died on 27th December 1938.

It is not entirely clear what became of all of James's family. We know that his mother continued to run the umbrella business from Tontine Street for many years after her husband's death and it was only when her health was clearly failing that James managed to extricate her from the family home and take her into his own house in Halewood (which in those days was largely surrounded by farmland). She finally passed away at the age of 76 in 1914. His two younger sisters died in the next few years, which according to James, left him as the sole surviving member of the family. What happened to his four younger brothers does not seem to be recorded anywhere.

Sir James Sexton was yet another unsung hero of the town of St Helens, a man who played a major part in shaping British 19th and 20th century industrial relations but whose name would today be recognised by few. He was a man whose integrity was questioned by none, who was passionate to the end in his role as an agitator but also someone who could name many with vastly differing political views as personal friends. Lloyd George wrote that he was honoured to have known James and that his life and work were "woven into the very texture of the social conditions of our land". His autobiography *Sir James Sexton: Agitator* is a worthy read, chronicling the journey he made from humble beginnings, the years of striving for social justice and the achievements which he played such a huge part in bringing about. In the light of this I think there are few that could argue that Sir James is not another very credible candidate for St Helens finest!

Ken Shuttleworth

My teenage years coincided with a major upsurge in interest in cricket, fuelled primarily by the popularity of the relatively new concept of one day cricket. My friends and I all had a healthy interest in the game, many of us played, albeit at varying standards, and it was of course to Lancashire that our allegiance naturally gravitated. These were pre-Merseyside days so St Helens was unequivocally a part of Lancashire and I suspect the sense of belonging was somewhat greater than it is now. Anyway in those days Lancashire were generally regarded as the kings of one day cricket and playing for them during this golden era was Ken Shuttleworth, who we all knew was one

Image courtesy of Malcolm Lorimer of Lancashire Heritage Society

of our own, having been born and raised in Parr, as well as being an alumnus of the club where many of us played at some time or other, St Helens Recs.

Ken was born on 13th November 1944 and was raised on Charnwood Street, the youngest of three children and the only boy. His father Arthur Shuttleworth had as a young man played for West Bromwich Albion but in those days top flight football was not the passport to early riches that it is now and he later worked down the mines in St Helens. His mother, Ellen, sadly died when Ken was 13. Ken's schooling began at Allanson Street Primary School and then Parr Central which he left at the age of 16 and went to work at Pilkington's.

In the 1950s and 1960s cricket often featured in the leisure activities of young boys in the town who would create their own pitches whether in the street, waste land or playing fields. Ken excelled from a very early age but as a batsman rather than a bowler. John Walsh, who was a schoolboy friend of Ken, recalls that they made him bat left-handed because he was impossible to get out right-handed. Ken himself recalls a friend buying bags of salt to try and melt the ice in mid-winter so they could pitch the stumps and play. And while cricket did not form a major part of the sports curriculum at Parr Central, Ken did receive plenty of encouragement from his school sports teacher, Sid Green, and by the time he left school he was playing weekend cricket at Earlestown CC.

Soon after he started work at Pilkington's, he was persuaded to play for St Helens Recs at Ruskin Drive, which in those days fell under the Pilkington umbrella. He made his first team debut at the age of 17 in 1962 against Formby and he was soon building a reputation as a genuinely fast young bowler. On arrival at work one day in August 1963, there was a message waiting for him that Lancashire wanted to give him a trial. He made his way to Old Trafford, played for the second eleven against Cheshire and four wickets for 36 runs was enough to get him a second chance. In the next match against Cumberland he took another four wickets, this time for 43 runs, and that was enough to secure him a professional contract. Thus began a career in first class cricket which was to take him to the very top of the professional game.

Ken did not however abandon St Helens Recs and continued to turn out for them until the end of the 1965 season. However by then he had already appeared for the Lancashire first eleven, making his debut in the Roses Match against Yorkshire at Old Trafford in 1964. Playing second fiddle to established opening bowlers Brian Statham and Ken Higgs, Ken succeeded where they had not and claimed as his first ever victim in first class cricket, the great Geoff Boycott (Boycott had however scored 131 runs at the time but let's ignore that!) His progress from this point was slow but sure and he soon became a regular in the Lancashire side. His first representative honours were not far away either and after taking 50 wickets in the 1967 season he was selected to tour Pakistan with the Commonwealth XI.

The next three seasons were Ken's most successful in first class cricket. He played for England against the Rest of the World at Lords in 1970 and, after taking 74 wickets that season, was selected for the Ashes Tour to Australia. He made his test debut at Brisbane where he took five wickets for 47 runs in the second innings. He retained his place for the second test match and would have played in the third had it not been abandoned without a ball being bowled. Instead, Ken played in a hastily arranged one-day match against Australia which was later recognised as the first ever one-day international.

Unfortunately Ken then suffered a groin injury and was replaced by a young Bob Willis for the fourth test. He wasn't able to recover his place for the last three test matches (yes there were seven in that series!) but he did go on to play in the two subsequent test matches in New Zealand.

Back in the UK, Ken had a decent season in 1971, taking 59 wickets and he kept his place for the first test match against Pakistan. Unfortunately this was the match when Zaheer Abbas announced his arrival on the international scene with a score of 274 and Ken definitely came off second best. This was to be his final test match and his career from there took a downward path, with loss of form and injury taking its toll. His appearances became less frequent and after missing the whole of the 1976 season, he took his leave of Lancashire and between 1977 and 1980 played for Leicestershire.

By then however the persistent injuries finally got the better of him – he was suffering from back problems, fallen arches and arthritis, so it was hardly surprising that his body could no longer meet the demands required by fast bowling in cricket at the top level. He decided to retire from the first class game having made 177 appearances for Lancashire, 40 for Leicestershire and played in five test matches. He had taken in total 623 first class wickets at an average of 24.51. His batting statistics were less impressive but he was capable of some big hits, as befitted a tailender in those days, leading one commentator to describe his style as "spectacular"! He did not disappear from the game completely, playing initially in the North Staffs and South Cheshire League for Sneyd and then for Norton before ending his career at Congleton (by now as a batsman!), the town where he had made his home.

Ken worked in a number of different arenas once he was no longer playing full-time. He briefly ran a wines and spirits shop in Congleton, worked for several years in marketing for British Coal and latterly in partnership with a friend in a "dewatering" company. In the year 2000 he returned to the world of first class cricket as an umpire and continued in this role until 2005.

Married to Barbara since 1969, (who hails from Leicester), Ken has two daughters and three grandchildren. He still lives in Congleton where golf has taken over from cricket as his sport of participation. But whilst his cricket days may be a distant memory, he will be forever the first, and for the time being only, international cricketer produced by the town of St Helens.

Prior to Andy Murray becoming world number one in November 2016, the only British person to have reached number one in the world at any level of tennis (since the rankings were introduced) was Mark Eccleston from St Helens.

Michael "Bully Boy" Smith

I t could be argued that we are currently in a golden era for St Helens darts players with two locally-born players featuring in the top ten in the world darts rankings throughout 2016 and most of 2017.* Clearly some achievement. Indeed, the introduction of Michael "Bully Boy" Smith to the sport, has uncanny echoes of Dave Chisnall's introduction. Michael too threw his first darts as a consequence of an injury which prevented him indulging in outdoor activities. In his case it was all down to a wheelie on a bike that went wrong and he ended up, at the age of 15, with a broken hip and 16 weeks on crutches. Totally bored, he borrowed his dad's darts and dartboard and practised constantly for the whole time he was injured. He even scored his first 180 whilst on crutches!

Michael was born on 18th September 1990. His father Ian was a truck driver and his mother Sara a manager at various pubs and clubs including St Anne's Social Club. Michael had an elder brother and sister and the family lived in Sutton, with Michael attending St Cuthbert's school. His father played darts at St Joseph's Club in Peasley Cross so there was a darts tradition in the family (hence the darts lying around the house when Michael had his injury) and after the crutches came off in 2006, Michael soon became pretty well-known on the local darts scene. When he left school he took a joinery course at St Helens Technical College but didn't turn up for the final exam because he was playing in a darts competition – he lost but it was a decision he has certainly not had any cause to regret!

It turned out that success was not too far away: in 2008 he played in the New Kids on the Oche tournament, reaching the semi-final before losing to the eventual winner Arron Monk and that same year he signed for the Professional Darts Corporation. Adopting the nickname by which he was already known, Bully Boy (after wrestling with a calf whilst working on a farm!), he made his debut in a major tournament when still only 18 in the 2009 UK Open. He made a pretty decent fist of his first game but ended up on the wrong end of a 6-5 defeat.

It wasn't all plain sailing however – money was tight and Michael was starting to fall out of love with the game. However on Christmas Eve 2009, he fell and broke both wrists which meant an enforced 20 week lay-off (although he continued to play with broken hands and indeed won a number of games that way!) It was during this period that his resolve to succeed hardened and on returning to the game, he made the last 32 of the UK Open in June 2010. More progress was made in 2011 with his first PDC Pro Tour win in the UK Open Qualifier (beating Dave Chisnall in the final), shortly followed by another win in the Players Championship Event 2 in Benidorm in January 2012. He qualified that year for the World Matchplay, The World Grand Prix and the Players Championship Finals, and finished the year in 25th place in the Order of Merit.

2013 was a big year with Michael qualifying for the World Championships for the first time and also winning the PDC World Youth Championship. He reached the semi-finals of the Players Championship and qualified for the Grand Slam of Darts which took place in November 2013. The next month, just as his fellow townsman Dave Chisnall had done two years previously, he created a major upset by defeating 16-time world champion Phil "The Power" Taylor in the second round of the 2014 World Championships – and then, just as Chizzy had done, fell at the next hurdle. His success had not gone unnoticed however and he was awarded the PDC Young Player of the Year in January 2014.

The rest of the year was pretty busy, with Michael reaching five major finals, losing the first four but finally winning in the European Darts Trophy in Leipzig in September, beating Michael van Gerwen in the final to notch up his first European tour event win. The following year saw him break into the world top 16 for the first time, win the UK Open Qualifier and clock up two more European event wins, first at the International Darts Open in Riesa in Germany before retaining the European Darts Trophy, once again in Germany, and once again beating Michael van Gerwen in the final.

In January 2016 Michael managed his best showing in the World Championships, reaching the quarter finals, and he went on that year to qualify for the Premier League for the first time. He finished bottom of the pile, but, now at number eight in the world rankings he qualified for the inaugural Champions League of Darts, played by the top eight players in the world and which was held in September 2016. The tournament was notable as the first PDC event to be broadcast on BBC. And finally, on 24th September 2016, Michael took another accolade when he was officially announced as a Guinness World Record Holder for the highest score in one minute – 581 as it happens, beating on the way all seven of those above him in the world rankings!

Michael suffered a bit of a slump towards the end of 2016, losing a number of games on the bounce, but he managed to turn the tide in the World Championships in January 2017, winning his first two contests before going out against James Wade after being 3-1 up. In May 2017 he took his first title for nearly two years when he won the Gibraltar Darts trophy with a 132 finish when the game was tied and his opponent waiting on 56!

So, for the most part it has been onward and upward for Michael in his career so far – still only 27, he has been tipped by many as a future world champion and, importantly, believes himself that he can do it. In 2014 he predicted in an interview that within the next two years, he would be in the Premier League, in the top ten in the world and have won a major title. He has ticked off two of those but the third still eludes him.

He was managed, and is now mentored by Gary Anderson who was his childhood hero and who still sits above him in the world rankings, but Gary too believes that Michael will go the distance. Time will tell – in the meantime, Michael and his partner Dagmara (also a darts player, yet another parallel with Dave Chisnall!) have their two young sons, Michael and Kasper to look after and, as Michael put it in another interview, "If I don't win, my boy doesn't eat!" – yet another incentive to achieve his goals!

---

*   There is a third St Helens-based player in the top twenty, Stephen Bunting, but he does not qualify for inclusion as he was neither born, brought up nor educated in the town.

Dr Michael Smurfit KBE

P ossibly more than anyone else, whenever I have mentioned to people that Michael Smurfit is from St Helens, eyebrows are raised and the look of faint scepticism suggests that they think I've got that one wrong. But it isn't wrong; Michael was born in St Helens on 7th August 1936, as a consequence of the fact that his father, Jefferson Smurfit, moved to St Helens at the age of 17 from his birthplace of Sunderland to work in his uncle's tailoring business.

The background to the move was that Jefferson's father died when he was ten years old. His mother was originally from St Helens (and was an

Image reproduced courtesy of Oak Tree Press and Justin Macinnes

enterprising sort of person – she set up a moneylending business with the £90 she was left with after her husband's death) and had named her son Jefferson after her elder sister Mary's first husband who had already passed away. In return, her sister had promised that she would always look after young Jefferson. After one of her regular visits to Sunderland, Mary offered him the opportunity to work in her present husband's tailoring business in St Helens, an offer which he readily accepted. This venture started well enough and all the indications were that this was going to be a successful arrangement. Everything went sour however after Jefferson converted to Catholicism in order to marry a Catholic girl from Belfast. Both Mary and Jim were staunch members of the Salvation Army and had a strong aversion to Catholics and the bust up finally came in 1936 with Jefferson storming out of the business.

Fortunately by this point, funded in part by his wife Ann's mother, they were already living in a decent home in Devonshire Road in Denton's Green with a quarter of an acre of garden and a further loan from his mother-in-law enabled Jefferson to set up his own business in Hardshaw Street with the signage "Jeff Smurfit, Creator of Good Clothes". Two months later Michael was born. Despite the efforts of his previous employer to disrupt the business, Jefferson did pretty well and soon became, in Michael's words, the "self-styled squire of Eccleston".

It was around about this time that the first move to Ireland was made. The priest who had conducted his wedding introduced Jefferson to a box-making business in Dublin which he ended up buying. He then spent a number of years splitting his time between St Helens and Dublin. Michael's recollection of those days is understandably patchy but he does recall a number of events which took place after the Second World War had broken out: the death of his baby sister Ann from convulsions and a family friend who died with all his family when his house was subject to a direct hit by a German bomb. These events prompted Jefferson and Ann to up sticks in 1942 and move the family over to Dublin.

Michael was brought up as a Catholic and educated at St Michael's College in Rathmines before going as a boarder to Clongowes Wood College in County Kildare, Ireland's oldest Catholic school (which James Joyce had attended) where he was taught by Jesuits. After the war, Michael and his brother Jeff would return during the school holidays to St Helens to stay with their cousins but also started to undertake trips overseas with their father, as the box making business expanded internationally. The business had already been named Jefferson Smurfit and Sons Limited, so the expectation was clear that Michael and his brothers would enter the business. However this was to take place earlier than Michael had anticipated. Jefferson made the decision to take Michael and Jeff out of school at the age of 16, gave them some overalls and set them to work in the factory – something of a shock to Michael who had assumed that he would be going on to study at university. However Michael accepted his father's decision without putting up anything of a fight – at this stage of his life he was a quiet shy boy, and not one that you would necessarily have picked out as being a future captain of industry.

After three years working on the shop floor, fed up and bored, Michael decided to go to work with a friend in Canada. Indirectly this decision was to save his life as tuberculosis was detected in the medical he was required to undergo. Had it remained undetected, Michael would most likely have died within six months. In the event he was confined to a sanatorium for nine months before emerging pale, overweight but critically, free of tuberculosis and well enough to return to work. He had spent much of his time in hospital reading business publications and once back at work was elevated into an office role rather than working in the factory.

He now had the travel bug however and persuaded his father to arrange for him to work for a period for the business's main supplier of paper, Continental Can, in Connecticut. He moved out to the US on his own, a lonely time initially, but he took the opportunity to travel widely (on one occasion spending a night in a police cell in Alabama after having fallen asleep on a bus in a seat reserved for non-whites - Michael at the time knew nothing about racial segregation). Once back in Ireland he found himself increasingly frustrated that his father would not listen to his ideas about the business. He spent six months in London where he met his future wife Norma although they kept their relationship under wraps for some time; she was Jewish and he Catholic so neither family would have been happy. They decided to marry at just about the time, in 1962, when Michael's frustrations were coming to a head and he had decided to set up his own packaging business in England. He was to find suitable premises in the area he still regarded as the ancestral home – or at least not far away, as the site was just a few miles away in Bryn. Michael married Norma in London, and although neither set of parents attended, Jefferson did provide some invaluable financial support in setting up the Bryn operation.

Michael and Norma's first home was a bungalow near the factory, and within two years they had two sons, Tony and Michael Junior (who was born in St Helens Hospital, as had been Michael himself). Michael however was working 14 or 15 hour days so Norma bore the brunt of the work bringing up the children in those early days. The factory however was thriving and was soon moved to St Helens, followed shortly afterwards by the family who bought a house in Forest Grove, Eccleston Park. So in one way, Michael had now come full circle – but in many ways this was just the beginning.

His subsequent rise into the upper echelons of Irish society was prompted in the first instance by a visit to St Helens by his father. Sitting in the pub outside Michael's factory, his father invited him back to run the business in Ireland which in the meantime had been floated on the Irish Stock Exchange. Michael readily accepted, moved back to Ireland with his family and the St Helens business was merged into the Irish public company. The springboard was now in place for the Smurfit business to become Ireland's first multinational company and the first Irish company to become the world leader in any major industry. It became in fact the largest packaging company in the world and the single biggest factor in its success was the strategy adopted by, and the drive and determination of Michael Smurfit.

On the way he was to break the Protestant stranglehold on Ireland's biggest companies (which did of course make him very unpopular in some circles) and he is credited also with providing the inspiration to a whole new generation to take on the risks and rewards of entrepreneurial activity. Nobody in Ireland had ever pursued takeover activity and international expansion in the way that Michael did. He was involved in two of the biggest corporate transactions ever to occur in the Irish history – the first when he took the company private* in a deal funded by the US private equity firm Madison Dearborn and the second, the subsequent merger with the Dutch company Kappa Packaging BV. Michael was also at the helm as Chairman when the company was refloated in 2007, before finally standing down in 2008.

His reputation spread far and wide – it was said that everyone with Irish connections in Wall Street was asked, "Do you know Michael Smurfit?" He was without doubt one of the iconic figures in the Irish business community in the latter part of the 20th century and the early part of the 21st.

---

*   This is a process whereby the shares held by the public in a listed company are bought back, often by the original founder of the business who has retained a significant shareholding.

A successful career such as this does of course also involve a considerable accumulation of wealth (estimated in 2017 in the Irish Independent Rich List as €399 million) and the opportunity to live a lifestyle about which others can only dream. Michael has lived outside Ireland since leaving his first wife Norma (with whom he had four children) in 1985. He married his second wife, Birgitta in 1988 and they lived first in St Tropez, then Cannes and from there on to Monaco where he still bases himself (although his second marriage was also to end in divorce, two children and ten years later).

He was always a keen sportsman, skiing and golf being two of his particular passions and he is part-owner of the K Club in Dublin, fulfilling a dream when he was instrumental in bringing the Ryder Cup there in 2006. He has his own superyacht named *Lady Ann Magee* after his mother, was a prominent racehorse owner and has a valuable art collection. He has collected a whole string of honours, ranging from the KBE awarded to him by the Queen in 2005 for services to British business, various awards from the Irish state and other governments around the world, honorary degrees from universities and several orders from churches and other religious organisations. His autobiography includes photographs of him with the Queen, Princes Albert and Rainier of Monaco, Tiger Woods, Seve Ballesteros, Bono, Naomi Campbell, Nelson Mandela, Warren Buffet, Bill Gates, President of Ireland Mary McAleese, and Bill Clinton. Mention also needs to be made of his extensive philanthropic activities, with the naming of the postgraduate business school at University College Dublin as the Michael Smurfit School of Business being a mark of recognition of the financial support that he has provided.

The main qualities which one associates with Michael Smurfit are leadership and vision. He was never afraid to take a risk and although he would inevitably upset some of those he encountered, he inspired a fierce loyalty in others, particularly those who worked for him. He prided himself also on the integrity which he brought to both his personal and business life.

His autobiography *A Life Worth Living* begins with his reflection that it is 815 miles from St Helens to his current home in Monaco but that his journey there has been much longer. It is doubtful if there have been many from St Helens whose journey in life has been longer than his.

Gary Stretch

I have commented elsewhere in this book that one cannot always control the circumstances in which one finds oneself but that it is the way you respond to these circumstances that defines you as a person. However if we look at the converse situation, that is, where someone unexpectedly finds himself in a position of opportunity, the ability to grab it with both hands can also be critical in determining one's path in life. Gary Stretch is a good case in point.

Gary's credentials for inclusion in this book are two or arguably threefold. He was a successful boxer who doubled as a male model before making a relatively seamless transition into the film business - somewhat less dangerous an activity and with at least a prospect of greater longevity. He was not of course the first boxer to make this career move but he has definitely made as good a fist of it as anyone.

Gary was born in Haresfinch on 4th November 1965. His father, Ronnie, ran a plumbing business and raised Gary and his two brothers alone – Gary's mum walked out when he was ten and he has barely had any contact with her since. Gary went to Cowley School but whilst there developed a reputation as a troublemaker and was threatened with expulsion. As a last resort, he went to a boxing gym and fortunately, loved every minute of it. From then on, there was no looking back and at the age of 16 he had his first lucky break when he was drawn to fight against a young boxer who was going for a place in the Guinness Book of Records for the longest winning run (he was on 75 at the time). Because of that, the fight was televised and after Gary had won with a round 1 knockout, he was offered the opportunity to turn professional, an offer which he eagerly accepted.

Gary was to stay in the fight game for some ten years and retired with a very respectable record behind him. By September 1998 he was British Light Middleweight Champion and in 1990 he won the WBC International Light Middleweight title (not quite a world championship but the next stage down). Of his 25 professional fights, he won 23 and lost only two, the second of these being the much-hyped showdown against Chris Eubank for the WBO World Middleweight Championship in 1991, a fight billed in advance as "Beauty v The Beast". Gary lost, although the outcome was not without controversy. The doctor had advised the referee to stop the fight at the end of round 5 because of a cut to Eubank's forehead, but the referee allowed him to continue and when he did stop the fight after Gary had taken a standing count of eight in Round 6, all three judges had Gary ahead on the scorecard. That was pretty much it for Gary as far as boxing was concerned. He did return briefly to the ring two years later for a relatively low-key bout but by now he was ready to move on.

During his boxing career, Gary had done some modelling work for, amongst others, Calvin Klein and Versace, although this was not the result of a career choice which he made; he had simply been sitting in a pub when he was approached by a lady who asked if he was a model and, when she found out he was not, she invited him to join her agency.

However after retirement his career was to take a different direction, albeit once again as a result of an opportunity which unexpectedly came his way. He was on holiday in New York and chanced upon an altercation in the street between an old lady and two young punks. Gary intervened on the old lady's behalf and it turned out that she was a famous acting coach, whose client list was littered with Hollywood names. They went to lunch together and on hearing he wanted to be an actor, she immediately took him under her wing and he has not looked back since.

At the time of writing Gary has some 39 acting credits to his name, the best-known of which are probably Oliver Stone's *Alexander* and *World Trade Center*. He was also nominated for a British Independent Film Award for his role in *Dead Man's Shoes*. In 2005 he auditioned for the James Bond role and was indeed one of the bookie's early favourites – I have no idea how well he might have performed in the role but I have to say that the idea of James Bond coming from St Helens does appeal to me. In the event he lost out to some chap called Daniel Craig so sadly it was not to be. Gary continues however to base himself in Hollywood whilst he has the opportunity to pick up film roles although he has stated that his long term intention is to move back to England.

According to the newspapers Gary has had liaisons with many well-known celebrities, including Kylie Minogue, Liz Hurley and Kelly Brook. He was also linked with Raquel Welch but denies that there was ever any relationship between them – they were, he says, simply classmates in the same acting school. He was married to the Puerto Rican singer and actress Roselyn Sanchez from 1998 to 2001 but is currently single and, it seems, happy to stay that way until the right person comes along.

Unsurprisingly, given his background, Gary has featured in numerous newspaper and magazine articles over the years. Most refer to his upbringing and many observe that he still sounds like a man from St Helens. A quick browse through YouTube however reveals that although there are certainly traces of his home town accent he has now grafted on to that a distinct mid-Atlantic drawl, of the sort which is not commonly heard in Haresfinch!

Gary is not the finest actor the town has produced but if the measure were done by reference to colourful lifestyle, he would be right up there with the best of them.

In the 1850s the
St Helens Cycling Club
was the largest outside London.

Sir Hugh Stott Taylor

S ir Hugh Stott Taylor was a chemist who made a landmark contribution to catalytic theory in 1925.

Born in St Helens on 6th February 1890 he was, like the eminent scientist John William Draper, destined to make his name in the United States rather than in his own country. However their approaches to the world of science differed somewhat – as we saw earlier, Dr Draper's publication, *The History of the Conflict between Religion and Science* was to find its way into the Catholic Church's list of proscribed publications whereas Sir Hugh was made a Knight

Photograph supplied by Anita Taylor

Commander of the Order of St Gregory the Great by Pope Pius XII. He was indeed a great believer in the doctrine promoted by St Thomas Aquinas that "Science is a revelation of the mind of God" and was President of Pax Romana, the international Catholic movement for intellectual and cultural affairs. So it is unlikely that he and Dr Draper would have agreed on very much, at least in this arena.

Hugh was the third of eight children of James and Ellen Taylor. James's occupation was a "glass technologist" and we are told that he was responsible for a number of improvements in the quality of plate glass and in the manufacture of coloured glass. He had his own laboratory at home which no doubt influenced the career choice of young Hugh. Ellen had been a headmistress before her marriage and both parents were very heavily involved in charity work, mainly for the local poor. James was also an organiser of the Co-operative movement, both locally and nationally. The family was raised in an atmosphere of strict observance of the Catholic faith.

The first school attended by Hugh was Notre Dame Convent School, followed by Lowe House Higher Grade and then Lowe House Elementary School. He won a scholarship to Cowley in 1902 (West Park did not open its doors until 1911 so there was at the time no Catholic secondary education available) and then a scholarship to Liverpool University which he attended from 1906. He obtained a BSc degree in 1909 (let's remember he was still only 19) and an MSc in 1910. He then spent three years doing post-graduate work in Liverpool before a year in Stockholm at the Nobel Institute and a further year in Hanover at the Technische Hochschule; at both of these institutions he worked under eminent scientists. In 1914 he was awarded a Doctor of Science degree from Liverpool on the basis of the nine papers which he had published whilst overseas.

His move to the United States arose as a consequence of a friendship he had developed with another young English chemist, JP Kendall, with whom he had worked in Stockholm. Kendall, who had gone to the United States to take up a post at Columbia University, was approached in 1914 by Princeton to see if he was prepared to move there. Kendall declined the invitation but suggested that Taylor would be an equally good candidate. Hugh accepted the offer; initially he saw this as just another brief spell working overseas but it was in fact a life-changing decision as he was to stay at Princeton (with the exception of a spell in London during the latter part of the First World War working for the interestingly named Munitions Inventions Department) until his death in 1974.

Hugh appears to have been a very popular addition to the teaching staff at Princeton: during one month in his first year he was the recipient of 28 dinner invitations. He was also regarded as something of a hero by the students, at least in part because he would allow them to accompany him whilst he drove at 80 mph on trips to New York, all the time chatting casually away. Hugh married in 1919, his wife being Elizabeth Sawyer from Southport who had attended Liverpool University at the same time as he had. They were to stay together until her death in 1958.

It was in 1919 that Hugh first gained international recognition with the publication of a book on catalysis, which he authored jointly with

Sir Eric Rideal, who had been wounded in the First World War and, after returning to England, had also worked in the Munitions Inventions Department. Hugh's landmark contribution came six years later. It has been said that his own words best describe the nature of the breakthrough: "In 1925, by a deductive leap in the dark, I suggested that catalyst surfaces could not be homogenous, that from the heterogeneity might stem some of the most characteristic properties of catalytic materials". This will no doubt mean a lot more to others than it does to me but it certainly cemented his reputation in the field of physical chemistry and as a consequence he was regularly consulted by both industry and government.

During the Second World War, he played a major part in the chemical activities associated with the production of the atom bomb. His British nationality (which he retained throughout his life) meant that in theory high security clearance was problematic but a circuitous way of solving this problem was found by appointing him as a liaison officer for the Canadian government (exactly why this made it easier is not clear but it seems to have done the trick).

From arriving at Princeton his progress up the academic ladder was swift. He was appointed assistant professor in 1915, associate professor in 1921 and full professor a year later at which point he was still only 32. From 1926 until 1951 he was Chairman of the Chemistry Department and from 1945 Dean of the Graduate School during which time he founded the Association of Princeton Graduate Alumni. His energy and dynamism were legendary – his movement resembled more of a run than a walk – and despite all his research commitments and the work he did with outside bodies, he never neglected his duties at Princeton, even during the stressful war years when he was spending significant amounts of time in New York. He was a decisive man (albeit some would say ruthless) but nonetheless was always regarded by the students as approachable, possessing the interpersonal skills which conveyed the impression that he always had time to deal with anything the students brought to him.

Hugh's achievements secured for him numerous honours. He was awarded the Nichols Medal of the American Chemical Society in 1928, elected a Fellow of the Royal Society of London in 1932, and made a Commander of the Belgian Order of Leopold II in 1937. The ensuing years brought him other medals, in addition to which he was awarded honorary degrees by 28 American and European institutions. In 1953 he was knighted by the young Queen Elizabeth, a month after he had been made a Knight of the Order of St Gregory by the Pope.

After his retirement, he remained active; a colleague joked that he reduced his workload to the average of two men, whereas he had previously carried the workload of three and served as president of the Woodrow Wilson National Fellowship Foundation, as well as editor-in-chief of *American Scientist,* the periodical publication of the Society of Sigma Xi, of which he had also been president.

As we have seen, the influence of Hugh's Catholic upbringing was to stay with him until the end of his life and alongside this he was equally devoted to his family. He had two daughters, each of whom graduated at Vassar College, a liberal arts institution in New York State. His wife's death in 1958, the same year as his retirement was a bitter blow, depriving them of the opportunity to travel and carry out other activities together – this may of course have contributed to his continued level of professional activity in the years until his death in 1974.

A lasting memorial to Sir Hugh's contribution to Princeton was established in 1962, when an anonymous donor made a $500,000 gift to create the Hugh Stott Taylor Chair of Chemistry.

Hugh Stott Taylor is at the very least one of the top two scientists to come out of St Helens, his only possible rival being the aforementioned John William Draper.

St.Helens Council

John Walsh

John Walsh in action.
Image courtesy of Saints Heritage Society.

Given my intention to keep entries for rugby league players to a minimum, many will think the inclusion of John Walsh a strange choice. I would defend it however on two counts. As a rugby player he was a World Cup winner who remains to this day one of the best centres I have had the privilege to witness, notwithstanding that we have seen the likes of Newlove, Meninga, Lyon, and Gidley in the centre since his retirement. Secondly, there was the extra-curricular dimension in that he was, uniquely in the rugby league world at the time, a graduate with a master's degree. In addition, he worked throughout his rugby league career as an actuary, before retiring from the game (twice!) at a time when he was arguably at his peak to concentrate on his career in the financial world.

John was born on 13th June 1946 and lived with his two brothers and sister in Richards Grove at the top of Boardmans Lane. His father was a warrant officer with the Royal Air Force and his mother a registered nurse at what was then known as Rainhill Mental Hospital.

He was educated initially at St Joseph's Infant School in Fingerpost and then Holy Cross Junior School before moving on to Grange Park for his secondary education. There are many there who recollect him as both a rebel and a high achiever. Whilst his academic achievements (A levels in Maths, Further Maths, Special Maths, Physics and Special Physics with four distinctions and one credit) provide the evidence of latter, the fact that he was the only student in the Upper 6th form who was not made a prefect, suggests that there may well be some truth in the former as well.

Unsurprisingly, John excelled as a rugby player for the school (union not league) but also played for Liverpool FC's junior teams, even spending a summer training with the first and reserve team under the supervision of Bill Shankly. However he concluded that football was not the career for him and in 1964 enrolled at Hull University to study Special Maths. It was here that he met fellow student Bill Bailey, who was in 2013 to publish the booklet *John Walsh: Saint and Winner*. John was by all accounts a very gifted student, gaining a BSc (2:1) with relative ease, whilst at the same time participating fully in the university social life as described in some detail in the aforementioned booklet.

After graduating in 1967, he moved back over the Pennines and did a Masters degree in Statistics at the University of Manchester which he obtained in 1968. Around about this time, he played briefly for St Helens Rugby Union club at Moss Lane, before joining the newly formed amateur rugby league club at Moss Bank where he played alongside Ken Gill, another destined to become a rugby league international.

In 1968 John married Liz Collins who had also attended Grange Park School and then toyed with the prospect of a teaching career after filling in for the father of a friend teaching maths to the 6th form at West Park. However he opted eventually for the somewhat unfashionable (but, at the time, extremely well paid!) career as an actuary and joined the Royal Insurance in Liverpool. That he subsequently went on to become a professional rugby player didn't register on his employer's radar (even after he had achieved international honours!)

In the meantime, the Moss Bank amateur side was doing rather well and John's performances had not gone unnoticed. This led to his selection for the Great Britain Amateur RL team for the tour of Australia. However before the tour took place, Saints were knocking on his door and he was to make his debut on 15th April 1968 on the left wing, away against Swinton. The following season he played 17 games at full-back and by the time the 1969/70 season came around, John had secured a regular place in the team, first as full-back but then as centre. He was from a very early stage a firm favourite of the fans, combining a wonderful creativity with the ball with some of the best defence we had ever seen from a centre three-quarter.

Honours started to accumulate, beginning with a win in the 1970 Championship Final against Leeds during which he scored a try and two crucial drop goals. The following year, the Championship was secured once again, this time against Wigan in the most thrilling of finales, when John's last minute dropkick went some way wide of the posts but bounced straight into the arms of the chasing Billy Benyon who went on to score the winning try in a game Saints had never looked like winning.

The 1971/2 season saw John play a key part in the Challenge Cup win at Wembley, again against Leeds, followed by a starring role in Great Britain's winning side in the World Cup in September 1972. In the final against Australia, John's defensive display, and in particular a crash tackle he executed on one of the opposition's danger men, big centre Mark Harris (which, in the university television room where I was watching the game, gave rise to huge cheers and almighty shudders in equal measure) still lives vividly in the memory.

It was shortly after this tournament that the unthinkable happened. John announced his retirement from rugby league to concentrate on his actuarial career, observing that he had won everything there was to win in the game. This coincided with a temporary slump in the club's fortunes with no silverware on display after each of the 1972/3 and 1973/4 seasons. Then, quite unexpectedly, in the pre-season charity game on 16th August 1974 against Blackpool Borough, who should appear at full-back but one John Walsh. Rumours abounded around the town – I remember being informed on great authority that John had failed his exams and decided to pack in his professional career in favour of rugby. The reality however was that Saints, knowing that he had the X factor that gave the team that extra dimension, simply got the cheque book out to entice him back. John duly worked his magic and the championship returned once again that season to Knowsley Road. Sadly however, John's last game for the club was a defeat in the Premiership Final against Leeds, just two weeks after arguably his best display ever when he inspired Saints to an amazing comeback against Wigan to win 22-16 in a semi-final they had been losing 2-16 with only about ten minutes to go. John did play for England in the World Cup in the summer in 1975 but injuries were now taking their toll and although there was no formal retirement announcement this time round, we did not get to see him on the rugby field again.

By this time John and Liz had two children and he was still working for the Royal Insurance in Liverpool. Somewhat disillusioned with life in Britain in the 1970s, they elected to emigrate to Canada. John went on to complete the separate qualification as a Canadian actuary and in 1977 he joined Mercers where he was to work until the end of his career.

He and his wife still live in Canada but return regularly to see family and to travel in the UK and Europe. John returned also for his induction into the St Helens Hall of Fame as well as a reunion of the 1972 Cup winning team. They have three children, the third having been born in Canada, and now have six grandchildren.

John Walsh has been described as many things – the "brainiest bloke in rugby league", an "enigma", and an "iconoclast" on the one hand, a "hard man" and an "enforcer" on the other. Bill Bailey tells us that he was extrovert, socially confident, down to earth, quick-witted but self-deprecating, had a sardonic sense of humour and loved a practical joke. For my own part, he is up there with the best rugby players St Helens has ever produced - had he been blessed with searing pace to go with the rest of his abilities, it would be difficult to think of a more complete player.

As an interesting aside John is occasionally confused with another John Walsh, a young Australian rugby league player who fractured his spine during a game in 1971 and ended up spending the rest of his life in a wheelchair. By a strange quirk of fate he too had been a star student at maths and physics and went on to qualify as an actuary (indeed he was one of my own partners at PwC before our respective retirements). In 2001 the St Helens John Walsh was informed by his daughter that she had seen on Google that he had been chosen as Actuary of the Year – something of a surprise to him but it was in fact the other John Walsh!

Colin Welland

Colin Welland is another who was raised within the Metropolitan Borough of St Helens, albeit some years before it actually came into existence. His rugby affiliation, it has to be conceded, was with Warrington rather than with the Mighty Saints but that has not prevented the inclusion of others in this collection and nor should it prevent his.

Colin was actually born in Kensington in Liverpool, on 4th July 1935, son of Jack, a crane driver on the docks, and Norah, a hospital worker. He had an elder sister, Beryl. He had vivid recollections of the blitz as a young child, although he was too young to take in the full horror of the regular bombing raids and recollects it as a thrilling time for all the young children. Escape came at the age of seven when his father secured a job at the US Air Base in Burtonwood and the family went to live in Whiteman Avenue in Newton-le-Willows. Colin attended school initially in Golborne where he soon shed his Liverpool accent and adopted the flat Lancashire vowels that would characterise him for the rest of his life.

It certainly wasn't an affluent upbringing, although pretty much everyone was in the same boat. Colin's father was constantly looking for ways of making money but it never quite came off for him so the family was rarely able to afford very much. However from a very young age, Colin saw himself as an entertainer, initially as a boy soprano and then later, after he passed the scholarship and went to Newton Grammar, he would get involved in all the school productions, whether it be Shakespeare or Gilbert and Sullivan.

At school Colin was a keen sportsman, his two main sports being rugby and athletics. He also loved English, history, geography and art but took little or no interest in subjects he didn't enjoy with the consequence that he did not have the academic qualifications to go to university. Instead he had to endure two years in the army completing his National Service, which he loathed. It did not help that whilst Colin was in the army, his father died of lung cancer and then his sister died, just two weeks later, at the age of 24 from a rare blood disease. His father had however encouraged Colin to become a teacher and after National Service finally came to an end, he enrolled at Teacher's Training College at Bretton Hall near Wakefield, followed by Goldsmiths College in London. Armed with a Teaching Diploma in Art and Drama he took a job as an art teacher at Manchester Road Secondary Modern School in Leigh where he was known by the pupils as "Ted" because of his Teddy Boy hairstyle. He continued to play rugby turning out regularly for Newton Rugby Club on Crow Lane.

Colin was however desperate to get into acting and it was his forthcoming marriage to Patricia which led to him taking the plunge. Thinking that it was now or never, in that once he had the responsibilities of a married man he was far less likely to take a risk, he decided to give up teaching in favour of a job at the Manchester Library Theatre as an assistant stage manager. Crucially however, although he was required to spend time sweeping the stage, he also got the opportunity to perform on it. Various roles came his way and the big break arrived when in 1962 he was offered a part in what was to become the legendary *Z Cars* series as PC David Graham. Now Colin Welland rather than Williams (there was already an actor Colin Williams), this was the role which fast tracked him into the nation's consciousness and which paved the way for further stage and some film work.

One of the directors of *Z Cars* at the time was Ken Loach and it was as a consequence of this that Colin was given the film role for which he was probably best-known, that of English teacher, Mr Farthing, in the highly acclaimed *Kes* in 1969, for which he won a BAFTA award. Other film roles were in *Villain* in 1971 alongside Richard Burton, *Straw Dogs* with Dustin Hoffman in 1971 and *Sweeney,* a spin-off from the television series, in 1977.

It was however Colin's screenwriting for which he became most renowned. He had started writing plays in the late 1960s, several of which went on to be aired on television. The most notable early ones were *Bangelstein's Boys, The Hallelujah Handshake,* and *Roll on 4 O'Clock.* In 1973 the TV play *Say Goodnight to Grandma* was later turned into a West End success, whilst in the same year he received a BAFTA for *Kisses at Fifty.* On three occasions he won Writers' Guild Awards for best TV playwright.

In the late 1970s Colin turned his attention to writing for the big screen and his first success came with *Yanks* in 1979 which drew on his experience of the US servicemen based in Burtonwood, whom Colin had encountered many times in his youth. The big one however was just around the corner. David Puttnam commissioned him to write the story of two British athletes in the 1924 Olympics, a task which Colin performed by undertaking an enormous amount of research, including placing advertisements in London newspapers seeking personal memories of the games. This clearly paid off; *Chariots of Fire* was nominated for seven Oscars and won four, including the award for the best original screenplay. This gave Colin particular satisfaction as he had been given short shrift in Hollywood when he had first tried to market the film. It led also to his famous acceptance speech in which he proclaimed, "The British are coming". (Nigel Havers, who played another athlete in the film, was convinced this was said tongue-in-cheek but it was for the most part taken as a serious expression of intent!) The film itself had a St Helens connection – the changing rooms at Cowley Girls School were used in one scene while another was filmed at the athletic track in Ruskin Drive.

There would have been another St Helens link had Colin succeeded with his next project. He wanted to script a film entitled *Rocket,* chronicling the story of the railway engineers George and Robert Stephenson which culminated with the famous Rainhill Trials in 1829. It appealed particularly as a story of the common man, with in the first instance George, who could neither read nor write till he was 18, and then Robert, taking on the establishment and winning. Sadly however, Hollywood could not be convinced and it never happened.

Chariots was certainly the highlight of Colin's career, although he did go on to script *War of the Buttons* in 1984 (which was also a David Puttnam film) and *Twice in a Lifetime* in 1985 which was tipped for an Oscar nomination but didn't actually receive one. He also wrote the original script for 1989's *A Dry White Season,* a film about the abuses and cruelty of the South African apartheid regime, although the script was considerably revised for the film by its director Euzhan Palcy.

For many years Colin was a regular writer in both *The Observer* and *The Independent* and he often used these columns to promote the game of rugby league and in particular its persecution at the hands of the

Rugby Union – Colin's own role coaching the juniors at Richmond was once challenged on the basis that he was an honorary director of Fulham Rugby League Club! He would also rail against the snobbishness of golf clubs although he gave an honorary exemption in this regard to Keswick Golf Club which he used to frequent during a period when he and his family were living close by in Threlkeld. Indeed, during a period when I was also a member there, I would encounter him in the bar on a Friday evening, this being the early days of Super League, watching (and indeed opining on) the day's televised match.

Colin passed away on 2nd November 2015 aged 81 after suffering from Alzheimers for several years. He was survived by his wife of more than 50 years, Pauline, three daughters, a son and six grandchildren.

The purists will argue that Colin was not a true son of the town and indeed he didn't see himself as such either, Newton having been an independent urban district for the first 40 years of his life. But it is of course now an integral part of the Borough of St Helens so he must take his rightful place amongst the great and the good that the town has produced. And few could argue that his place is anywhere other than in the upper echelons of that august grouping!

St.Helens Council

Elton Welsby

Those of a certain vintage will remember very clearly the man who fronted *Granada Sport* form 1978 to 2000. That man was Elton Welsby, born as Robert Elton Welsby, on 28th May 1951.

His father Dan was a bank manager and his mother Ruth (who once dated Geoff Duke!) was a

Elton Welsby punches the air as Mal Meninga intercepts in the Premiership Final 1985 – Elton's son Christopher is next to him.
© Copyright Photographer Brian Peers 1985

teacher and the family lived at Hamilton Road in Bleak Hill. Robert was educated initially at Bleak Hill Primary School, but the life of a bank manager is an itinerant one and the family moved to Meols in the Wirral, then to Macclesfield and finally to Liverpool where Robert attended Liverpool College for his secondary education.

Robert stayed on at school into the sixth form but didn't actually complete his A levels, leaving instead to take up a job with the Royal Insurance. He soon found that an office job was not to his liking, abandoned it and took a job as a hospital porter at Broad Green Hospital. He was to stay there for a year and still remembers it as one of the most enjoyable years of his life. His uncle however was giving him a hard time, believing he could do much better and, almost on a whim, in 1970 Roger decided to apply for a job as a sports reporter with the *Liverpool Weekly News* after coming across a copy and noting with interest that it had some ten pages of sport. He got the job straight away, and shortly thereafter disclosed his middle name to a fellow journalist. He was henceforth referred to as Elton and the name stuck.

Promotion soon came his way and he became the lead reporter on both Liverpool and Everton matches. A particular coup was spending a full day with Bill Shankly as part of a series of articles entitled *A Day in the Life of a Football Manager*. With his name becoming well-known on the Liverpool sporting scene, Elton was in 1994 offered a position at the newly founded Radio City and very soon his voice became familiar to all listening to the football commentaries on that station. His meteoric rise was to continue in January 1978 when he was offered a job by Granada, not as a commentator but as a presenter. He went on to host their main football programme *The Kick Off Match*, its successor *Match Night*, and was the ITV reporter attached to the Northern Ireland team in the World Cup both in Spain in 1982 and Mexico 1986. After ITV was granted the exclusive live football rights in 1988, Elton was appointed as chief presenter and at this time, his unique lively, sometimes described as dazzling, style of presenting made him a household name in football circles around the country.

Elton led the ITV coverage of the World Cup in Italy in 1990 and then again at the Euros in Sweden in 1992, when he worked alongside Jack Charlton. The two of them struck up a great relationship and had a huge amount of fun. However the body blow was not far away; it was that same year that Sky Sports outbid ITV for live football and this was to mark the beginning of the end of Elton's career as one of the country's premier football presenters. He was to stay at Granada for several more years and latterly presented a poorly funded football programme *Soccer Sunday*. He retained much of his popularity however and regularly outperformed Jim Rosenthal, one of his successors at ITV, in polls undertaken in the North West. The final parting of the ways was to come in May 2000, when ITV bosses decided that his contract would not renewed.

Elton's career had not consisted simply of presenting football – he stood in sometimes for Dicky Davies on *World of Sport*, presented both darts and snooker (indeed he was there on the occasion of the very first televised 147 by Steve Davies in 1982) and was one of the anchor men at the Seoul Olympics in 1988. He also made a lone foray outside the sporting world with a stint as host of the quiz show *Busman's Holiday* in the early 1990s.

After leaving ITV, his television appearances have been infrequent, although he did present *Crown Green Bowls* for Sky Sports in 2005. Initially it had been back to radio, taking up a role with Century Radio in Manchester presenting *Elton Welsby's Soccer Saturday* for three years. He also toured the country with Ricky Tomlinson where his role was to interview Ricky in character as Jim Royle of *The Royle Family*. Nowadays his appearances are restricted to after-dinner speaking and charity functions - on one occasion he shaved off his beard and dyed his hair red to raise money for Zoe's Hospice in West Derby (cheerfully admitting at the time he looked like a plonker!)

Sport was not however simply a day job as far as Elton was concerned. In his own time he has always been a passionate supporter of Everton FC, having been taken to see his first game by his father at the age of eleven, shortly after the family had moved to Liverpool. More pertinently, for this collection at least, he was a keen follower of the Mighty Saints and one of his fondest memories was the 1984/5 "Meninga" season. Elton was a good friend of coach Billy Benyon and he travelled with his son, Christopher, home and away for every match, more often than not on the team coach. Elton recalls being asked to reassure a terrified Sean Day in the dressing room prior to the Lancashire Cup Final against Wigan in front of a crowd of more than 26,000. He did a pretty good job as Sean went on to score a try and kick five goals in a 26-18 victory. Other less pleasing memories include being approached by a young Joe Lydon, who told Elton he didn't see himself staying at Widnes and would welcome a move to Saints. Elton passed this on to Billy Benyon who was unsurprisingly enthusiastic, seeing him as the perfect replacement for the departing Meninga. Sadly the Saints Board didn't share his enthusiasm and took the matter no further. The following year of course Wigan swooped and he became rugby league's first £100,000 transfer. And Elton's disillusionment with the Board was complete when they advised Billy Benyon that Elton was not part of the team set-up and should not therefore travel on the team coach.

Elton had married Joyce in 1976 and they had two children together, Christopher and Laura. There are currently two grandchildren on the scene, Dylan and Oscar. Elton and Joyce are now divorced and he is living out his retirement in Heswall on the Wirral.

He is still fondly remembered on many football fan websites, although inevitably there are others who are less kind, particularly those that accused him of bias towards Everton. Alongside Chris Foy, he appears in the list of "Celebrity Blues" on ToffeeWeb so his allegiance is there for all to see – indeed the fact that his cousin's grandson Danny Welsby, is now on Everton's books, is a source of extreme pride to him! And like any commentator of repute, he is remembered for some notable soundbites, two of the best-known of which were, "And now for the goals from Carrow Road where the game ended nil-nil" and, "that's Aston Villa's first goal since their last one!"

The inspiration for the
2012 Olympic
opening ceremony was
the St Helens town motto
"Ex Terra Lucem".

Paul Wilson

I had to think long and hard over the decision to include Paul Wilson in this collection. You might think that a long career as a journalist, which has included periods as chief football reporter with *The Observer* would naturally qualify him for inclusion. Looked at in isolation, that is probably correct but the picture is muddied by a stunning piece of misjudgement on his part (many will say I am being kind in calling it that). His rugby allegiance rested for a lengthy period in his life, with, of all clubs, Wigan rather than the town of his birth, St Helens. Now I have always assumed that those who were born in Wigan secretly wish they had been born in St Helens but feel obliged to support their hometown. The idea therefore that someone from elsewhere should actually choose to support Wigan is difficult to get your mind round. When that person hails from St Helens, the matter is beyond comprehension.

Paul defends his choice in an articulate manner, as befits someone who writes so eloquently for a living. Having been educated at Thatto Heath Primary School, Cowley and Lancaster University, he had taken up a job with the *St Helens Reporter* but because the pay was so poor, had abandoned this and was doing a series of manual jobs which were somewhat more lucrative. He was however approached by the editor of the *Reporter* who offered him a job as a writer for the new *Wigan Reporter*, which was a free handout set up in part as a response to the success of the *St Helens Star*. So far, so good you might think and an opportunity to do some missionary work in alien territory. However it did not quite work out like this.

One of Paul's tasks in his new job was to cover Wigan rugby league matches. As they were languishing in the second division at the time, having been relegated in the 1979/80 season, there was no direct conflict with any lingering St Helens allegiance. And in fairness to Paul, this took place at a point in time when the rivalry was probably at its lowest ebb. I recall, for example, a game in 1979, between the two sides shortly before

Wigan's fall from grace. Captaining St Helens was Bill Francis, ex-Wigan and still a baddie in the eyes of most St Helens fans, whilst tossing up with him in the centre circle, as captain of Wigan, was Tony Karalius, an ex-St Helens hero and an undoubted goodie. Confusing times indeed. I can even recall a conversation with fellow fans, in which we agreed that the matches against Widnes, then a top side, were probably now bigger than the traditional derbies against Wigan – unthinkable now but that was the reality of the time. This is not of course to excuse Paul in any way but more to put his conversion to the Wigan cause into some sort of context.

Paul took up his duty as rugby league reporter with relish, although he had previously been more of a football than rugby fan (an Everton supporter, as it happens, something he once described in a newspaper article as a "childhood affliction"). Travelling in the company of the supporters, getting to know the players, interviewing them and reporting their thoughts in the local paper, penning a column in the Wigan programme under the name Doug Stand – all this placed him very firmly in the Wigan camp and living in the border country that is Billinge meant he didn't have to put up with too much derision for what would have seemed to many as traitorous behaviour. And, in his own words, if Alex Murphy could make the change of allegiance, why couldn't he? (Whether Alex, off the pitch at least, is the sort of role model one might choose is another question, but Paul seemed to have no problem!)

Paul describes this as an exciting time to be associated with Wigan Rugby League Club and he attributes this in part to the involvement of Messrs Whelan and Lindsay, two characters to whom I will be generous by describing them merely as divisive. But while there are many critics of Wigan's period of dominance during the late eighties and early nineties (and the manner in which they attempted to maintain their dominance), Paul is certainly not one of them – as is evidenced by his book *The Best Years of our Lives* (yes, it really was called that!), which charted Wigan's rise from the Second Division to the end of their period of rugby league dominance in the mid-1990s. Paul did go as far as to concede that this dominance gave rise to great problems for the game, but he maintained that Wigan did not actually do anything wrong and that they could not be criticised for setting new standards which others were unable to achieve. This rather conveniently ignores the fact that the Wigan dominance came about at least in part because they mortgaged the future of the club on continued success and regularly enticed the best talent away from any rival clubs (using, in the view of many, foul means as well as fair). This was hardly the blueprint for success that other clubs would want to replicate. Interestingly, in his brief biography at the end of the book, the fact that Paul originated from St Helens was overlooked – funny that!

These days Paul lives in Wigan with his second wife (both of his wives were from Wigan!) and has three adult children, with the affiliation of all being to the town of their upbringing. Having moved to the *Wigan Evening Post* in 1983, he stepped up to cover rugby league for *The Independent* in 1987 and then on to *The Observer* in 1990. Thankfully for all concerned, he stopped covering rugby in 1995 and became football correspondent, a role which he occupies to this day and in which he seems to have discovered the ability to write thoughtful, insightful and intelligent articles. This might be of course because he no longer feels the need to attempt to poke fun at the town of his birth (was it really necessary to describe the BBC commentary team of Ray French and Alex Murphy as a "double dose of dreary St Helens accents"?) but perhaps also that he is now reporting on the sport which was his first love, before that fateful day when he took the job at the *Wigan Observer*. He claims now that he has a foot in both the St Helens and Wigan camps and his Twitter page makes the observation that he is the only person in the world who doesn't know whether he supports Wigan or St Helens. All I can say to this is that the answer to this question is pretty clear to me. You've made your bed, Paul, and you have to be prepared to lie in it – there's no jumping back into ours!

David Yates

I t is not difficult to identify the point in time at which David Yates, previously a respected and highly-regarded television director, was catapulted into the limelight. It was his appointment as director of *Harry Potter and the Order of the Phoenix,* the fifth in the series of *Harry Potter* films. He was in many ways an unlikely choice for the role, having virtually no previous experience in the world of feature films. And although it was the culmination of a childhood ambition to direct a major film, David was initially reluctant to take it on for a different reason: the way he saw it, there had already been three well-known directors involved in the series, Christopher Columbus, Mike Newall and Alfonso Couron, so had not the challenge of creating the Harry Potter world on screen already been achieved? However after meeting up with the film producer, David Heyman, he was immediately won over and the arrangement clearly worked for both parties as David went on to direct each of the final four films in the series.

David was born on 30th November 1963 and raised in Rainhill with his younger brother Andrew and elder sister Beverley. It was whilst he was a pupil at Grange Park that his love affair with film began, inspired specifically by Steven Spielberg's blockbuster *Jaws* which David saw at the cinema at the age of 12. He determined then that he wanted to be a film director and shortly afterwards his mother bought him an 8mm camera which David would use to make short films and videos at school and in Taylor Park, dragging relatives and friends along to appear in them. Film became an obsession which stayed with him throughout his schooldays at Grange Park and St Helens College (where he obtained A levels in Politics, English Literature and Sociology) and also at Essex University (where he studied for a degree in Government). Indeed whilst at Essex University he founded the Film and Video Production Society.

After graduation in 1987 it was back to making films and his first serious attempt *When I Was a Girl,* funded with grants from Southern Arts, won an award for the best short film at the San Francisco International Film Festival in 1988. This facilitated his entry into the National Film and Television School in Beaconsfield (NFTS) in 1989 where he studied for three years – in his own words, carrying on what he had been doing before but with better equipment! The film was also purchased by the BBC and on the back of that David got his first professional outing, directing a short film called *Oranges and Lemons*.

Over the next 15 or so years, David was prolific in his output, the best-known of which included the television adaptation of *The Way We Live Now* which won a BAFTA in 2002, the short film *Rank*, also nominated for a BAFTA in 2003, and the six-part multi-award winning thriller *State of Play*. Towards the end of this period his profile was steadily increasing and was further enhanced by the Channel 4 two-part drama *Sex Traffic* which won eight gongs at the 2004 BAFTAs and four at the Canadian equivalent, the Gemini Awards. There was also the television adaptation of *The Young Visiters* and a television film *The Girl in the Cafe* which collected three Emmy awards in 2005. So it has to be said that David wasn't doing at all badly when *Harry Potter* came calling – he was hardly what *The Guardian* described, albeit with tongue-in-cheek, as "a nobody from St Helens with a track record of making fine but low-budget television dramas". However his profile was about to be raised to a completely new level.

There can be no doubt that David's contribution to the continued success of the *Harry Potter* series was huge – indeed it would not be inappropriate to regard him as the second most important influence after JK Rowling herself. His performances impressed pretty much everyone involved, not least the actors themselves – Daniel Radcliffe in particular was fulsome in his praise for how David was able to get the best out of the cast and described him on one occasion simply as "brilliant"! JK Rowling herself commented after the final film that he had "steered us home magnificently". And of course, more accolades found their way to his door, including two Empire awards for the Best Director, a BAFTA award for Excellence in Directing and an Honorary Fellowship from the NFTS for his Outstanding Contribution to the British Film and Television Industry.

David had lived and breathed *Harry Potter* for the best part of six years but of course all good things must come to an end and once completed he was ready and eager to move on. There were discussions about him directing a *Dr Who* film and he directed a new *Tarzan* film which went on release in July 2016 and a US drama production *Tyrant* set in the Middle East. He did not however abandon the *Harry Potter* world completely – he went on to direct the trilogy *Fantastic Beasts and Where to Find Them* set in New York some 70 years earlier than the *Harry Potter* story began, the first instalment of which was released at the end of 2016. A few months later, in February 2017, he was named as one of Liverpool's Citizens of Honour and presented with a scroll at the City Hall.

Notwithstanding his success, the St Helens connection is alive and kicking – David still visits the town to see family and friends and he remains very close to his brother Andrew. A source of regret however is that neither of his parents survived to witness his achievements. He is married to Yvonne Walcott, aunt of the England footballer, Theo.

It is likely that there is plenty more mileage in David yet and that we will hear a lot more of him as the years go on. At times it can be difficult to equate the man with the softly spoken demeanour with the director who approaches his work with total dedication, a huge attention to detail and the fierce determination to get everything right, even when that means pushing the cast and production team to physical and emotional extremes. However it is these attributes which have marked him out amongst his peers and have helped him secure his position amongst the St Helens elite. There have been many from the town who have contributed to the rich history of television and film but none who has come anywhere near David Yates in his chosen field.

Pauline Yates

As noted previously, the acting profession has always had an attraction for the townsfolk of St Helens, both in television and in film. As a consequence it has been difficult to decide which persons to include and which not. However for sheer longevity – her acting career lasted over 50 years - as well as the quality of her performances and the fact that she was at the heart of British television comedy during its Golden Age in the 1960s and 1970s, Pauline Yates most definitely makes the cut.

Pauline was born in St Helens on 16th June 1929. Her father Thomas was a travelling salesman selling cough mixtures and lung tonic and her mother Marjorie ran a corner shop which sold pretty much everything else. Pauline was the eldest of three girls. At some stage they moved to Liverpool and Pauline attended Childwall Valley High School. Her mother wanted her to teach but from a very early age Pauline had determined that she wanted to be an actress. She left school at 16 and immediately took a job as assistant stage manager with the Chorley Rep, which gave her the opportunity to progress to roles on the stage itself. She made her first appearance at the age of 17 as Grace Poole in *Jane Eyre* and was soon travelling around the country with various repertory companies, often performing twice nightly and earning herself a reputation as a hard worker which was to stay with her for the rest of her life.

During the late 1950s Pauline became a popular choice with TV casting directors, her first appearance being in one of the first hospital soap operas *Emergency Ward 10*. She continued however to appear on stage and in Liverpool in 1960, met the writer and actor Donal Churchill (then working as a stage electrician) and they married that same year. Many more television appearances followed in the 1960s, including *Z-Cars, Softly, Softly, Dixon of Dock Green, Sentimental Education, Rumpole of the Bailey* and *Kavanagh QC*.

Into the 1970s and she secured a number of lead roles – for example in *Harriet's Back in Town*, where she played a divorcee returning to London to restart her career and in *My Honourable Mrs* where she played a housewife who became a Conservative Member of Parliament. In 1976 came the role for which she is best-known, that of Leonard Rossiter's wife Elizabeth in *The Rise and Fall of Reginald Perrin*, where her performance so impressed writer David Nobbs that he was inspired to give her a more active role in later episodes – there were three series in all between 1976 and 1979.

The 1980s brought appearances in the television sitcom *Keep it in the Family* and in the Julie Walters film *They'll Be Wearing Pink Pyjamas* whilst the early noughties brought her final television casting in the pilot for the crime series *Rose and Maloney*.

Pauline never abandoned the stage however and throughout her career continued to make appearances all over the country, the best-known of which was probably the stage adaptation of Jane Austen's *Pride and Prejudice* where she played Mrs Bennett.

After marrying Donald, with whom Pauline had two children, Jemma, also an actress and Polly, a writer, the family lived initially in Surrey but then moved to Primrose Hill in London. It was because of the demands of home life that Pauline turned down opportunities in Hollywood and also *The Avengers* role that found its way ultimately to Honor Blackman.

Well-known for her caustic sense of humour, her colourful language (the "F" word featured often it seems!) and her fondness for causing shock amongst her guests by talking about sex, the family home was a regular venue on the show business entertainment circuit. Donald died however of a heart attack in 1991 and Pauline's career was brought to an end by a stroke in 2002. She lived out her final days in a retirement home for actors before passing away in January 2015.

THE BEST OF THE REST

S o there we have it – the St Helens top 100, or, more correctly, my St Helens top 100.* Such lists are by their very nature subjective and no two people would of course choose exactly the same 100 as I have. It is not as if we have to scrape around to find possible entrants. Indeed there are many who could legitimately argue that their claims for inclusion are greater than those whose names appear on the list.

Those with the greatest grievance almost certainly belong to the rugby league fraternity and indeed I have been taken to task by several for my failure to include more rugby league players than I have. After all, I am told, St Helens is a rugby league town, it is rugby league that is the first thing that comes to mind for many when they hear the name and it is rugby league that has for the most part put the town's name on the map. I take the point but would defend my choice on the basis that it would be all too easy to fill these pages with stars from the 13-a-side code. There are simply too many of them and unfair as it may seem, to qualify for inclusion there has to be something else, over and above their rugby careers. However there are a few whose grievances I would have to concede have some legitimacy. These would include Alf Ellaby, arguably the first rugby league superstar, Harry Pinner, Great Britain RL captain, and more recently, ex-player and subsequent coach Keiron Cunningham and of course Paul Wellens, who has been referred to as "Mr St Helens" on numerous occasions.

The other code has not of course produced anything like the same number of internationals, although we should at least acknowledge the names of Alan Ashcroft who is, as far as I know, the only British Lion to hail from the town, and Dickie Guest, one of only three players to represent England both before and after the Second World War.

The acting profession is, after rugby, arguably the sector in which the town has made the biggest impact. Amongst those unlucky not to make the cut are Matthew Crompton, who was a fixture in *The Bill* for many years as well as playing parts in *Brookside* and *Coronation Street*; Emma Rigby, who made her name in the series *Hollyoaks* and won the award for Best Actress at the British Soap Awards in 2008 and Carley Stenson, another who shot to fame through her role, also in *Hollyoaks*. Staying with television, Michael Ahearne, better known to many as Warrior from the television series *Gladiators,* would most likely have appeared had this collection been published in the 1990s when he featured regularly on our weekend television screens. Even today the *Gladiators* website describes him as "one of the most mighty Gladiators".

It would have been easy as well to add names from the academic world. For example, Andrew Lees, professor of neurology and author, Sir John Turton Randall, physicist and Peter Critchley, philosopher. Authors John Vose and Rachel Lyon also merit an honourable mention.

One for the future is almost certainly George Mathias, still only eleven years old, but who has made national news with his initiative "Run with George", after he decided to run a mile for every month his younger brother has been alive. Funds raised go to Alder Hey Hospital, which had saved his brother's life after he had gone into a coma, and George has been joined in his runs by a whole list of celebrities. In November 2017 he won Young Fundraiser of the Year at the Pride of Britain Awards at which he attracted the attention of both Lord Sugar and Simon Cowell.

And of course if we go back into time, there are many many more, far too numerous to include. But I feel I should at the very least make reference to two particular historical characters whose legacy to the town has been far-reaching indeed and is evident still today: Sara Cowley, who bequeathed the fund that brought into existence what is now Cowley International College, and Samuel Taylor, whose land gift has enabled all of us to enjoy the delights of Taylor Park over the years.

But let's call a halt at this point. I will almost certainly have missed some who should have been included and there are others, whose merits I did not think warranted inclusion, but where others would take a very different view. But you can't please 'em all and I hope readers will acknowledge this as a genuine attempt to include those most worthy but accepting at the same time that such a list as compiled by others, might have a very different look about it!

---

*   This is not strictly correct – there was one person who was on the original list who insisted that neither their name nor anything about them should feature in the book. On the basis that it is not my intention to upset anyone, nor to cause any distress, I have respected that person's views and removed all references to them.

NOT FROM ST HELENS

On the face of it, this category is somewhat wide-ranging and has the potential to be quite lengthy. However it is in fact reserved for a select number of individuals who have been associated, sometimes mistakenly, with the town or who have some connection with the town which is unfortunately, from their point of view, not strong enough to justify inclusion in the main section.

Dan Gauthier

The commercial has been described as one of the best ever made. An old guy is travelling through the US desert with his daughter (at least I think she's his daughter though I suppose she could be his wife – either way she is dark, sultry and stunningly attractive) when his car breaks down. A younger guy in a truck comes to his assistance. He removes his jeans (Levi's, of course), uses them to tie the two vehicles together and then gives a knowing wink to the young woman. She joins him in his truck which starts to tow away the older guy's car. Unsurprisingly, the tow rope (aka the pair of Levi's jeans) gives way and the two of them drive off into the sunset.

You might think this has little or nothing to do with St Helens and you would be right. However it was widely believed in St Helens when this commercial was released in the late 1980s that the younger man was Keith van Hoven, born in St Helens and the son of the legendary St Helens Springbok winger, Tom van Vollenhoven. I remember Keith as a child – simply known as "Voll's kid". We used to gawp as he demonstrated how athletic he was as he messed around with his friends (there is in fact a history of gymnastics in the Vollenhoven family which persists to this day – Tom's granddaughter Bianca has represented South Africa in the 2014 Commonwealth Games).

It is true that Keith did go to Hollywood to seek out fame and fortune as an actor but it didn't work out that way – googling the name Keith van Hoven will give you about 30,000 hits and a few film credits but will tell you little else. The person who actually played the part was the somewhat better known American actor Dan Gauthier (2,640,000 hits and a lot more film credits) who had first made his name around about the same time as the commercial was released in the film *Teen Witch*. For what it's worth he's from Prineville in Oregon and not from St Helens.

Peter Greenall

Were he still alive, Peter Greenall might well feel aggrieved that he has not been included in the main section of the book. After all, both his father and grandfather were from St Helens, he spent the majority of his life in the town and his contribution to its development and wellbeing during the 19th century was enormous. The problem however is that he does not meet the very strict criteria – he was born, raised and educated in Warrington before seeing the light (or being shown the light) and returning to the original seat of the Greenall family in St Helens. He is as close to a native of the town as you can get without actually being one. It follows that I cannot ignore him entirely, hence his entry in this part of the book.

Peter was born in Warrington in 1796, the second son of Edward Greenall and the grandson of the founder of the Greenalls brewery, Thomas Greenall. He was initially employed at the Widlerspool brewery and worked under the supervision of his father and Thomas Lyon. However with the latter's death in late 1817, Edward was forced into a management restructure somewhat earlier than he would ideally have preferred and Peter was despatched to St Helens to take over the management of the brewery there.

His ties to the town were further cemented when in 1821 he married Eleanor Pilkington, sister of William and Richard, with whom Peter went into partnership in 1826 as the St Helens Crown Glass Company, later to change its name to Greenall and Pilkington. Somewhat ironically, given that Peter's involvement was to cease in 1845, it was his influence at the Warrington bank of Parr, Lyon and Greenall which enabled the business to survive the depression of the early 1840s. The company's name was changed to Pilkington Brothers following Peter's departure and it went on to do rather well. But even if he did make the wrong call on that one, his legacy to St Helens was nonetheless very substantial indeed.

Peter's early days were understandably devoted to ensuring the prosperity and growth of the brewery but he clearly took note during this time of the problems which rapid industrialisation was causing and the failure of the four townships to work together to create any sort of infrastructure to address these. Given the status of Greenalls, not just as brewers but as major landowners in St Helens, Peter was understandably regarded as a leading resident and he took his responsibilities very seriously. Indeed he played such a prominent role in public life that the period up to his death in 1845 at the age of 49 is often referred to as "The Age of Peter Greenall".

Peter's first foray into public life was to arrange and fund the construction of a system of pipes to provide the main areas of St Helens with an unpolluted water supply, which was sourced from the brewery ponds in Eccleston and for which he charged residents a minimal amount. This was later supplemented by an agreement with Samuel Taylor of Eccleston Hall under which the two families merged their water resources and then the formation of the St Helens Waterworks Company via an Act of Parliament promoted by Peter who was by then an MP. He was the leading spirit in the formation of the St Helens Building Society in 1824, became involved in several transport ventures, both coach and railway (notably the St Helens and Runcorn Gap Railway of which his family had a significant shareholding and of which Peter was chairman) and was a shareholder in a local gaslight company which was floated on the stock market in 1832. He also financed the construction of St Thomas's Church in Greenbank, and was head of the local Oddfellows Lodge when it opened in 1825.

Over and above his business interests Peter had political ambitions. He failed in his first attempt at election as a Member of Parliament in 1837, but succeeded in 1841 when he was elected as a Tory for the Wigan area (not many of those these days!) In 1845, despite considerable opposition from landowners in St Helens, who feared that they would ultimately bear the cost, he managed to push through the St Helens Improvement Bill, though not before he had been forced to accept the exclusion of the St Helens Crown

Glassworks (of which he was still a partner) and the British Plate Glassworks from the area covered by the Bill. Peter's reasons for leaving the Crown business are not recorded but may well have been connected to disagreements over the St Helens Improvement Bill.

Peter's death was quite unexpected – he was only 49. According to the death certificate he died of "apoplexy" or what we would now term a stroke. All shops in St Helens closed on the day of Peter's funeral and many flocked to pay their respects to a man who had dominated the growth of the town for some 25 years. In February 2014, a William IV silver dinner service went to auction. It bore the inscription "Presented to Peter Greenall Esquire by the Inhabitants of St Helens and Neighbourhood as a Token of their Esteem for his Private Worth and of Gratitude for his Public Services". It sold for £21,000.

Ricky Hatton

Most people know that Ricky Hatton is from East Manchester. His background was widely publicised when he was at the height of his fame, as was his support for the Manchester City football team. It is difficult to believe therefore that he could have been included on any list of famous people from St Helens. That is exactly what happened though, in the early 2000s, when his name featured on a plaque in the foyer at the World of Glass (remember from the introduction - "one of the country's most remarkable visitor attractions"?)

I recall feeling compelled to query this with the lady on the counter. "Oh I know, luv…" she responded, "…a few people have mentioned this. I think we got him mixed up with that other boxer, though I can't think of his name at the moment". After a little bit of prompting it became clear that she was thinking of Gary Stretch, although that doesn't really make it any easier to understand how an error of this magnitude came about.

All that said, Ricky Hatton is the type of person whom I can imagine as coming from St Helens. I never actually met him but did share a shuttle flight to London with an aeroplane full of his mates who were on their way to Las Vegas to watch him fight Floyd Mayweather Jnr. Most of these guys were not slimline – indeed the two sitting next to me both found it impossible to put the tray table in front of them down horizontally as their body shape proved too much of an impediment. But they were all fantastic value and this made for certainly the most entertaining shuttle flight it has been my pleasure to experience. And hats off to the guy who informed all his friends in a disappointed voice that he could not sit with them on the London to Vegas flight as he had been told he had to sit with the businessmen. Having finally been convinced by one of his friends that travelling in business class was actually a good thing as you were plied with unlimited booze (and he did take some convincing "What? I can drink anything I like? And as much as I like? No, I'm not that daft, you're all having me on"), he then announced in a loud voice to the whole aircraft, "I am gonna be the drunkest f******g bloke ever arrived in America". And he meant it. Ricky did of course lose and I suspect the journey home was more subdued. But probably just as alcoholic.

Brian Labone

It was late in 2013 that it was drawn to my attention that Wikipedia recorded the birthplace of Brian Labone, (footballer with Everton and England) as Parr, St Helens. This was news to me but was a welcome revelation – the idea of including the "Last of the Corinthians" (which was how his celebrated manager, Harry Catterick referred to him on account of his free spirit) quite appealed to me.

This was a guy who was definitely something of a maverick and who turned down, for example, the chance of playing for England in the 1966 World Cup because he had arranged to get married. However I could trace no other evidence of a St Helens connection – schooling, relatives, background and so on. And friends with a close allegiance to Everton all expressed surprise and indeed some scepticism when I probed for more information. It occurred to me that it might have had something to do with the Second World War. Did his mother perhaps think that giving birth in St Helens would be safer than at home in Liverpool? But his date of birth, 23rd January 1940 was some eight months before the Blitz commenced in earnest. It turned out in the end that the scepticism of my Everton supporting friends was well-founded.

Patsy, Brian's widow, confirmed to me that he had been born in Walton Hospital, had been schooled at Liverpool Collegiate and had lived in Walton itself before moving to Lydiate. So no grounds for inclusion other than in the "Not from St Helens" section. And for the record, the misinformation was removed from Wikipedia some time in 2014 – whether by the person who made the original incorrect posting or by somebody else, we do not know.

Rory McGrath

Whilst Rory himself does not fulfil the criteria for entry – he was neither born nor educated in St Helens – his mum and dad did. Unfortunately neither was particularly well-known, at least outside the McGrath family and outside the Ministry of Defence research laboratory in which his dad worked. It was in fact as a consequence of his work that the family moved from St Helens to Cornwall in the early 1950s. I felt it nonetheless important that the St Helens connection should not be ignored for, whilst there are many who might be indifferent to the town of their father's birth, Rory is definitely not one of them. This is clear from the repeated references to the town in his book *The Father, the Son and the Ghostly Hole*, which tells his story of being brought up in a Catholic household and the long-term effect this had on his life – something else which resonated with me, given that I had gone through pretty much the same experience.

Rory, you may remember, was one of the resident comedians on the sporting quiz show *They Think It's All Over* and I recall him on one occasion giving a little cheer when St Helens RLFC was mentioned. This clearly marked him out as being a good guy and helpfully, he explains in his book the connection in some detail – in fact he devotes the whole of Chapter 29 (the chapters are not very long!) to a visit to the town to stay with his relatives. Admittedly the chapter does begin, "A piece of shit floated quickly into sight and disappeared down the watery drain," (this was Rory's first experience of an outside loo) but he then goes on to namecheck Hardshaw Street, the Greenall Whitley brewery in Hall Street, Pilkington's, UGB, Triplex, The Bridge in Rainford, Lowe House, Sacred Heart and Holy Cross. It was also his first experience of a pub crawl, courtesy of his two uncles and a cousin. Shortly after this visit however, Rory's grandmother moved down to Cornwall to join the family, leaving Rory to reflect on this visit to St Helens as "that strange, exciting and friendly place way up in the north of a country called England".

Catherine Parr

As anyone who studied any sort of history at school knows, Catherine Parr was final wife of Henry VIII and the one who survived him. One can only assume that this was from her perspective something of a result, given the fate of some of her predecessors. It is difficult to imagine her going into the marriage with anything other than apprehension.

The St Helens connection is that it was widely believed when I was at school that Catherine Parr was actually Catherine *of* Parr and that the Parr concerned was the village which together with Sutton, Eccleston and Windle, made up the original township of St Helens. As an aside, inhabitants of Parr with whom I was schooled often referred to themselves as Parisians, which I rather liked – Wikipedia however uses the term "Parrite", although that is not one I have encountered personally.

Catherine Parr was not actually from Parr which is probably no surprise but the assumption is not as far from the truth as it might at first blush seem. The Parr family did in fact originate there although they were originally known as the Halsalls, changing their name to Parr around the beginning of the fourteenth century. One of their number, Sir William de Parre, in 1383 married Elizabeth de Ros, daughter of John de Ros and granddaughter and heiress of Sir Thomas de Ros, Baron of Kendal. Sir William, it seems, had something of a shady background. He was a mercenary and was allegedly convicted of murder but pardoned after volunteering to fight for John of Gaunt, Duke of Lancaster (younger brother of the Black Prince), who was one of England's principal military commanders in France in the 1370s and 1380s. Sir William's marriage kicked off the Lancaster branch of the Parr family and Catherine, sixth and final wife of Henry VIII was his great-great-great-granddaughter.

The Parr family connection with the village of Parr did however survive until the mid-16ᵗʰ century when the widow of one of the Parr family married John Byrom, who had inherited the Byrom estate in Lowton. He managed to pick up most of the Parr inheritance by this move and indeed Parr Hall was henceforth to become the main seat of the Byroms.

Sir Alastair Pilkington

Lionel Alexander Bethune Pilkington (known as Alastair), who was born in 1920, is widely regarded as the inventor of the float glass technology that revolutionised the world of glass. He was employed by Pilkington from 1947 when he joined as a technical officer, until 1985 when he retired after twelve years as Chairman of the Pilkington Group. What was remarkable however was that not only was he not from St Helens, but he had no connection at all with the St Helens branch of the Pilkington family.

The story, as related by Professor TC Barker in *The Glassmakers: Pilkington 1826–1976*, is that Sir Richard Pilkington, one of the family shareholders (though not a director) was indulging in a little genealogy as part of which, circa 1945, he contacted a Colonel Lionel Pilkington, who was a businessman in Reading. Whilst it soon became clear that there was no obvious link between their respective families, the conversation apparently turned to the next generation and specifically, Lionel's second son Alastair, who after returning from the war had resumed his studies at Cambridge and would in due course be looking for a job.

Lionel (rather than Alastair) was in due course interviewed by two family directors and on 29ᵗʰ November 1945 the board considered the possibility of offering young Alastair a position. It seems they reached the conclusion that, because Alastair was a Pilkington (the assumption was made that Lionel's branch of the family must have broken away from the mainstream over 15 generations earlier, which was as far back as Richard Pilkington had been able to trace), he could only be employed as a family member and therefore as a potential director. Reservations were expressed that life in the North of England was very different from life in the South and it was important that Alastair understood this. It was also stressed that it was important to take steps to learn more about Colonel Lionel Pilkington, his business and his family background before any formal offer was made. However all of this was clearly addressed to the satisfaction of the Board and as a consequence, on completion of his studies, Alastair Pilkington began work in St Helens in August 1947.

The rest is history, as the saying goes. Alastair Pilkington, who had already fought in the Desert, Greek and Crete Campaigns with the Royal Artillery, spent three years in Germany as a prisoner of war, returned and completed his university education, then went on to a glittering career as an industrialist during which he received a knighthood as well as a multitude of honours and awards for his work on the invention and development of float glass. These included no less than 13 doctorates and fellowships from academic institutions. It is no exaggeration to say that he, more than any one other single person, was responsible for the rise of Pilkington to the undisputed position of the world's leading glassmaker.

Sir Alastair, as he then was, died in 1995. After leaving Pilkington he had been extremely active in the academic world as Chairman of the Cambridge Foundation, Pro-Chancellor of Lancaster University and Chancellor of Liverpool University. And he left a final mark on St Helens by creating the UK's first enterprise agency, the Community of St Helens Trust which was the forerunner of Business in The Community of which he was founder chairman. He may not have been from St Helens but he certainly could not have played a bigger role in putting St Helens onto the world map.

Saint Helena

It would have been quite fitting had St Helen, more commonly known as St Helena, mother of Constantine the Great, actually come from St Helens. She didn't. Or rather I don't think she did although historians don't seem to be able to agree on where she actually did come from. The majority view seems to be in favour of Drepana in what was then known as Asia Minor but is now part of Turkey. There are however rival claims that she was born in Colchester (and so was an Essex girl!)

This was on the basis that she was the daughter of Coilus, the ruler of a tribe in Colchester, who arranged for her to marry Constantine's father who was at that time a Roman general posted to Britain. The Welsh and Greeks have also claimed her so perhaps we shouldn't rule out completely the possibility that she is one of our own. Certainly nobody seems to be very clear why the chapel of ease from which the town supposedly derived its name was called St Elyn (and indeed whether it had anything at all to do with St Helen!)

As mentioned in the introduction, James Hibbs, (*The First Tourist – Travels in Search of St Helena)* actually began his search in St Helens and indeed devoted the whole of the first chapter to his visit to the town in order to research the origins of the town's name. He left no wiser than he had arrived, noting merely the "ignorance or forgetfulness, the lack of any concern…" and the "absence of curiosity" which he had encountered when making his enquiries into the town's heritage. I rather liked his conclusion: "I felt that the answers really lay elsewhere". Quite.

St Helen however is a figure who is right at the very heart of the Christian faith and it is no exaggeration to say that she changed the course of history by providing the impetus which transformed Christianity into a major world force. This is based upon the belief that she travelled to the Holy Land in the year 327AD (by which time she was in her 70s) and whilst there somehow managed to unearth the True Cross upon which Jesus had been crucified. The Cross was then divided into pieces and fragments were transported to all parts of the globe, as a result of which the Cross became a symbol of salvation rather than defeat. And in the fullness of time, one of these fragments materialised in the Church of St Helen and the Holy Cross in Corporation Street in St Helens. Nobody is quite sure how it got there, although there is a suggestion that it might have been brought by a local woman, Mary Stapleton, who travelled to Rome in 1862 and apparently procured from the Pope some religious mementoes to mark the opening of the Holy Cross Church and these included a relic of the True Cross. Interestingly however the Jesuit archives in London contain an official certificate confirming that the relic in St Helens is authentic which is dated December 1852, some ten years earlier. Another Jesuit publication claims that a fragment of the True Cross was in fact located at St Mary's Lowe House, rather than Holy Cross Church, although there seems little evidence to support this claim.

Of course, all of this presupposes that St Helen did indeed find the True Cross but on the basis that at least one report claimed she located it by taking a local wise

*The sarcophagus of St Helena at
St Paul's Basilica in Rome.
© Copyright Brian Leyland 2018*

man captive and throwing him into a dungeon without food until he told her where the cross was buried, some might conclude there is some doubt about the matter. In fact there seems to be very little consensus at all, even in relation to the reason that she made the trip. Many believe it was related in some way to a little minor turmoil in the household, as Constantine had just had his son Crispus (supposedly Helena's favourite) and his second wife Fausta executed as he believed they were having an affair. Others believe that she travelled at the bidding of Constantine who had attributed a recent victory in battle to a vision he had seen of the Cross in the sky.

Given that numerous learned scholars have over the centuries carried out enormous amounts of research into the legend of St Helena and the Cross with little or no meeting of minds, it may well be that the townsfolk in St Helens with their "lack of concern" and "absence of curiosity" have got it spot on – why waste time when it is clearly impossible to arrive at the truth with any certainty?

CONCLUSION

What then, have we learnt from our scrutiny of the lives of those who have emerged from the town and made their mark on a national and in some cases international stage? Are there any common themes that we can detect? Does it tell us whether or not there is indeed any validity in the research mentioned in the introduction, that different geographical places in the United Kingdom have distinct personality traits?

Well it is certainly the case that writing this book has reinforced in my mind the theory that there is a genuine St Helens gene, which for the most part, prevents us from taking ourselves too seriously. Time and again this was evident in the responses I had from, and the discussions with, the persons who feature in this book. It is probably fair to say that in many cases this gene sits side by side with a cynical gene, although I suspect the distribution of such a gene is somewhat more widely spread than just our town boundaries.

Are there any other common themes? Well something else we encounter time and again, is a sense of self-belief, possibly not on a conscious level but certainly detectable from the outside looking in, that we are as good as anyone else at anything that we want to be or do. It doesn't seem to occur to those from the town making their way through life, that they might be in any way at a disadvantage to others that they meet, however different their background, wealth or accent. This translates for many into an ability to move effortlessly between different sectors of society, comfortable in whatever surroundings they find themselves, whether it be in a PLC boardroom or on the terraces at rugby league game. Such persons simply have the confidence to be themselves and it would never occur to them to try to be someone totally different. Indeed the Chief Executive at the Arts Council commented in 2017 that St Helens has never been "overwhelmed by its proximity to the two major metropolitan centres of Liverpool and Manchester". And that same personality trait means that when they do encounter snobbery, it doesn't get to them – they simply regard it either with amusement or as something not worth getting worked up about, and move on.

Why should this be so? Well this may be pure speculation, but from my own experience the town is one of the few places I have encountered where snobbery is virtually non-existent. Of course, it would be easy to say that there is nothing to be snobbish about and there is certainly an element of truth in that. But that hasn't stopped snobbery rearing its ugly head in many other places which you might also conclude have nothing to be snobbish about. This may well go back to the fact that if you don't take yourself seriously, then snobbery almost by definition is not part of your DNA. But whatever the reason, we have arguably all grown up in a true meritocracy which will certainly not be the case in every other town in the land.

Are there any other characteristics which we can identify in the townsfolk? Well, it seems to me that everyone in the town is pretty much agreed that our expectations from life are not high. Nobody expects anything to be handed to them on a plate – life simply isn't like that if you are from St Helens. There may be a sense that progress in life is easier if you are born elsewhere, in a more fashionable place perhaps, but interestingly this sentiment rarely translates into a simmering resentment, nor into the sort of bitter, "chip on the shoulder" attitude which defines those who inhabit some other parts of the North. Instead we encounter a more philosophical response. On the positive side, for some it simply means that you just get on with life and take satisfaction that whatever you achieve is down to you and you alone. On the less positive side, it engenders in some a sense of resignation that nothing is ever going to work to your benefit and that any initiative designed to help will inevitably end in failure. This indeed has the potential to be a major stumbling block for those trying to effect positive change – the "I've heard it all before" and "I'll believe that when I bloody see it" mentality.

Another question worth posing is whether or not St Helens folk have more of an attachment to their hometown than those from elsewhere do. Once again, the comparison is difficult to make but it is certainly the case that the vast majority feel a sense of belonging which they never lose. To succeed in their chosen field, most of the entries in this book had to leave the town – that is inevitable if you are to make progress and become a national or international figure. But the great majority retain both a sense of identity and an affiliation with the town. The rugby league team plays an enormous part in this – it gives everyone something to hold on to, whether by returning to watch them play, viewing them on television or simply looking out for the results. And critically it means that many whom we encounter in the course of our lives will already be aware of the town and its sporting heritage, which in turn helps every single one of us establish our own identity and credentials.

Is St Helens a special place? According to Richard Donald Lewis in *The Billingers*, everyone believes there is something special about the place in which he or she is born. I'm not sure I actually subscribe to this theory, unless by "something special" he simply means a sense of belonging. If the history of St Helens and its contribution to the nation over the years had been better recognised, you might indeed conclude that it is special but the reality is that very few, even from the town itself, fully appreciate their heritage and nobody ever talks about the town as being special. Perhaps the real question which we should address is whether or not the town's production line is more or less prolific than those of similar sized towns with the same demographic. We will never know the answer to this for sure but we can certainly speculate and I for one would wager my money on St Helens being in the upper quartile of any league table comprising such towns (I rather like venturing opinions in situations such as this where nobody will ever be able to prove me wrong – it is the sort of assertion that could be prefaced by an expression beloved of many in the town "For me, ...", after which all sorts of outrageous views are aired but on the basis that they are presented as opinions rather than facts, you cannot deny anyone the right to express them!)

A second, but equally pertinent question is, will the town continue to produce and export the same levels of talent in future years? That is in fact a far more difficult question to answer. During the last 30 years or so, the country has undergone dramatic social and economic change and whilst there have been many winners, including those cities which have undergone a major revival and where inner city living is now a major feature – many areas, and in particular the old industrial towns, have been left a long way behind. St Helens is undoubtedly one of these. The old industries, mainly glass and coal, which bound everyone together and were instrumental in creating a sense of community in the town, have largely disappeared and there has been little to take their place. The town centre, like many others, has suffered from chronic underinvestment, the increased popularity of online shopping and the pull of large, successful, out of town shopping centres. On top of that there has been an influx of residents into areas of the Metropolitan Borough, who do not regard St Helens as their hometown, whose offspring grow up with an accent which is alien to the town and who have yet to establish the sense of belonging which is critical to the development of a thriving and close knit community. There is a real risk, it seems to me, that St Helens could evolve, not just into a dormitory town from which everyone travels elsewhere to go to work, but worse, a Merseyside suburb without a distinct identity. At the time of going to press, the Council has announced a very ambitious vision for the transformation of the town centre with a view to halting the decline. It is important that this is followed up with decisive action in the short to medium term. If not, the tendency towards negativity amongst the townsfolk is likely to kick in again, making the task much more difficult than it need be. Any change for the better will be aided and abetted by the continuing success of the St Helens RLFC, the institution which has played such a major part both in the past in establishing the town's identity and which continues to this day to act as the glue which binds us together, whether we live in the town or not. If the community does fight back, as it can and should, then let us all hope that we will continue to observe a succession of famous, successful and distinguished citizens emerge from the town who will grace the national and international stage for many years to come.

I will finish by reproducing in full the final paragraphs of the first chapter of the autobiography of Sir James Sexton. The words were written in the 1930s but carry the same weight today as they did then.

> *"Beecham's Pills were probably the first influence in bringing St Helens before the eyes of the world, but since then – I do not claim this as a result of the famous pills! – the town has made remarkable contributions to the historic and industrial history of the world. The subject tempts me to digress, and to quote an incident in the House of Commons. I was then the representative of St Helens in the House, and when a young sprig of the nobility interjected in the course of a debate "St Helens? Isn't that the place from which the pills come?" I replied*

that compared with the constituency he represented, whose only contribution to history so far was not a very progressive one, being confined, in fact, to his presence in that House, St Helens had not only a national but an international reputation which did not rest solely upon Beecham's Pills, even though they ministered to the cure of most of the ills of humanity and yielded profits which in turn provided food for the intellect and music which soothed the savage breast.

Many rivers, tributaries to the seven seas, I informed the noble lordling, were spanned by bridges that came from St Helens; the Prime Minister of one of our colonies also came from St Helens, and though the town might boast no palaces lifting to the eternal skies, it had helped, through its staple trade, the manufacture of glass, to spread light throughout the civilised world, including the Chamber in which we were sitting, and, last but perhaps not least, it had produced me as a politician. That seemed to satisfy the House, and, like Mark Antony, I paused in vain for a reply from the member who had provoked the little outburst."

We can only hope fervently that in eighty years' time, readers of these words will conclude that they still stand the test of time!

ACKNOWLEDGEMENTS

This book was conceived a long time ago. In fact, it was so long ago that I cannot recall precisely when nor what prompted it. I had always had in mind that I might write a book at some point – after all it is often said that every single person has at least one book in them (although I was also conscious of the observation by Christopher Hitchens, the English-born American author and columnist, that "in most cases that is exactly where it should stay!") But once having resolved that this should be the subject, it then took on a life of its own and, notwithstanding that I have written it in what little spare time I have, and also that it turned out to be a far larger project than I ever anticipated, I was determined to see it through to the very end. But all that said, I have enjoyed the experience tremendously – the thrill of unearthing new characters, the satisfaction of filling in gaps through different forms of research and, perhaps most of all, the privilege of engaging directly with many of those still living who appear in these pages.

And that I think is where I should start the long list of thanks – with those persons who gave freely of their time (or in a few cases their secretaries' time), some uncomfortable that their names and achievements were to appear in print, others perhaps a little more used to featuring in the media and others still, who expressed surprise but a certain pleasure that they had been accorded a place amongst the great and the good of the town. By far the majority of the persons I approached were willing to help and I am indebted to them in that regard. Sadly, a small number did not want to participate and whilst all but one still retain their rightful place in the collection, I can only apologise if the information I am able to supply is not as comprehensive as it might otherwise have been.

Next in the list of thanks must come the relatives of those already deceased, too numerous to mention individually but whose help and assistance was invaluable – they helped fill in the many gaps that I encountered along the way and also to bring to life the stories surrounding their deceased relatives.

In third place I have to thank all those who provided introductions, assistance and information. There are very many of these but it is important that their role is acknowledged. So, in no particular order, thanks go to Eamonn McManus, (St Helens RLFC chairman), Alex Service, (Saints official historian), Charles Nevin and David Lawrenson, (journalists), Mike Critchley and Chris Coffey (from the *St Helens Star*), Keith Atherton, (author of *Surprising Connections Between the World of Aviation and the Town of St Helens*), Mary Presland (from the St Helens Historical Society), Karl Holden (A180 Darts), Stephen Wainwright (of Sutton Beauty), Linzi Prescott, (widow of Steve), my brother John, who fed me a constant stream of articles from local newspapers, and all those contributors to St Helens Connect who answered my enquiries.

Next I must thank those with whom I shared my idea more years ago than I care to remember. First and foremost amongst these is my wife Linsey (who has had to live with this book for much longer than either she or I expected when I began) and then all those friends and acquaintances who have had to put up with lengthy progress reports and conversations over many many beers in that same period. But whilst the length of time I devoted to the book became something of a joke (I lost count of the number of times I was asked if it would end up being published posthumously), I have greatly appreciated the help and encouragement provided – it certainly hardened my resolve to get to the finish. If nothing else, my credibility was at stake!!

Last but by no means least, my thanks go to Patsy Byron from Stellar Books for all her help, guidance and hand holding throughout the publishing process and for helping me package a jumble of material into the book you now have before you.